Text Book Of

CONTROL SYSTEM

(17538)

For
Semester – V

Third Year Diploma Courses in
Instrumentation / Instrumentation and Control /
Industrial Electronics

As Per MSBTE's 'G' Scheme Syllabus

MRS. PRATIBHA D. KULKARNI
M.Tech. (E & TC)
Lecturer, E & TC Deptt.
Pimpri-Chinchwad Education Trust's
Pimpri-Chinchwad Polytechnic
Nigdi. Pune – 44

N3148

CONTROL SYSTEM
First Edition : June 2014
© : **Author**

The text of this publication, or any part thereof, should not be reproduced or transmitted in any form or stored in any computer storage system or device for distribution including photocopy, recording, taping or information retrieval system or reproduced on any disc, tape, perforated media or other information storage device etc., without the written permission of Author with whom the rights are reserved. Breach of this condition is liable for legal action.

Every effort has been made to avoid errors or omissions in this publication. In spite of this, errors may have crept in. Any mistake, error or discrepancy so noted and shall be brought to our notice shall be taken care of in the next edition. It is notified that neither the publisher nor the author or seller shall be responsible for any damage or loss of action to any one, of any kind, in any manner, therefrom.

ISBN 978-93-5164-080-6

Published By :
NIRALI PRAKASHAN
Abhyudaya Pragati, 1312, Shivaji Nagar,
Off J.M. Road, PUNE – 411005
Tel - (020) 25512336/37/39, Fax - (020) 25511379
Email : niralipune@pragationline.com

Printed at
Repro Knowledgecast Limited
India

DISTRIBUTION CENTRES
PUNE

Nirali Prakashan
119, Budhwar Peth, Jogeshwari Mandir Lane
Pune 411002, Maharashtra
Tel : (020) 2445 2044, 66022708, Fax : (020) 2445 1538
Email : niralilocal@pragationline.com

Nirali Prakashan
S. No. 28/25, Dhyari,
Near Pari Company, Pune 411041
Tel : (020) 24690204Fax : (020) 24690316
Email : bookorder@pragationline.com

MUMBAI
Nirali Prakashan
385, S.V.P. Road, Rasdhara Co-op. Hsg. Society Ltd.,
Girgaum, Mumbai 400004, Maharashtra
Tel : (022) 2385 6339 / 2386 9976, Fax : (022) 2386 9976
Email : niralimumbai@pragationline.com

DISTRIBUTION BRANCHES

NAGPUR
Pratibha Book Distributors
Above Maratha Mandir, Shop No. 3, First Floor,
Rani Jhanshi Square, Sitabuldi, Nagpur 440012,
Maharashtra, Tel : (0712) 254 7129

BENGALURU
Pragati Book House
House No. 1, Sanjeevappa Lane, Avenue Road Cross,
Opp. Rice Church, Bengaluru – 560002.
Tel : (080) 64513344, 64513355,
Mob : 9880582331, 9845021552
Email:bharatsavla@yahoo.com

JALGAON
Nirali Prakashan
34, V. V. Golani Market, Navi Peth, Jalgaon 425001,
Maharashtra, Tel : (0257) 222 0395
Mob : 9423491860

KOLHAPUR
Nirali Prakashan
New Mahadvar Road,
Kedar Plaza, 1st Floor Opp. IDBI Bank
Kolhapur 416 012, Maharashtra. Mob : 9850046155

CHENNAI
Pragati Books
9/1, Montieth Road, Behind Taas Mahal, Egmore,
Chennai 600008 Tamil Nadu, Tel : (044) 6518 3535,
Mob : 94440 01782 / 98450 21552 / 98805 82331, Email : bharatsavla@yahoo.com

RETAIL OUTLETS
PUNE

Pragati Book Centre
157, Budhwar Peth, Opp. Ratan Talkies,
Pune 411002, Maharashtra
Tel : (020) 2445 8887 / 6602 2707, Fax : (020) 2445 8887

Pragati Book Centre
Amber Chamber, 28/A, Budhwar Peth,
Appa Balwant Chowk, Pune : 411002, Maharashtra,
Tel : (020) 20240335 / 66281669
Email : pbcpune@pragationline.com

Pragati Book Centre
676/B, Budhwar Peth, Opp. Jogeshwari Mandir,
Pune 411002, Maharashtra
Tel : (020) 6601 7784 / 6602 0855

PBC Book Sellers & Stationers
152, Budhwar Peth, Pune 411002, Maharashtra
Tel : (020) 2445 2254 / 6609 2463

MUMBAI
Pragati Book Corner
Indira Niwas, 111 - A, Bhavani Shankar Road, Dadar (W), Mumbai 400028, Maharashtra
Tel : (022) 2422 3526 / 6662 5254, Email : pbcmumbai@pragationline.com

Dedicated to

My beloved father Shri. Krishnaji A. Deshpande (Principal)

Mother Late Sau. Sunita K. Deshpande

– Mrs. Pratibha D. Kulkarni

Preface ...

It gives me great pleasure and immense satisfaction in presenting this text book of **'Control System'** for students of Fifth Semester Diploma courses in Instrumentation, Instrumentation and Control and Industrial Electronics Branches. This text has been written as per MBTE's 'G' scheme syllabus.

This subject is presented in a simple language considering the requirements of all the students regarding the changing trends of examination. Utmost care has been taken to check the mistakes and misprints, yet it is very difficult to claim perfection.

I take this opportunity to thank **Hon. Secretary Shri. V. S. Kalbhor, Hon. A. O. Shri. Vispute** and **Hon. Principal Mrs. V. S. Byakod, Vice-Principal Hon. Shri. B. V. Mane** for their moral support and encouragement.

I also thank **Shri. M. P. Munde** whose inspirational words and constant motivation helped me in completing this book in a short period. I am also thankful to the publisher **Shri. Dineshbhai Furia** and **Shri. Jignesh Furia**. I am also thankful to Mr. Malik Shaikh, Mrs. Anagha Kaware (Co-ordination and Proof Reading), Mrs. Deepa Sawant (Figure Drawing) and staff of Nirali Prakashan for bringing out this book.

A very special thanks my husband **Shri. Dipak Kulkarni**, daughter **Chi. Sharvari and** Son **Chi. Shriprasad** for their support and co-operation.

Any undetected and unintentional error, omissions, suggestions etc. from students and teachers for improvement brought to our notice in good spirit are most welcome.

Pune. **Author**

Syllabus ...

Chapter 1 : Introduction to Control System   [Hrs. : 08, Mks. : 16]

1.1   [8 Marks]

- **Control system:** Definition and practical examples
- **Classifications:** Open Loop and Closed Loop Systems – definition, Block Diagram, practical example and Comparison; Linear and Non-linear System; Time Variant and Time Invariant Systems.
- **Laplace Transform:** Laplace Transform for Standard Functions
- **Transfer Function:** Definition, Derivation of Transfer Functions for Closed Loop and Open Loop Control System, Differential Equations and Transfer Functions of R-C and R-L-C Electrical Circuits.

1.2   [8 Marks]

- **Order of a System:** Definition 0, 1, 2 Order System, Standard Equations, Simple Numericals
- **Block Diagram Reduction Technique:** Need, Reduction Rules, Numerical Problems.

Chapter 2 : Time Response Analysis   [Hrs. : 12, Mks. 24]

2.1   [12 Marks]

- **Time Domain Analysis:** Transient and Steady State Response
- **Standard Test Inputs:** Step, Ramp, Parabolic and Impulse: Need of them, Significance, and Corresponding Laplace Representation
- **Poles and zeros:** Definition, S-plane Representation
- **First Order Control System:** Analysis for Unit Step Input, Concept of Time Constant
- **Second Order Control System:** Analysis for Unit Step Input, Concept, Definition and Effect of Damping

2.2   [12 Marks]

- **Time Response Specifications** (No Derivations)
- T_p, T_s, T_r, T_d, M_p, e_{ss}; Numerical Problems
- **Steady State Analysis:** Type 0, 1, 2 Systems, Steady State Error and Error Constants, Numerical Problems

Chapter 3 : Stability   [Hrs. : 08, Mks. 16]

- **Stability:** Definition of Stability, Analysis of Stable, Unstable, Critically Stable and Conditionally Stable System, Relative Stability, Root Locations in S-plane for Stable and Unstable Systems.
- **Routh's Stability Criterion:** Different Cases and Conditions (Statement Method), Numerical Problems.

Chapter 4 : Frequency Response [Hrs. : 08, Mks. 10]

4.1 [4 Marks]

- **Frequency Response Analysis:** Introduction, Advantages and Disadvantages; Frequency Response Specifications.

4.2 **Bode Plot:** [6 Marks]

- Need of Bode Plot
- Straight Line Magnitude Plot
- Straight Line Phase Angle Plot
- Bode Plot for Gain K, Poles and Zeros at Origin, 1st Order Poles System (1/(as+c)) and Zero
- Analyze Stability from Bode Plot using Gain Margin and Phase Margin.

Chapter 5 : Process Control and Control Actions [Hrs. : 06, Mks. 16]

- **Process Control System:** Block Diagram and Explanation of Each Block.
- **Control Actions**
- **Discontinuous Modes:** ON-OFF Controllers: Equation, Neutral Zone
- **Continuous Modes:** Proportional Controllers (Offset, Proportional Band), Integral and Derivative Controllers: o/p Equations, Corresponding Laplace Transforms, Response Graph of P, I and D Controllers
- **Composite Controllers:** PI, PD, PID controllers - O/P Equations, Response, Comparison, Application, Electronic op-amp based circuits

Chapter 6 : Servo System [Hrs. : 06, Mks. 18]

6.1 [4 Marks]

- **Servo System:** Definition, Block Diagram
- AC and DC Servo Systems: Concept and Principle, Comparison, Schematic Diagram.

6.2 Servo components [14 Marks]

Draw, describe the working and state the applications of following

- Potentiometer as Error Detector
- Synchro as Error Detector
- Stepper Motor - PM and Variable Reluctance Type, Comparison of Stepper Motor with DC Servo Motor
- DC Servo Motor - Characteristic, Difference from a Normal DC Motor
- AC Servo Motor - Characteristic, Difference from a Normal 2 Phase Induction Motor.

***

CONTENTS

1. Introduction to Control System 1.1 - 1.74

    1.1   Introduction   1.1

    1.2   Control System   1.2

           1.2.1 Practical Examples   1.3

    1.3 Control System Classification   1.4

           1.3.1 Open Loop System   1.5

           1.3.2 Closed Loop System   1.6

           1.3.3 Comparison Between Open Loop and Closed Loop Systems   1.10

    1.4   Mathematical Foundation   1.10

           1.4.1 Complex-Variable Concept   1.10

           1.4.2 Differential Equations   1.12

           1.4.3 Linear and Non-Linear System   1.12

           1.4.4 Time Variable and Time Invariant System   1.14

    1.5   Laplace Transform (L.T.)   1.14

           1.5.1 Significance of Laplace Transform in Control System   1.14

           1.5.2 Important Theorems of Laplace Transform   1.16

           1.5.3 Inverse Laplace Transform   1.17

           1.5.4 Laplace Transform for Standaed Functions   1.19

           1.5.5 Application of Laplace Transform to the solution of Linear System   1.20

    1.6   Transfer Function   1.21

           1.6.1 Derivation of Transfer Function for Open-Loop Control System   1.23

           1.6.2 Derivation of Transfer Function for Close Loop Control System   1.23

           1.6.3 Properties of the Transfer Function   1.24

           1.6.4 Transfer Function of R-C and R-L-C Electrical Circuits   1.24

           1.6.5 Developing Differential Equations of R-C and R-L-C Electrical Circuits   1.25

           1.6.6 Advantages and Disadvantages of Transfer Function   1.29

1.7	Order of a System	1.29
1.8	Block Diagram Representation	1.30
	1.8.1 Need	1.30
	1.8.2 Block Diagram Fundamentals	1.31
	1.8.3 Block Diagram Reduction of Closed Loop Control System	1.32
	1.8.4 Multiple-Input Multiple-Output Systems	1.32
	1.8.5 Rules of Block Diagram Reduction	1.34
	1.8.6 Advantages and Disadvantages of Block Diagram	1.39
•	Important Points	1.68
•	Practice Questions	1.70
•	Previous Year MSBTE Questions and Answers (As Per 'E' Scheme)	1.73

2. Time Response Analysis   2.1 - 2.66

2.1	Introduction	2.1
2.2	Time Domain Analysis	2.2
	2.2.1 Transient Response	2.3
	2.2.2 Steady State Response	2.3
	2.2.3 Steady State Error	2.3
2.3	Standard Test Inputs (Signals)	2.4
	2.3.1 Step Input	2.5
	2.3.2 Ramp Input	2.5
	2.3.3 Parabolic Input	2.6
	2.3.4 Impulse Input	2.6
2.4	Poles and Zeros	2.7
2.5	Analysis of First Order System for Unit Step Input	2.9
	2.5.1 Concept of Time Constant	2.11
2.6	Analysis of Second-Order Control System	2.12
	2.6.1 Response of Second-Order System to the Unit-Step	2.13
	2.6.2 Effect of Damping	2.15

2.7	Time Response Specifications	2.15
2.8	Steady State Errors and Error Constants	2.23
	2.8.1 Derivation of Steady-State Error	2.23
	2.8.2 Unit Step Input	2.24
	2.8.3 Unit Ramp Input	2.25
	2.8.4 Unit Parabolic (Acceleration) Input	2.26
2.9	Types of Feedback Control System	2.26
	2.9.1 Analysis of Type 0, 1, 2 Systems for Standard Inputs	2.27
•	Important Points	2.61
•	Practice Questions	2.62
•	Previous Year MSBTE Questions and Answers (As Per 'E' Scheme)	2.63

3. Stability   3.1 - 3.42

3.1	Introduction to Stability	3.1
3.2	The Concept of Stability	3.2
3.3	Analysis of Stability	3.2
	3.3.1 Stable System	3.3
	3.3.2 Unstable system	3.3
	3.3.3 Absolutely Stable System	3.4
	3.3.4 Relatively Stable System	3.4
	3.3.5 Marginally or Limitedly Stable System (Critically)	3.4
3.4	Root Locations in s-Plane for Stable and Unstable System	3.5
	3.4.1 Special Cases	3.6
3.5	Routh's Stability Criterion (Routh's Hurwitz Criterion)	3.6
•	Important Points	3.40
•	Practice Questions	3.40
•	Previous Year MSBTE Questions and Answers (As Per 'E' Scheme)	3.41

4. Frequency Response   4.1 - 4.36

4.1	Introduction	4.1
4.2	Frequency Response Specifications	4.2
4.3	Frequency Response of Closed Loop System	4.4

4.4	Methods Used in Frequency Response	4.5
4.5	Advantages and Disadvantages of Frequency Response Analysis	4.5
4.6	Bode Plot	4.5
	4.6.1 Standard Form of G (jω)	4.9
	4.6.2 To Plot the Slop Lines and Angles on Bode Plot	4.10
	4.6.3 Steps for Constructing Bode Plot	4.10
	4.6.4 Bode Plot for Gain K	4.11
	4.6.5 Bode Plot for Poles and Zeros at Origin	4.12
•	Important Points	4.35
•	Practice Questions	4.35
•	Previous Year MSBTE Questions and Answers (As Per 'E' Scheme)	4.36

5. Process Control and Control Actions — 5.1 - 5.22

5.1	Introduction	5.1
5.2	Process Control System	5.2
5.3	Modes of Control Action	5.3
5.4	Discontinuous Mode	5.4
	5.4.1 ON-OFF Controllers	5.4
5.5	Continuous Mode	5.6
	5.5.1 Proportional Controller	5.6
	5.5.2 Integral Controller	5.11
	5.5.3 Derivative Controller	5.12
5.6	Composite Controllers (Control Action)	5.14
	5.6.1 PI Control Action	5.14
	5.6.2 Proportional and Derivative (PD) Controller	5.16
	5.6.3 PID Control Action	5.17
5.7	Comparison of P, PI, PD and PID Controller	5.19
•	Important Points	5.19
•	Practice Questions	5.20
•	Previous Year MSBTE Questions and Answers (As Per 'E' Scheme)	5.21

6. Servo System — 6.1 - 6.26

- 6.1 Introduction — 6.1
- 6.2 Servo System — 6.2
- 6.3 A.C. and D.C. Servo Systems — 6.2
  - 6.3.1 D.C. Position Control System (D.C. Servosystem) — 6.2
  - 6.3.2 (A.C. Position Control System) A.C. Servosystem) — 6.3
- 6.4 Servo-Components — 6.4
  - 6.4.1 Potentiometer as Error Detector — 6.5
- 6.5 Synchros — 6.6
  - 6.5.1 Synchro Error Detector — 6.6
- 6.6 Servomotors — 6.8
  - 6.6.1 Difference from Normal 2 Phase Induction Motor — 6.8
  - 6.6.2 Two-phase A.C. Servo Motors — 6.10
  - 6.6.3 Torque-speed Characteristics of A.C. Servomotor — 6.10
- 6.7 D.C. Servomotor — 6.11
  - 6.7.1 Armature Controlled d.c. Servomotor — 6.12
  - 6.7.2 Field Controlled d.c. Servomotor — 6.14
  - 6.7.3 Comparison between Armature Controlled and Field Controlled d.c. Servomotors — 6.16
  - 6.7.4 Comparison between D.C. and A.C. Servomotor — 6.16
- 6.8 Stepper Motor — 6.17
  - 6.8.1 Variable Reluctance Stepper Motor — 6.17
  - 6.8.2 Permanent-Magnet Stepper Motor — 6.21
  - 6.8.3 Use of Stepper Motor in Control System — 6.22
  - 6.8.4 Comparison between Stepper Motor and D.C. Servomotor — 6.23
- • Important Points — 6.24
- • Practice Questions — 6.24
- • Previous Year MSBTE Questions and Answers (As Per 'E' Scheme) — 6.25

***

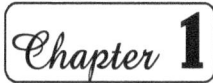

INTRODUCTION TO CONTROL SYSTEM

About This Chapter ...

After reading this chapter students can understand –
- Introduction
- Control System
- Control System Classification
- Mathematical Foundation
- Laplace Transform (L.T.)
- Transfer Function
- Order of a System
- Block Diagram Representation

1.1 INTRODUCTION

- Automatic control system play an important role in the development and advancement of modern civilisation and technology.
- But industrially, control systems have numerous applications such as quality control of manufactured products, machine tool control, space technology and weapons systems etc.
- Before studying control systems we should know what is a system ?
- **A system is a combination of individual elements or components that act together in performing a specific function.**
- **Thus, a system is a collection of objects in such a manner so as to achieve an aim or output.**
- Thus, we can say that, a system, has an input, an output and a way to achieve this input-output combination.

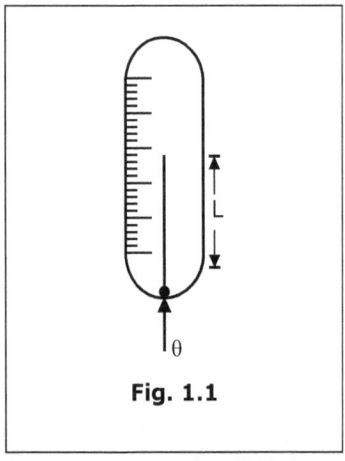

Fig. 1.1

- So, electrical, mechanical, hydraulic, pneumatic, chemical, analog, digital or any other elements, devices or processes may be regarded as a system.
- Example – Consider a mercury thermometer shown in Fig. 1.1.
- As temperature around the mercury bulb increases, the length of the mercury column increases proportionally.
- Thus, a thermometer is identified as a system whose input is temperature (θ) and output is length (L) of the mercury column.

System Classification:

A general system is classified in two types.

(i) SISO (Single Input Single Output). (ii) MIMO (Multi-Input Multi-Output).

(i) Single Input Single Output System (SISO):

A system which gives single (only one) output corresponding to a single input is called as a Single Input Single Output System (SISO).

Example – Thermometer System (as explained above).

(ii) Multi-Input Multi-Output (MIMO):

A system which has more than one inputs and outputs is called Multi-Input Multi-Output System (MIMO).

Example – Driving an automobile.

- Here, the position of the steering wheel is one input producing an output as direction of two front wheels.
- The second input is the pressure exerted on the accelerator which produces output as speed variation of the automobile.
- So automobile has two inputs and two outputs, thus it is an MIMO system.

1.2 CONTROL SYSTEM

Definition:

The control system is a system, in which any quantity of interest in a machine, mechanism or other equipment is maintained or changed in with a desired manner.

So, control system must have –
1. One or more inputs.
2. One or more outputs.
3. An arrangement to achieve this input-output combination.

1. Input: *Input is the excitation applied to a control system from an external source in order to produce an output.*

2. **Output:** *The actual response obtained from a system is called output.*

3. **Control:** Control means to regulate, direct or command a system so that the desired objective is attained.

1.2.1 Practical Examples

QUESTIONS

1. Draw the block diagram of a temperature control system and state the function of each block. **(4M)**

---

1. **Liquid Level Controller:**
   - Fig. 1.2 shows the liquid level control system which can maintain the liquid level 'h' (controlled output) of tank even though the output flow rate through the valve V_1 is varied.
   - The liquid level is sensed by float (which is the feedback path element) which positions the slider arm B on a potentiometer.

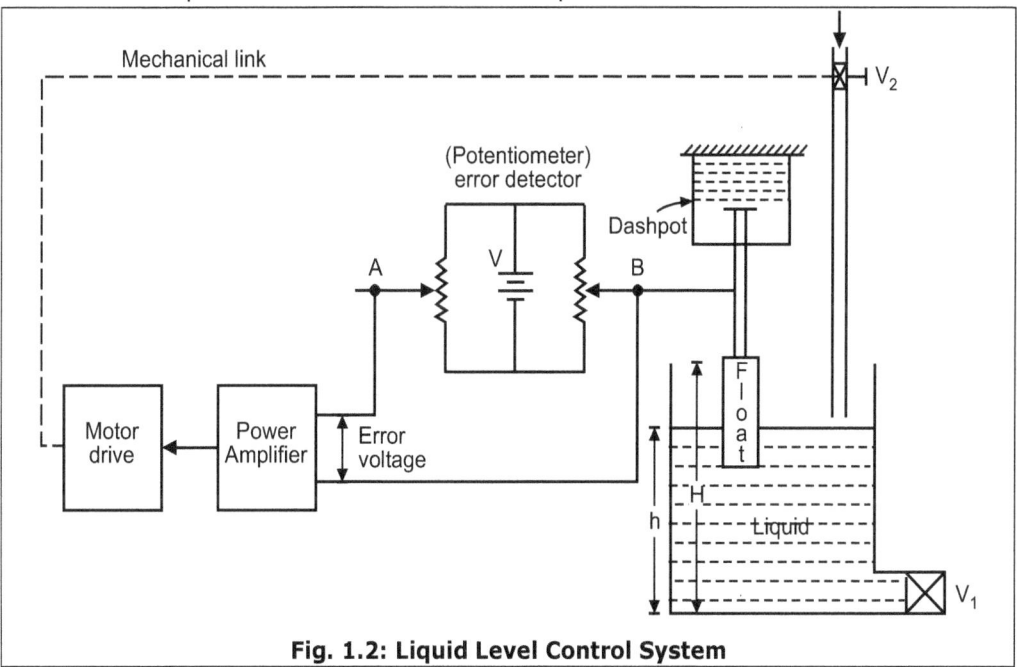

Fig. 1.2: Liquid Level Control System

- The slider arm A of the other potentiometer is positioned corresponding to the desired liquid level H (which is the reference input).

- When the liquid level rises or falls, the potentiometer or error detector gives an error voltage (which is the actuating signal) proportional to the change in the liquid level.

- This error signal actuates the motor through the power amplifier (which is the control element) which then conditions the plant (i.e. opening or closing the valve V_2) in order to restore the desired liquid level.
- Thus, the control system automatically attempts to correct any deviation between actual and desired liquid level.

2. **Temperature Controller:**
- Consider a thermal system as shown in Fig. 1.3, where temperature of the hot water is to be maintained at a desired value.
- The desired temperature or the reference input is set on the dial of the automatic controller.
- The output, that is the temperature of the outgoing hot water is compared with the desired value in the controller.
- Then, the controller generates an actuating signal which positions the control valve opening for steam supply. If the temperature of the hot water is greater than the desired value, the control valve is closed proportionally.

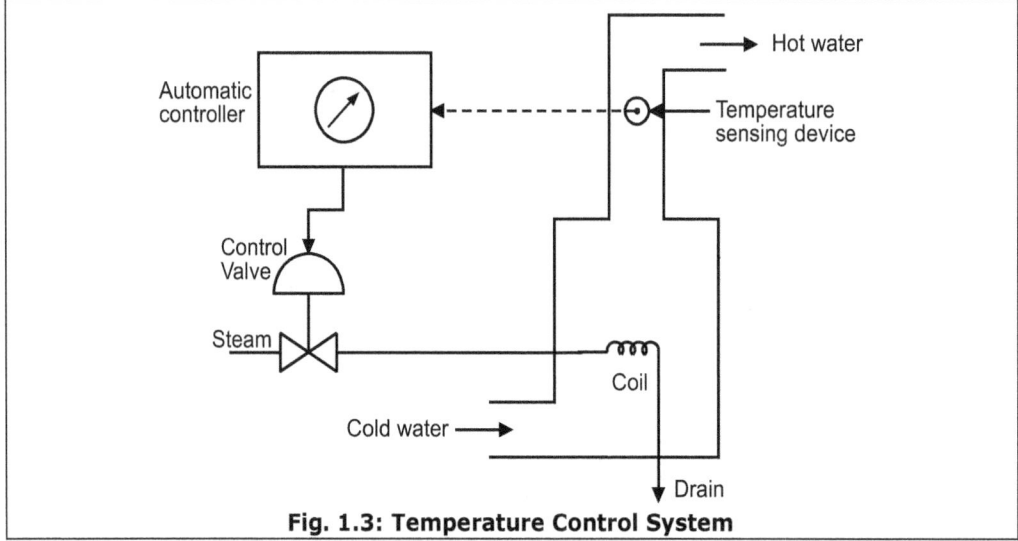

Fig. 1.3: Temperature Control System

- If the temperature of the hot water is less than the desired value, the control valve is opened proportionally.

1.3 CONTROL SYSTEM CLASSIFICATION

- Control action is a quantity which produces desired output.
- Depending on whether the control action is dependent on the output or not, the control systems are classified as –
    (1) Open Loop System (Non-feedback).
    (2) Closed Loop System (Feedback).

1.3.1 Open Loop System

QUESTIONS

1. Define open loop control system. Give two examples. **(2M)**
2. Define open loop control and closed loop system. Draw the block diagram of open loop system. **(4M)**
3. State and describe the advantages of open loop system. **(4M)**

- In an open loop system, the input is directly applied to the system through a controller and the output known as controlled output is obtained.
- In this case, the input to the controller or the control action is in no way affected by the value of controlled output i.e. the output is neither measured nor feedback for comparison with the input.

Definition:

A system in which the control action is totally independent of the output of the system is called as an open loop system.

Fig. 1.4 shows the block diagram of an open loop system.

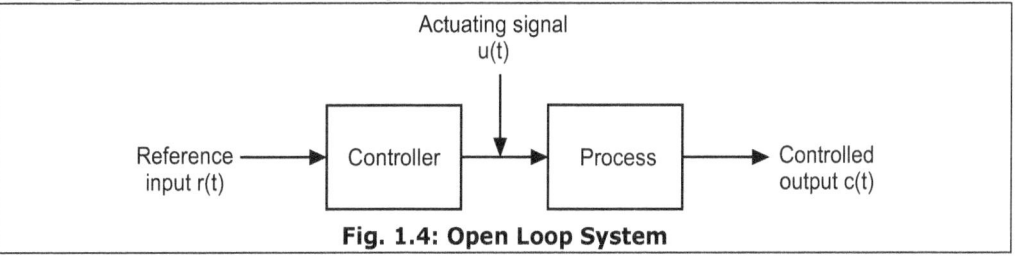

Fig. 1.4: Open Loop System

As shown in Fig. 1.4,

- Reference input r(t) is applied to the controller which generates the actuating signal u(t).
- Actuating signal u(t) actuates the process to give controlled output c(t).
- The control action has nothing to do with the output c(t) i.e. there is no relation between input and output that can form a loop.
- Hence, the system is open loop.
- It is also known as a non-feedback system.

Examples:

1. **Washing Machine:**
    - In washing machine, the *input is dirty clothes* and *output is clean clothes*. The water, soap etc. can also be considered as inputs.
    - The *control action* is *determined by the timer* (time set). But at the particular time set we can not get 100% clean cloths i.e. control action is

not responsible for the desired output. **Hence, washing machine action is open loop.**

2. **Control of Traffic by Road Traffic Lamps:**
   - The glowing of red and green lamps is the *input*.
   - When red lamp glows, the traffic in that direction stops.
   - When green lamp glows, the traffic flow starts in that direction.
   - So, the traffic action (flow or stop) is the *output*.
   - The *control action* is determined by the time set to glow the red or green lamp.
   - But the control action has nothing to do with the actual status of the output. i.e. suppose, suddenly an accident happens on the road, the traffic will stop there, but the red and green lamp will glow alternately at the set time. Hence, it is an *open loop* system.

3. **Bread Toaster:**
   - A toaster simply heats the bread for some time. This time determines the quality of bread i.e. either soft or hard.
   - Therefore, the bread is *input*.
   - The quality of bread soft or hard is *output*.
   - The time required for determining the quality of bread is the *control action*.
   - This control action, has nothing to do with the status of output.
   - Hence, it is an *open loop system*.

- **Advantages of open loop system:**
  1. Simple design and construction.
  2. Economical.
  3. Easy maintenance.
  4. Stable.

- **Disadvantages of open loop system:**
  1. Inaccurate and unreliable.
  2. To maintain quality and accuracy, recalibration is necessary every time.

1.3.2 Closed Loop System

QUESTIONS	
1. Draw the block diagram of closed loop control system.	(4M)
2. Define a closed loop control system. Give two examples of each.	(2M)

Closed loop system is one in which the output signal has direct effect upon the control action i.e. the closed loop systems are feedback system.

Definition:

A system in which the control action is dependent on the output is called a closed loop system.

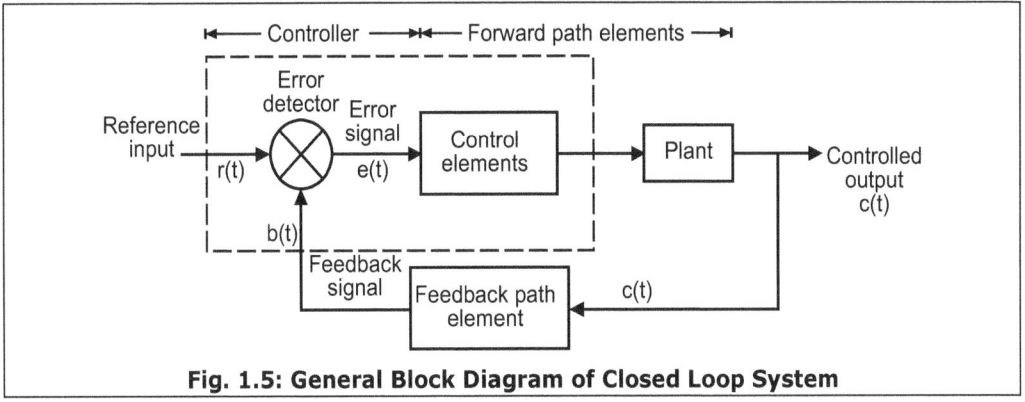

Fig. 1.5: General Block Diagram of Closed Loop System

Fig. 1.5 shows the general block diagram of the closed loop system.

$r(t)$ = Reference input,

$e(t)$ = Error or actuating signal,

$b(t)$ = Feedback system

- **Error detector:** Error detector compares the reference input r(t) and feedback signal b(t) and gives the result as error signal e(t).

Note: When feedback signal is positive, i.e. system is called **positive feedback system** and e(t) = r(t) + b(t).

When the feedback signal is negative, system is called **negative feedback system** and e(t) = r(t) – b(t).

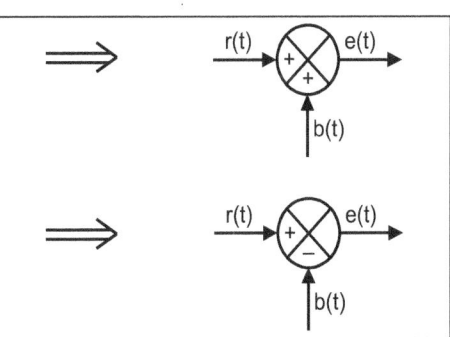

- **Control elements:** The error signal r(t) is applied to the control element which is used to activate the control element. Therefore, error signal is also called actuating signal.

- **Feedback path element:** It is the transducer that produces feedback signal b(t) proportional to the controlled output c(t).

- **Controller:** The action of the controller will be to drive the controlled element in such a manner that the error is reduced to zero i.e. the feedback signal is equal to reference input r(t).

- **Plant:** It is the body or process or machine whose condition is controlled.

Some important terms in closed loop system are –

(1) Reference input r(t): It is an external signal applied to a closed loop control system in order to obtain a desired output.

(2) Feedback signal b(t): It is the signal proportional to the controlled output c(t).

(3) Error signal e(t): It is difference or sum of r(t) and b(t).

(4) Controller: It produces a controlled output based on the error signal.

(5) Forward path: It is the transmission path from the actuating signal to the controlled output.

Examples:

1. Human Beings

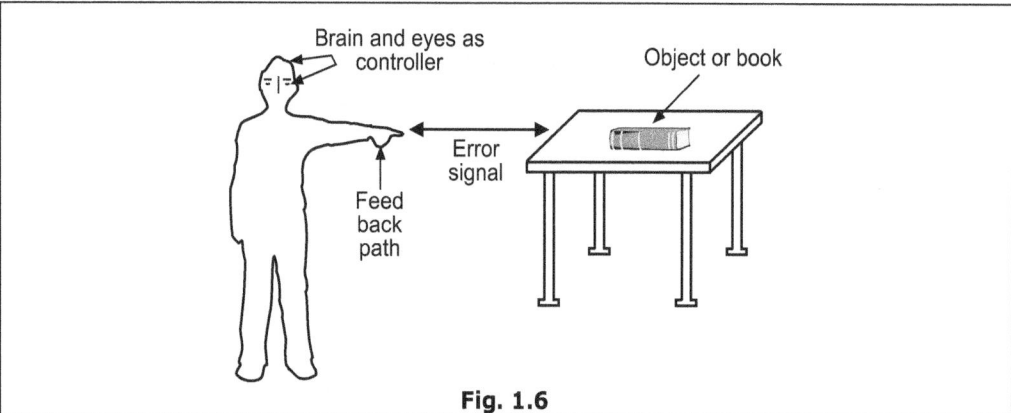

Fig. 1.6

- Human being is the best example of a closed-loop system. Consider that the objective (human being) has to reach an object (e.g. book) on table.
- In this case, the *brain* performs the work of the controller and the eyes serve as the measuring element which gives continuous feedback regarding the position of hand which is the output.
- Here, the reference input is the object (book).
- The distance between the hand and the object is the error which is brought to zero by the controller i.e. brain by giving instructions to the hand to move closer to the object.
- When error i.e. distance between the book and hand is zero, we get the desired output.

2. Automatic Electric Irons

- An automatic iron regulates the temperature of the iron such that for a given quality of cloth selection, the temperature remains in a specified range.
- Suppose the temperature is set at 40°C.
- When the temperature falls below 40°C, heating starts and when it exceeds 40°C, the heating stops. Hence, it is a closed loop system with temperature as the control action which depends on output temperature.

- It is shown in Fig. 1.7.

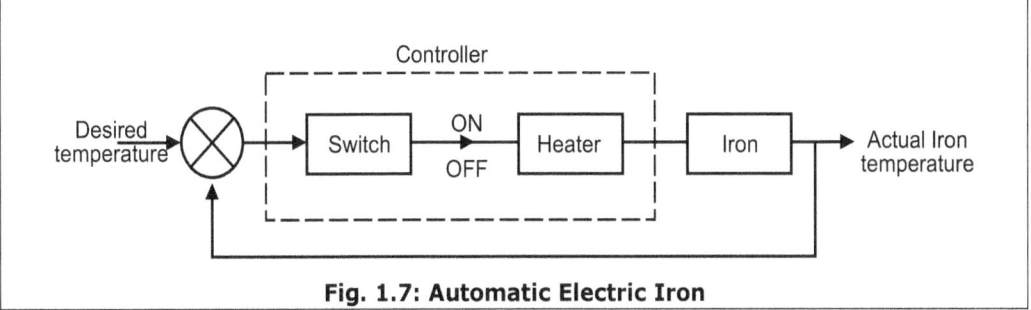

Fig. 1.7: Automatic Electric Iron

3. Driving an Automobile

A simple block diagram of an automobile steering mechanism is shown in Fig. 1.8.

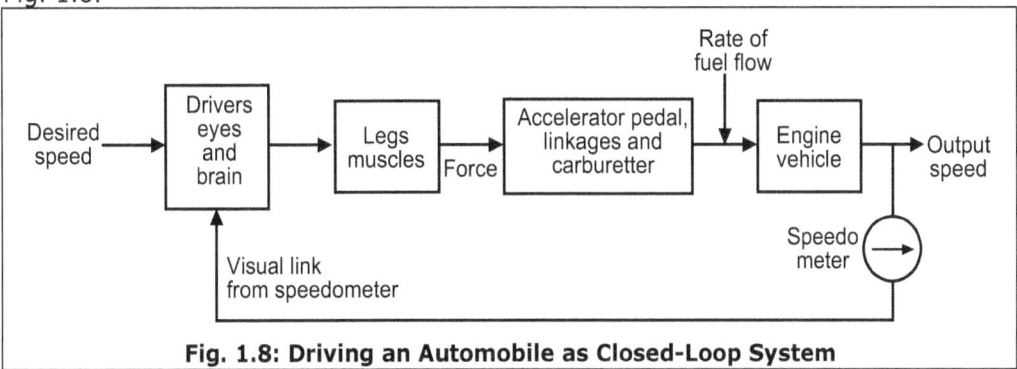

Fig. 1.8: Driving an Automobile as Closed-Loop System

- The driver senses visually and by body movement the error between the actual and the desired directions of the automobile.

- Additional information is also available to the driver who senses the movement of the steering wheel through his hands. This information forms the feedback signal, which are interpreted by the driver's brain, who then signals his hands to adjust the steering wheel accordingly. Hence, the closed loop system.

- **Advantages of Closed Loop System:**
    1. High accuracy.
    2. High bandwidth.
    3. Facilitates automation.
    4. Reduced effects of non-linearities.
    5. It senses changes in outputs.

- **Disadvantages of Closed Loop System:**
    1. Complex design.
    2. Costly maintenance.
    3. Unstable system.

1.3.3 Comparison Between Open Loop and Closed Loop Systems

QUESTION
1. Compare open loop and closed loop control system. (any six points)   **(4M)**

Sr. No.	Open Loop System	Closed Loop System
1.	Non-feedback system, so feedback element is absent.	Feedback system, so feed back element is present.
2.	No error detector.	Error detector is present.
3.	Highly sensitive to parameter changes.	Less sensitive to parameter changes.
4.	Inaccurate.	Accurate.
5.	Small bandwidth.	Large bandwidth.
6.	Stable.	Can be unstable.
7.	Economical.	Costly.
8.	**Examples:** Traffic lamps on road, automatic toaster, coffee maker, hair dryer.	**Examples:** Human begins, temperature control of oven, automatic electric iron, voltage stabilizers.

1.4 MATHEMATICAL FOUNDATION

- For the analysis and design of practical control systems, we need to use applied mathematics.
- However, one of the major purpose of control-systems study is to develop a set of analytical tools so that the designer can arrive at reasonably predictable and reliable designs without depending completely on the drudgery (means unpleasant and uninteresting) of experimentation or computer simulation.
- For study of control theory, the required mathematical background includes *complex-variable theory, differential and differential equations, Laplace transformation and z-transformation* and so on.

1.4.1 Complex-Variable Concept

- **Complex Variable:**
  - Complex means the combination of real and imaginary components.
  - The classical control-system theory is based on the application of complex variables and their functions, since both the transform variable s and the z-transform variable z are complex variables.
  - A complex variable s has two components –
  - A real component σ and an imaginary component ω.

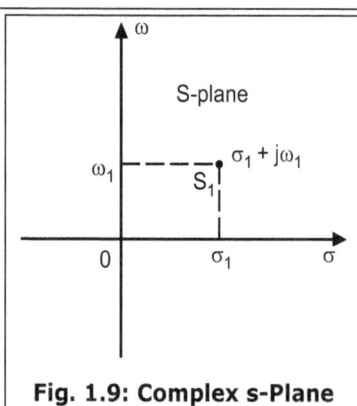

Fig. 1.9: Complex s-Plane

- For graphical representation, the real component of s is represented by a σ axis in the horizontal direction, and the imaginary component is measured along the vertical jω axis, in the complex s-plane as shown in Fig. 1.10. Here any arbitrary point $s = s_1$ is defined by the co-ordinates $\sigma = \sigma_1$ and $\omega = \omega_1$ or simply $s_1 = \sigma_1 + j\omega_1$.

- **Functions of Complex Variables:**
  - The function G(s) is said to be a function of the complex variable s if for every value of s, there is one or more corresponding values of G(s).
  - Since s is defined to have real and imaginary parts, the function G(s) is also represented by its real and imaginary parts,

    i.e. $\quad G(s) = \text{Re } G(s) + j\text{Im } G(s) \quad \ldots (1.1)$

- where,

  Re G(s) denotes the real part of G(s), and

  Im G(s) denotes the imaginary part of G(s). Thus, the function G(s) can also be represented by the complex G(s) plane, whose horizontal axis represents Re G(s) and the vertical axis represents the imaginary component of G(s).

- If for every value of s, there is only one corresponding value for G(s), then G(s) is said to be a *single-valued function* and the mapping from points in the s-plane onto points in the G(s) plane is described as single-values as shown in Fig. 1.11.

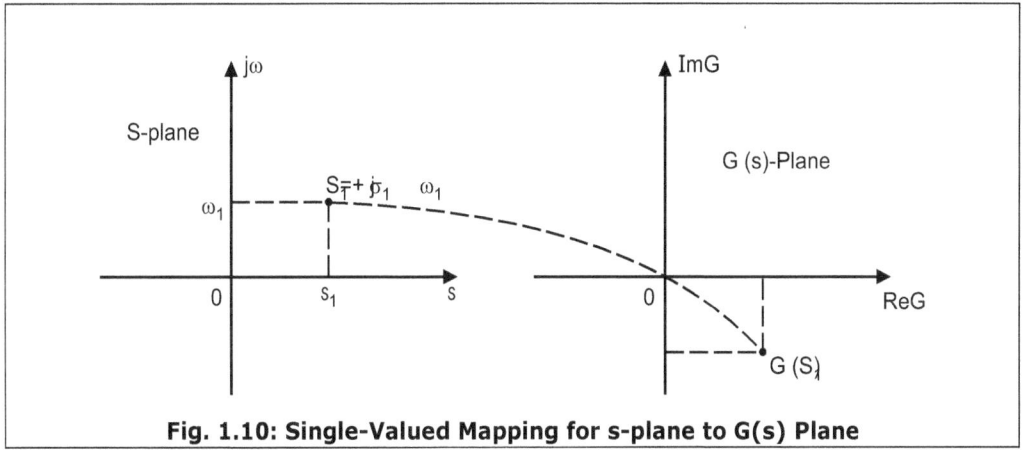

Fig. 1.10: Single-Valued Mapping for s-plane to G(s) Plane

- If the mapping from G(s) plane to the s-plane is also single valued, the mapping is called one-to-one.

  For example, for the function,

  $$G(s) = \frac{1}{s(s+1)} \quad \ldots (1.2)$$

- It is shown that, for each value of s, there is only one (unique) corresponding value for G(s).

- However, the reverse mapping is not true, for instance, the point $G(s) = \infty$ is mapped onto two points, $s = 0$ and $s = -1$ in the s-plane.

1.4.2 Differential Equations

- One class of equations which has a broad application in the description of physical laws is **differential equations**.

Definition:

A *differential equation is any algebraic or transcendental equality which involves either differentials or derivatives.*

- Differential equations are useful for relating rates of change of variables and other parameters.

1.4.3 Linear and Non-Linear System

Definition:

- **A linear system is one whose differential equation consisting of the dependent variables and their derivatives in first degree.**
- **A linear ordinary differential equation is one in which the dependent variables and their derivatives have the first degree.**
- A large class of systems and phenomena in engineering are mostly formulated in terms of differential equations.
- These equations generally involves derivatives and integrals of dependent variables with respect to the independent variable.
- For example, a series electric RLC network can be represented by the equation,

$$Ri(t) + L\frac{di(t)}{dt} + \frac{1}{C}\int i(t)\,dt = v(t) \qquad \ldots (1.3)$$

where,

    R = Resistance; Ω

    L = Inductance; H

    C = Capacitance; F

    i(t) = Current in the network; A

    v(t) = Applied voltage; v

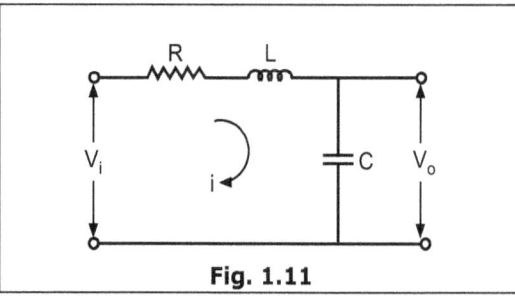

Fig. 1.11

- In this case, v(t) is the forcing function, v(t) the independent variable and i(t) the dependent variable or the unknown that is to be determined by solving the differential equation.
- Similarly, for a series mechanical mass-spring-damper system, the differential equation of the system may be written as – (Refer Fig. 1.13).

$$M\frac{d^2y(t)}{dt^2} + B\frac{dy(t)}{dt} + ky(t) = f(t) \qquad \ldots (1.4)$$

where,

$$f(t) = \text{Applied force}$$
$$M = \text{Mass}$$
$$B = \text{Damping coefficient}$$
$$k = \text{Linear spring constant}$$
$$y(t) = \text{Displacement}$$

- Equation (1.4) is a *second order **linear differential equation*** and we refer to the system as a *second order system*.
- Equation (1.3) is known as *integrodifferential equation* since the integral is also involved.
- Also it is known as *first order differential equation*.

  The differential equation of an nth order system is written as,

$$a_{n+1}\frac{d y^n(t)}{dt^n} + a_n\frac{d y^{n-1}(t)}{dt^{n-1}} + \ldots\ldots + a_2\frac{dy(t)}{dt} + a_1 y(t) = f(t) \qquad \ldots (1.5)$$

- The differential equations (1.3) to (1.5) are also known as **linear ordinary differential equations** where the coefficients $a_1, a_2, \ldots\ldots a_{n+1}$ are not functions of y(t) and since y(t) and its derivatives are all of first order.
- **Non-Linear System:**

Definition:

A non-linear system is one whose differential equation consisting other than linear terms.

A linear differential equation is a differential equation consisting of a sum of linear terms. All the others are non-linear differential equations.

Many of the physical and non-linear systems are described by non-linear differential equation.

For example, the differential equation that describes the motion of the pendulum as shown in Fig. 1.13 is:

$$ML\frac{d^2\theta(t)}{dt^2} + Mg\sin\theta(t) = 0 \qquad \ldots (1.6)$$

As the $\theta(t)$ appears as a sine function, equation (1.6) is non-linear and hence the system is called a ***non-linear system***.

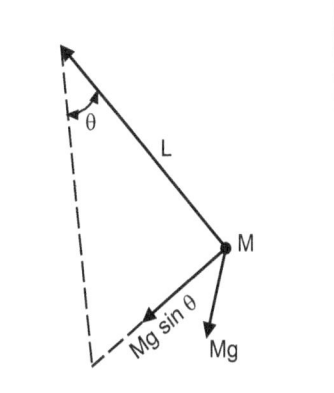

Fig. 1.12: A Simple Pendulum

1.4.4 Time Variable and Time Invariant System

- The differential equations are either dependent or independent of time. There are two types of systems.
    1. Time variable system
    2. Time invariant system
- **Time Variable Systems:**

Definition:

A time variable system is one whose differential equation having one or more terms depends explicity on the dependent variable time 't'.

A time-variable differential equation is a differential equation in which one or more terms depend explicitly on the independent variable time 't'.

Example:

The differential equation $t^2 \frac{d^2y}{dt^2} + y = x$ where, x and y are dependent variables, is time-variable since the term $t^2 \frac{d^2y}{dt^2}$ depend explicitly on t through the coefficient t^2.

- **Time Invariant System:**

Definition:

A time invariant system is one whose differential equation having one of the terms depend implicity on the independent variable time 't'.

A time-invariant differential equation is a differential equation in which none of the terms depends implicitly on the independent variable time t.

- This definition implies that the process defined by a time-invariant differential equation does not vary with time.

- **Example:**

Any differential equation of the form

$$\sum_{i=0}^{n} a_i \frac{d^i y}{dt^i} = \sum_{i=0}^{m} b_i \frac{d^i x}{dt^i} \qquad \ldots (1.7)$$

where, the coefficients $a_0, a_1, \ldots, a_n, b_0, b_1, \ldots, b_m$ are constants is **time-invariant**, since the equation depends only implicitly on 't' through the dependent variables x and y and their derivatives.

1.5 LAPLACE TRANSFORM (L.T.)

The Laplace transform is one of the mathematical tools used for the solution of *linear ordinary differential equation.*

1.5.1 Significance of Laplace Transform in Control System

1. *The homogeneous equation and the particular integral of the solution are obtained in one operation.*

2. *The Laplace transform converts the differential equation into an algebraic equation in s. Then it is possible to manipulate the algebraic equation by simple algebraic rules to obtain the solution in the s-domain. The final solution is obtained by taking the inverse Laplace transform.*

Definition of the Laplace Transform:

Given the real function f(t) that satisfies the condition,

$$\int_0^\infty |f(t) e^{-\sigma t}| \, dt < \infty \qquad \ldots (1.8)$$

For some finite σ, the Laplace transform of f (t) is defined as,

$$F(s) = \int_0^\infty f(t) e^{-st} \, dt \qquad \ldots (1.9)$$

or

$$F(s) = \text{L.T. of } f(t) = L[f(t)] \qquad \ldots (1.10)$$

Laplace Operator:

The variable s is known as **Laplace operator**, which is a complex variable, i.e. $s = \sigma + j\omega$.

The equation (1.9) is also known as the **one-sided Laplace Transform**, since the integration is taken from t = 0 to ∞.

SOLVED EXAMPLES

Example 1.1: Let f (t) be a unit-step function that is defined as

$$f(t) = u_s(t) = 1 \; ; \quad t > 0$$
$$= 0 \quad\quad\quad ; \quad t < 0 \qquad \ldots (1)$$

The L.T. of f(t) is obtained as,

$$F(s) = L[u_s(t)] = \int_0^\infty u_s(t) e^{-st} \, dt$$

$$= -\frac{1}{s} e^{-st} \Big|_0^\infty$$

$$= \frac{1}{s} \qquad \ldots (2)$$

$$\therefore \quad f(t) = 1$$

Then, L.T. is,

$$\boxed{F(s) = \frac{1}{s}}$$

Example 1.2: Consider the exponential function,

$$f(t) = e^{-\alpha t} \; ; \; t \geq 0 \qquad \ldots (1)$$

where, α is constant.

Then the L.T. of f(t) is written as [From equation (1.9)].

$$F(s) = \int_0^\infty e^{-\alpha t} \cdot e^{-st} \, dt$$

$$= -\frac{e^{-(s+\alpha)t}}{s+\alpha} \bigg|_0^\infty$$

$$= \frac{1}{s+\alpha}$$

Therefore,

For $f(t) = e^{-\alpha t}$

The L.T. is,

$$\boxed{F(s) = \frac{1}{s+\alpha}}$$

1.5.2 Important Theorems of Laplace Transform

The application of the Laplace transform in many instances are simplified by the utilisation of the properties of some theorems. These properties are given by the following theorems –

Theorem 1: Multiplication by a constant

Let k is a constant, and F(s) is the Laplace transform of f(t). Then,

$$L[k \, f(t)] = k \, F(s) \qquad \ldots (1.11)$$

Theorem 2: Sum and difference

Let $F_1(s)$ and $F_2(s)$ are Laplace transform of the functions $f_1(t)$ and $f_2(t)$. Then,

$$L[f_1(t) \pm f_2(t)] = F_1(s) \pm F_2(s) \qquad \ldots (1.12)$$

Theorem 3: Differentiation

Let F(s) is the Laplace transform of f(t), and f(0) is the limit of f(t) as t approaches 0. Then, the Laplace transform of the time derivative of f(t) is,

$$L\left(\frac{d \, f(t)}{dt}\right) = s \, F(s) - \lim_{t \to 0} f(t) = s \, F(s) - f(0) \qquad \ldots (1.13)$$

Also, for higher order derivatives of f(t)

$$L\left(\frac{d^n f(t)}{dt^n}\right) = s^n F(s) - \lim_{t \to 0}\left(s^{n-1} f(t) + s^{n-2}\frac{d\,f(t)}{dt} + \ldots + \frac{d^{n-1} f(t)}{dt^{n-1}}\right)$$

$$= s^n F(s) - s^{n-1} f(0) - s^{n-2} f^{(1)}(0) \ldots f^{(n-1)}(0) \qquad \ldots (1.14)$$

Theorem 4: Integration

The Laplace transform of the first order integral of f (t) is,

$$L\left(\int_0^t f(t)\,dt\right) = \frac{F(s)}{s} \qquad \ldots(1.15)$$

Also, for n^{th} order integration,

$$L\int_0^{t_1}\int_0^{t_2}\ldots\int_0^{t_n} f(\tau)\,d\tau\,dt_1\,dt_2\,dt_{n-1} = \frac{F(s)}{s^n} \qquad \ldots (1.16)$$

Theorem 5: Initial Value Theorem

If the Laplace transform of f(t) is F(s), then,

$$\lim_{t \to 0} f(t) = \lim_{s \to \infty} s\,F(s) \qquad \ldots (1.17)$$

This exists, if the time limit exists.

Theorem 6: Final Value Theorem

If the Laplace transform of f(t) is F(s), and if s F(s) is analytic on the imaginary axis and also in the right half of the s-plane, then,

$$\lim_{t \to \infty} f(t) = \lim_{s \to 0} s\,F(s) \qquad \ldots (1.18)$$

Theorem 7: Complex Shifting

The Laplace transform of f(t) multiplied by $e^{\alpha t}$, where α is constant,

$$L[e^{\pm \alpha t} f(t)] = F(s \pm \alpha) \qquad \ldots (1.19)$$

1.5.3 Inverse Laplace Transform

- The operation of obtaining f(t) from the L.T. of F(s) is termed as **Inverse Laplace Transform** which is given as,

$$f(t) = L^{-1}[F(s)] \qquad \ldots (1.20)$$

- **Inverse Laplace Transform by Partial Fraction Expansion:**
  - The Laplace transform operation containing rational functions can be carried out using a Laplace transform table and partial fraction expansion.
  - When the Laplace transform solution of a differential equation is a rational function in s, it can be written as –

$$X(s) = \frac{Q(s)}{P(s)} \qquad \ldots (1.21)$$

- where, P(s) and Q(s) are polynomials of s. The assumption is that the order of P(s) is greater than that of Q(s). Then the polynomial P(s) may be written as –

$$P(s) = s^n + a_1 s^{n-1} + \ldots + a_{n-1} s + a_n \quad \ldots (1.22)$$

where, $a_1, a_2 \ldots, a_n$ are real coefficients.

- The zeros of Q(s) are either real or complex cases of simple poles, multiple-order poles and complex-conjugate pairs.
- The methods of partial-fraction expansion will be given for the cases of simple poles, multiple-order and complex-conjugate poles of X(s).

For all the poles of X(s) which are simple and real, the partial-fraction expansion is,

Equation (1.21) can be written as,

$$X(s) = \frac{Q(s)}{P(s)} = \frac{Q(s)}{(s + s_1)(s + s_2) \ldots (s + s_n)} \quad \ldots (1.23)$$

where, $s_1 \neq s_2 \neq \ldots \neq s_n$.

Apply partial-fraction expansion, equation (1.23) becomes,

$$X(s) = \frac{A_1}{s + s_1} + \frac{A_2}{s + s_2} + \frac{A_3}{s + s_3} + \ldots + \frac{A_n}{s + s_n} \quad \ldots (1.24)$$

The coefficients A_i ($\because i = 1, 2, \ldots, n$) is determined by multiplying both sides of equation (1.23) or (1.24) by $(s + s_i)$ and then setting s equal to $-s_i$.

To find coefficient A_1, we have to multiply both sides of equation (1.23) by $(s + s_1)$ and let $s = -s_1$.

Thus,

$$A_1 = \left[(s + s_1) \frac{Q(s)}{P(s)}\right]_{s = -s_1} = \frac{Q(-s_1)}{(s_2 - s_1)(s_3 - s_1) \ldots (s_n - s_1)} \quad \ldots (1.25)$$

Example 1.2: Consider the given function is,

$$X(s) = \frac{7s + 3}{(s + 1)(s + 2)(s + 3)} \quad \ldots (1)$$

This equation is written in the partial-fraction expanded form as,

$$X(s) = \frac{A_1}{s + 1} + \frac{A_2}{s + 2} + \frac{A_3}{s + 3} \quad \ldots (2)$$

Then, the coefficients A_1, A_2, A_3 are determined as,

$$A_1 = [(s + 1) \cdot X(s)]_{s = -1}$$

$$= \left[(s + 1) \cdot \frac{7s + 3}{(s + 1)(s + 2)(s + 3)}\right]_{s = -1}$$

$$= \frac{7(-1) + 3}{(-1 + 2)(-1 + 3)} = \frac{-4}{2} = -2$$

$$A_2 = [(s + 2) \cdot X(s)]_{s = -2}$$

$$= \left[(s+2) \cdot \frac{7s+3}{(s+1)(s+2)(s+3)}\right]_{s=-2}$$

$$= \frac{7(-2)+3}{(-2+1)(-2+3)} = \frac{-14+3}{(-1)(1)}$$

$$= 11$$

$$A_3 = [(s+3) \cdot X(s)]_{s=-3}$$

$$= \left[(s+3) \cdot \frac{7s+3}{(s+1)(s+2)(s+3)}\right]_{s=-3}$$

$$= \frac{7(-3)+3}{(-3+1)(-3+2)} = \frac{-18}{2}$$

$$= -9$$

Thus, equation (2) becomes,

$$X(s) = \frac{-2}{(s+1)} + \frac{11}{(s+2)} + \frac{-9}{(s+3)} \quad \ldots (3)$$

1.5.4 Laplace Transform for Standaed Functions

Laplace Transform F(s)	Time Function f(t)
1	Unit impulse function $\delta(t)$
$\frac{1}{s}$	Unit step function $u_s(t)$
$\frac{1}{s^2}$	Unit ramp function t
$\frac{n!}{s^{n+1}}$	t^n (n is positive integer)
$\frac{1}{s+\alpha}$	$e^{-\alpha t}$
$\frac{1}{(s+\alpha)^2}$	$t e^{-\alpha t}$
$\frac{n!}{(s+\alpha)^{n+1}}$	$t^n e^{-\alpha t}$ (n is positive integer)
$\frac{1}{(s+\alpha)(s+\beta)}$	$\frac{1}{\beta-\alpha}(e^{-\alpha t} - e^{-\beta t})$ $(\alpha \neq \beta)$
$\frac{s}{(s+\alpha)(s+\beta)}$	$\frac{1}{\beta-\alpha}(\beta e^{-\beta t} - \alpha e^{-\alpha t})$ $(\alpha \neq \beta)$
$\frac{1}{(s+\alpha)^2}$	$\frac{1}{\alpha}(1 - e^{-\alpha t})$

Laplace Transform F(s)	Time Function f(t)
$\dfrac{1}{s(s+\alpha)^2}$	$(-\alpha t)\,e^{-\alpha t}$
$\dfrac{\omega_n^2}{s^2+\omega_n^2}$	$\sin \omega_n t$
$\dfrac{s}{s^2+\omega_n^2}$	$\cos \omega_n t$
$\dfrac{\omega_n^2}{s^2+2\xi\omega_n s+\omega_n^2}$	$\dfrac{\omega_n}{\sqrt{1-\xi^2}}\,e^{-\xi\omega_n t}\sin\omega_n\sqrt{1-\xi^2}\,t\ (\xi<1)$

1.5.5 Application of Laplace Transform to the solution of Linear System

Linear differential equations can be solved using theorem of Laplace transform and table of Laplace transform.

The procedure for solution –

1. Transform the differential equation to the s-domain by Laplace transform using Laplace transform table.
2. Manipulate the transformed algebraic equation and solve for the output variable.
3. Perform partial fraction expansion i.e. by obtaining inverse Laplace transform from L.T. table.
4. Perform the inverse Laplace transform.

Example 1.3: Given the differential equation.

$$\dfrac{d^2x(t)}{dt^2} + 3\dfrac{dx(t)}{dt} + 2x(t) = 5\,u_s(t) \qquad \ldots (1)$$

where, $u_s(t)$ is the unit step function.

The initial conditions are $X(0) = -1$ and $X^{(1)}(0) = \dfrac{dx(t)}{dt}\bigg|_{t=0}^{t=2}$

To solve the differential equation,

Take L.T. on both sides of the equation (1.32).

$$s^2 x(s) - s x(0) - x^{(1)}(0) + 3s x(s) - 3x(0) + 2x(s) = \dfrac{5}{s} \qquad \ldots (2)$$

Substituting the values of initial conditions,

$$X(s) = \dfrac{-s^2 - s + 5}{s(s^2+3s+2)} = \dfrac{-s^2 - s + 5}{s(s+1)(s+2)} \qquad \ldots (3)$$

Equation (3) is expanded by partial fraction expansion,

$$X(s) = \frac{5}{2s} - \frac{5}{s+1} + \frac{3}{s(s+2)} \qquad \ldots (4)$$

Taking inverse L.T. of equation (4),

$$x(t) = \frac{5}{2} - 5e^{-t} + \frac{3}{2}e^{-2t} \quad (\text{for } t \geq 0) \qquad \ldots (5)$$

If only magnitude of the steady state equation is to be found, then by final value theorem,

$$\lim_{t \to \infty} X(t) = \lim_{s \to 0} sX(s) = \lim_{s \to 0} \frac{-s^2 - s + 5}{s^2 + 3s + 2} = \frac{5}{2}$$

1.6 TRANSFER FUNCTION

- The first and the most important step in the analysis and design of control systems is the mathematical modelling of controlled process.
- Suppose, for a given controlled process, the set of variables that identify the dynamic characteristics of the process should first be defined.
- For example, consider a motor used for control purposes.
- We have to identify the applied voltage, current in the armature windings, developed torque, angular displacement and velocity etc.
- These variables are interrelated through established physical laws that lead to mathematical equations that describe the dynamics of the motor.
- Depending on the operating conditions of the motor, the system equation may be linear, non-linear, time-varying or time invariant.
- For practical reasons, assumptions and approximations are made to physical systems.
- Whenever possible these systems are studied using linear systems theory because non-linear systems are difficult to solve.
- Note that, the analysis is applicable only for the range of variables in which the linearization is valid.

Definition:

Transfer function of a linear time-invariant system is defined as the ratio of the Laplace transform of the output variable to the Laplace transform of the input variable assuming that all the initial conditions are zero.

$$\text{T.F.} = \frac{\text{L.T. of output}}{\text{L.T. of input}}$$

Consider the mass-spring dash pot system shown in Fig. 1.13.

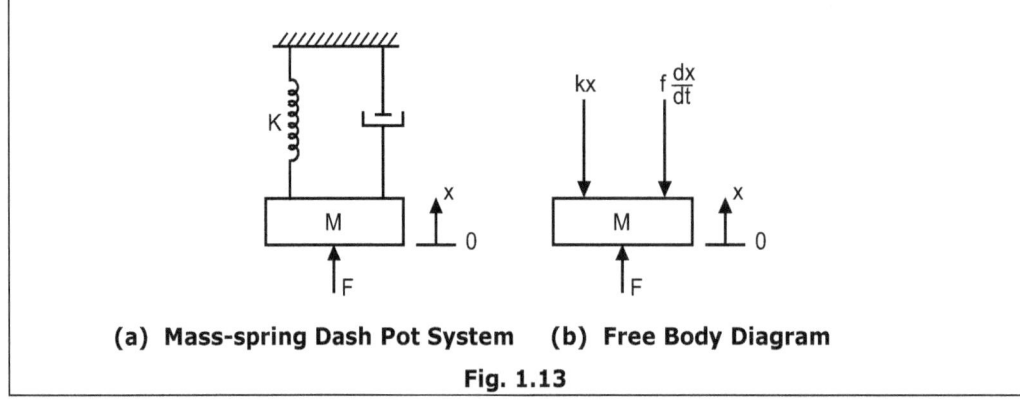

(a) Mass-spring Dash Pot System   **(b) Free Body Diagram**

Fig. 1.13

- Here, a mass M is attached to a spring (stiffness k) and a dashpot (viscous friction coefficient f) on which the force F acts, whereas displacement x is positive.

- The zero position is taken to be at the point where the spring and mass are in static equilibrium.

Apply the Newton's Law of motion to the free-body diagram, then the force equation is,

$$F - f\frac{dx}{dt} - kx = M\frac{d^2x}{dt^2}$$

∴ $$F = M\frac{d^2x}{dt^2} + f\frac{dx}{dt} + kx \qquad \ldots (1.26)$$

This equation is a second order differential equation.

$$F(s) = Ms^2 X(s) + f s X(s) + kX(s)$$

Then the transfer function is,

$$G(s) = \frac{X(s)}{F(s)}$$

∴ $$G(s) = \frac{1}{Ms^2 + fs + k} \qquad \ldots (1.27)$$

- The highest power of the complex variable s in the denominator of transfer function determines the order of the system.

- Thus, mass-spring dash pot system is a second-order system.

- **Impulse Response:**

    - Consider a linear time-invariant system having the input r(t) and the output c(t).

    - Then, the system can be characterised by its **impulse response g(t)**, which is defined as the output when the input is a unit-impulse function $\delta(t)$.

    - Once the impulse response of a linear system is known, the output of the system, c(t) with input r(t), and can be found using **transfer function.**

1.6.1 Derivation of Transfer Function for Open-Loop Control System

The transfer function of a linear time-invariant system is defined as the Laplace transform of the impulse response, with all initial conditions set to zero. Fig. 1.14 shows the open loop control system or single input single output system.

Let, $G(s)$ = Transfer function of a single input single output system

$r(t)$ = Input

$c(t)$ = Output

$g(t)$ = Impulse response

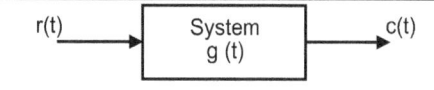

Fig. 1.14: Block Diagram of Open Loop System

Then, the transfer function $G(s)$ is defined as,

$$G(s) = L[g(t)] \qquad \ldots (1.28)$$

The transfer function $G(s)$ is a ratio of L.T. of the transfer function $G(s)$ for Fig. 1.14 is,

$$G(s) = \frac{\text{L.T. of output}}{\text{L.T. of input}}$$

$$\boxed{G(s) = \frac{C(s)}{R(s)}} \qquad \ldots (1.29)$$

1.6.2 Derivation of Transfer Function for Close Loop Control System

Fig. 1.15 (a) shows the block diagram of a negative feedback system

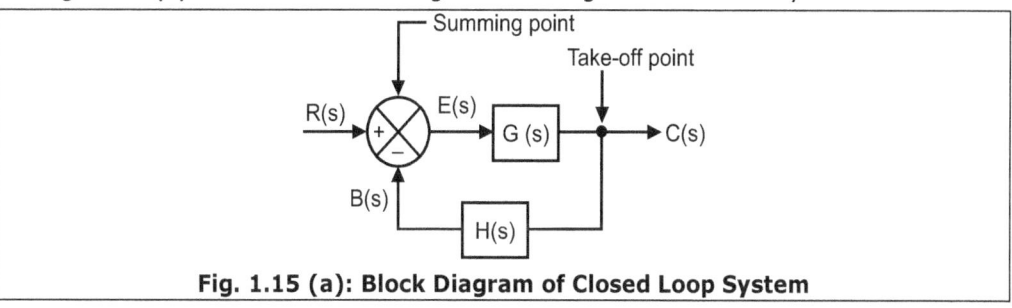

Fig. 1.15 (a): Block Diagram of Closed Loop System

where,
- $R(s)$ = Reference input
- $C(s)$ = Output signal
- $B(s)$ = Feedback signal
- $E(s)$ = Actuating signal
- $G(s) = \dfrac{C(s)}{E(s)}$ = Forward path transfer function
- $H(s)$ = Transfer function of feedback element
- $G(s)\,H(s) = \dfrac{B(s)}{E(s)}$ = loop transfer function
- $T(s) = \dfrac{C(s)}{R(s)}$ = Closed-loop transfer function

From Fig. 1.15 (a),

$$C(s) = G(s) E(s) \quad [\because \text{Output} = \text{gain} \times \text{input}] \quad \ldots (1.30)$$

$$\therefore \quad E(s) = R(s) - B(s) [\because \text{Error signal} = \text{subtraction of two inputs}]$$

$$= R(s) - H(s) C(s) \quad \ldots (1.31)$$

Eliminating $E(s)$ from equation (1.30) and (1.31), we have,

$$C(s) = G(s) R(s) - G(s) H(s) C(s)$$

$$\therefore C(s) [1 + G(s) H(s)] = G(s) R(s)$$

$$\therefore \quad \boxed{\frac{C(s)}{R(s)} = T(s) = \frac{G(s)}{1 + G(s) H(s)}} \quad \ldots (1.32)$$

$$R(s) \longrightarrow \boxed{\frac{G(s)}{1 + G(s) R(s)}} \longrightarrow C(s)$$

Fig. 1.15: (b) Reduction of Block Diagram of Fig. 1.15 (a)

Therefore, the system shown in Fig. 1.15 (a) can be reduced to a single block as shown in Fig. 1.15 (b).

For positive feedback, transfer function is,

$$\boxed{T(s) = \frac{C(s)}{R(s)} = \frac{G(s)}{1 - G(s) H(s)}} \quad \ldots (1.33)$$

1.6.3 Properties of the Transfer Function

1. The transfer function is defined only for a linear time-invariant system and not for non-linear systems.
2. The transfer function is the ratio of Laplace transform of output to the Laplace transform of input.
3. All initial conditions of the system are set to zero.
4. The transfer function is independent of the input of the system.
5. The transfer function of a continuous data system is expressed only as a function of complex variable s.

1.6.4 Transfer Function of R-C and R-L-C Electrical Circuits

The three basic elements in electrical systems are –

1. **Resistor**: By Ohm's Law,

$$V_R(t) = R i(t)$$

$\therefore$ Laplace transform is

$$V_R(s) = R I(s) \quad \ldots (1.34)$$

2. Inductor:

$$V_L(t) = L \cdot \frac{di(t)}{dt}$$

∴ Laplace transform is

$$V_L(s) = Ls\,I(s) \qquad \ldots (1.35)$$

3. Capacitor:

$$V_C(t) = \frac{1}{C}\int i(t)\,dt$$

∴ Laplace transform is,

$$V_C(s) = \frac{1}{Cs} I(s) \qquad \ldots (1.36)$$

1.6.5 Developing Differential Equations of R-C and R-L-C Electrical Circuits

Example 1.4: Find the transfer function of the given R-C circuit.

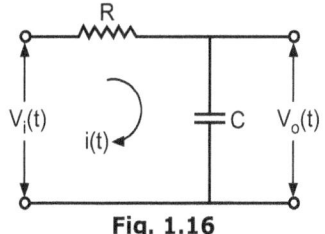

Fig. 1.16

Solution: Apply Kirchoff's Voltage Law (KVL) to loop

$$V_i(t) = R\,i(t) + \frac{1}{C}\int_0^t i(t)\,dt \qquad \ldots (1)$$

and output voltage across capacitor is,

$$V_o(t) = \frac{1}{C}\int_0^t i(t)\,dt \qquad \ldots (2)$$

Taking L.T. of equations (1) and (2) under zero initial conditions.

$$V_i(s) = R\,I(s) + \frac{1}{sC} I(s) \qquad \ldots (3)$$

∴
$$V_i(s) = \left(R + \frac{1}{sC}\right) I(s) \qquad \ldots (4)$$

$$V_o(s) = \frac{1}{sC} I(s) \qquad \ldots (5)$$

Take the ratio of equation (5) and (4),

∴ Transfer function,
$$G(s) = \frac{V_o(s)}{V_i(s)} = \frac{1}{sc\left(R + \frac{1}{sC}\right)}$$

$$G(s) = \frac{1}{scR + 1}$$

i.e. $V_i(s) \longrightarrow \boxed{\frac{1}{scR + 1}} \longrightarrow V_o(s)$

Example 1.5: Find the transfer function of the given R-L circuit.

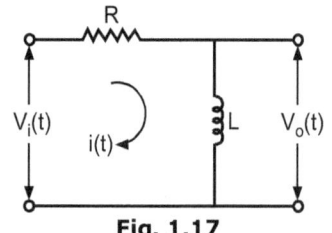

Fig. 1.17

Solution: Apply KVL to loop,

∴ $$V_i(t) = R\,i(t) + L\frac{di(t)}{dt} \qquad \ldots (1)$$

Taking Laplace transform,
$$V_i(s) = R\,I(s) + Ls\,I(s) \qquad \ldots (2)$$

Output voltage across L is,
$$V_L(t) = L \cdot \frac{di(t)}{dt} \qquad \ldots (3)$$

Taking L.T.,
$$V_o(s) = V_L(s) = Ls\,I(s) \qquad \ldots (4)$$

Taking the ratio of equation (4) and (2),

Transfer function is,
$$G(s) = \frac{V_o(s)}{V_i(s)}$$
$$= \frac{Ls\,I(s)}{(R + Ls)\,I(s)}$$

∴ $$\boxed{G(s) = \frac{Ls}{R + Ls}}$$

$$\boxed{G(s) = \frac{1}{\frac{R}{Ls} + 1}}$$

Example 1.6: Find the transfer function of the given R-L-C circuit.

OR

For the electrical system given below, derive the transfer function $\frac{V_o(s)}{V_i(s)}$. **(S-10) (4M)**

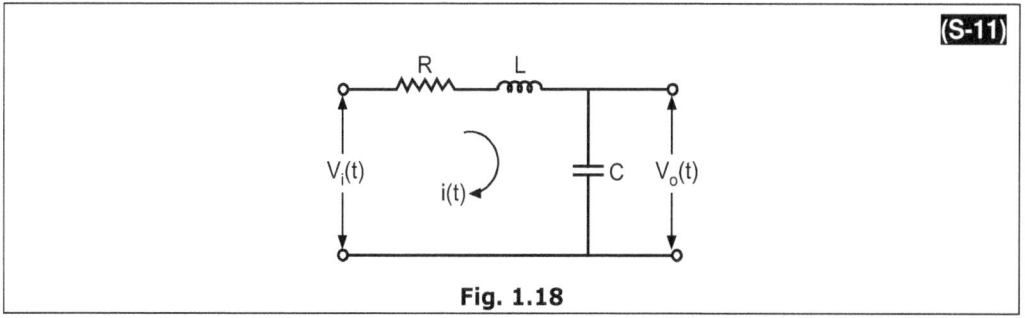

Fig. 1.18

Solution: Apply KVL to loop.

$$V_i(t) = R_i(t) + L\frac{di(t)}{dt} + \frac{1}{C}\int i(t)\, dt \quad \ldots (1)$$

Taking L.T.

$$V_i(s) = R\, I(s) + Ls\, I(s) + \frac{1}{sC} I(s)$$

$$= \left(R + Ls + \frac{1}{sC}\right) I(s) \quad \ldots (2)$$

Output voltage across capacitor is,

$$V_o(t) = \frac{1}{C}\int i(t)\, dt \quad \ldots (3)$$

Taking L.T.

$$V_o(s) = \frac{1}{sC} I(s) \quad \ldots (4)$$

Take the ratio of equation (2) and (4),

∴ **Transfer function is,**

$$G(s) = \frac{V_o(s)}{V_i(s)}$$

∴ $$\boxed{G(s) = \frac{1}{RCs + LCs^2 + 1}}$$

Example 1.7: For the given differential equation with input x, and output y, find the transfer function.

$$\frac{dy}{dt} + 3y = \frac{dx}{dt} + 2x$$

Solution: The given differential equation is,

$$\frac{dy}{dt} + 3y = \frac{dx}{dt} + 2x$$

Taking Laplace transform

$$s\, y(s) + 3y(s) = s\, x(s) + 2x(s)$$

∴ $$(s + 3)\, y(s) = (s + 2)\, x(s)$$

∴ $$\boxed{G(s) = \frac{y(s)}{x(s)} = \frac{(s + 1)}{(s + 2)}} = \text{Transfer function}$$

Example 1.8: For the given transfer function
$$G(s) = \frac{5s + 1}{s^2 + 2s + 1}$$
Find the differential equation.

Solution: $G(s) = \frac{y(s)}{x(s)} = \frac{5s + 1}{s^2 + 2s + 1}$

i.e. $(s^2 + 2s + 1) y(s) = (5s + 1) x(s)$

$\therefore$ $\boxed{\dfrac{d^2y}{dt^2} + 2\dfrac{dy}{dt} + y = 5\dfrac{dx}{dt} + x}$ is the differential equation.

Example 1.9: Find the transfer function of the circuit shown in Fig. 1.19 (a).

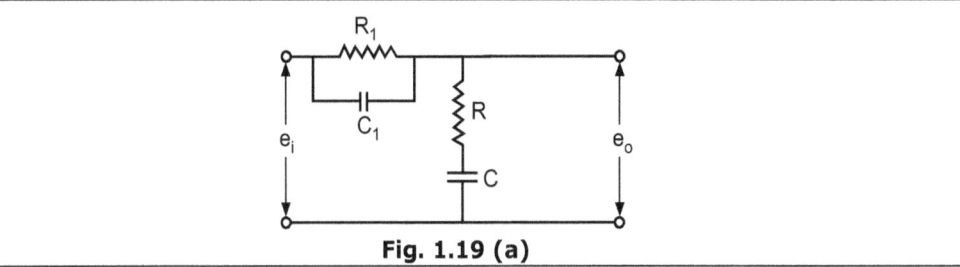

Fig. 1.19 (a)

Solution: Transforming the circuit components in s form as shown in Fig. 1.19 (b).

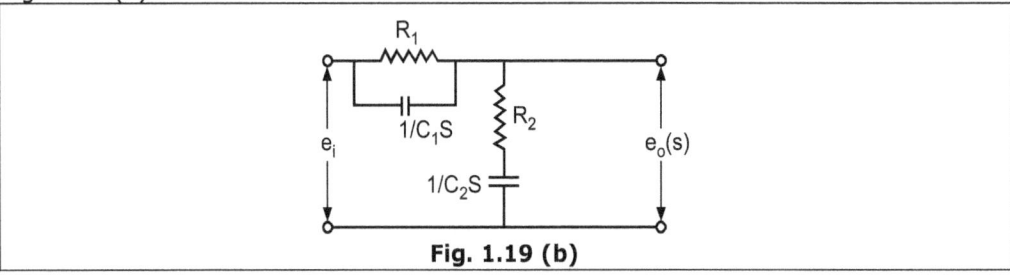

Fig. 1.19 (b)

Suppose $I(s)$ is the L.T. of the current flowing in circuit.
We have,

$$E_i(s) = \left[\left\{R_1\left(\frac{1}{C_1 s}\right) / \left(R_1 + \frac{1}{C_1 s}\right)\right\} + R_2 + \frac{1}{C_2 s}\right] I(s)$$

$= [R_1/(R_1 C_1 s + 1) + R_2 + 1/C_2 s] I(s)$

$= [R_1/(R_1 C_1 s + 1) + (R_2 + C_2 s + 1)/C_2 s] I(s)$

$= [R_1 C_2(s) + (R_1 C_1 s + 1)(R_2 C_2 s + 1)]/(R_1 C_1 s + 1) C_2(s)$

$I(s) = [(R_1 C_1 s + 1) C_2 s] e_i(s)/R_1 C_2 s + (R_1 C_1 s + 1)(R_2 C_2 s)]$

$E_0(s) = (R_2 + 1/C_2 s) I(s)$

$= [(R_2 C_2 s + 1)/C_2 s] I(s)$

Putting value of $I(s)$,

$E_0(s) = [(R_2 C_2 s + 1)/C_2 s] [(R_1 C_1 s + 1) C_2 s] E_1(s)/$
$\qquad R_1 C_2 s + (R_1 C_1 s + 1)(R_2 C_2 s + 1)]$

$\therefore \quad \dfrac{E_0(s)}{E_i(s)} = \dfrac{[R_2 C_2 s + 1][(R_1 C_1 s + 1)]}{[R_1 C_2 s + (R_1 C_1 s + 1)(R_2 C_2 s + 1)]}$

1.6.6 Advantages and Disadvantages of Transfer Function

- **Advantages:**
    1. It is a mathematical model which gives the gain of the given system.
    2. It uses Laplace transform, so the terms are simple algebraic expressions.
    3. Once the transfer function is known, the input and output can be known.
    4. From the transfer function, the poles and zero's of system can be found out.
    5. From the characteristic equation, stability of the system can be found.
- **Disadvantages:**
    1. Initial conditions loses its significance.
    2. It is valid only for linear time invariant systems.

1.7 ORDER OF A SYSTEM

Definition:

The order of a system is being the highest power of derivative in the differential equation or characteristic equation standard equation of close loop transfer function is

$$\text{T.F.} = \frac{G(s)}{1 + G(s)\,H(s)}$$

where, $1 + G(s)\,H(s) = 0$ is characteristic equation.

The transfer function of the feedback system can be written as

$$G(s) = \frac{b_m s^m + b_{m-1} s^{m-1} + \ldots + b_0}{s^n + a_{n-1} s^{n-1} + \ldots + a_0}$$

$$= \frac{K(s + b_1)(s + b_2)}{s^n (s + a_1)(s + a_2)}$$

The denominator term is equated to zero and is known as characteristic equation.

Here, $s^n + a_{n-1} s^{n-1} + \ldots + a_0 = 0$ is the characteristic equation.

The highest power in the characteristic equation is 'n' so that **order of the system is 'n'**.

In this equation if n = 0 is called 0th **order system**.

if n = 1 is called **first order system**.

if n = 2 is called **second order system**.

The nth order differential equation is,

$$a_{n+1} \cdot \frac{d y^n(t)}{dt^n} + a_n \frac{d y^{n-1}(t)}{dt^{n-1}} + \ldots + a_2 \frac{d y(t)}{dt} + a_1 y(t) = f(t)$$

Example 1.10:

Given the differential equation as,

$$\frac{d^2x(t)}{dt^2} + 3\frac{dx(t)}{dt} + 2x(t) = 5\,u(s)$$

Find the order of system.

Solution: Highest power of differential equation is 2 so that the order of the system is **2**.

Example 1.11:

A unity feedback system is characterized by the open loop transfer function is,

$$G(s) = \frac{k(s+B)}{s(s+3)(s+7)}$$

Find the order of the system.

Solution: Given: $G(s) = \dfrac{k(s+13)}{s(s+3)(s+7)}$

$$H(s) = 1$$

The characteristic equation of the closed loop system is,

$$1 + G(s)\,H(s) = 0$$

$$1 + \frac{k(s+13)}{s(s+3)(s+7)} = 0$$

$$s(s+3)(s+7) + k(s+13) = 0$$

$$\therefore\ s^3 + 10s^2 + (21+k)s + 3k = 0$$

In this characteristic equation highest power is 3 so that **order of the system is 3**.

1.8 BLOCK DIAGRAM REPRESENTATION

- **Block diagram is a pictorial representation of the control system.**
- Here, each block is arranged sequentially.
- Block diagram represents the relationship between the linear and non-linear physical systems.

  Block diagram shows more realistically the signal flow in the actual system.

1.8.1 Need

- For complex systems, schematic diagrams are difficult to draw. Hence, to represent this complex system a shorthand symbol called block-diagram is used.
- It provides a pictorial representation of the relationship between input and output of the system.
- If we use block diagram reduction method, then we come to know directly the input and output relationship, and it also gives an easy way to find out the transfer function i.e., a complex system is converted into only one block, so analysis is easy.
- Feedback control systems consist of many non-interactive elements whose transfer function is determined independently.
- By interconnection of the blocks of individual elements, the whole system is represented.

1.8.2 Block Diagram Fundamentals

1. Block diagram:

A block diagram consists of the following representing the transfer function of the individual elements.

The arrow head pointing towards the block indicates input and the one pointing away indicates output.

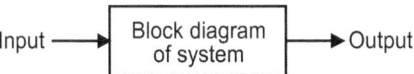

2. Output:

The value of input multiplied by block gain forms the output of the system.

Output = Gain × Input

Input → Gain → Output

3. Summing point:

More than one signal is added or subtracted at the summing point.

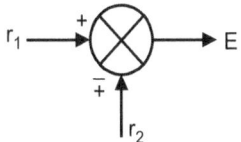

Negative sign indicates subtraction
i.e. $E = r_1 - r_2$

Positive sign indicates addition
i.e. $E = r_1 + r_2$

4. Take-off point:

The output signal can be applied to two or more than two inputs from a take-off point.

Take-off point

Take-off point

5. Feedback path: The signal flows from output to input.

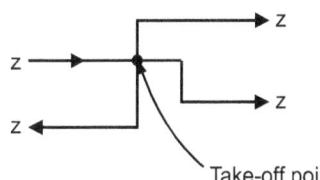

← Feedback path

Feedback path

6. Forward path: The signal flows from input to output.

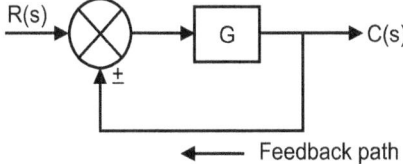

→ Forward path

1.8.3 Block Diagram Reduction of Closed Loop Control System

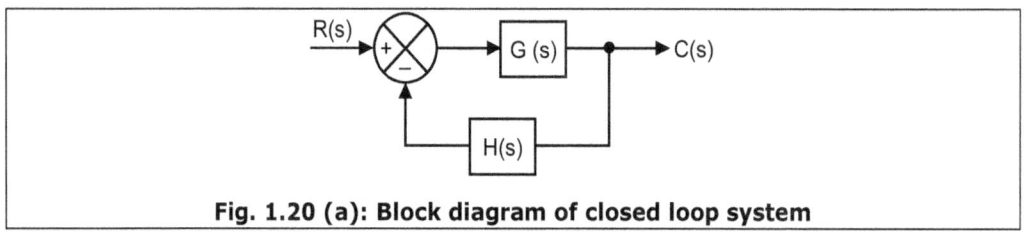

Fig. 1.20 (a): Block diagram of closed loop system

Fig. 1.20 (a) shows the negative positive feedback control system.

T.F. of closed loop system.

$$T(s) = \frac{C(s)}{R(s)} = \frac{G(s)}{1 \pm G(s)\,H(s)}$$

∴ Reduced block diagram of Fig. 1.20 (b) is

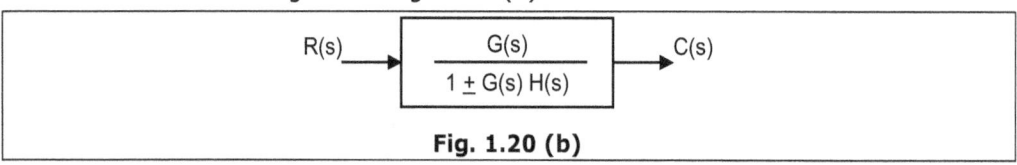

Fig. 1.20 (b)

1.8.4 Multiple-Input Multiple-Output Systems

When a linear system has multiple inputs, each input can be treated independently of the others. The complete output of the system can be obtained by superposition i.e. outputs corresponding to each input are added together.

Consider a two input linear system as shown in Fig. 1.21 (a).

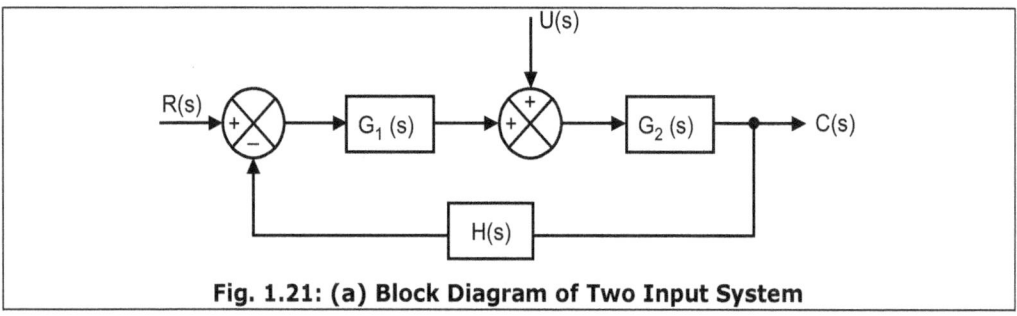

Fig. 1.21: (a) Block Diagram of Two Input System

The response to the reference input can be obtained by assuming $U(s) = 0$.

Now, the block diagram is shown in Fig. 1.21 (b).

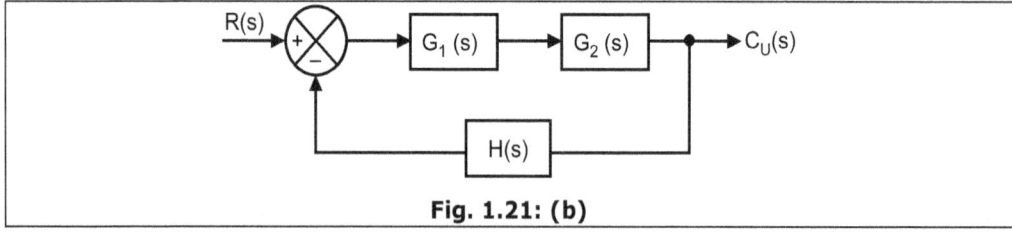

Fig. 1.21: (b)

where, $C_R(s)$ = Output due to R(s) acting alone

$$\therefore \quad C_R(s) = \frac{G_1(s)\,G_2(s)}{1 + G_1(s)\,G_2(s)\,H(s)} R(s) \quad \ldots (1.37)$$

Similarly, response to the input U(s) can be obtained by assuming R(s) = 0. Now, the block diagram is shown in Fig. 1.21 (c).

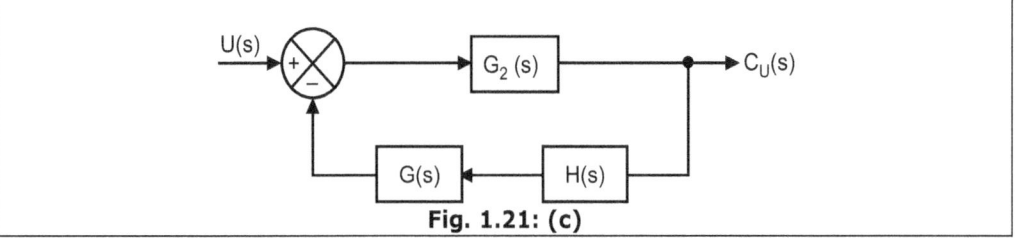

Fig. 1.21: (c)

$C_U(s)$ = Output due to U(s) acting alone

$$\therefore \quad C_U(s) = \frac{G_2(s)}{1 + G_1(s)\,G_2(s)\,H(s)} U(s) \quad \ldots (1.38)$$

- Then, the response to the simultaneous application of R(s) and U(s) can be obtained by adding the two individual responses.

Adding equations (1.51) and (1.52), we get,

$$C(s) = C_R(s) + C_U(s)$$

$$C(s) = \frac{G_2(s)}{1 + G_1(s)\,G_2(s)\,H(s)} [G_1(s)\,R(s) + U(s)] \ldots (1.39)$$

In case of multiple-input multiple-output system as shown in Fig. 1.22 which have r inputs and m output.

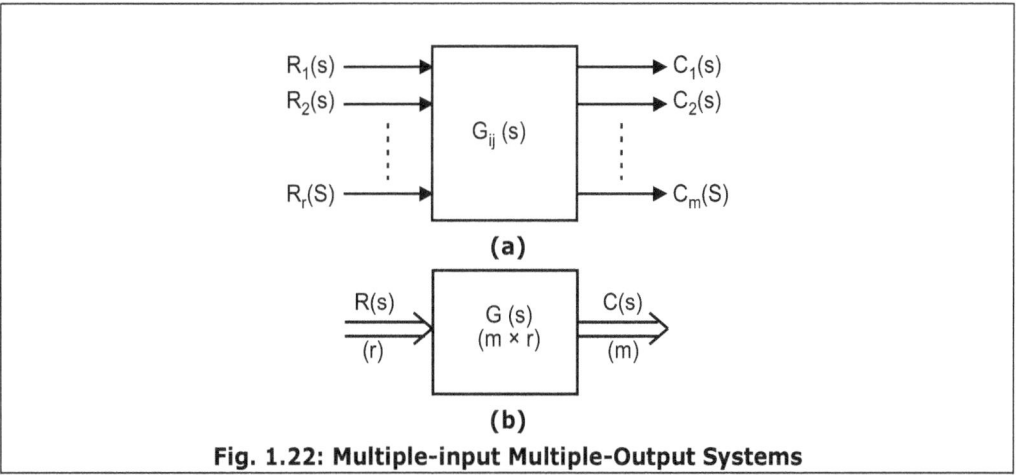

Fig. 1.22: Multiple-input Multiple-Output Systems

Then, the ith output $C_i(s)$ is given by the principle of superposition as,

$$C_i(s) = \sum_{j=1}^{r} G_{ij}(s)\,R_j(s)\,; \qquad [i = 1, 2, \ldots m] \ldots (1.40)$$

★ Steps for drawing the block diagram:
1. Write the differential equation for all components of the system.
2. Take Laplace transform of the differential equation.
3. Find the transfer function for the various parts.
4. Combine the transfer functions and draw the block diagram.
5. Reduce the block diagram to simple form.
6. Find the closed loop transfer function.
7. Take inverse Laplace transform to study the system response.

1.8.5 Rules of Block Diagram Reduction

(Block Diagram Algebra)

QUESTION

1. Describe the eight rules of block diagram reduction. **(4M)**

- As indicated earlier, a complex diagram configuration can be simplified by a certain rearrangement of the block diagram using the rules of **block diagram algebra.**
- The rules are given below. All these rules are derived by simple algebraic manipulations of the equations representing the blocks.
- The rules mostly used for block diagram reduction are –

Rule 1: Blocks in Series or Cascade

Any finite number of blocks in cascade (series) may be algebraically combined by multiplication.

The flow of the signal is unidirectional from input to output.

$$\therefore \quad R_2(s) = G_1 R_1(s)$$
$$\text{and} \quad C(s) = G_2 R_2(s)$$
$$\mathbf{C(s) = G_1 G_2 R_1(s)} \quad \ldots (1.41)$$

Rule 2: Blocks in Parallel

The blocks connected in parallel get added algebraically (considering the polarity of the signal).

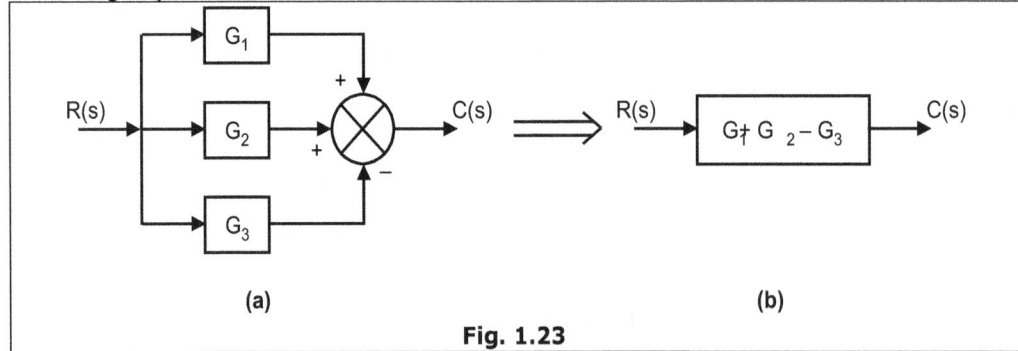

Fig. 1.23

The output is,

$$C(s) = R(s) G_1 + R(s) G_2 - R(s) G_3$$
$$= R(s) (G_1 + G_2 - G_3)$$

Now, replace all the three blocks by an equivalent single block as shown in Fig. 1.23 (b).

Rule 3: Moving a Summing Point After a Block

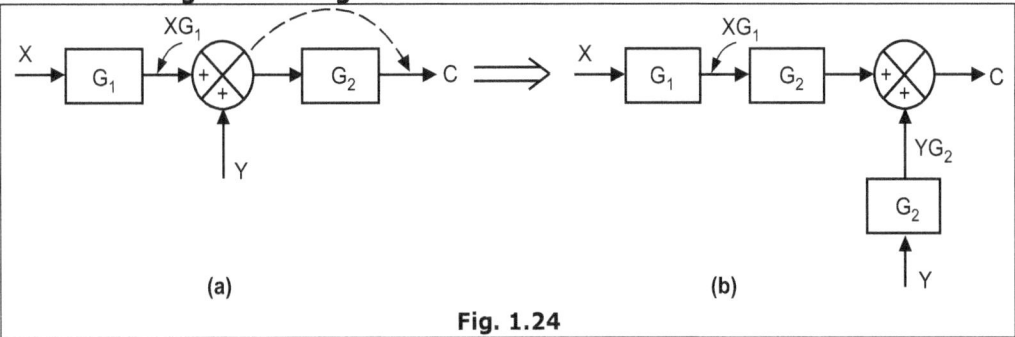

Fig. 1.24

As shown in Fig. 1.24 (a),

$$C = (X G_1 + Y) G_2$$
$$C = X G_1 G_2 + Y G_2 \qquad \ldots (1.42)$$

Now, shift the summing point after block G_2 without changing its output. So, the block G_2 is added at the summing point as shown in Fig. 1.24 (b).

Now, the blocks G_1 and G_2 are in series.

Rule 4: Moving a summing point before a block

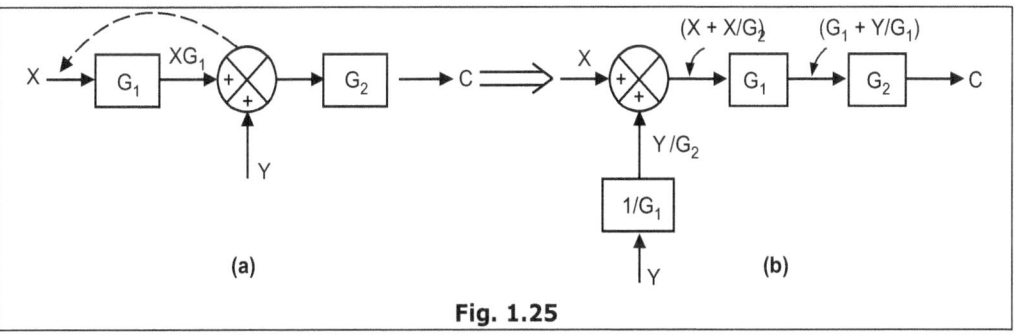

Fig. 1.25

Given the block arrangement as shown in Fig. 1.25 (a),

$$C = (X G_1 + Y) G_2 \qquad \ldots (1.43)$$

We have to shift the summing point before block G_1 but the output should be the same as equation (1.43).

∴ Fig. 1.25 (b) shows the equivalent block diagram.

where,

$$C = G_1 \left(X + \frac{Y}{G_1} \right) G_2$$

$$\mathbf{C = G_1 X + G_2}$$

Rule 5: Moving a Take-off Point After a Block

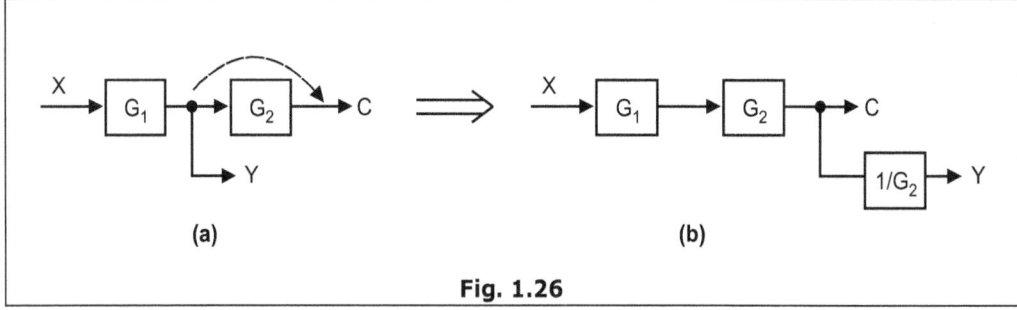

Fig. 1.26

In Fig. 1.26 (a),

$$Y = X G_1$$

Shifting take-off point after G_2,

$$Y = (X G_1 G_2) \left(\frac{1}{G_2}\right)$$

$$Y = X G_1$$

∴ Equivalent block arrangement is shown in Fig. 1.26 (b).

Rule 6: Moving Take-off Point Before a Block

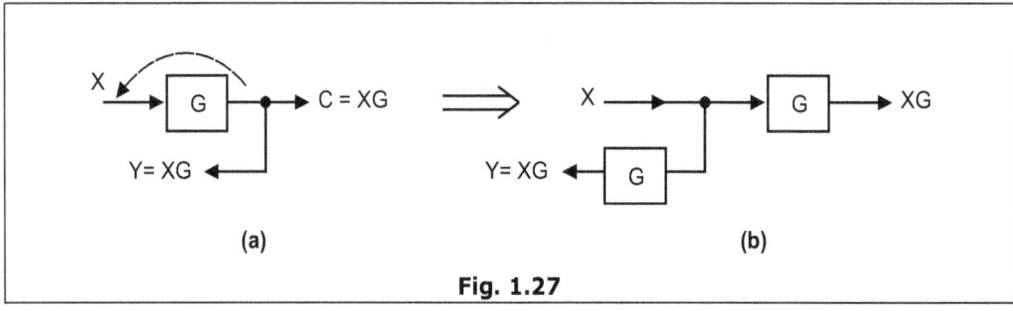

Fig. 1.27

In Fig. 1.27 (a),

$$C = X G$$
$$Y = X G$$

By adding block G in X_2 and shifting take-off point before G gives,

$$Y = XG$$

Rule 7: Eliminating a Feedback Loop

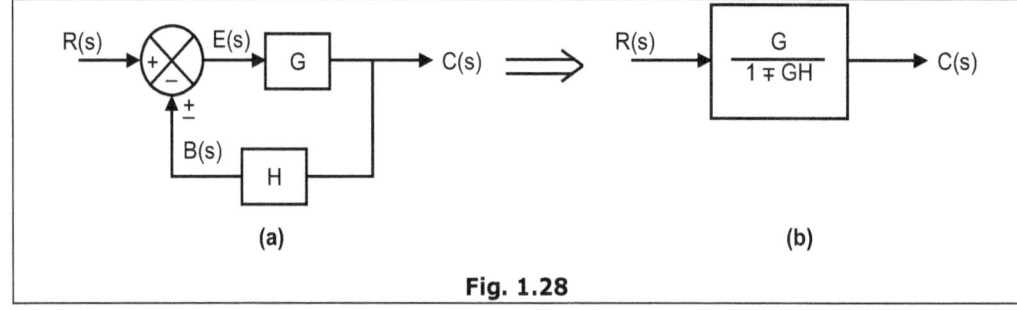

Fig. 1.28

As shown in Fig. 1.28 (a),

$$E(s) = R(s) \pm B(s) \quad \ldots (1.44)$$
$$B(s) = C(s) H \quad \ldots (1.45)$$
$$C(s) = E(s) G \quad \text{[From equation (1.46)]}$$
$$= G [R(s) \pm B(s)]$$
$$= G R(s) \pm G B(s)$$

$$\therefore \quad C(s) = G R(s) \pm G C(s) \cdot H \quad \text{[From equation (1.47)]}$$
$$\therefore \quad C(s) \pm G \cdot H C(s) = G R(s)$$
$$\therefore \quad C(s) [1 \pm G H] = G R(s)$$
$$\therefore \quad \frac{C(s)}{R(s)} = \frac{G}{1 \pm G H}$$

$$\therefore \quad \boxed{\frac{C(s)}{R(s)} = \frac{G}{1 + G H}} \quad \text{For negative feedback} \quad \ldots (1.48)$$

$$\boxed{\frac{C(s)}{R(s)} = \frac{G}{1 - G H}} \quad \text{For positive feedback} \quad \ldots (1.49)$$

Rule 8: Associative Law for Summing Point

The order of the summing point can be changed if two or more summing points are arranged in series.

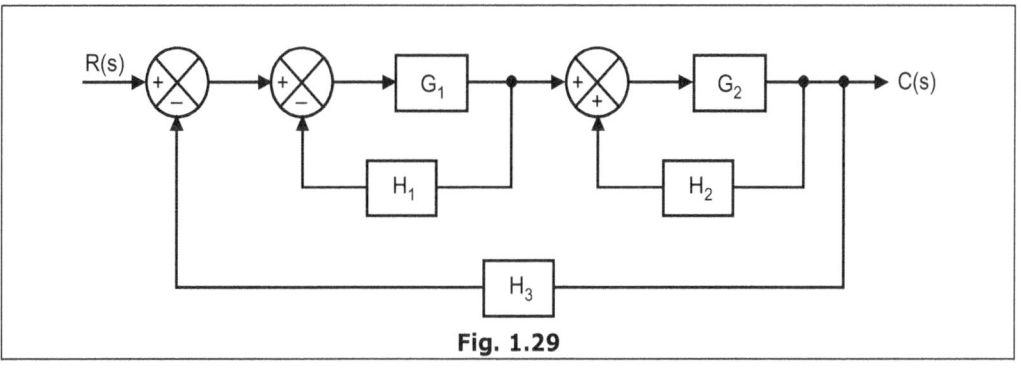

Fig. 1.29

$$Z = R(s) - X \qquad\qquad Z = R(s) - Y$$
$$\therefore \quad C(s) = Z - Y \qquad\qquad \therefore \quad C(s) = Z - X$$
$$= R(s) - X - Y \qquad\qquad = R(s) - Y - X$$

★ **Procedure for Reduction of Blocks:**
1. Reduce blocks in series.
2. Reduce blocks in parallel.
3. Eliminate the feedback path.
4. Shifting summing point and take-off point before or after block (as per requirement).
5. Repeat the above procedure till you get the simplest form.
6. Find the transfer function for the complete system.

Table 1.2: Rules of Block diagram Algebra (Reduction) (W-10)

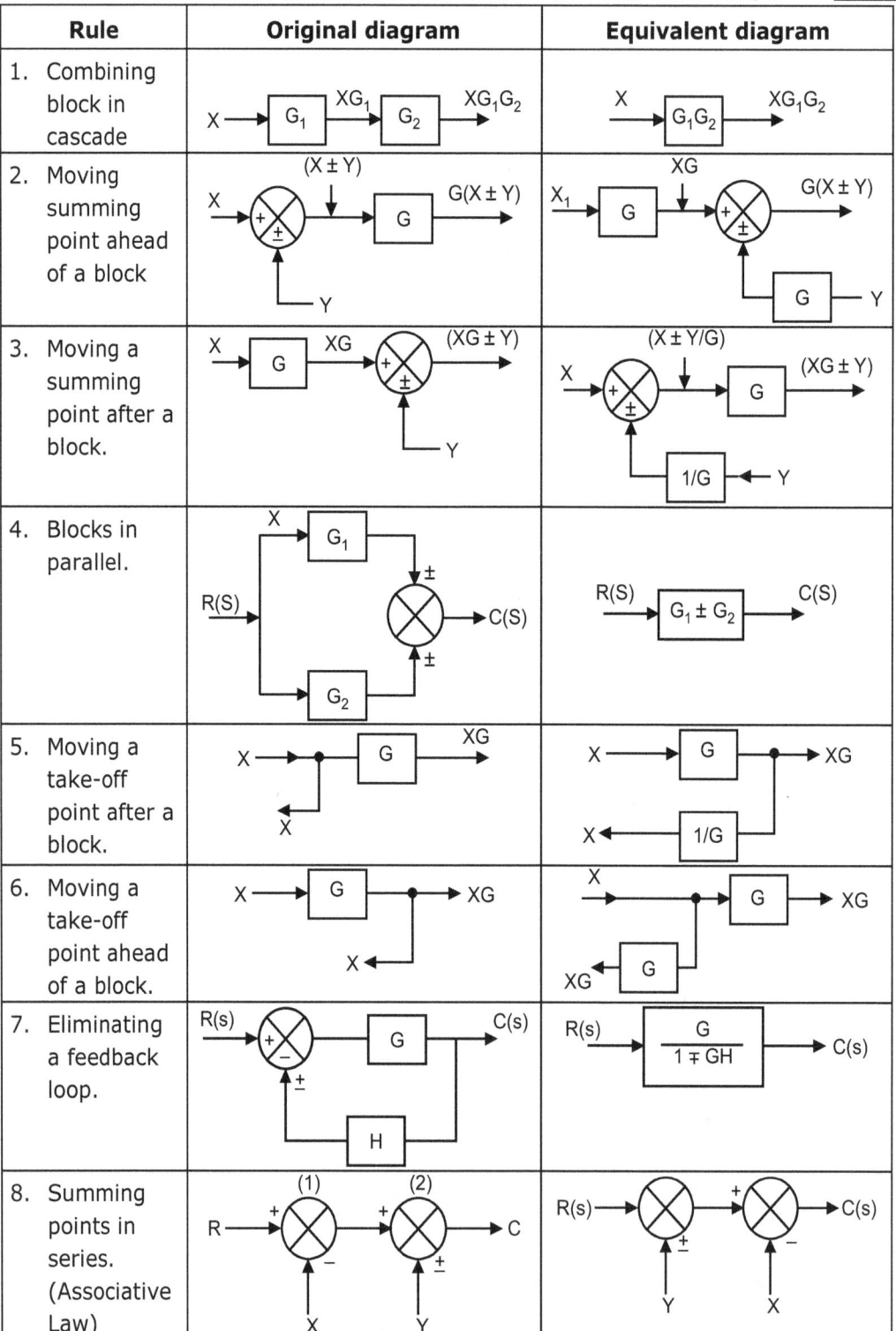

1.8.6 Advantages and Disadvantages of Block Diagram

- **Advantages:**
  1. The functional operation of the system can be observed from block diagram.
  2. Block diagram gives information about input and output of the system.
  3. Block diagram is used in the analysis and design of control system.
  4. Complicated systems can be reduced into a single block which then helps to find the transfer function.

- **Disadvantages:**
  1. Source of energy flow in the system is not shown on the diagram.
  2. There is no interaction between the various blocks.
  3. In the procedure of reduction of block diagram algebra, some important functions are omitted and there is no check for it.

Example 1.12: Find the closed-loop transfer function of the system below in Fig. 1.30.

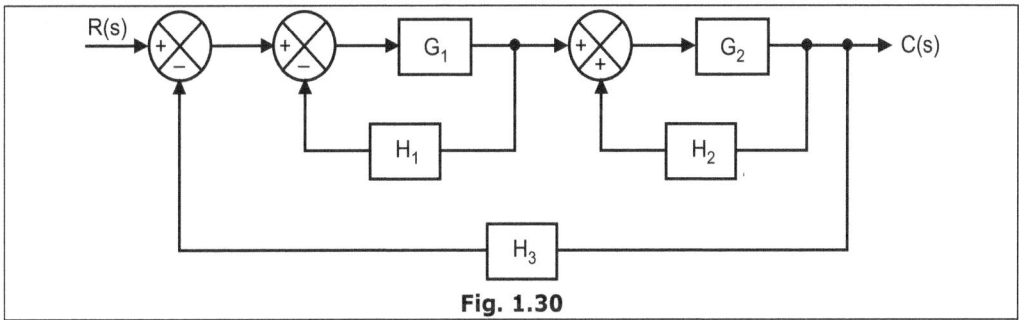

Fig. 1.30

Solution: Step 1: Redraw given block diagram

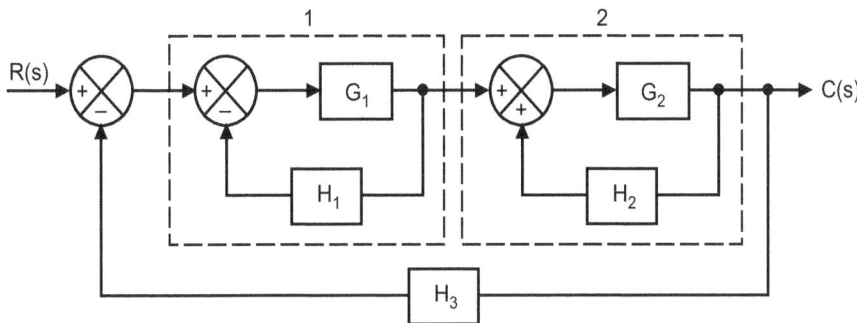

Step 2:

Rule – Eliminating feedback loop 1 and loop 2 as shown by dotted lines in Step 1.

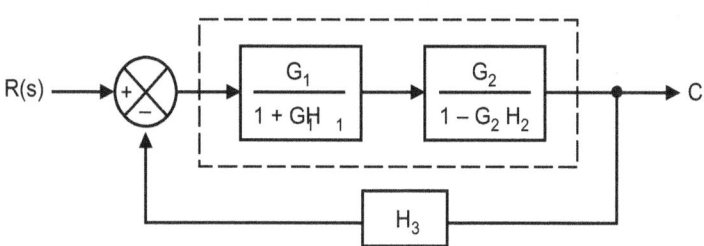

Step 3:

Rule – Combining blocks in cascade as shown by dotted lines in Step 2.

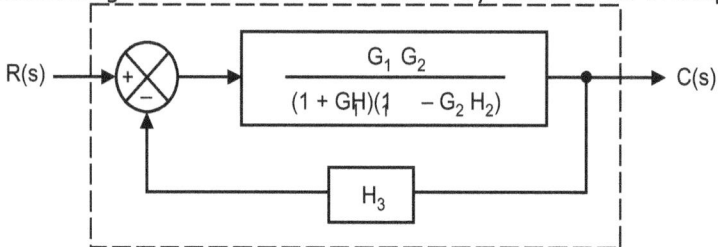

Step 4:

Rule – Elimination of feedback loop shown by dotted lines in Step 3.

$$\text{T.F.} = \frac{C(s)}{R(s)} = \frac{\dfrac{G_1 G_2}{(1 + G_1 H_1)(1 - G_2 H_2)}}{1 + \dfrac{G_1 G_2}{(1 + G_1 H_1)(1 - G_2 H_2)} \cdot H_3}$$

$$= \frac{G_1 G_2}{(1 + G_1 H_1)(1 - G_2 H_2) + G_1 G_2 H_3}$$

$$R(s) \longrightarrow \boxed{\frac{G_1 G_2}{(1 + G_1 H_1)(1 - G_2 H_2) + G_1 G_2 H_3}} \longrightarrow C(s)$$

Example 1.13: Determine the overall transfer function of the given block diagram (Fig. 1.31).

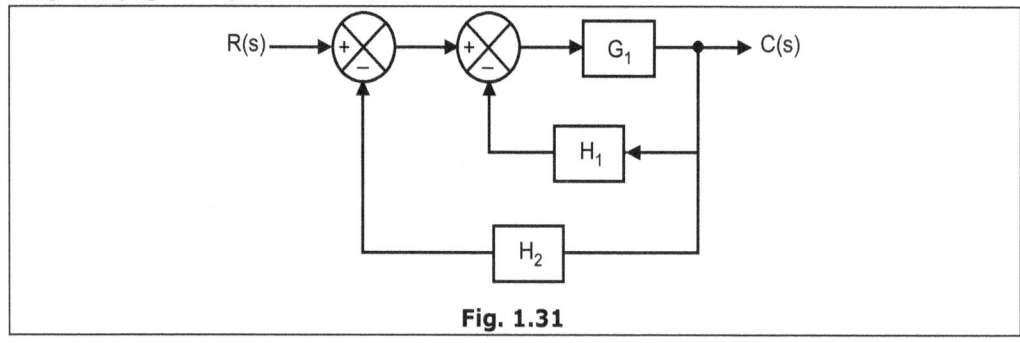

Fig. 1.31

Solution: Step 1: Redraw given block diagram.

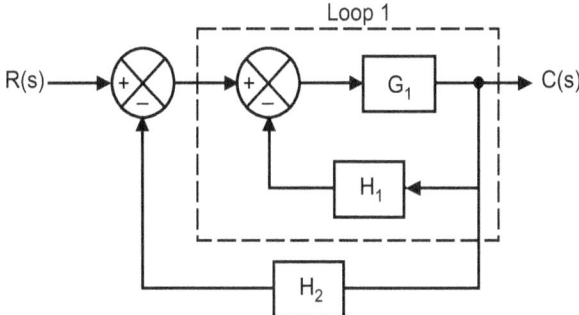

Step 2: Rule – Eliminate feedback loop (marked loop 1).

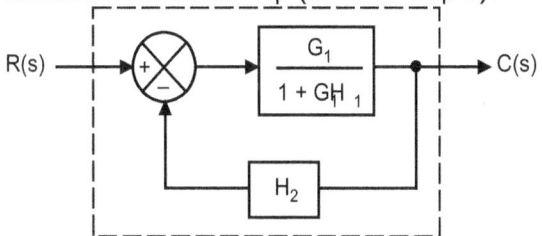

Step 3: Rule – Eliminating feedback loop

$$\text{T.F.} = \frac{C(s)}{R(s)} = \frac{\frac{G_1}{1 + G_1 H_1}}{1 + \frac{G_1}{1 + G_1 H_1} H_2}$$

$$\boxed{\text{T. F.} = \frac{C(s)}{R(s)} = \frac{G_1}{1 + G_1 H_1 + G_1 H_2}}$$

Thus, the reduced block diagram is,

$$R(s) \longrightarrow \boxed{\frac{G_1}{1 + G_1 H_1 + G_1 H_2}} \longrightarrow C(s)$$

Example 1.14: Determine $\dfrac{C(s)}{R(s)}$ for the given block diagram in Fig. 1.32.

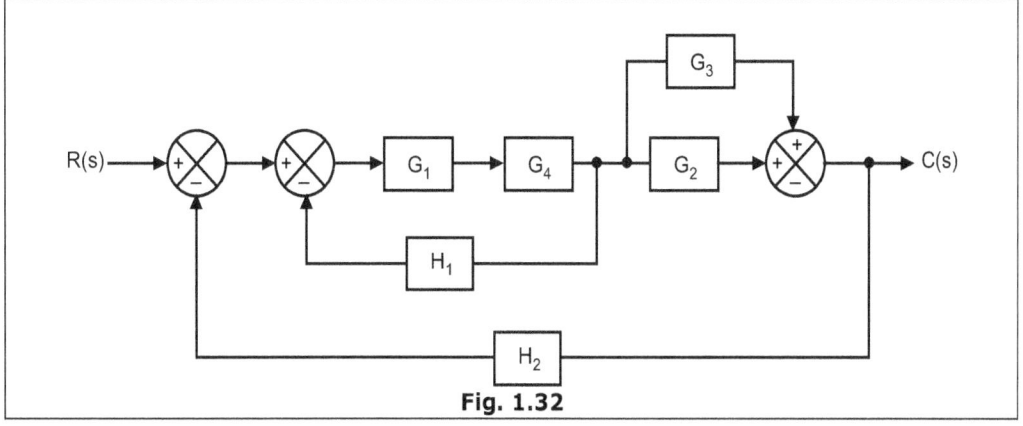

Fig. 1.32

Solution: Step 1: Redraw the given block diagram.

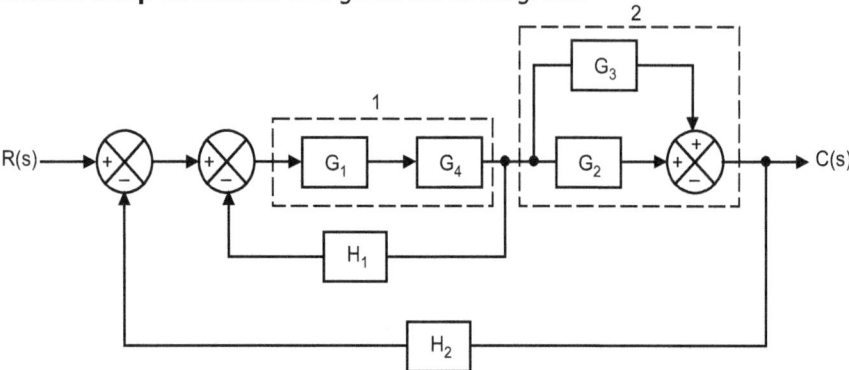

Step 2:

Rule – For 1 – Combine blocks in cascade.
For 2 – Blocks in parallel

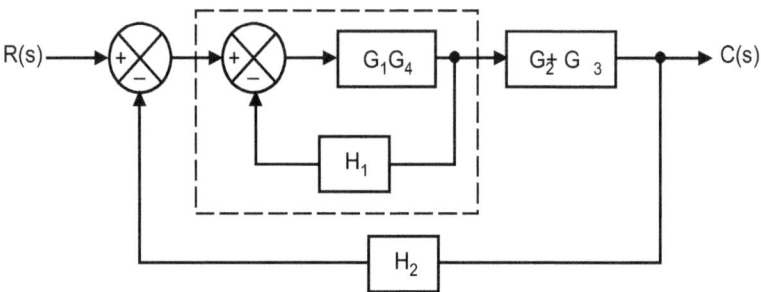

Step 3:

Rule – Eliminate the feedback loop.

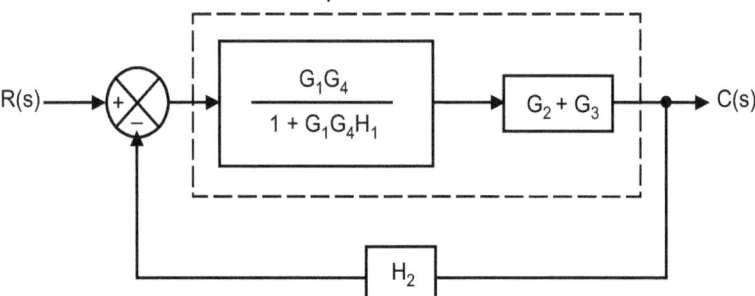

Step 4:

Rule – Combine blocks in cascade

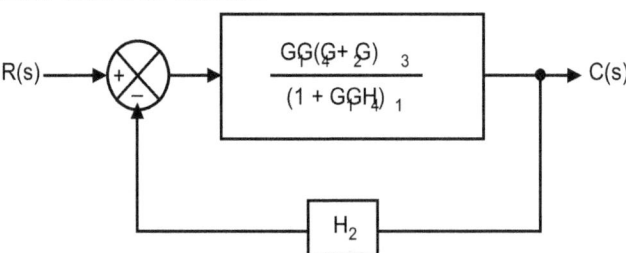

Step 5:

Find the transfer function by eliminating feedback loop.

$$\text{T.F.} = \frac{C(s)}{R(s)} = \frac{\dfrac{G_1 G_4 (G_2 + G_3)}{(1 + G_1 G_4 H_1)}}{1 + \dfrac{G_1 G_4 (G_2 + G_3)}{1 + G_1 G_4 H_1} H_2}$$

$$\boxed{\text{T.F.} = \frac{C(s)}{R(s)} = \frac{G_1 G_4 (G_2 + G_3)}{(1 + G_1 G_4 H_1) + G_1 G_4 (G_2 + G_3) H_2}}$$

Thus, the reduced block diagram is,

$$R(s) \longrightarrow \boxed{\frac{G_1 G_4 (G_2 + G_3)}{(1 + G_1 G_4 H_1) + G_1 G_4 (G_2 + G_3) H_2}} \longrightarrow C(s)$$

Example 1.15: Determine the transfer function of the given block diagram as shown in Fig. 1.33.

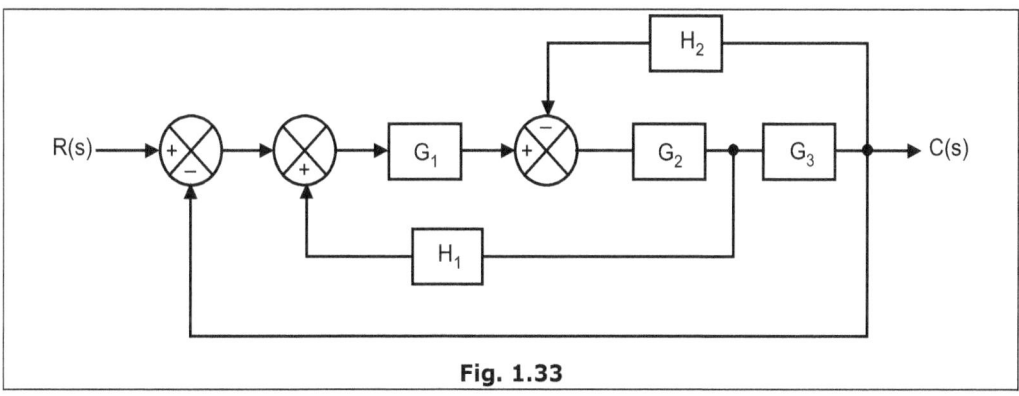

Fig. 1.33

Solution: Step 1: Redraw the given block diagram.

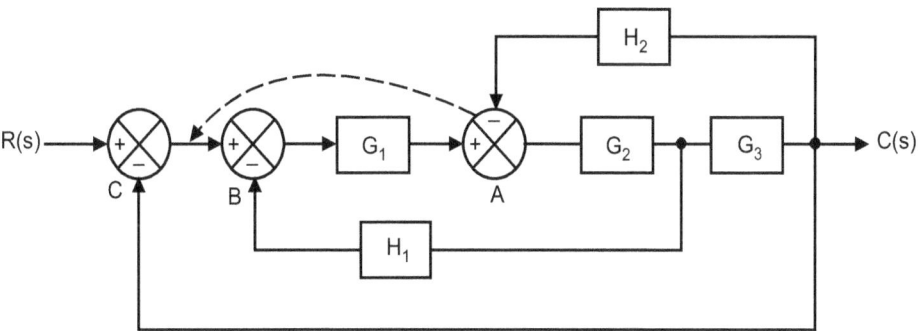

Step 2:

Rule – Moving summing point ahead of a block.

Here move the summing point A ahead of summing point B as shown by dotted line.

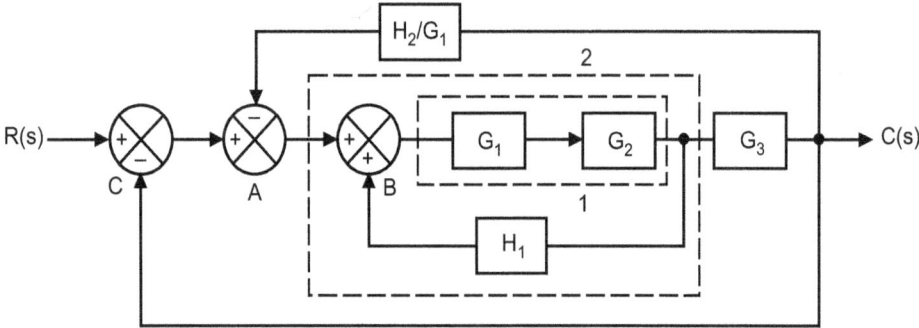

Step 3:
Rule – For 1 – Blocks in cascade

i.e.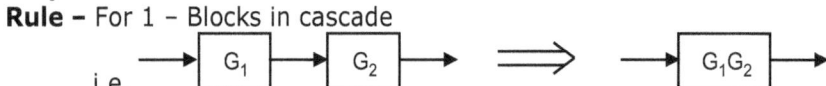

For 2 - Eliminating positive feedback loop.

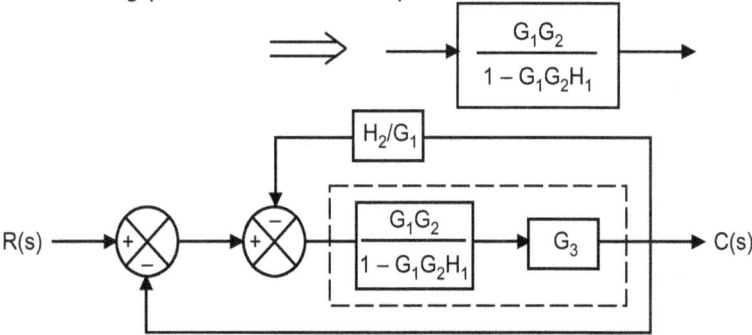

Step 4:
Rule – Blocks in cascade.

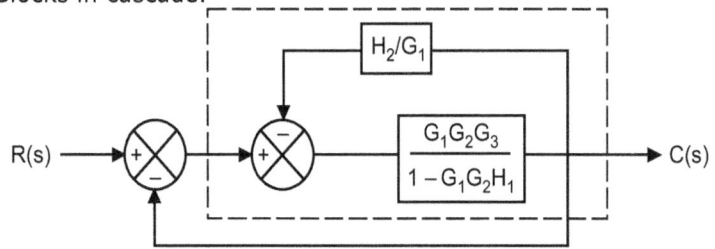

Step 5:
Rule: Eliminating feed back loop.

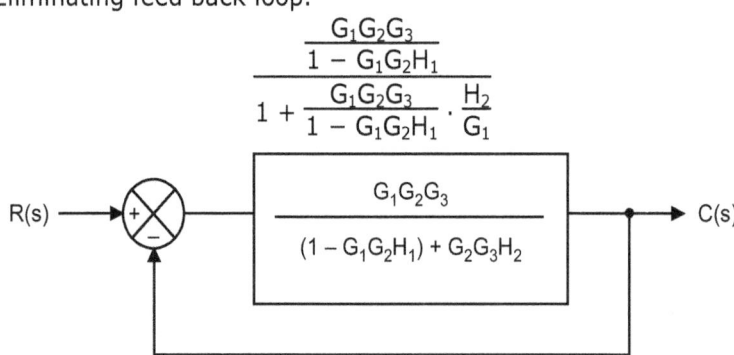

Step 6:

Rule – Eliminating unity feedback loop.

i.e. feedback element H (s) = 1.

and find the transfer function

$$T.F. = \frac{C(s)}{R(s)} = \frac{\dfrac{G_1 G_2 G_3}{1 - G_1 G_2 H_1 + G_2 G_3 H_2}}{1 + \dfrac{G_1 G_2 G_3}{1 - G_1 G_2 H_1 + G_2 G_3 H_2}}$$

$$= \frac{G_1 G_2 G_3}{1 - G_1 G_2 H_1 + G_2 G_3 H_2 + G_2 G_2 G_3}$$

Thus, Reduced block diagram is,

R(s) → [$\dfrac{G_1 G_2 G_3}{1 - G_1G_2H_1 + G_2G_3H_2 + G_2G_2G_3}$] → C(s)

Example 1.16: Obtain the transfer function for the block diagram shown in Fig. 1.34.

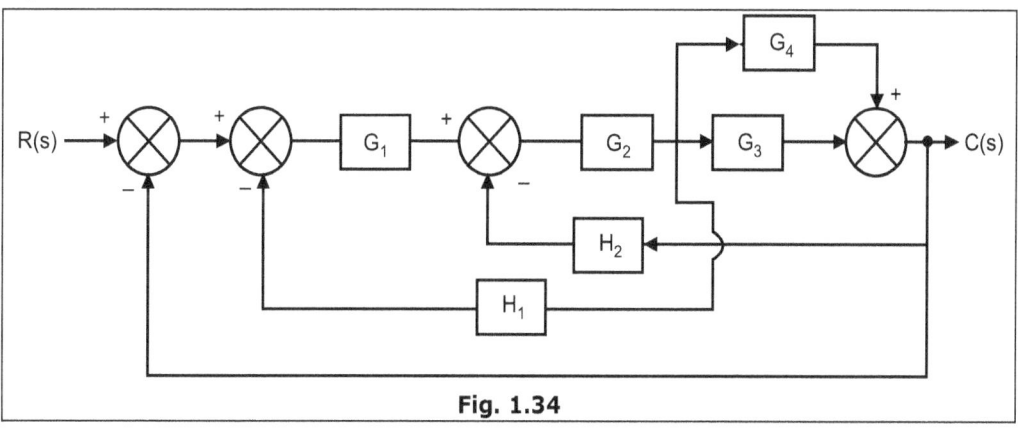

Fig. 1.34

Solution: Step 1: Redraw the given block diagram as given below.

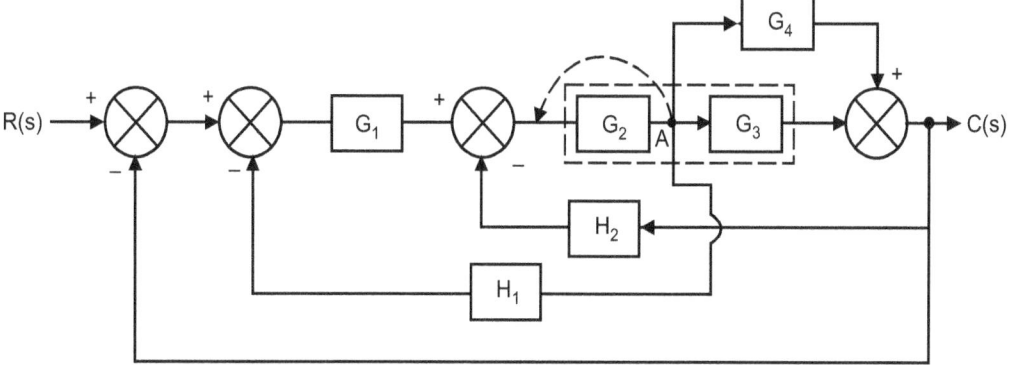

Step 2:

1. Moving take-off point A ahead of block G_2.
2. Now blocks G_2 and G_3 are in cascade. So, combining the blocks in cascade.

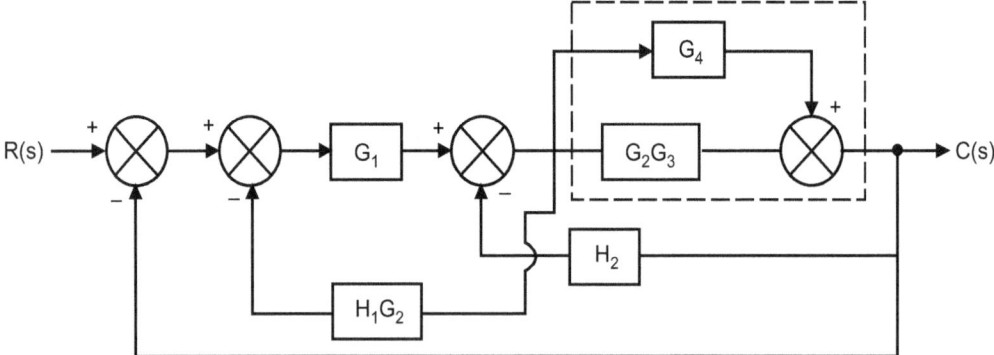

Step 3: Eliminating blocks in parallel

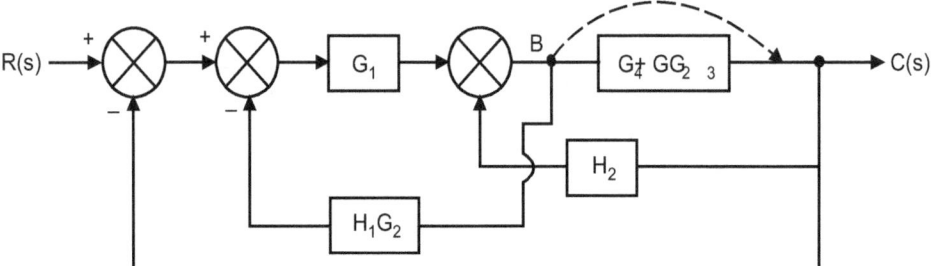

Step 4: Moving take-off point B beyond block $(G_4 + G_2 G_3)$

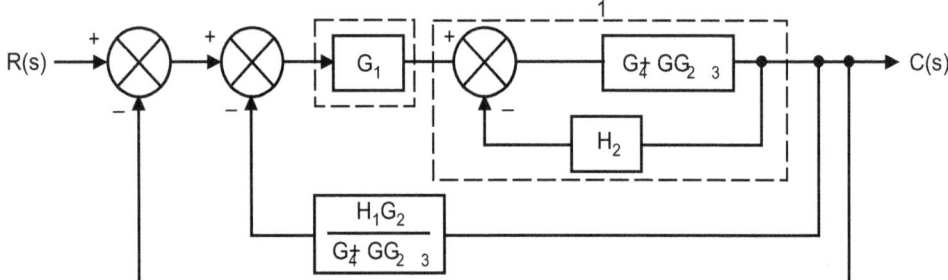

Step 5: Eliminating feedback loop 1.

$$\Rightarrow \quad \frac{G_4 + G_2 G_3}{1 + (G_4 + G_2 G_3)H_2}$$

Combining blocks in cascade.

$$G_1 \rightarrow \frac{G_4 + G_2 G_3}{1 + (G_4 + G_2 G_3)H_2} \quad \Rightarrow \quad \frac{G_1(G_4 + G_2 G_3)}{1 + (G_4 + G_2 G_3)H_2}$$

Step 6: Elimination of feedback loop.

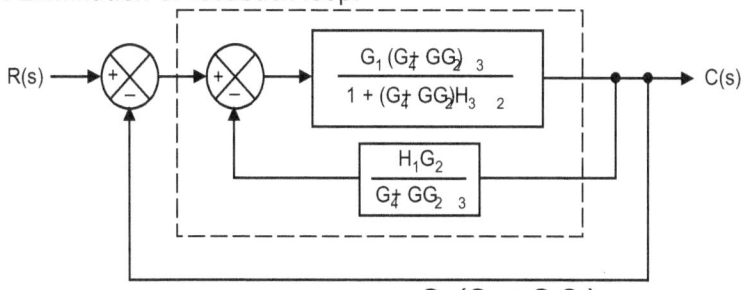

$$\text{T.F.} = \frac{C(s)}{R(s)} = \frac{\dfrac{G_1 (G_4 + G_2G_3)}{1 + (G_4 + G_2G_3) H_2}}{1 + \dfrac{(G_4 + G_2G_3) G_1}{1 + (G_4 + G_2G_3) H_2} \cdot \dfrac{H_1G_2}{G_4 + G_2G_3}}$$

$$\therefore \quad \text{T.F} = \frac{C(s)}{R(s)} = \frac{G_1 (G_4 + G_2G_3)}{1 + H_2 (G_4 + G_2G_3) + H_1G_1G_2}$$

Reduced block diagram is,

$$R(s) \rightarrow \boxed{\frac{G_1 (G_4 + G_2G_3)}{1 + (G_4 + G_2G_3) H_2 + G_1G_2H_1 + G_1(G_4 + G_2G_3)}} \rightarrow C(s)$$

Step 7: Finding transfer function and eliminating unity feedback loop.

$$\text{T.F.} = \frac{C(s)}{R(s)} = \frac{\dfrac{G_1 (G_4 + G_2 G_3)}{1 + H_2 (G_4 + G_2 G_3) + H_1 G_1 G_2}}{1 + \dfrac{G_1 (G_4 + G_2 G_3)}{1 + H_2 (G_4 + G_2 G_3) + H_1 G_1 G_2}}$$

$$= \frac{G_1 (G_4 + G_2 G_3)}{1 + H_2 (G_4 + G_2 G_3) + H_1 G_1 G_2 + G_1 (G_4 + G_2 G_3)}$$

$$\therefore \quad \boxed{\text{T.F.} = \frac{C(s)}{R(s)} = \frac{G_1 (G_4 + G_2 G_3)}{1 + (G_4 + G_2 G_3) H_2 + G_1 G_2 H_1 + G_1 (G_4 + G_2 G_3)}}$$

Reduced block diagram is,

$$R(s) \longrightarrow \boxed{\frac{G_1 (G_4 + G_2 G_3)}{1 + (G_4 + G_2 G_3) H_2 + G_1 G_2 H_1 + G_1 (G_4 + G_3 G_3)}} \longrightarrow C(s)$$

Example 1.17: Evaluate $\dfrac{C}{R_1}$ and $\dfrac{C}{R_2}$ for a system whose block diagram is shown in Fig. 1.35.

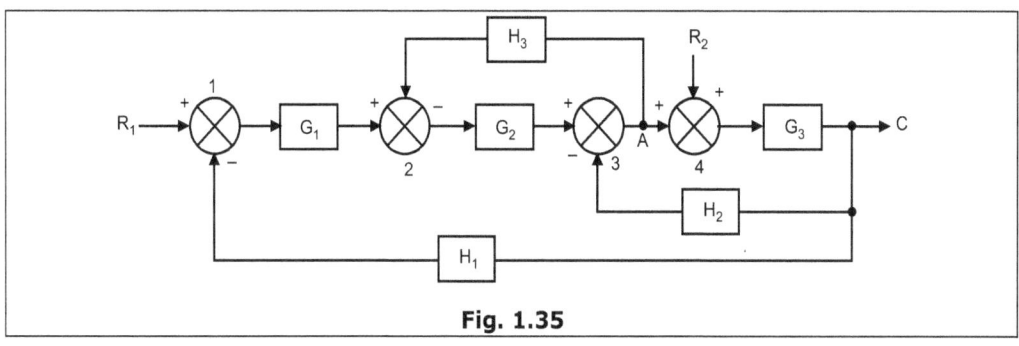

Fig. 1.35

Solution: The given block diagram has two inputs. So, it is a multiple-input multiple output system.

Step 1: For evaluation of $\dfrac{C}{R_1}$, assume $R_2 = 0$.

Therefore, summing point No. 4 can be removed.

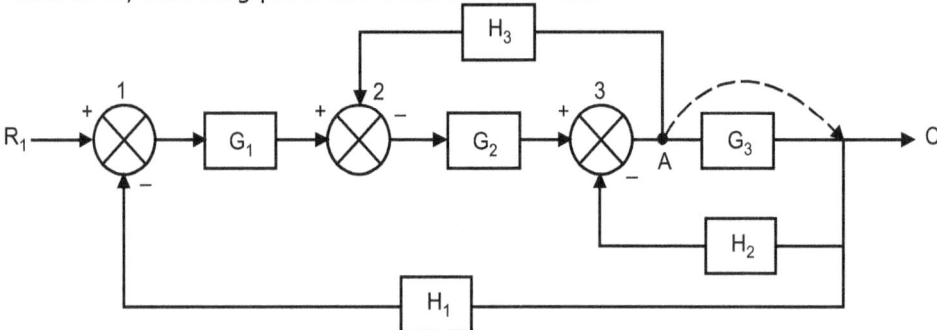

Step 2: Move take-off point A beyond block G_3.

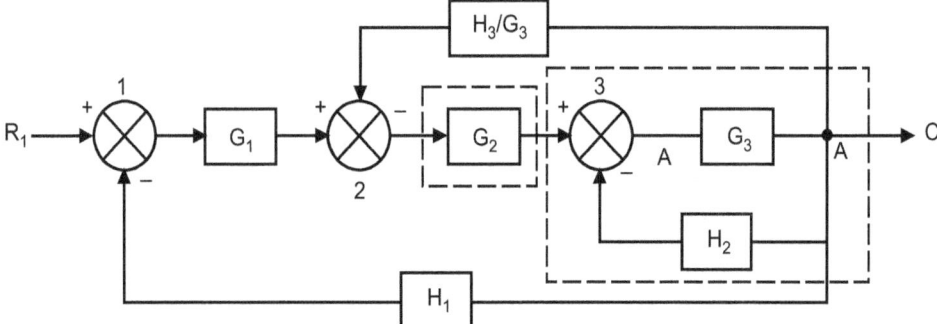

Step 3: Eliminating feedback loop and combining blocks in cascade.

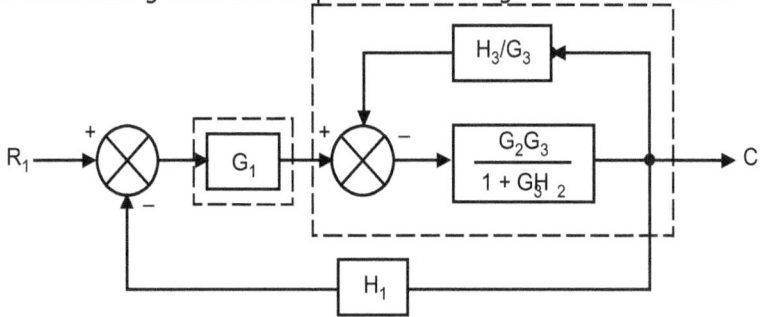

Step 4: Eliminating the feedback loop again and combining with block G_1 which is in cascade.

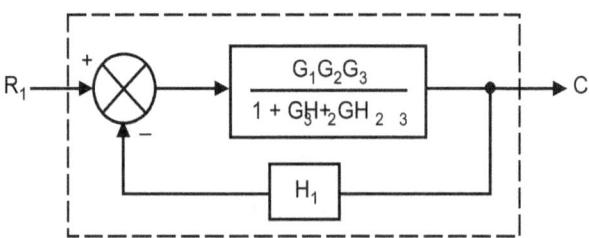

Step 5: Eliminate feedback loop and find T.F.

$$\therefore \quad \boxed{\frac{C}{R_1} = \frac{G_1 G_2 G_3}{1 + G_3 H_2 + H_3 G_2 + G_1 G_2 G_3 H_1}}$$

- **For Evaluation of** $\dfrac{C}{R_2}$

Step 1: Assume $R_1 = 0$. Thus summing point No. 1 is removed.

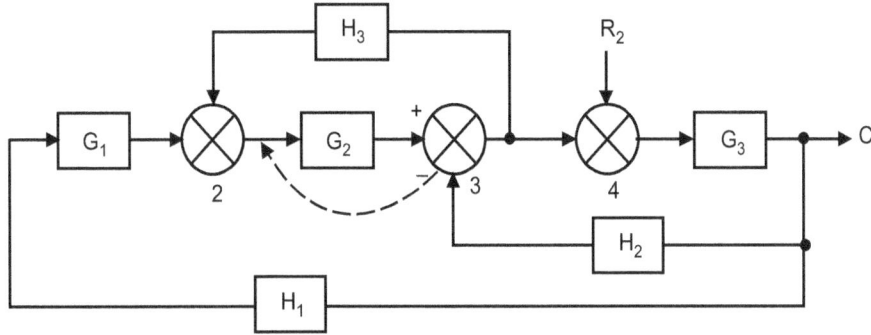

Step 2: Moving summing point No. 3 beyond G_2.

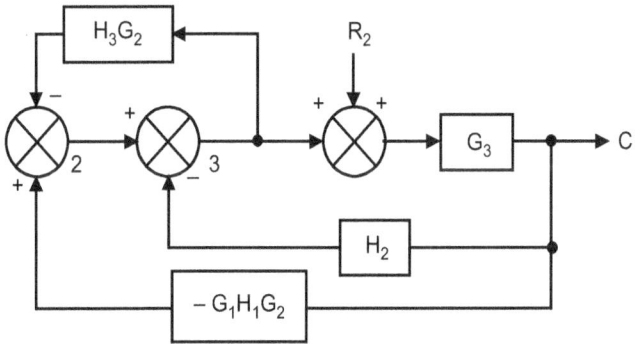

Step 3: Rearranging, we get

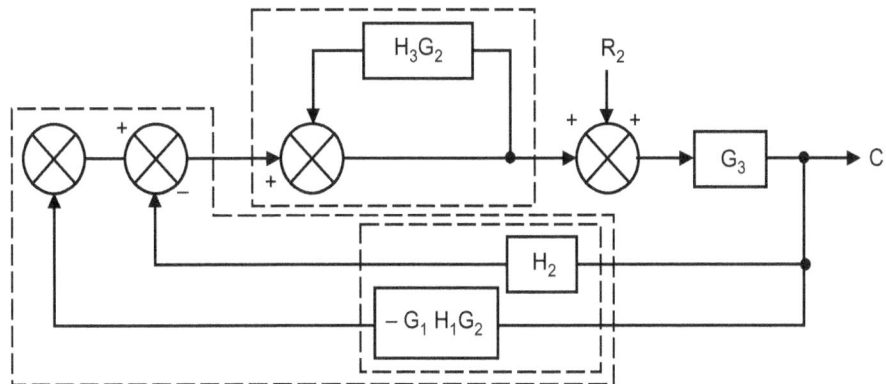

Step 4: Rearranging and eliminating the feedback loop and combining blocks in parallel.

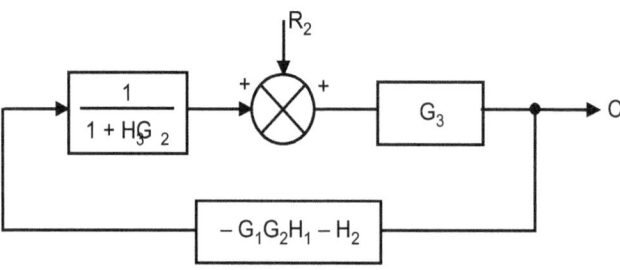

Step 5: Rearranging,

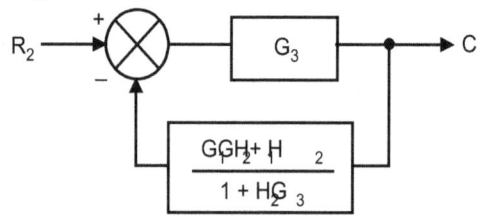

Eliminating feedback loop

$$\frac{C}{R_2} = \frac{G_3(1 + H_3 G_2)}{1 + H_3 G_2 + G_3(G_1 G_2 H_1 + H_2)}$$

Example 1.18: Find the closed loop transfer function of the system shown in Fig. 1.36.

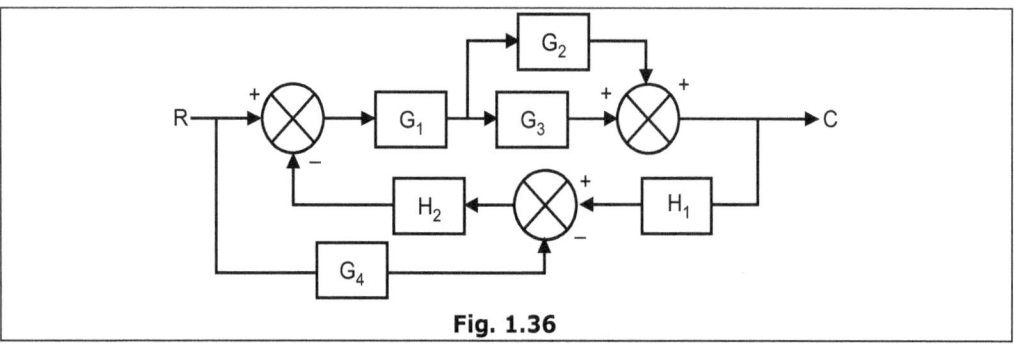

Fig. 1.36

Solution: Step 1: Redraw the given block diagram.

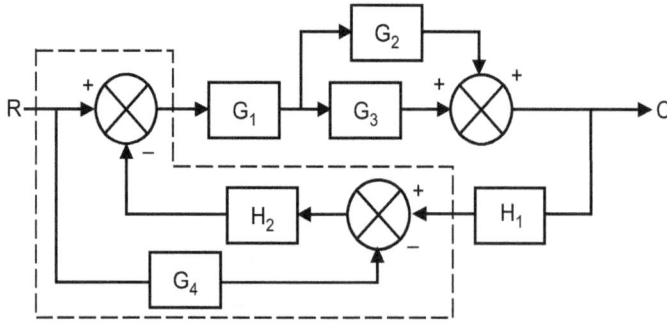

Step 2: Use common summing point and combine blocks in cascade.

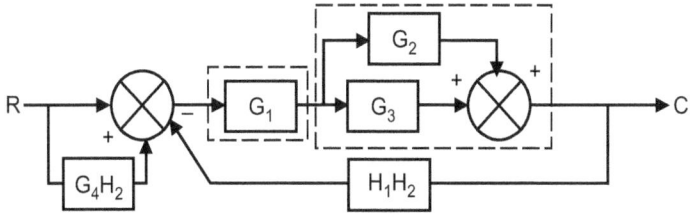

Step 3: Eliminating blocks in parallel and cascading with G_1.

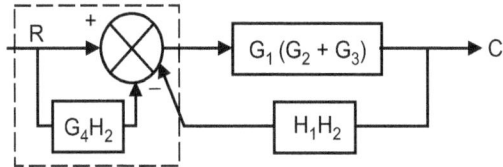

Step 4: Eliminating blocks in parallel (No block means consider G = 1).

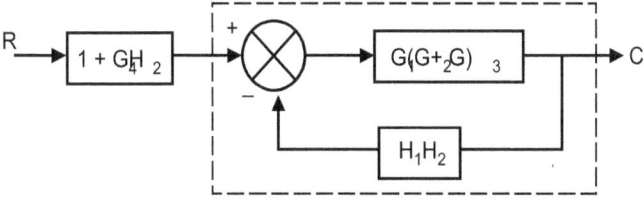

Step 5: Eliminating close-loop.

$$R \longrightarrow \boxed{1 + G_4 H_2} \longrightarrow \boxed{\frac{G_1 (G_2 + G_3)}{1 + G_1 G_2 H_1 H_2 + G_1 G_3 H_1 H_2}} \longrightarrow C$$

Step 6: Block in cascade.

$$R \longrightarrow \boxed{\frac{(1 + G_4 H_2) G_1 (G_2 + G_3)}{1 + G_1 G_2 H_1 H_2 + G_1 G_3 H_1 H_2}} \longrightarrow C$$

$$\therefore \quad \boxed{\text{T.F.} = \frac{C}{R} = \frac{G_1 (G_2 + G_3)(1 + G_4 H_4)}{1 + G_1 H_1 H_2 (G_2 + G_3)}}$$

Example 1.19: Determine the transfer function of Fig. 1.37 below by the block diagram reduction technique.

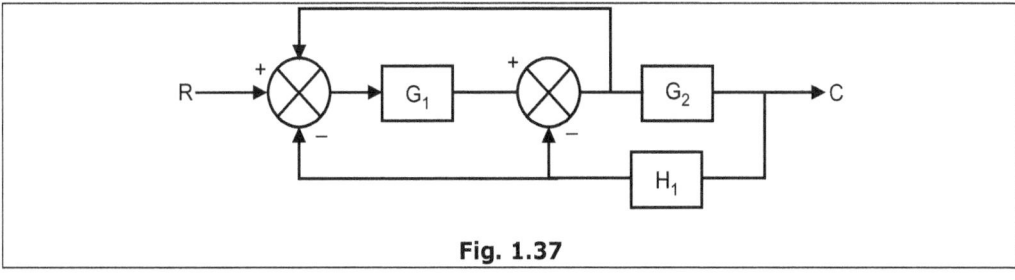

Fig. 1.37

Solution: Step 1: Redraw the given block diagram.

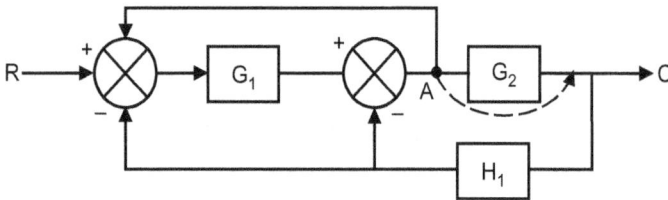

Step 2: Shifting take-off point A after G_2 (shown by dotted line in Step 1).

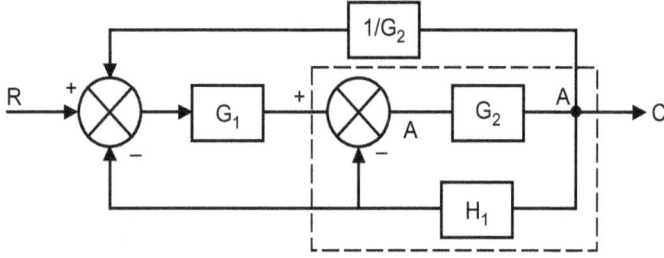

Step 3: Eliminating close-loop (marked by dotted line in Step 3).

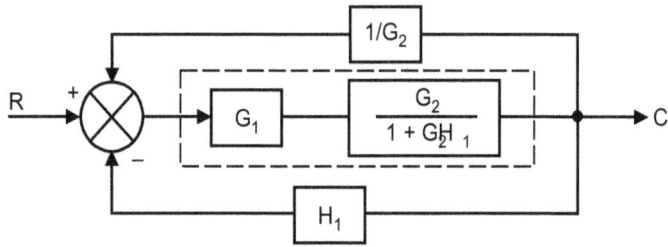

Step 4: Combining blocks in cascade (dotted lines shown in Step 3).

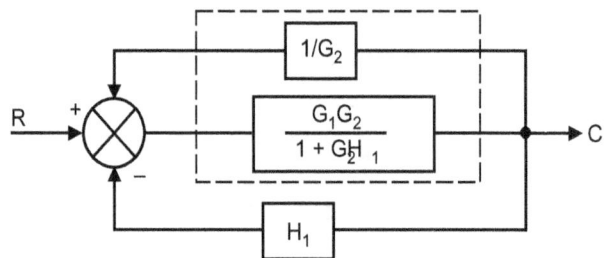

Step 5: Blocks in parallel.

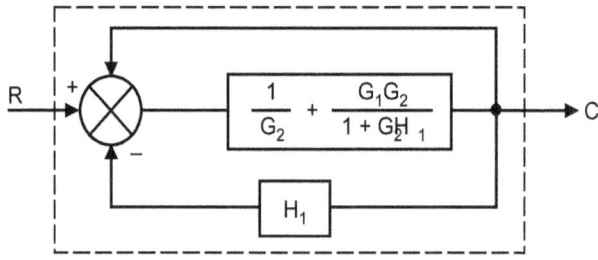

Step 6: Eliminating close-loop.

$$\text{T.F.} = \frac{C}{R} = \frac{\dfrac{1 + G_2H_1 + G_1G_2^2}{G_2(1 + G_2H_1)}}{1 + \dfrac{(1 + G_2H_1 + G_1G_2^2)}{G_2(1 + G_2H_1)} H_1}$$

$$\boxed{T = \frac{C}{R} = \frac{1 + G_2H_1 + G_1G_2^2}{G_2(1 + G_2H_1) + (1 + G_2H_1 + G_1G_2^2) H_1}}$$

$$R_B \longrightarrow \boxed{\frac{1 + G_2 H_1 + G_1 G_2^2}{G_2(1 + G_2 H_1) + (1 + G_2 H_1 + G_1 G_2^2) H_1}} \longrightarrow C$$

Example 1.20: Obtain the transfer function for the block diagram shown in Fig. 1.38 using block diagram reduction technique.

Solution:

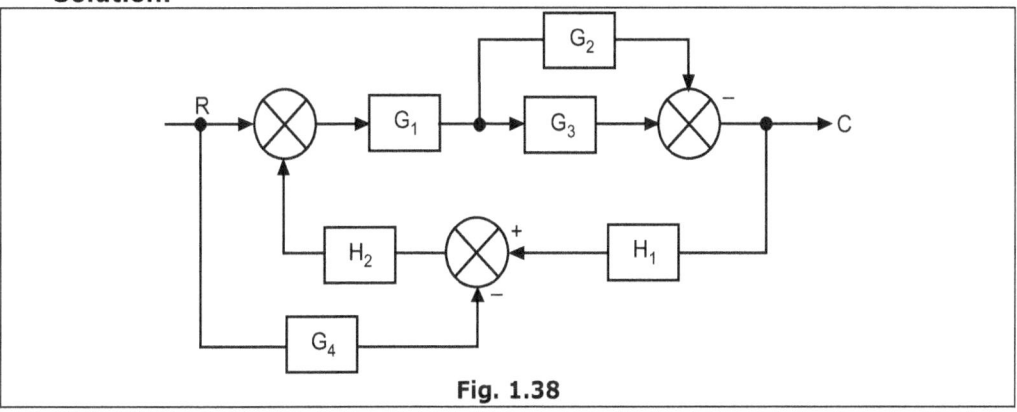

Fig. 1.38

Step 1: Block G_2 and G_3 are in parallel.

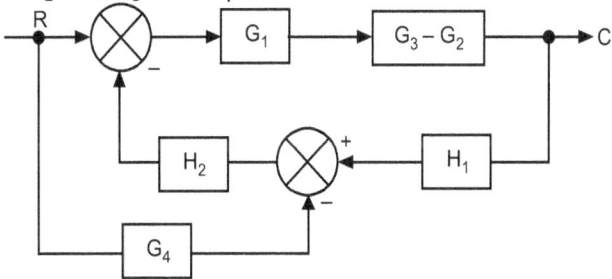

Step 2: Combining blocks in cascade G_1 and $(G_3 - G_2)$.

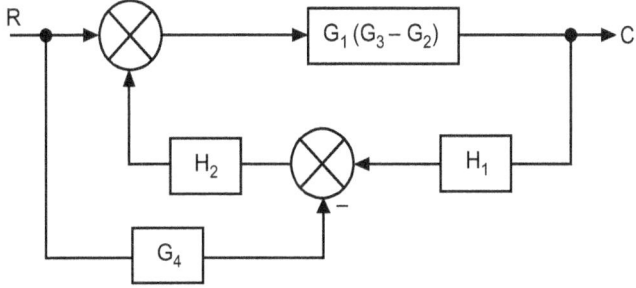

Step 3: Moving block ahead of summing point.

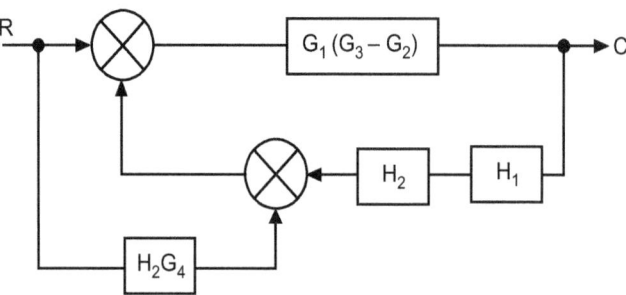

Step 4: Combining two summing points.

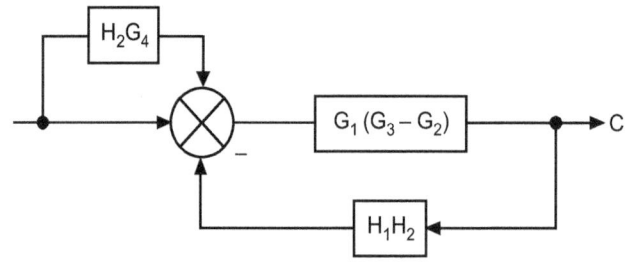

Step 5: Combining blocks in parallel.

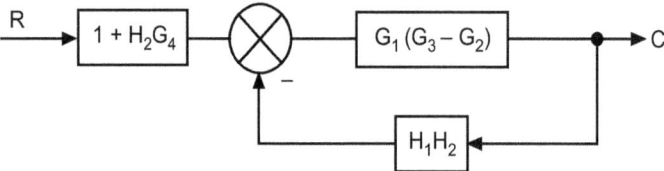

Step 6: Removing close loop.

$$R \longrightarrow \boxed{1 + H_2G_4} \longrightarrow \boxed{\frac{G_1(G_3 - G_2)}{1 + G_1(G_3 - G_2)(H_1H_2)}} \longrightarrow C$$

Step 7: Blocks in cascade.

$$R \longrightarrow \boxed{\frac{(1 + H_2G_2)\, G_1(G_3 - G_2)}{1 + H_1H_2G_1(G_3 - G_2)}} \longrightarrow C$$

Transfer function

$$\therefore \quad \frac{C}{R} = \frac{G_1(1 + H_2G_2)(G_3 - G_2)}{1 + H_1H_2G_1(G_3 - G_2)}$$

Example 1.21: Find the transfer function of the following block diagram as shown in Fig. 1.39. **(S-10)**

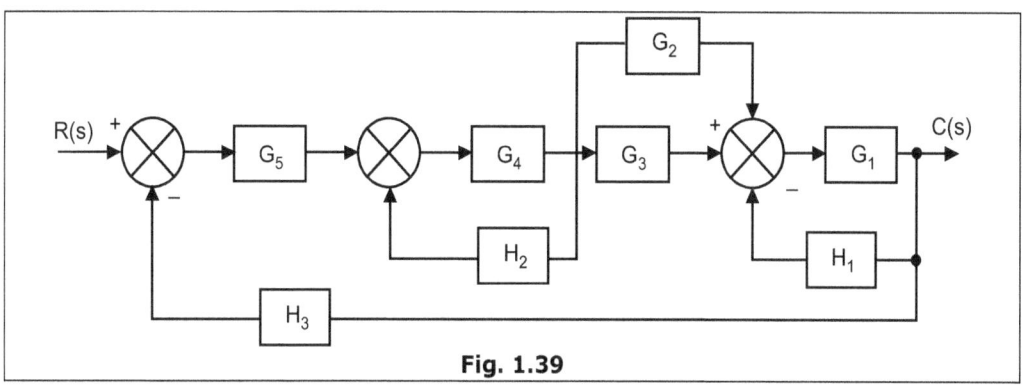

Fig. 1.39

Solution:

Step 1: Close-loop T.F. and blocks in parallel.

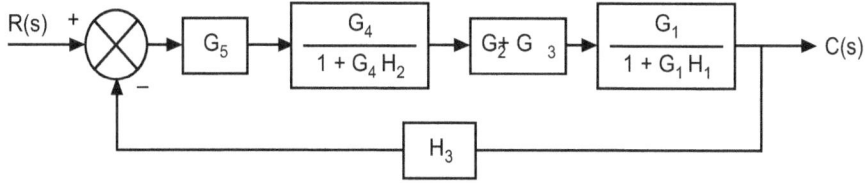

Step 2: Blocks in cascade.

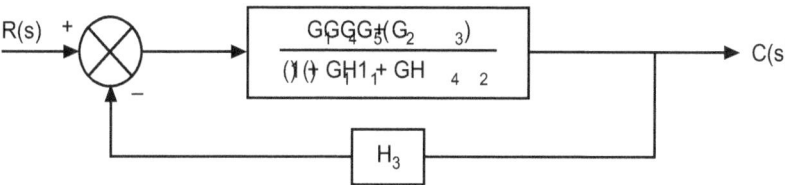

Step 3: Closed-loop T.F.

$$\therefore \quad \frac{C(s)}{R(s)} = \frac{G_1 G_4 G_5 (G_2 + G_3)}{[(1 + G_1 H_1)(1 + G_4 H_2) + G_1 G_4 G_5 (G_2 + G_3) H_3]}$$

Example 1.22: Find the transfer function in the following block diagram as shown in Fig. 1.40.

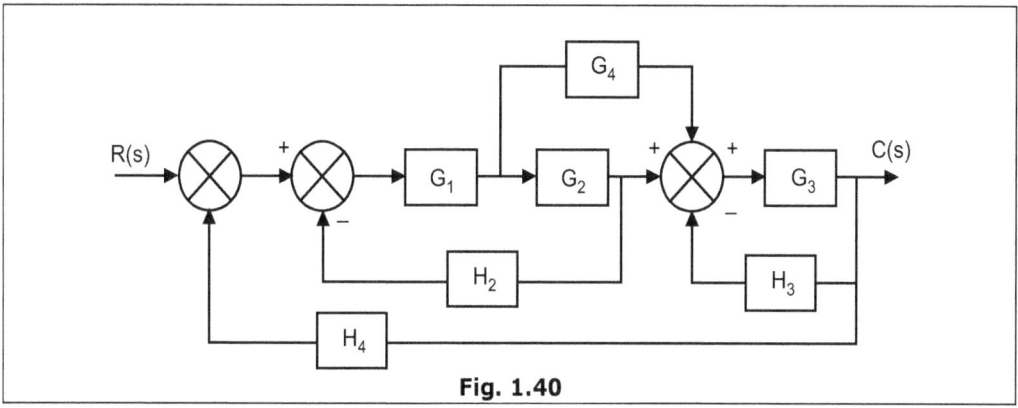

Fig. 1.40

Solution:

Step 1: Shifting take-off point before block G_2.

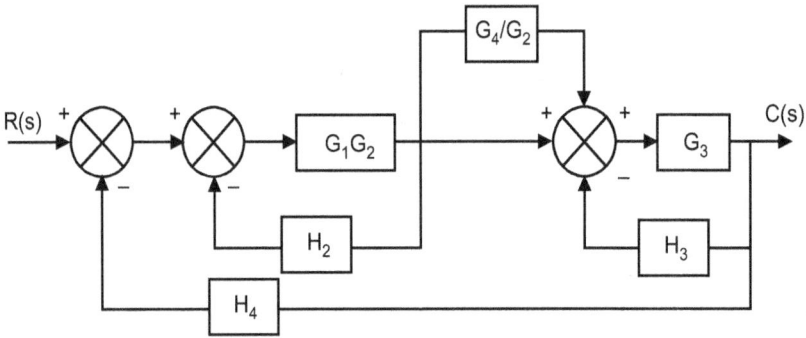

Step 2: Close loop T.F. and blocks in parallel.

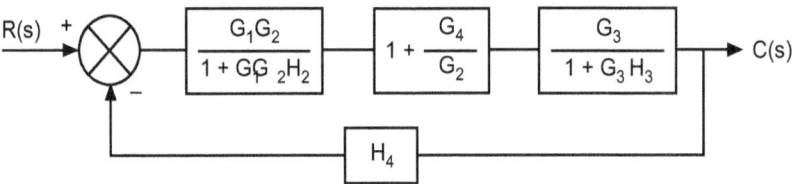

Step 3: Blocks in cascade.

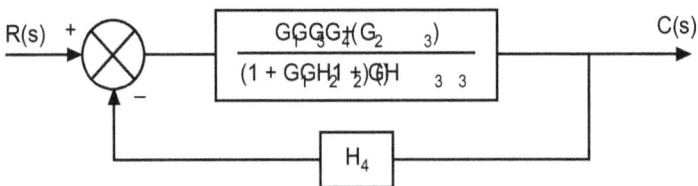

∴ Closed-loop T.F.

$$\frac{C(s)}{R(s)} = \frac{G_1 G_3 (G_2 + G_4)}{[(1 + G_1 G_3 H_2)(1 + G_3 H_3) + G_1 G_3 (G_2 + G_4) H_4]}$$

Example 1.23: Determine the transfer function of Fig. 1.41 (a) below by block diagram reduction method.

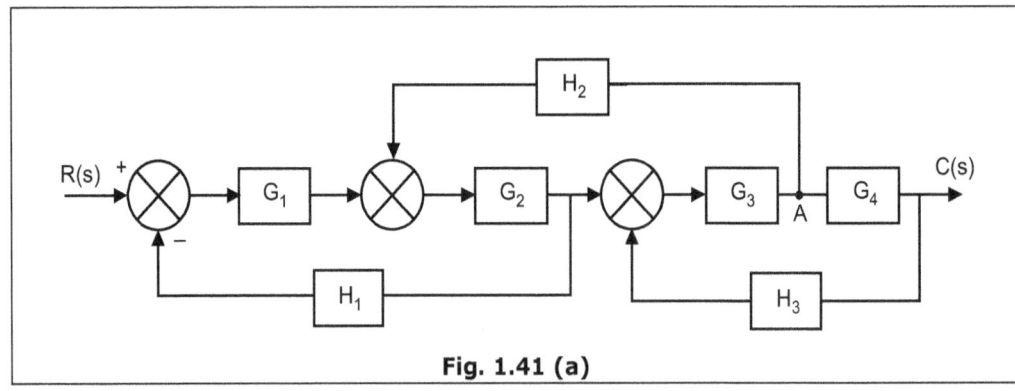

Fig. 1.41 (a)

Solution:

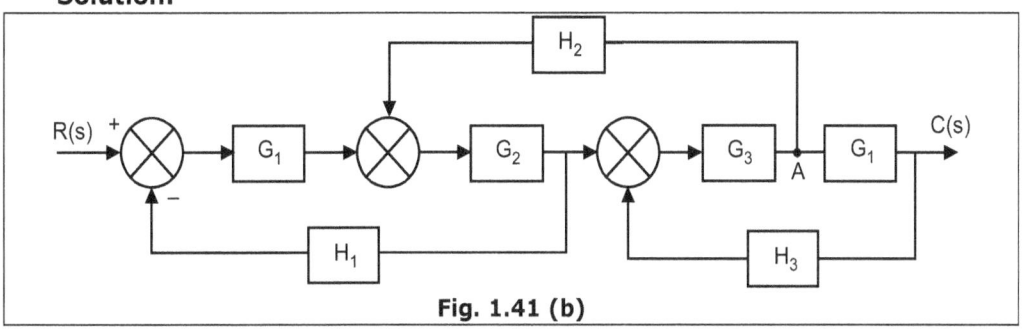

Fig. 1.41 (b)

Step 1: Shifting take-off point A ahead of block G_4.

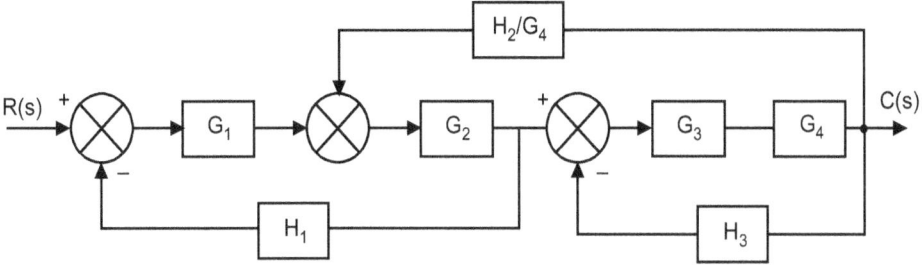

Step 2: Blocks in cascade (G_3 and G_4) and closed-loop T.F.

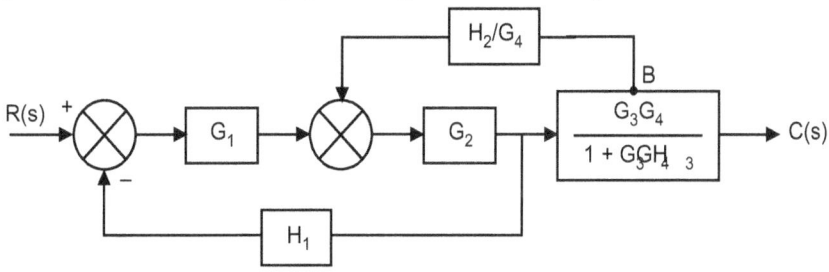

Step 3: Shifting point B.

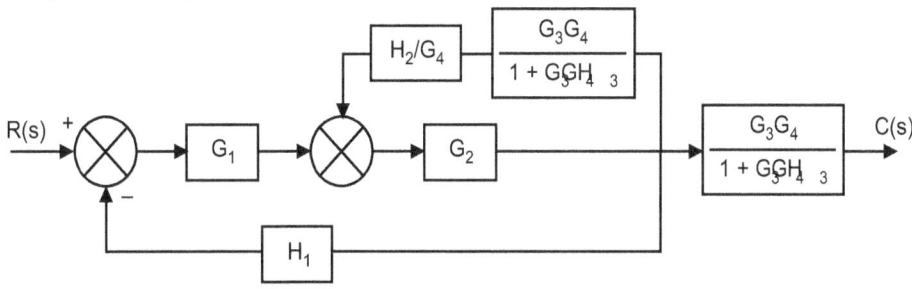

Step 4: Blocks in cascade and close-loop.

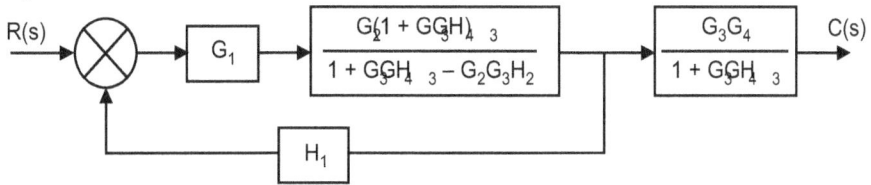

Step 5: Blocks in cascade.

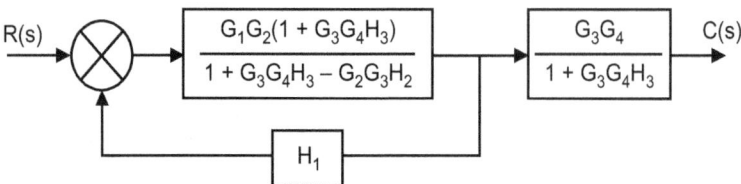

Step 6: Closed loop.

R(s) → ⊗ → [G₁G₂(1 + G₃G₄H₃) / (G₄H₃ − G₂G₃H₂ + G₁G₂H₁(1 + G₃G₄H₃))] → [G₃G₄ / (1 + G₃G₄H₃)] → C(s)

∴ Transfer function is

$$\frac{C(s)}{R(s)} = \frac{G_1 G_2 G_3 G_4}{[1 + G_3 G_4 H_3 - G_2 G_3 H_2 + G_1 G_2 H_1 (1 + G_3 G_4 H_3)]}$$

Example 1.24: Determine the transfer function of the block diagram given below in Fig. 1.42 (a).

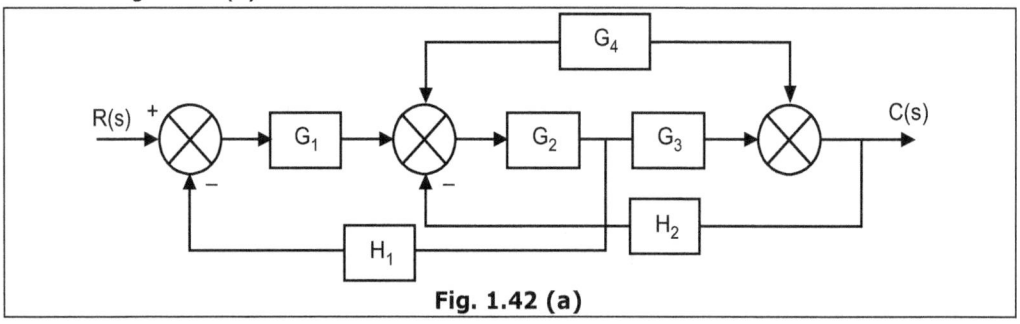

Fig. 1.42 (a)

Solution:

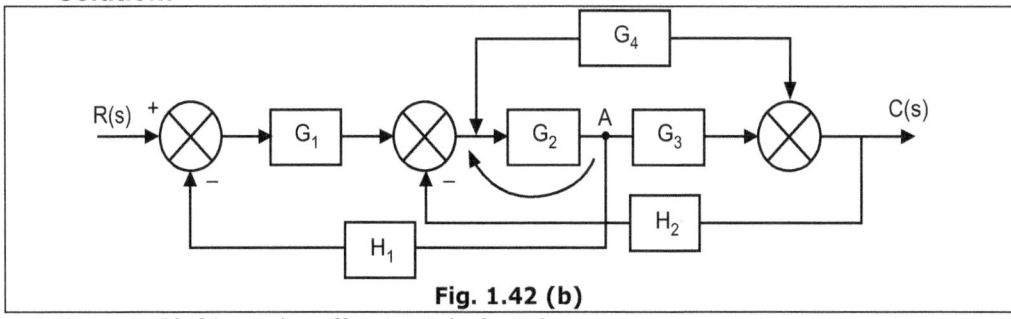

Fig. 1.42 (b)

Step 1: Shifting take-off point A before G_2.

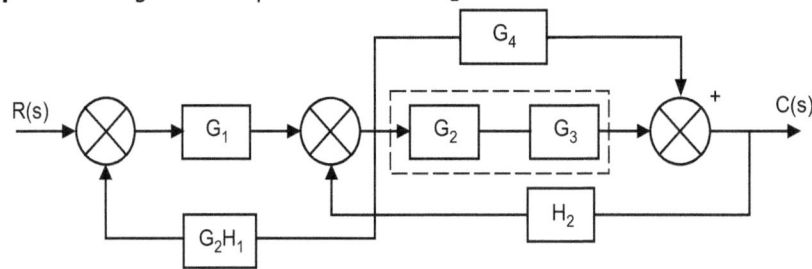

Step 2: Blocks in cascade G_2, G_3 and blocks in parallel G_2G_3 and G_4.

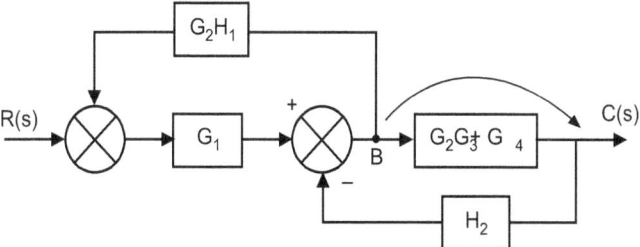

Step 3: Shifting take-off point B.

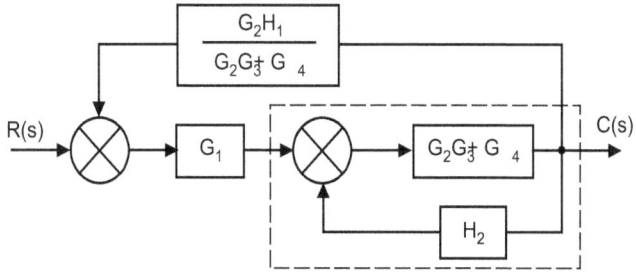

Step 4: Close-loop and blocks in cascade.

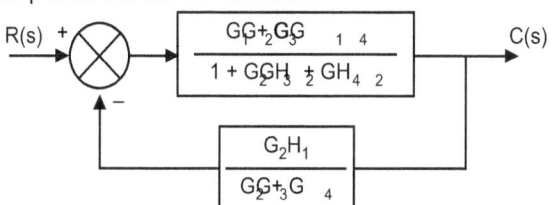

Step 5: Closed-loop.

$$R(s) \longrightarrow \boxed{\frac{G_1G_2G_3 + G_1G_4}{1 + G_2G_3H_2 + G_4H_2 + G_1G_2H_1}} \longrightarrow C(s)$$

So, transfer function is,

$$\frac{C(s)}{R(s)} = \frac{(G_1G_2G_3 + G_1G_4)}{(1 + H_2G_2G_3 + H_1G_1G_2 + H_2G_4)}$$

Example 1.25: Reduce the block diagram as shown in Fig. 1.43 (a) and find T.F.

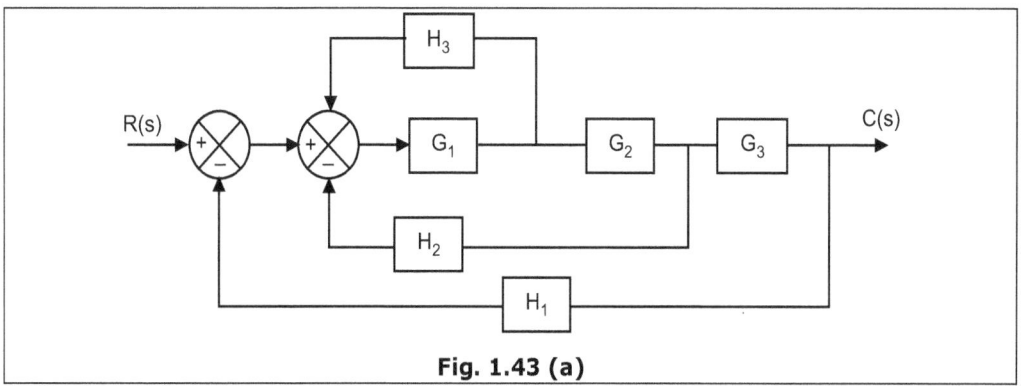

Fig. 1.43 (a)

Solution:

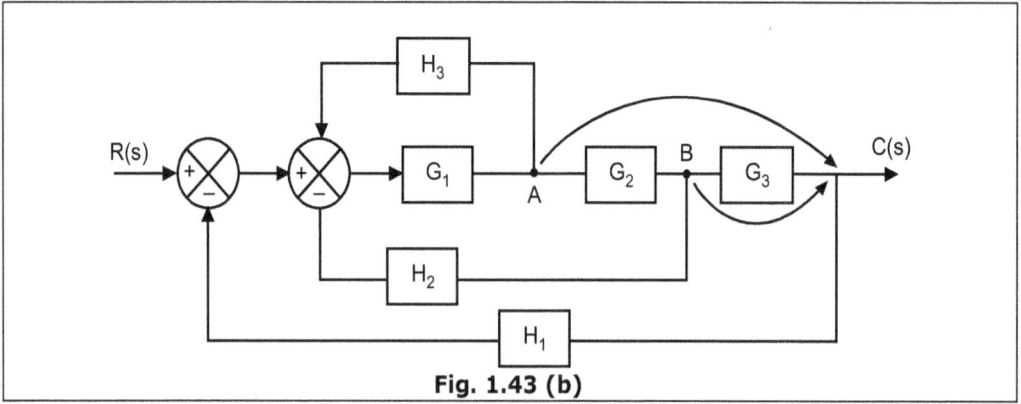

Fig. 1.43 (b)

Step 1: Shifting take-off point A and B ahead of G_3.

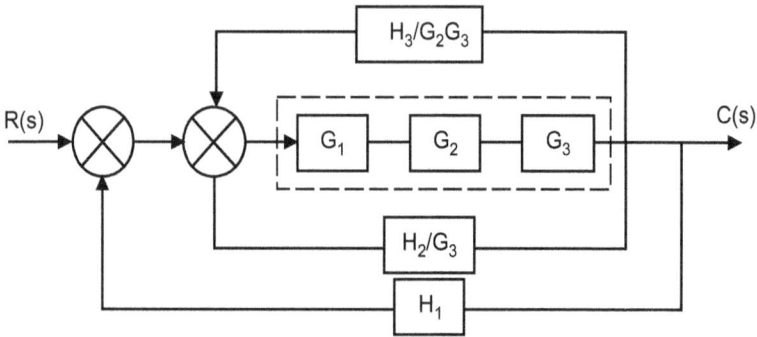

Step 2: Blocks in cascade.

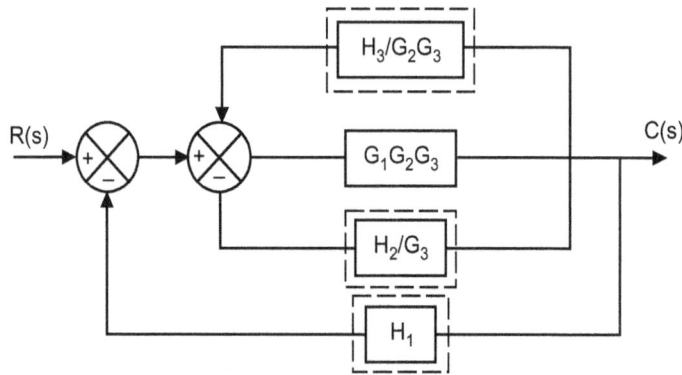

Step 3: Blocks in parallel.

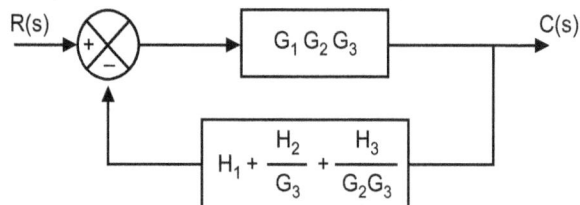

∴ Transfer function is

$$\frac{C(s)}{R(s)} = \frac{G_1G_2G_3}{1 + G_1G_2G_3\left(H_1 + \frac{H_2}{G_3} + \frac{H_3}{G_2G_3}\right)}$$

$$\frac{C(s)}{R(s)} = \frac{G_1G_2H_1}{1 + G_1G_2G_3H_1 + G_1G_2H_2 + G_1H_3}$$

Example 1.26: Find C/R of the system shown below in Fig. 1.44 (a).

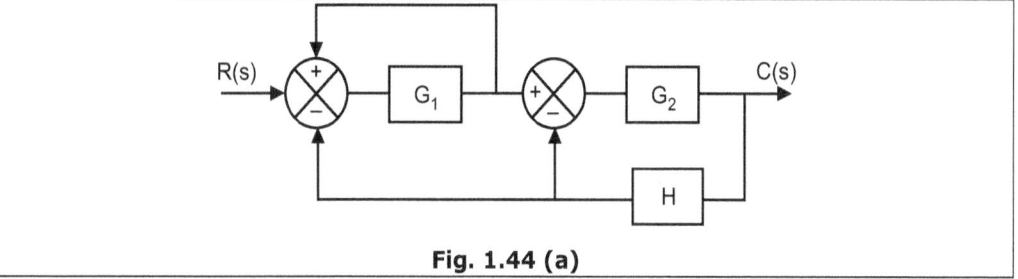

Fig. 1.44 (a)

Solution:

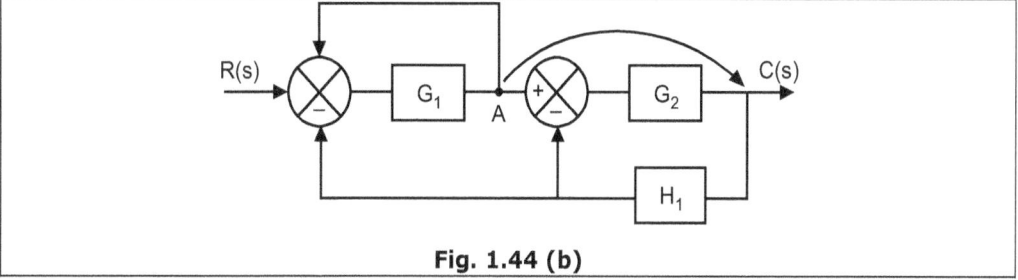

Fig. 1.44 (b)

Step 1: Shifting take-off point A ahead of G_2.

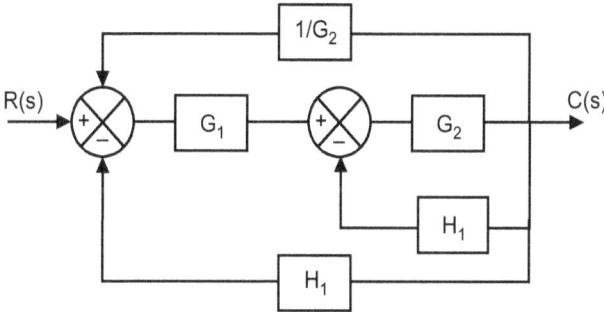

Step 2: Blocks in parallel $\frac{1}{G_2}$ and H_1 and close-loop.

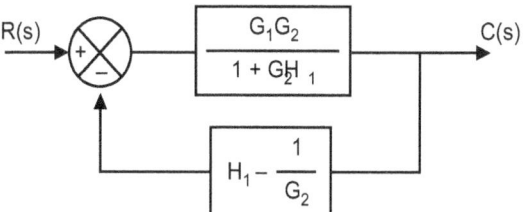

∴ Transfer function.

$$\frac{C}{R} = \frac{\dfrac{G_1 G_2}{1 + G_2 H_1}}{1 + \dfrac{G_1 G_2}{1 + G_2 H_1} \times \dfrac{H_1 G_2 - 1}{G_2}}$$

∴ $$\boxed{\dfrac{C}{R} = \dfrac{G_1 G_2}{1 + G_1 H_1 + G_1(H_1 G_2 - 1)}}$$

Example 1.27: Find the transfer function of the electrical network in the Fig. 1.45 shown below.

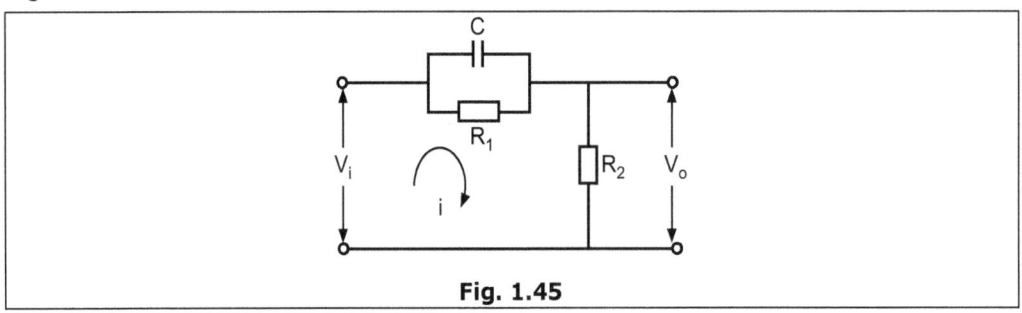

Fig. 1.45

Solution: Suppose Z_1 is the equivalent impedance of the parallel combination.

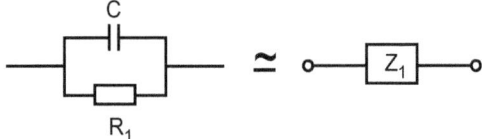

Then,

$$\frac{1}{Z_1} = \frac{1}{R_1} + \frac{j\omega c}{1}$$

∴ $$Z_1 = \frac{R_1}{1 + j\omega c R_1}$$

$$= \frac{R_1}{1 + SCR_1} \qquad (\because j\omega = S)$$

Applying Kirchoff's voltage law,

$$V_i(t) = Z_1 i(t) + R_2 i(t) \qquad \ldots (1)$$

and $$V_o(t) = R_2 i(t) \qquad \ldots (2)$$

Taking Laplace transform of equations (1) and (2), we get,

$$V_i(s) = Z_1 I(s) + R_2 I(s)$$

$$V_i(s) = \frac{R_1}{1 + SCR_1} I(s) + R_2 I(s) \qquad \left(\because Z_1 = \frac{R_1}{1 + SCR_1}\right)$$

$$V_i(s) = \left(\frac{R_1}{1 + SCR_1} + R_2\right) I(s) \qquad \ldots (3)$$

and $$V_o(s) = R_2 I(s) \qquad \ldots (4)$$

Transfer function of the network is,

$$\text{T.F.} = \frac{V_o(s)}{V_i(s)} = \frac{R_2 \, I(s)}{\left(\frac{R_1}{1 + SCR_1} + R_2\right) I(s)}$$

$$\therefore \quad \boxed{\frac{V_o(s)}{V_i(s)} = \frac{R_2 \,(1 + SCR)}{R_1 + R_2 \,(1 + SCR)}}$$

Example 1.28: Find the transfer function of the electrical network shown in Fig. 1.46.

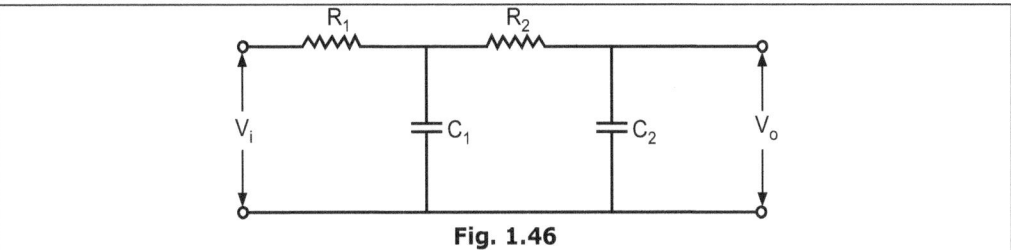

Fig. 1.46

Solution: Let
$$R_1 = Z_1$$
$$\frac{1}{SC_1} = Z_2$$
$$R_2 = Z_3$$
$$\frac{1}{SC_2} = Z_4$$

Redraw above figure.

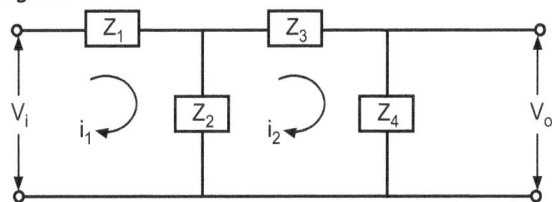

Apply KVL and take Laplace transform.
Loop I: $\quad V_i(s) = (Z_1 + Z_2) I_1(s) - Z_2 I_2(s)$ ... (1)
Loop II: $\quad V_o(s) = Z_3 I_2(s) + Z_4 I_2(s) + Z_2 I_2(s) - Z_2 I_1(s)$ ... (2)
$\quad V_o(s) = Z_4 I_2(s)$ ... (3)

From equation (2),
$$I_1(s) = \frac{(Z_2 + Z_3 + Z_4) I_2(s)}{Z_2} \quad \ldots (4)$$

Substitute the value of $I_1(s)$ in equation (1).
$$V_i(s) = \frac{(Z_1 + Z_2)(Z_2 + Z_3 + Z_4) I_2(s) - Z_2 I_2(s)}{Z_2} \quad \ldots (5)$$

Transfer function from equations (3) and (5).
$$\frac{V_o(s)}{V_i(s)} = \frac{Z_4 I_2(s)}{\frac{[(Z_1 + Z_2)(Z_2 + Z_3 + Z_4) - Z_2^2] I(s)}{Z_2}}$$

$$= \frac{Z_2 Z_4}{(Z_1 + Z_2)(Z_2 + Z_3 + Z_4) - Z_2^2}$$

Substitute values of Z_1, Z_2, Z_3 and Z_4.

$$\frac{V_o(s)}{V_i(s)} = \frac{\frac{1}{SC_1} \cdot \frac{1}{SC_2}}{\left(R_1 + \frac{1}{SC_1}\right)\left(\frac{1}{SC_1} + R_2 + \frac{1}{SC_2}\right) - \frac{1}{S^2 C_1 C_2}}$$

$$\frac{V_o(s)}{V_i(s)} = \frac{1}{1 + S(R_1 C_1 + R_2 C_2 + R_1 C_2) + (S^2 R_1 R_2 C_1 C_2)}$$

Example 1.29: Define transfer function. Find the transfer function of the network shown in Fig. 1.47. **(W-10)**

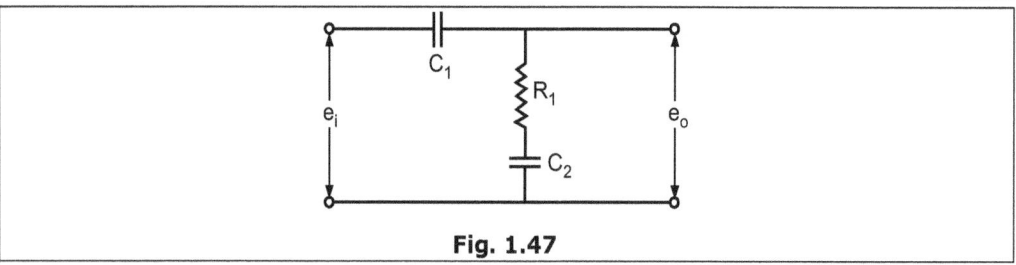

Fig. 1.47

Ans. Definition: Transfer function of a linear linear time-invariant system is defined as the ratio of L.T. of output variable to the L.T. of input variables assuming all initial conditions are zero.

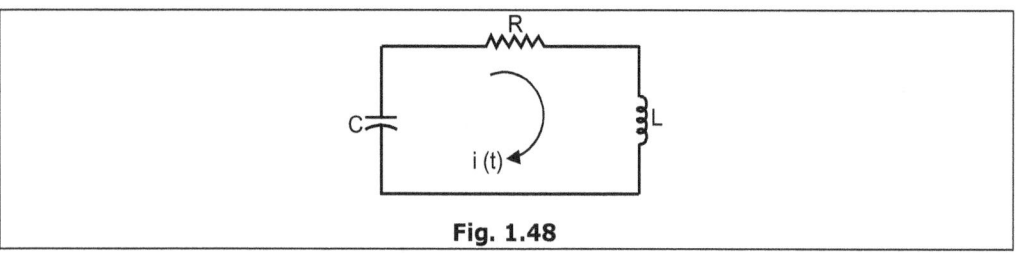

Fig. 1.48

Apply kVL to loop to Fig. 1.47.

$$E_i(t) = R_1 i(t) + R_2 i(t) + \frac{1}{C}\int_c^t i(t) \cdot dt \qquad \ldots (1)$$

Taking L.T.

$$E_i(s) = R_1 I(s) + R_2 I(s) + \frac{1}{SC} I(s)$$

$$= \left(R_1 + R_2 + \frac{1}{SC}\right) I(s) \qquad \ldots (2)$$

Output voltage is across $\frac{1}{C}\int i(t) \cdot dt \qquad \ldots (3)$

Taking L.T.

$$V_o(s) = R_2 I(s) + \frac{1}{SC} I(s)$$

$$= \left(R_2 + \frac{1}{SC}\right) I(s) \qquad \ldots (4)$$

Take the ratio of equation (2) and (4)

∴ Transfer function is,

$$G(s) = \frac{E_o(s)}{E_i(s)}$$

$$= \frac{\left(R_2 + \frac{1}{SC}\right)I(s)}{\left(R_1 + R_2 + \frac{1}{SC}\right)I(s)}$$

$$G(s) = \frac{R_2 + \frac{1}{SC}}{R_1 + R_2 + \frac{1}{SC}}$$

Example 1.30: Obtain transfer function for the following block diagram using block diagram reduction technique as shown in Fig. 1.49 below. **(S-05)**

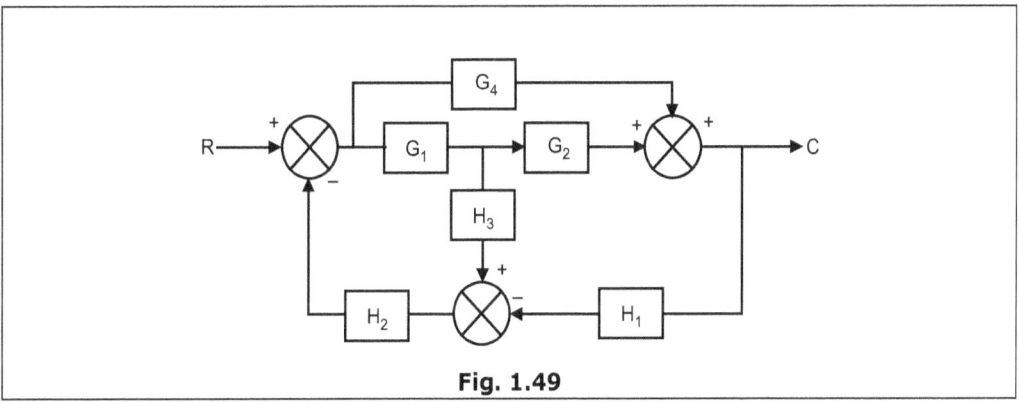

Fig. 1.49

Ans. Step 1: Blocks in parallel and eliminating the close loop.

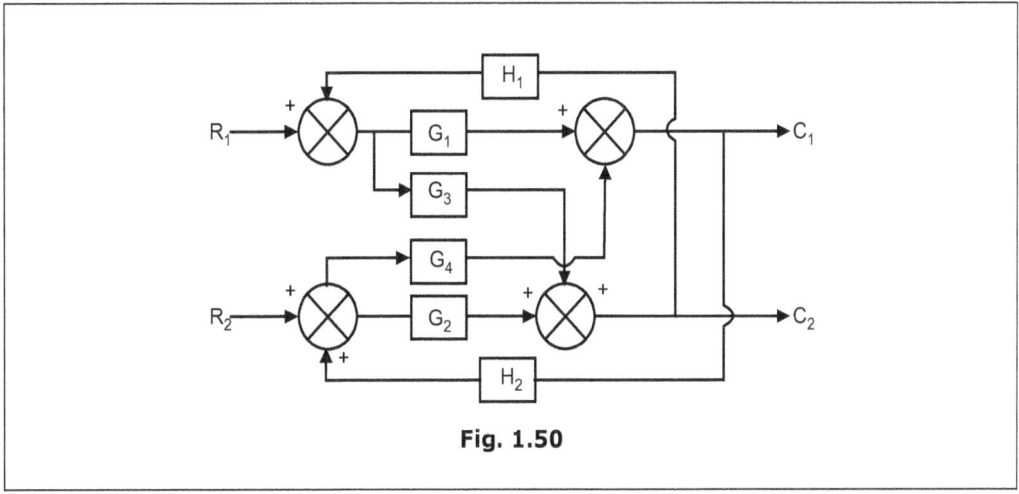

Fig. 1.50

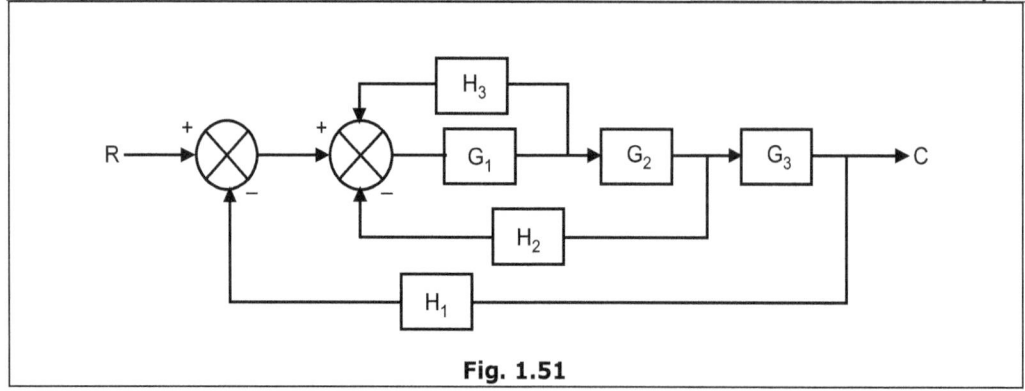

Fig. 1.51

Step 2: Blocks in cascade.

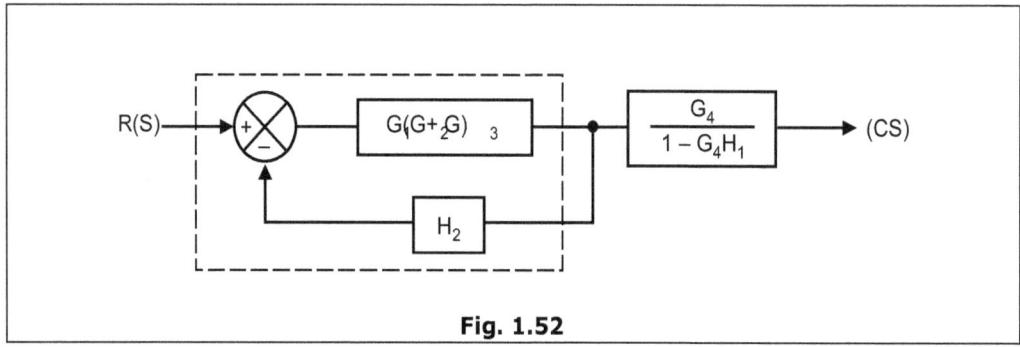

Fig. 1.52

Step 3: Eliminating closed loop.

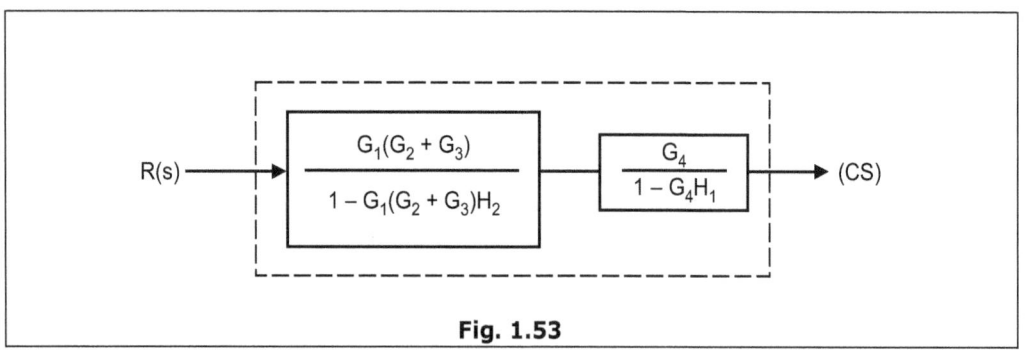

Fig. 1.53

Step 4: Again blocks in cascade.

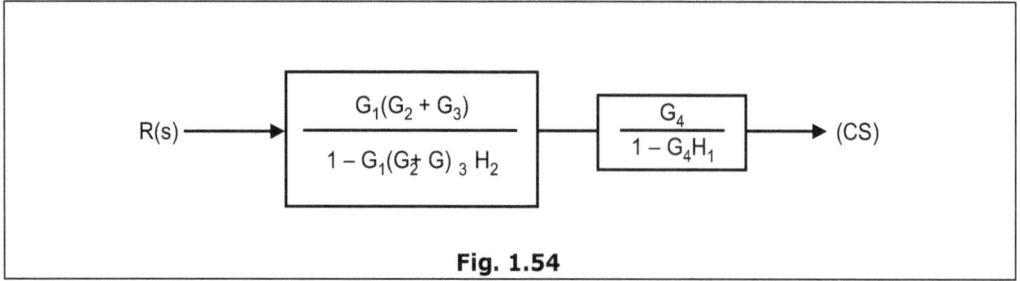

Fig. 1.54

Example 1.31: Derive the transfer function of the system shown in Fig. 1.55 using block diagram reduction method. **(S-09) (4M)**

Solution:

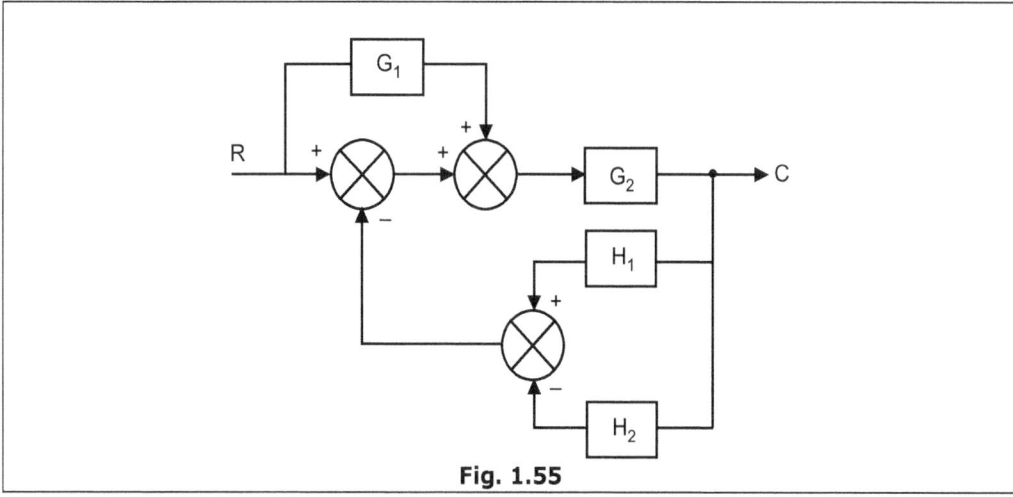

Fig. 1.55

Solution: Given:

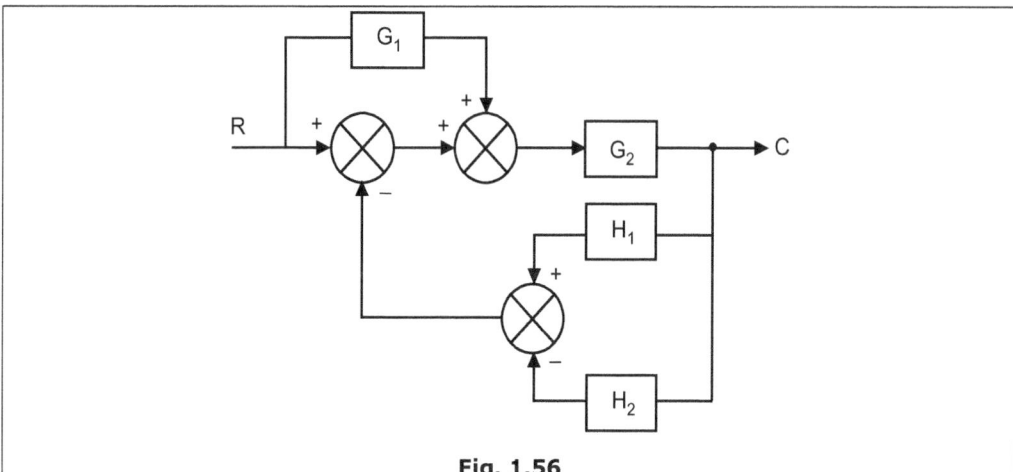

Fig. 1.56

Step 1: Blocks in parallel

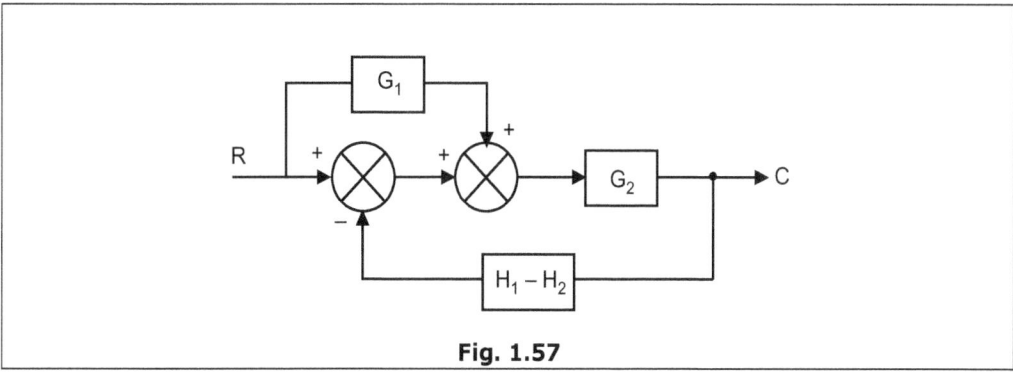

Fig. 1.57

Step 2: Shifting summing point ahead of block.

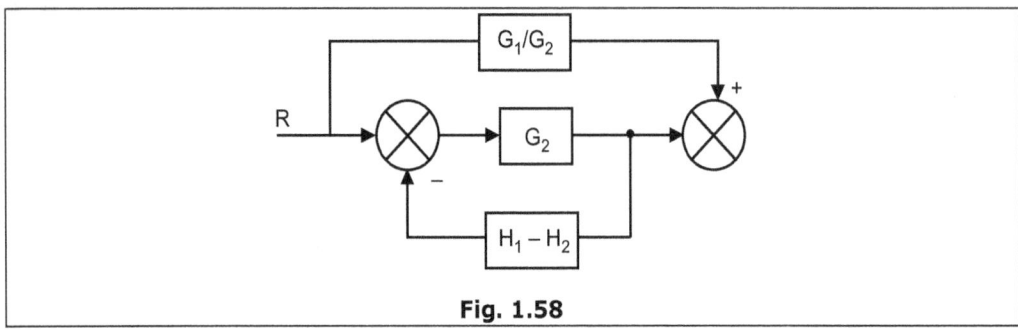

Fig. 1.58

Step 3: Close loop T.F.

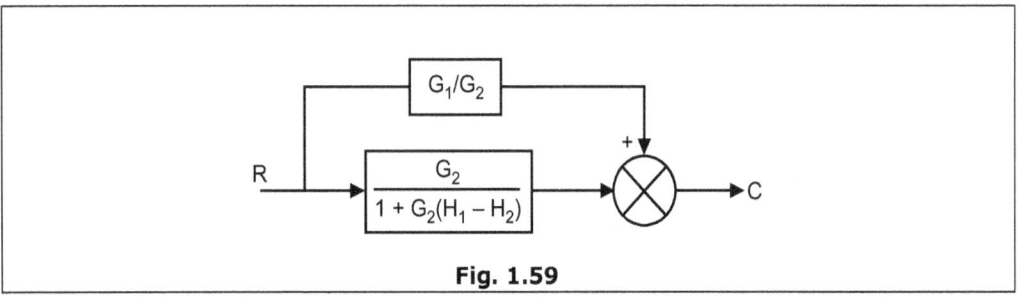

Fig. 1.59

Step 4: Close loop T.F.

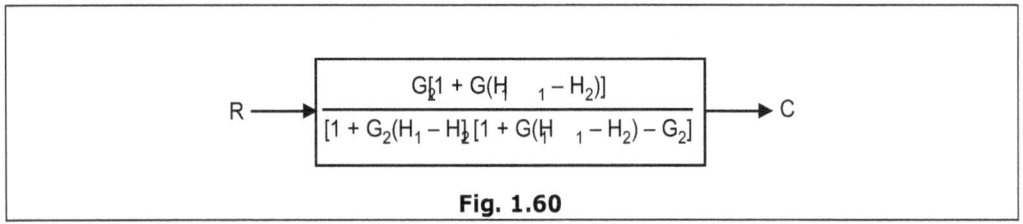

Fig. 1.60

Important Points

- **A system** is a combination of individual elements or components that act together in performing a specific function.

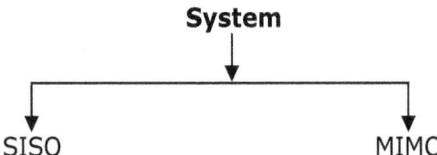

- The **control system** is a system in which any quantity of interest in a machine, mechanism or other equipment is maintained or changed in a desired.
- A system in which control action is totally independent of the output of the system is called an **open loop system.** For example, Automatic Washing Machine, Traffic lamps.

- A system in which the control action is dependent on the output is called a **closed loop system.** For example, Human beings, Driving an automobile.
- **Error detector** compares the reference input and feed back signal.
- A system in which the effect of the disturbance must show up in the error before the controller can take proper corrective action is called **feedback system.**
- A system in which corrective action is taken before disturbances affect the output is called **feedforward system.**
- For analysis and design of practical control systems **applied mathematics** is required.
- For study of control theory the required mathematical background includes complex-variable theory, differential equations, Laplace transform and Z-transformation.
- **Complex** means a combination of real and imaginary components.
- A **differential equation** is any algebraic or transcendental equality which involves either differentials or derivatives.
- A **linear** term is one which is first degree in the dependent variables and their derivatives.
- A **linear differential** equation is a differential equation consisting of a sum of linear term and all the others are **non-linear differential equations.**
- A **time variable differential equations** in which one or more terms depend explicitly on the independent variable time 't'.
- A **time-invariant differential equation** is one is a differential equation in which none of the terms depends implicitly on the independent variable time 't'.
- The **Laplace transform** is one of the mathematical tool used for the solution of linear ordinary differential equation.
- Mathematically, L.T. is defined as,

$$F(s) = \int_0^\infty f(t)\, e^{-st}\, dt$$

- The variable 's' is known as **Laplace operator** which is a complex variable $s = \sigma + j\omega$.
- **Important Theorems of Laplace Transform:**

Sr. No.	Theorem	Mathematical Representation
1.	Multiplication by a constant	$L[k\, f(t)] = k\, f(s)$
2.	Sum and difference	$L[f_1(t) \pm f_2(t)] = f_1(s) + f_2(s)$
3.	Differentiation	$L\left(\dfrac{df(t)}{dt}\right) = s\, f(s) - \lim_{t \to 0} f_1(t)$ $= s\, f(s) - f(0)$

Sr. No.	Theorem	Mathematical Representation
4.	Integration	$L\left[\int_0^t f(t)\,d\tau\right] = \dfrac{f(s)}{s}$
5.	Initial Value Theorem	$\lim\limits_{t \to 0} f(t) = \lim\limits_{s \to \infty} s\,f(s)$
6.	Final Value Theorem	$\lim\limits_{t \to \infty} f(t) = \lim\limits_{s \to 0} s\,f(s)$
7.	Complex Shifting	$L[e^{\pm \alpha t} f(t)] = F(s \pm \alpha)$

- **Transfer function of a linear time-variant system** is defined as the ratio of the Laplace transform of the output variable to the Laplace transform of the input variable assuming that all initial conditions are zero.
- The system can be characterized by its **impulse response** $g(t)$, which is defined as the output when the input is unit-impulse function $\delta(t)$.
- The transfer function of a **linear time-invariant system** is defined as the Laplace transform of the impulse response, with all initial conditions set to zero.

$$G(s) = \dfrac{\text{L.T. of output}}{\text{L.T. of output}}$$

$$G(s) = \dfrac{C(s)}{R(s)}$$

- **Block diagram** is a pictorial representation of the control system.
- Block diagram represents the relationship between the linear and non-linear physical systems.
- **Transfer function** for a closed loop system is,

$$T(s) = \dfrac{G(s)}{1 \pm G(s)\,H(s)}$$

$$R(s) \longrightarrow \boxed{\dfrac{G(s)}{1 \pm G(s)\,H(s)}} \longrightarrow C(s)$$

Practice Questions

1. Define the terms:
   (i) System, (ii) SISO, (iii) MIMO.
2. Define system. Give its classification with examples.
3. Define the terms:
   (i) Control system, (ii) Input, (iii) Output, (iv) Control.
4. Give the classification of control system and define each.
5. Draw the basic block diagram of open loop system and explain.

6. Give the examples of open loop system and explain any one.
7. List the advantages and disadvantages of the open-loop system.
8. Draw and explain the block diagram of closed loop system.
9. Give the examples of closed loop system and explain any one.
10. List the advantages and disadvantages of closed-loop system.
11. Give the comparison between open-loop and closed-loop system.
12. What are the various variables and components of a control system ? Define each component.
13. Draw the diagram for liquid level controller and explain.
14. Draw and explain the temperature controller.
15. What is meant by linear and non-linear differential equation ?
16. What is Laplace transform ? Or define laplace transform and state its features.
17. Define transfer function.
18. State the properties of transfer function.
19. Derive the transfer function of the given R-C circuit as shown in Fig. 1.61.

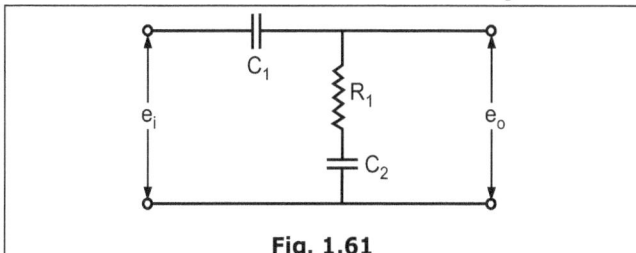

Ans.: T.F. $= \dfrac{R_2 + \dfrac{1}{C_2 s}}{R + \dfrac{1}{C_1 s} + \dfrac{1}{C_2 s}}$

Fig. 1.61

20. For a given network, find expression for i (t) if capacitor is initially charged to a voltage V_0.

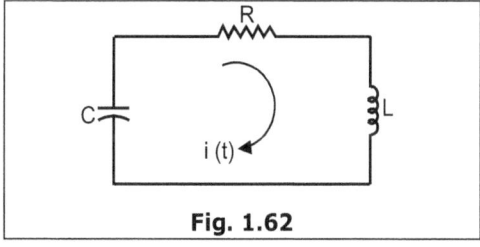

Fig. 1.62

Ans.: $i(t) = 4 t e^{-2t}$

21. For a given transfer function

$$G(s) = \dfrac{8s + 1}{s^2 + 2s + 1}$$

Find the differential equation.

Ans.: $\dfrac{d^2 y}{dt^2} + \dfrac{dy}{dt} + 1 = 8 \dfrac{dx}{dt} + x$

22. State the advantages and disadvantages of transfer function.
23. What is meant by block diagram representation ?

24. Draw the basic block diagram of a closed system and derive its transfer function for negative feedback.
25. Give any four rules of block diagram algebra.
26. Find the close loop transfer function of the system shown in Fig. 1.63.

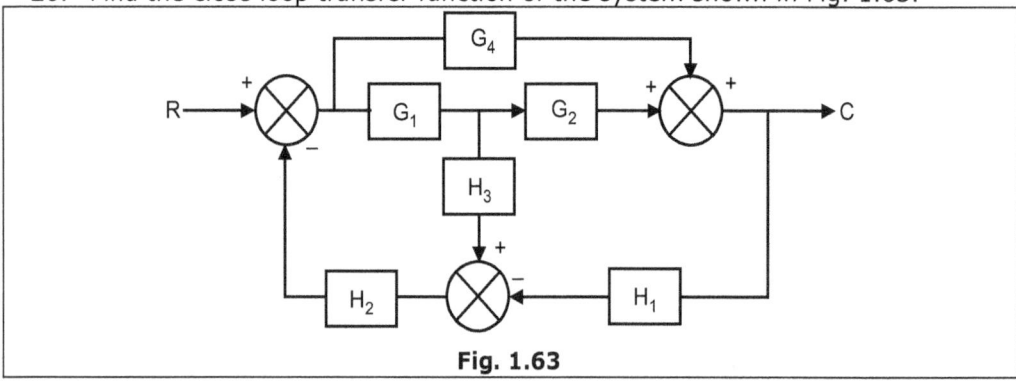

Fig. 1.63

Ans.: T.F. $= \dfrac{(G_1 G_2 + G_4) G_3}{1 + G_1 H_2 (H_3 - G_2 G_3 H_1) - G_3 G_4 H_1 H_2}$

27. Evaluate $\dfrac{G_2}{R_1}$ for the system whose block diagram is shown in Fig. 1.64.

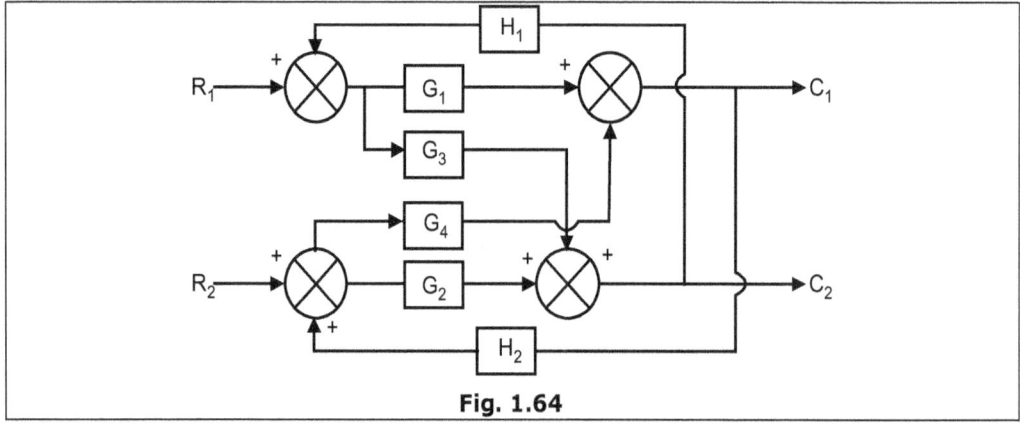

Fig. 1.64

Ans.: $\dfrac{C_2}{R_1} = \dfrac{G_3 (1 - H_2 G_4) + G_1 G_2 H_2}{(1 - G_4 H_2) + H_1 [G_3 (H_2 G_4 - 1) - G_1 G_2 H_2]}$

28. Reduce the block diagram shown in Fig. 1.65 and find the closed loop transfer function.

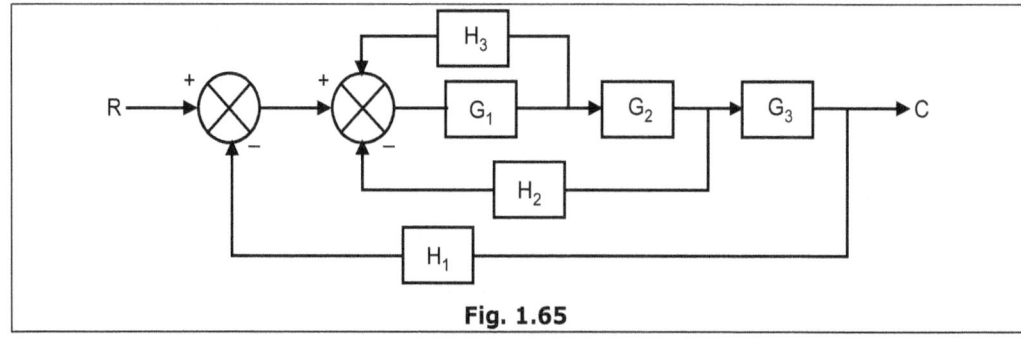

Fig. 1.65

Previous Year MSBTE Questions and Answers (As Per 'E' Scheme)

1. For the electrical system shown in Fig. 1.66. Derive the transfer function $\frac{V_o(s)}{V_i(s)}$. **(S-11) (4M)**

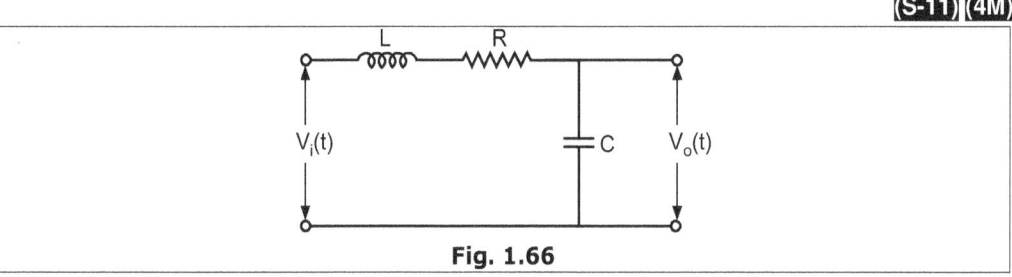

Fig. 1.66

Ans. Refer Example 1.3.

2. Derive the transfer function of closed loop control system. **(S-11) (4M)**

Ans. Refer Section 1.6.2.

3. Obtain the transfer function $\frac{C(s)}{R(s)}$ of the block diagram shown in Fig. 1.67. **(S-11) (4M)**

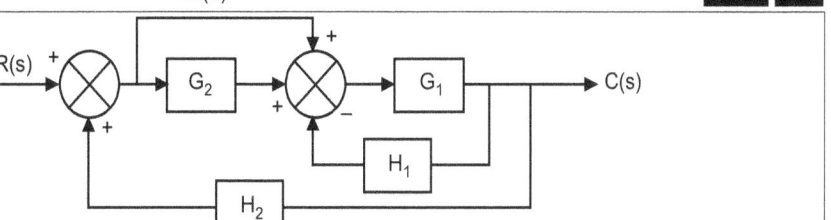

Fig. 1.67

Ans. Similar to Example 1.14.

4. State and describe the advantages of open loop system (any six points). **(S-12) (4M)**

Ans. Refer Section 1.3.1.

5. Reduce the given complex block diagram in its simple form using reduction rules. Find overall T.F. $\frac{C(S)}{R(S)}$. **(S-12)**

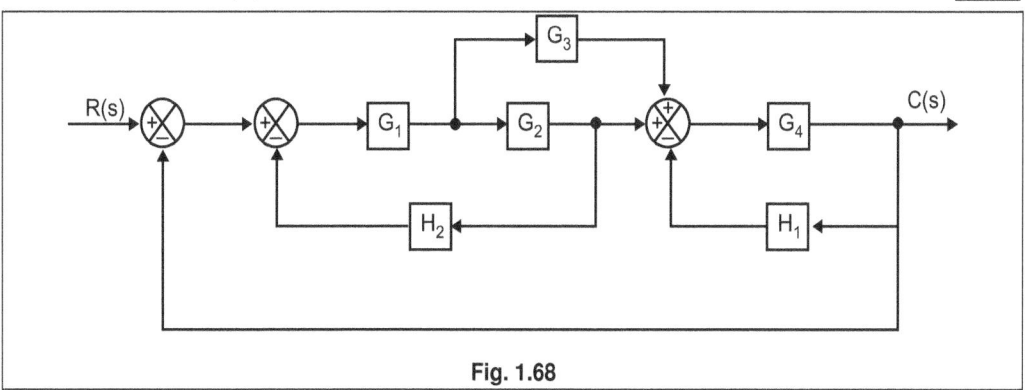

Fig. 1.68

Ans. Similar to Example 1.17, for this example put $H_4 = 1$.

6. Find T.F. of following electrical R.C. circuit. (Refer Fig. 1.69). **(S-12) (4M)**

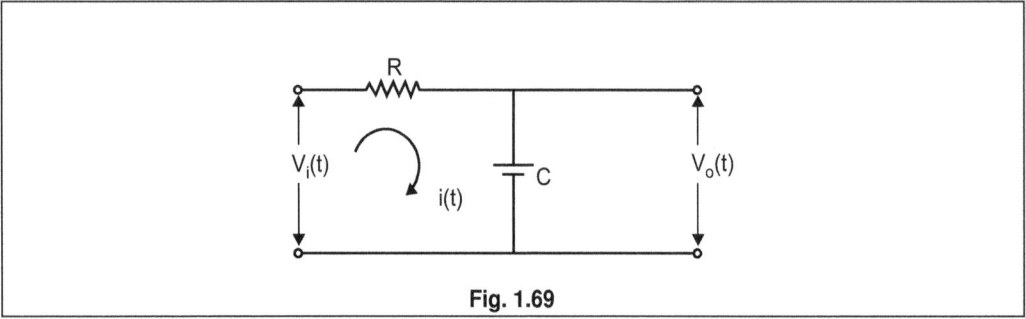

Fig. 1.69

Ans. Refer Example 1.1.4.

7. Derive the transfer function of closed loop system **(W-12) (4M)**

Ans. Refer Section 1.6.2.

8. Derive the transfer function of following electrical circuit. **(W-12) (4M)**

Ans. Refer Example 1.6.

9. Derive the transfer function of the block diagram, shown in Fig. 1.70.

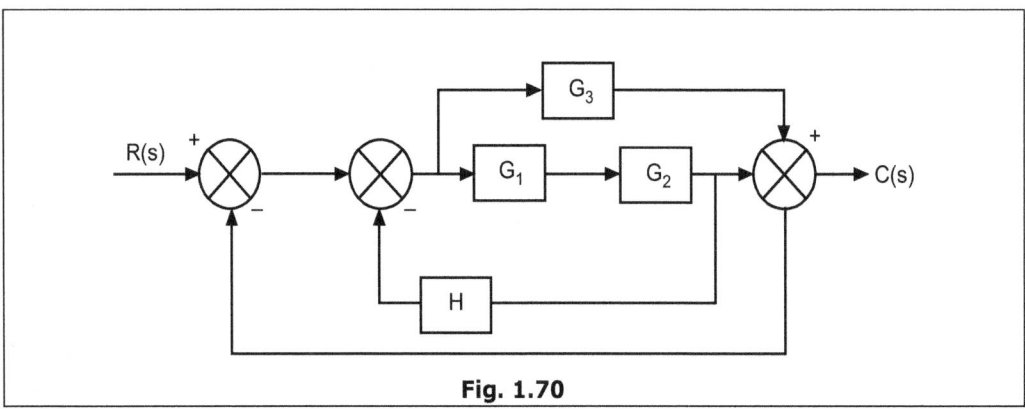

Fig. 1.70

Ans. Similar to Section 1.22.

***

TIME RESPONSE ANALYSIS

About This Chapter ...

After reading this chapter students can understand —
- Introduction
- Time Domain Analysis
- Standard Test Inputs
- Poles and Zeros
- Analysis of First Order System
- Analysis of Second Order System
- Time Response Specifications
- Types of Feedback Control System
- Steady State Errors and Error Constants

2.1 INTRODUCTION

- Control systems are generally called upon to perform both under transient (i.e. dynamic) and steady conditions.
- A feedback control system has the inherent capability that its parameters can be adjusted to change both, transient as well as steady-state behaviour.
- In order to analyse the transient and steady-state behaviour of control systems, the first step always is to obtain a mathematical model of the system.
- For any specific input signal, a complete time response expression can be obtained through laplace transform inversion.
- This expression yields the steady-state behaviour of the system with the time tending to infinity.
- Before proceeding with the time response analysis of a control system, it is necessary to test the stability of the system.

- System stability can be tested through indirect tests without actually obtaining the transient response.
- In case the system happens to be unstable, we need not proceed with its transient response analysis.
- Usually, the input signals to control systems are not known fully ahead of time.
- In most of the cases, these signals may be random in nature for example, in radar tracking system, the position and speed of the target to be tracked may vary randomly.
- Thus, it is difficult to express the actual signals mathematically by simple equations.
- System dynamic behaviour for analysis and design is, therefore, judged and compared under the application of standard test signals.
- The nature of the transient response is revealed by any of these test signals as this nature depends on system poles and not upon the type of input.

2.2 TIME DOMAIN ANALYSIS

- Time response is the analysis of control system or the analysis of an output of the control system with respect to time.
- In control system, the system is not directly put into operation.
- The system is either stimulated and tested.
- One of the method of testing such a system is to study the input behaviour of the system with respect to time for different types of input signals.
- These input signals are known as standard test signals.
- Also in analysis, a reference input signal is applied to the system and the performance of the system is evaluated by studying the time-response.
- For analysis, proper selection of the input signal is a must i.e. the selected input signal should match the process parameter that the control system will face.
- It is necessary to compare the input and output responses as a function of time. Thus, for most control system problems, the final evaluation of the performance of the system is based on the time response.

Time Response:

Since time is used as an independent variable in most control systems, it is usually of interest to evaluate the state and output responses with respect to time. This is known as Time response.

The response of a system to an applied excitation is called time response and it is a function of time, C(t).

The time response of a control system consists of two parts:
(i) Transient Response,
(ii) Steady State Response.

Let C (t) is the time response of a continuous-data system, then,

$$C(t) = C_t(t) + C_{ss}(t) \qquad \ldots (2.1)$$

where,

$C_t(t)$ = Transient response
$C_{ss}(t)$ = Steady state response

2.2.1 Transient Response

Definition:

In control systems, the transient response is defined as the part of the time response that goes to zero as time becomes very large.

Thus,

$C_t(t)$ has the property.

$$\lim_{t \to \infty} C_t(t) = 0 \qquad \ldots (2.2)$$

Transient response gives hints about,
(i) When the system begins to respond after the input is given ?
(ii) How much time it takes to reach the output ?
(iii) Oscillations of output about its final value.

2.2.2 Steady State Response

The steady state response of a control system, indicates where the system output ends up at which time becomes large.

Definition:

The part of the response that remains after the transient have died out is called steady state response C_{ss} (t).

In position control system, the steady state response when compared with the reference input gives an indication of the final accuracy of the system.

The steady state gives hints about,
(i) How much time it takes before steady state was reached ?
(ii) Actual value (If any) error between the desired, value and
(iii) Whether this error is constant, zero or finite.

2.2.3 Steady State Error

QUESTION

1. Define steady state error.

If the steady-state response of the output does not agree with the steady state input exactly, the system is said to have steady-state error.

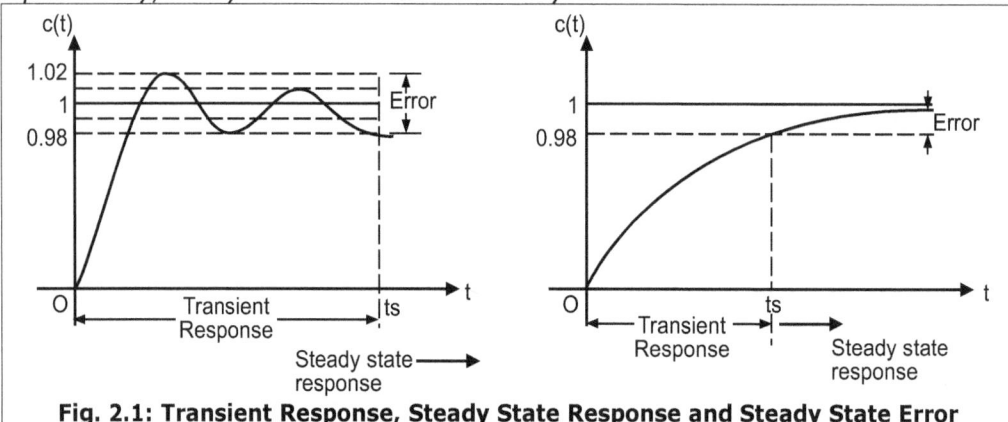

Fig. 2.1: Transient Response, Steady State Response and Steady State Error

2.3 STANDARD TEST INPUTS (SIGNALS)

QUESTIONS
1. What are the different standard test inputs ? Draw them and give their laplace representation. **(4M)**
2. What is meant by standard test signal ? State its necessity. Define step and ramp input. **(4M)**

Need:

- Usually, the input signals to control systems are not known fully ahead of time. In many cases, these signals are of random nature.
- For example, In radar tracking system, the position and speed of target to be tracked may vary randomly.
- Thus, it is difficult to express the actual input signals mathematically in simple equations.
- The dynamic behaviour of the system for analysis and design is judged and compared under applications of some signals, these signals are known as standard test signals or inputs.

These standard test signals are: 1. Step, 2. Ramp, 3. Parabolic, 4. Impulse.

- **Significance:**

The proper selection of the test signal is very important, for example, if a control system is designed to control a 'steadily increasing temperature', then the ramp input can be selected as the standard test signal. However, if the temperature increases in steps, then a 'step-input' will be the selected standard test signal.

To test the output response or result of particular system, it is necessary to apply some form of input. According to the system, we have to select proper input signal like step, ramp etc.

These signals are used to test the response of system and hence the name test signals.

2.3.1 Step Input

The step is a signal whose value changes from one level (usually zero) to another level A in zero time.

It is shown in Fig. 2.2 (a) below.

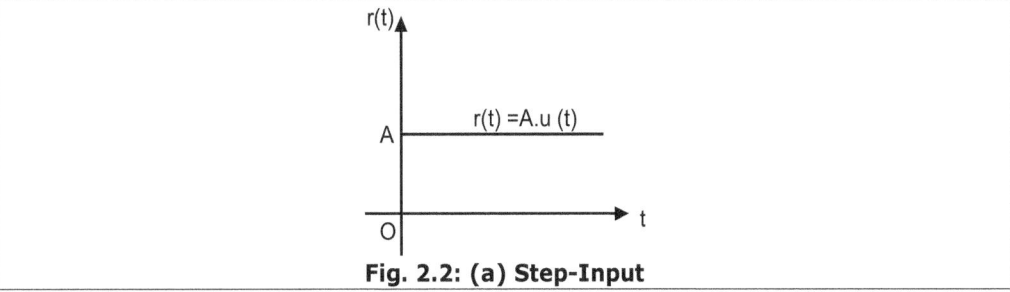

Fig. 2.2: (a) Step-Input

The mathematical representation of the step function is,

$$r(t) = A\, u(t)$$
$$u(t) = \text{Unit step function}$$

where,

$$u(t) = 1 \; ; \; t \geq 0$$
$$= 0 \; ; \; t < 0$$

Taking Laplace Transform,

$$R(s) = \frac{A}{s}$$

2.3.2 Ramp Input

Definition:

The ramp is a signal which starts at a value of zero and increases linearly with time.

$$r(t) = At \; ; \; \text{for } t > 0$$
$$= 0 \; ; \; \text{for } t < 0$$

Taking Laplace Transform,

$$R(s) = \frac{A}{s^2}$$

The graphical representation is shown in Fig. 2.2 (b).

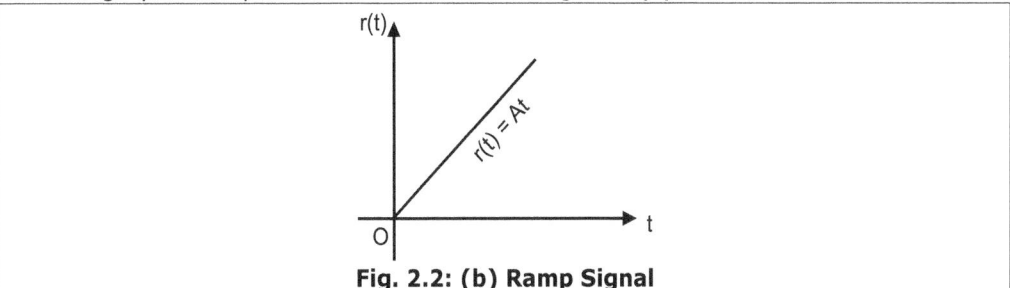

Fig. 2.2: (b) Ramp Signal

2.3.3 Parabolic Input

Parabolic signal is the integral of ramp input.

Mathematically,
$$r(t) = \frac{At^2}{2} \quad ; \quad \text{for } t > 0$$
$$= 0 \quad ; \quad \text{for } t < 0$$

Taking Laplace Transform,
$$R(s) = \frac{A}{s^3}$$

The graphical representation is shown in Fig. 2.2 (c).

Fig. 2.2: (c) Parabolic Signal

2.3.4 Impulse Input

Definition:

A unit impulse is defined as a signal which has zero value everywhere except at $t = 0$, where its magnitude is infinite. It is generally called the δ-function and is represented as,

$$\delta(t) = 0 \quad \text{for } t \neq 0$$

$$\int_{+\varepsilon}^{-\varepsilon} \delta(t)\, dt = 1$$

where,

ε tends to zero.

The graphical representation is shown in Fig. 2.2 (d).

Fig. 2.2: (d) Impulse Signal

Mathematically, the impulse function is the derivative of step function,
$$\delta(t) = u(t)$$
Taking Laplace transform of a unit-impulse is,
$$L\,\delta(t) = 1 = R(s)$$
The impulse response of a system with transfer function $\dfrac{C(s)}{R(s)} = G(s)$ is given by,

$$C(s) = G(s)\,R(s)$$
$$= G(s)$$
or $\quad C(t) = L^{-1}\,G(s) = g(t)$

Thus, the impulse response of a system, indicated by g(t), is the inverse Laplace of the transfer function.

2.4 POLES AND ZEROS

QUESTION
1. What do you mean by pole and zero ? Explain with example. **(4M)**

The open loop transfer function of a unity feedback system can be written as,
$$G(s) = \frac{C(s)}{R(s)}$$
Both C(s) and R(s) are polynomials in s.
$$G(s) = \frac{b_m s^m + b_{m-1} s^{m-1} + \ldots + b_0}{s^n + a_{n-1} s^{n-1} + \ldots + a_0}$$

$\therefore \quad G(s) = \dfrac{k\,(s + b_1)\,(s + b_2)}{s^n\,(s + a_1)\,(s + a_2)}$

This form of equation is known as *pole-zero form* where k is the gain factor.

Poles
Definition:
The values of 's' for which the transfer function magnitude $|G(s)|$ becomes infinite after substitution in the denominator of the system is called as poles of transfer function.

For example, $s = a_1, a_2, \ldots$ are called the poles of G (s). To get these values, equate the denominator function to zero.

When the pole values are not repeated, those poles are called **simple poles** but when pole values are repeated then those poles are called **multiple poles**.

For example, $\quad F(s) = \dfrac{2s^2 - 2s - 4}{s^3 + 5s^2 + 8s + 6}$

$$= \frac{2\,(s + 1)\,(s - 2)}{(s + 3)\,(s + 1 + j)\,(s + 1 - j)}$$

Equate denominator functions to zero.

$(s + 3) = 0 \quad s + 1 + j = 0 \qquad\qquad s + 1 - j = 0$
$\therefore \quad s = -3 \qquad s = -1 - j \qquad\qquad s = -1 + j$

Thus, F (s) has finite poles at s = − 3, s = − 1 + j and s = − 1 + j.

If we have to plot these poles on s-plane then they are marked by cross (X).

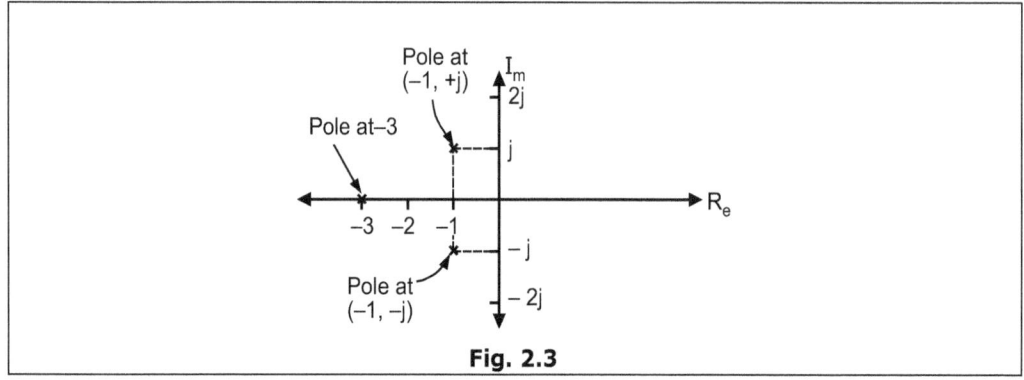

Fig. 2.3

Zeros

Definition:

The values of complex variable s for which the value of |F(s)| is zero and are called zeros of F(s).

In equation, s = b_1, b_2, b_3 ...... are zeros.

To get these values, equate the numerator to zero.

When zeros are not repeated, they are called **simple zeros** and when zeros are repeated then they are called **multiple zeros.**

In the above example, equate numerator to zero.

$$2(s + 1) = 0, \qquad (s - 2) = 0$$
$$\therefore \quad s = -1, \qquad s = 2$$

The function have zeros at s = − 1, 2.

The zeros are represented by a small circle (O) on the s-plane.

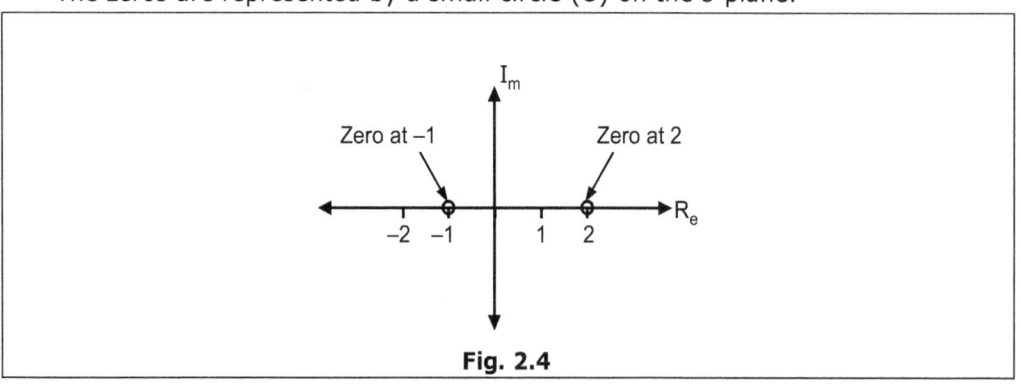

Fig. 2.4

SOLVED EXAMPLES

Example 2.1: The function,

$$F(s) = \frac{(s + 2)(s + 3)}{(s + 4)(s + 1 + j)(s + 1 - j)}$$

Find the poles and zeros present and mark them on the s-plane.

Sol.: Equate numerator to zero.

∴ $\quad (s + 2) = 0, \quad\quad (s + 3) = 0$
$\quad\quad s = -2, \quad\quad s = -3$

∴ $F(s)$ has zeros at $s = -2, -3$.

Equate denominator to zero.

$s + 4 = 0, \quad s + 1 + j = 0, \quad s + 1 - j = 0$
$s = -4, \quad s = -1 - j, \quad s = -1 + j$

∴ $F(s)$ has poles at $s = -4, -1-j, -1+j$

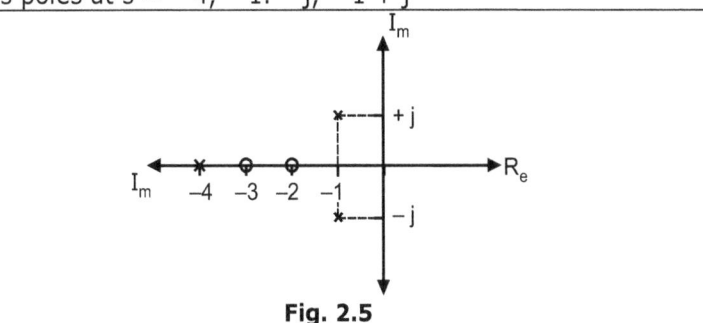

Fig. 2.5

Example 2.2: Sketch the,

$\quad$ zeros $= -3, 2 + j3, 2 - j3$
$\quad$ poles $= -4, j2 - 3, -2 + j2$ on s-plane.

Sol.:

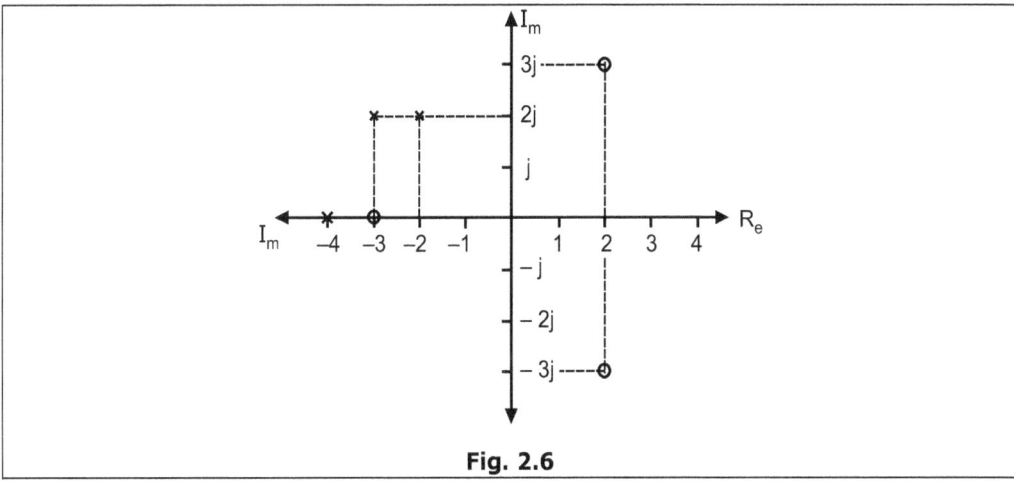

Fig. 2.6

2.5 ANALYSIS OF FIRST ORDER SYSTEM FOR UNIT STEP INPUT

QUESTIONS

1. Draw the unit step response of the first order control system.
2. Derive the expression of output response of a 1st order system for unit step input.

Let us consider the first order system shown in Fig. 2.7 with unity feedback.

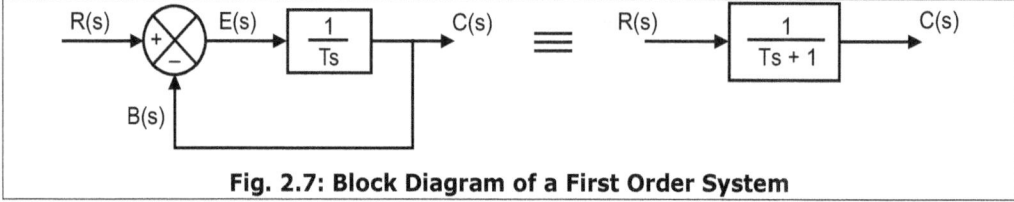

Fig. 2.7: Block Diagram of a First Order System

Here, the transfer function of the system shown in Fig. 2.7 is,

$$\frac{C(s)}{R(s)} = \frac{1}{Ts + 1} \qquad \ldots (2.3)$$

We shall analyse the system response to unit-step and unit-ramp inputs assuming zero initial conditions.

1. **Response to Unit Step Input:**

For the unit-step input. i.e. $R(s) = \frac{1}{s}$,

From equation (2.3), the output response is given by,

$$C(s) = \frac{1}{s(Ts + 1)} \qquad \ldots (2.4)$$

and by partial fraction,

$$C(s) = \frac{A}{s} + \frac{B}{Ts + 1}$$

$$A = \left[s \cdot \frac{1}{s(Ts + 1)} \right]_{s = 0} = 1$$

$$B = \left[(Ts + 1) \cdot \frac{1}{s(Ts + 1)} \right]_{s = -\frac{1}{T}} \quad \ldots \quad \begin{bmatrix} \text{Equating} \\ Ts + 1 = 0 \\ \therefore s = -\frac{1}{T} \end{bmatrix}$$

$$= \left. \frac{1}{s} \right|_{s = -\frac{1}{T}} = \frac{1}{-\frac{1}{T}} = -T$$

Equation (2.4) becomes,

$$C(s) = \frac{1}{s} - \frac{T}{Ts + 1} \text{ or } C(s) \frac{1}{s} - \frac{1}{s + \frac{1}{T}}$$

Taking Inverse Laplace Transform,

$$C(t) = 1 - e^{-t/T} \qquad \ldots (2.5)$$

Using,

e(t)	e(s)
1	$\frac{1}{s}$
$\frac{1}{s + \alpha}$	$e^{-\alpha t}$

which is plotted in Fig. 2.8.

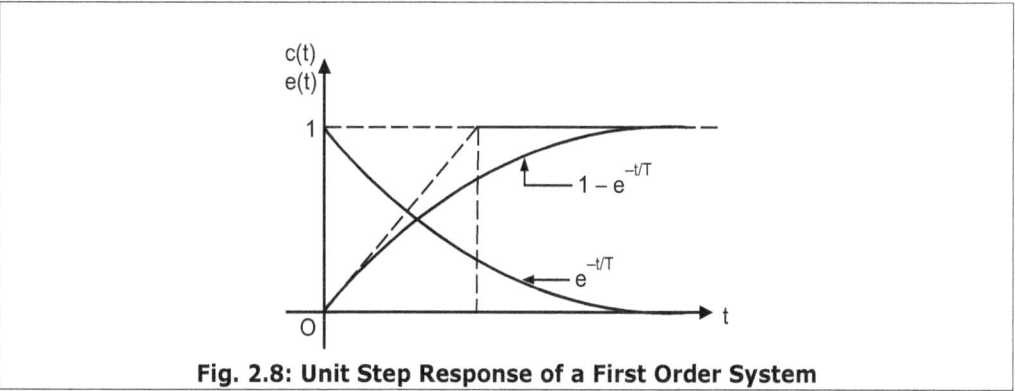

Fig. 2.8: Unit Step Response of a First Order System

From the response, it is shown that the output rises exponentially from zero value to the final value of unity.

where the initial slope at t = 0 is given by,

$$\left.\frac{dc}{dt}\right|_{t=0} = \left.\frac{1}{T}e^{-t/T}\right|_{t=0} = \frac{1}{T}$$

where, T is known as the **time-constant** of the system.

2.5.1 Concept of Time Constant

The **time constant** gives an indication as to how fast the system tends to reach the final value.

- The speed of the response can be defined as the time for the output to reach a particular percentage of its final value.
- A large time constant corresponds to a **sluggish** i.e. **(slow) system** and a small time constant corresponds to a **fast response** as shown in Fig. 2.9.

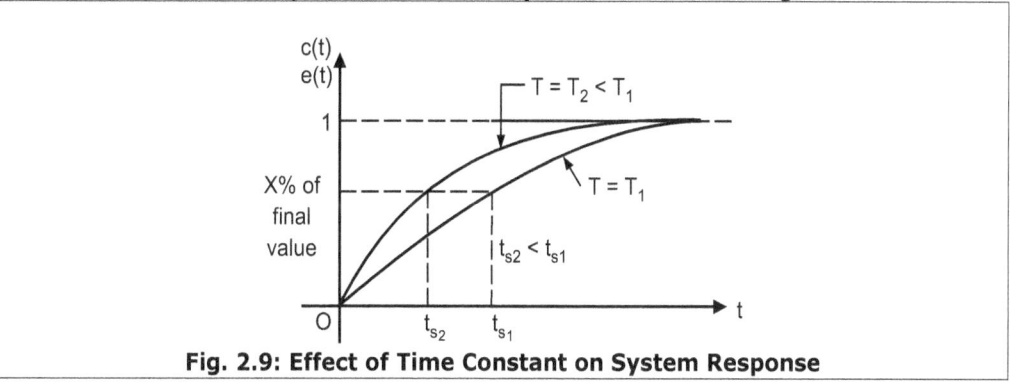

Fig. 2.9: Effect of Time Constant on System Response

Now, consider the error response of the system which is,

$$e(t) = r(t) - c(t)$$
$$= 1 - [1 - e^{-t/T}] \qquad \left(\because \begin{array}{l} r(t) = 1 \\ c(t) = 1 - e^{-t/T} \end{array}\right)$$
$$= e^{-t/T}$$

which is plotted in Fig. 2.16.

The steady state error is given by,

$$e_{ss} = \lim_{t \to \infty} e(t) \quad \text{[Using initial value theorem]}$$

∴ $e_{ss} = 0$

Thus, *this system tracks the unit-step input with zero steady-state error.*

2.6 ANALYSIS OF SECOND-ORDER CONTROL SYSTEM

Consider the servomechanism shown in Fig. 2.10 which controls the position of a mechanical load in accordance with the position of the reference shaft.

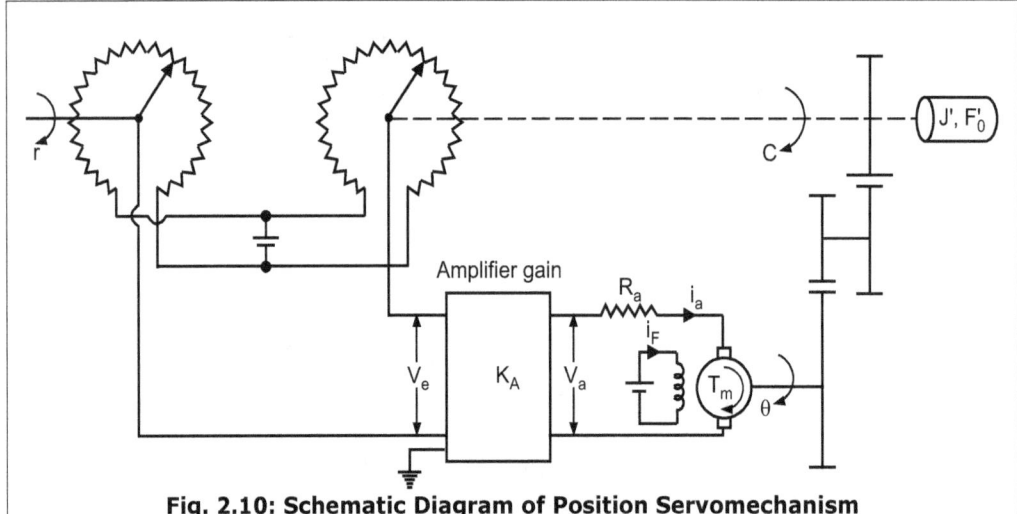

Fig. 2.10: Schematic Diagram of Position Servomechanism

- Here, the potentiometer converts the input and output positions into proportional electrical signals, which are then compared and the error signal (equal to difference of the two) appears at the potentiometer wiper arms.

The error signal (voltage) is,

$$V_e = k_p (r - c)$$

where,

r = Reference shaft position; rad.
c = Output shaft position; rad.
k_p = Potentiometer sensitivity; volts/rad.

- This error signal is amplified by a factor k_A by the amplifier and applied to the armature of d.c. motor whose field winding is excited with a constant voltage.
- By the existing error, the motor develops a torque which is transmitted to the output shaft through a gear train of ratio n (∵ n = load shaft speed $\dot{C}$/motor shaft speed $\dot{\theta}$).
- The transmitted torque rotates the output shaft in such a direction so as to reduce the error to zero.

The block diagram of the system shown in Fig. 2.11 (a) where, J and f_o are the equivalent inertia and friction at the motor shaft.

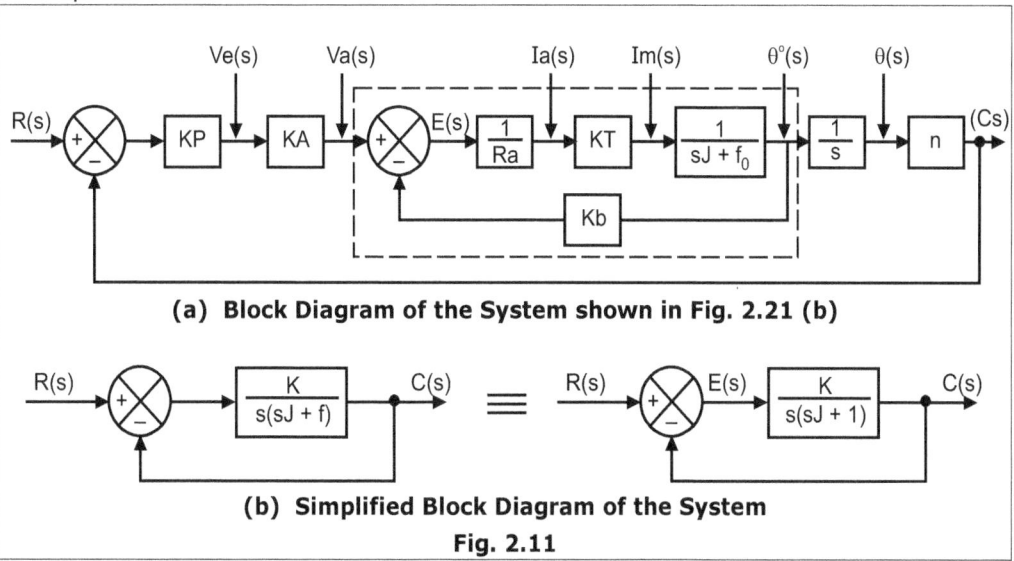

(a) Block Diagram of the System shown in Fig. 2.21 (b)

(b) Simplified Block Diagram of the System

Fig. 2.11

The inner loop shown by dotted lines can be reduced to give the motor transfer function as,

$$\frac{\theta(s)}{V_a(s)} = \frac{k_T/R_a}{s(sJ+f)} \quad \ldots (2.6)$$

where,

$$f = f_o + \frac{k_T k_b}{R_a}$$

The block diagram can be simplified to Fig. 2.21 (b).
where,

$$k = k_P k_A k_T \frac{n}{R_a}$$

The forward transfer function can be written in the time constant form,

$$G(s) = \frac{k_v}{s(\tau s + 1)}$$

where,

$$k_v = \frac{k}{f}, \quad \tau = \frac{J}{f}$$

Thus, Fig. 2.21 (b) is a second-order system involving one forward path.

2.6.1 Response of Second-Order System to the Unit-Step

From Fig. 2.11 (b), the overall transfer function of the system is,

$$\frac{C(s)}{R(s)} = \frac{k_v}{\tau s^2 + s + k_v}$$

∴ $$\frac{C(s)}{R(s)} = \frac{k_v}{s^2 + \frac{1}{\tau}s + \frac{k_v}{\tau}} \qquad \ldots (2.7)$$

This can be written in standard form.

$$\frac{C(s)}{R(s)} = \frac{\omega_n^2}{s^2 + 2\xi\omega_n s + \omega_n^2} = \frac{p(s)}{q(s)} \qquad \ldots (2.8)$$

where, ξ = Damping factor or damping ratio $= \dfrac{1}{2\sqrt{k_v \tau}} = \dfrac{f}{2\sqrt{kJ}}$

and ω_n = Undamped natural frequency $= \sqrt{\dfrac{k_v}{\tau}} = \sqrt{\dfrac{k_v}{J}}$

This time response of any system can be characterised by the roots of the denominator polynomial q(s), which are the poles of the transfer function.

The denominator polynomial q(s) is thus, called the *characteristic polynomial* and
$$q(s) = 0$$
is called characteristic equation.

Thus, the characteristic equation of the system is,

$$\boxed{s^2 + 2\xi\omega_n s + \omega_n^2 = 0} \qquad \ldots (2.9)$$

The roots of this characteristic equation are,

$$(s^2 + 2\xi\omega_n s + \omega_n^2) = (s - s_1)(s - s_2)$$

For $\xi < 1$,

$$\boxed{s_1, s_2 = -\xi\omega_n \pm j\omega_n\sqrt{(1-\xi^2)} = -\xi\omega_n \pm j\omega_d}$$

where,

$\boxed{\omega_d = \omega_n\sqrt{(1-\xi^2)}}$ is called the *damped natural frequency*.

From equation (2.7), for **unit-step input**,
the output response is given by,

$$C(s) = \frac{\omega_n^2}{s[s + \xi\omega_n - j\omega_n\sqrt{(1-\xi^2)}][s + \xi\omega_n + j\omega_n\sqrt{(1-\xi^2)}]} \qquad \ldots (2.10)$$

Taking inverse Laplace transform,

$$C(t) = \frac{\omega_n^2}{s^2 + 2\xi\omega_n s + \omega_n^2}\bigg|_{s=0}$$

$$+ 2\operatorname{Re}\left[\frac{\omega_n^2}{s[s + \xi\omega_n - j\omega_n J\sqrt{(1-\xi^2)}]}\right]_{s = -j\xi\omega_n - j\omega_n\sqrt{(1-\xi^2)}} - e^{-\xi\omega_n t} e^{-j\omega_n\sqrt{(1-\xi)^2}\,t}$$

$$\ldots (2.11)$$

$$= 1 - \frac{e^{-\xi \omega_n t}}{\sqrt{(1-\xi)^2}} \sin\left[\omega_n \sqrt{(1-\xi^2)}\, t + \tan^{-1} \frac{\sqrt{(1-\xi^2)}}{\xi}\right] \quad \ldots (2.12)$$

The steady-state value C (t) is given as,

$$\boxed{C_{ss} = \lim_{t \to \infty} C(t) = 1}$$

2.6.2 Effect of Damping

QUESTION
1. Explain the effect of damping on response of control system with neat sketch **(4M)**

Definition of Damping:
The oscillatory nature of the response is known as damping.

The time response of an underdamped (for $\xi < 1$) second-order system is shown in Fig. 2.12.

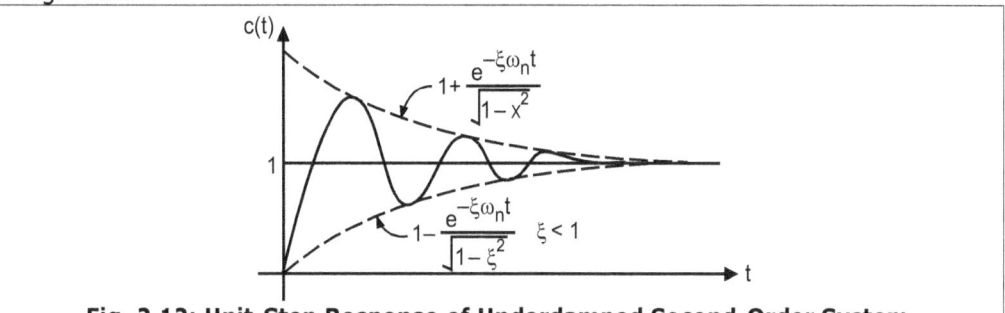

Fig. 2.12: Unit-Step Response of Underdamped Second-Order System

- It is a damped sinusoid.
- The response reaches a steady-state value $C_{ss} = 1$ i.e. steady-state error of this system approaches zero.
  As ξ is increased, the response is progressively less oscillatory, till it becomes critically damped i.e. just non-oscillatory for $\xi = 1$ and is overdamped for $\xi > 1$.
- Robotic control systems cannot be allowed to have oscillatory response otherwise the end effector would strike against the object that the robot is meant to manipulate.
- Highest possible speed of response and non-oscillating response dictates that a robotic control system shall be designed to have a damping factor $\xi = 1$ or close to unity.

2.7 TIME RESPONSE SPECIFICATIONS

QUESTIONS
1. Draw the time response of second order damped control system with neat labeling. **(4M)**
2. Define the following w.r.t. second order system when tested for unit step input.
   (i) Rise time, (ii) Peak time, (ii) Settling time, (iv) Peak overshoot **(4M)**

The control systems are generally designed with damping less than one ($\xi < 1$) i.e. the oscillatory step response. The time response of second and higher order control systems to a step response is damped oscillatory as shown in Fig. 2.13.

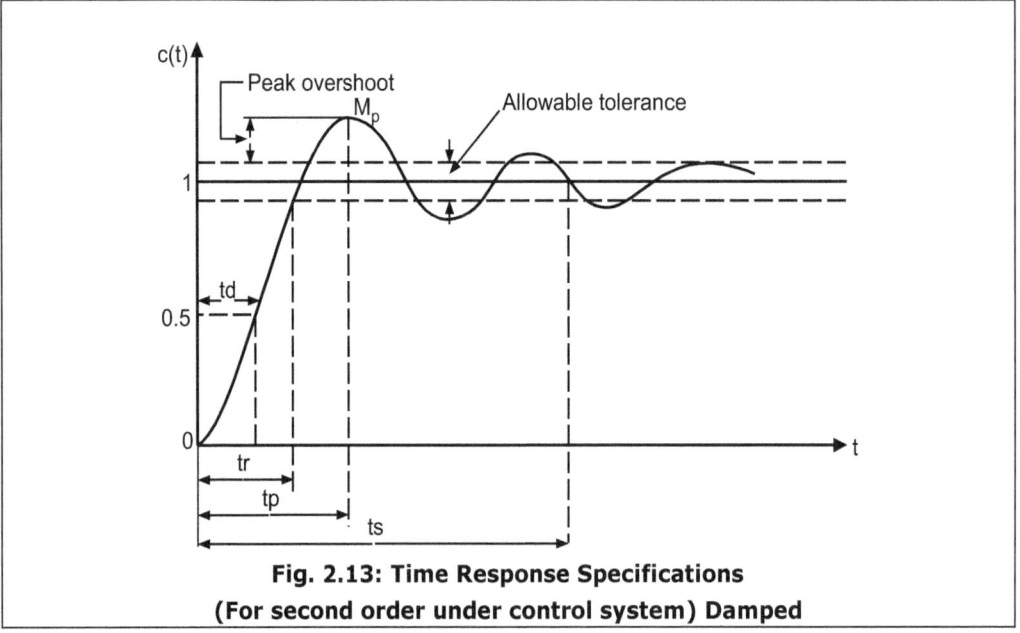

Fig. 2.13: Time Response Specifications
(For second order under control system) Damped

Observations from the time response:
- The step response has a number of overshoots and undershoots with respect to the final steady value.
- The overshoots and undershots decay exponentially, thus, the peak overshoot is the first overshoot and is the peak of complete time response.

This type of step-response is characterised by some performance indices as –

1. How fast the system moves to follow the input ?
2. How oscillatory it is ?
3. How much time it takes to reach the final value ?

The various indices are not independent of each other or the time response. The **specifications** are as follows –

1. **Delay time t_d:**

It is the time required for the response to reach 50% of its final value in the first attempt.

2. **Rise time t_r:**

It is the time required for the response to reach from 10% to 90% of the final value for **overdamped systems** and 0 to 100% of the final value for **underdamped** systems.

$$t_r = \frac{\pi - \beta}{\omega_d}$$

3. **Peak time t_p:**

It is the time required for the response to reach the peak of the time response or the peak overshoot.

$$t_p = \frac{\pi}{\omega_d}$$

4. Peak overshoot M_p:

It gives the normalized difference between the time resonse peak and the steady output and is defined as –

$$\text{Peak percent overshoot} = \frac{C(t_p) - C(\infty)}{C(\infty)} \times 100\% \qquad \ldots (2.13)$$

$$\boxed{M_p = e^{\frac{-\pi\xi}{\sqrt{1-\xi^2}}}}$$

Except type – 0 system, the steady output for step input is the same as input.

For example, for the second-order system of Fig. 2.21 (b) $C(\infty) = C_{ss} = 1$ i.e. same as input.

5. Settling time t_s:

It is the time required for the response to reach and stay within a specified tolerance band (usually 2% or 5%) of its final value.

$$\boxed{t_s = \frac{4}{\xi w n}}$$

6. Steady-state error e_{ss}:

It gives the error between the actual output and desired output as t tends to infinity, i.e.,

$$\boxed{e_{ss} = \lim_{t \to \infty} [r(t) - C(t)]} \qquad \ldots (2.14)$$

From Fig., it is seen that by specifying t_d, t_p, t_r, m_p t_s and e_{ss}, the shape of the unit-step time response curve is virtually fixed.

SOLVED EXAMPLES

Example 2.3: Measurement conducted on servomechanism showed the system response to be,

$$C(t) = 1 + 0.2\, e^{-60t} - 1.2\, e^{-10t}$$

when subjected to a unit step input. Obtain the expression for closed loop transfer function, the damping ratio and undamped natural frequency.

Sol.: Given,

$$C(t) = 1 + 0.2\, e^{-60t} - 1.2\, e^{-10t}$$

Take Laplace Transform,

$$C(s) = \frac{5}{2s} + \frac{5}{s^2} - \frac{5/2}{(s+2)}$$

$$C(s) = \frac{1}{s} + \frac{0.2}{s+60} - \frac{1.2}{s+10}$$

Rearrange the equation so, it will be a second order response.

$$C(s) = \frac{600/s}{s^2 + 70s + 600}$$

Where,

C(t)	C(s)
1	$\frac{1}{s}$
$e^{-\alpha t}$	$\frac{1}{s+\alpha}$

For unit step input,
$$R(s) = \frac{1}{s}$$

$$\therefore \quad T.F. = \frac{C(s)}{R(s)} = \frac{1}{s} \cdot \frac{600/s}{s^2 + 70s + 600}$$

Equate this equation with second order T.F. which is,
$$\frac{C(s)}{R(s)} = \frac{\omega_n^2}{s^2 + 2\xi\omega_n s + \omega_n^2}$$

Thus,
$$\omega_n^2 = 600$$
$$\therefore \quad \omega_n = 24.49 \text{ rad/sec.}$$

and
$$2\xi\omega_n = 70$$
$$\therefore \quad \xi = \frac{70}{2\omega_n} = \frac{70}{2 \times 24.49} = \mathbf{1.43} \qquad (\because \omega_n = 24.49)$$

Ans.

$$T.F. = \frac{600}{s^2 + 70s + 600}$$
Damping ratio, $\xi = 1.43$
Undamped natural frequency, $\omega_n = 24.49$ rad/sec.

Example 2.4: A unity feedback system is characterised by an open loop transfer function $G(s) = \frac{k}{s(s+10)}$. Damping ratio is 0.5. For the gain k, find settling time, peak overshoot.

Sol.: Given,
$$G(s) = \frac{k}{s(s+10)}$$

For unity feedback $\quad H(s) = 1$

$$\therefore \quad \frac{C(s)}{R(s)} = \frac{G(s)}{1 + G(s)H(s)} = \frac{k}{s^2 + 10s + k}$$

Compare this equation with standard second order transfer function which is,
$$\frac{C(s)}{R(s)} = \frac{\omega_n^2}{s^2 + 2\xi\omega_n + \omega_n^2}$$

$$\therefore \quad 2\xi\omega_n = 10$$

$$\therefore \quad \omega_n = \frac{10}{2\xi} \quad (\xi = 0.5 \text{ given})$$

$$= \frac{10}{2 \times 0.5}$$

$$\omega_n = 10 \text{ rad/sec.}$$

Also,
$$k = \omega_n^2$$
$$k = 10^2$$
$$k = 100$$

Settling time,
$$t_s = \frac{4}{\xi \omega_n} = \frac{4}{0.5 \times 10} = 0.8 \text{ sec.}$$

Peak overshoot
$$M_p = e^{\frac{-\pi \xi}{\sqrt{1-\xi^2}}} = e^{-\frac{0.5\pi}{\sqrt{1-(0.5)^2}}} = 16.3\%$$

Ans.

| Gain, k = 10 |
| Settling time, t_s = 0.8 sec. |
| Peak overshoot, M_p = 16.3% |

Example 2.5: A feedback system having transfer function.
$$G(s) = \frac{16}{s^2 + 4s + 16}, \quad H(s) = ks$$

The damping factor of the system is 0.8 Determine the, (i) Undamped natural frequency, ω_n and settling time t_s. (ii) Peak overshoot. (iii) Peak time t_p. (iv) Damped natural frequency, ω_d.

Sol.: The transfer function of the system is,
$$\frac{C(s)}{R(s)} = \frac{G(s)}{1 + G(s) H(s)}$$

Put the values of G(s) and H(s), so we get T.F.
$$\frac{C(s)}{R(s)} = \frac{16}{s^2 + (4 + 16k)s + 16}$$

Compare this equation with the standard second order T.F. which is,
$$\frac{C(s)}{R(s)} = \frac{\omega_n^2}{s^2 + 2\xi\omega_n s + 16}$$

Here,
$$\omega_n^2 = 16 \quad \therefore \omega_n = 4 \text{ (undamped natural frequency)}$$

and
$$2\xi\omega_n = 4 + 16k$$
$$2 \times 0.8 \times 4 = 4 + 16k$$
$$\therefore k = 0.15$$

Thus, the T.F. is,
$$\frac{C(s)}{R(s)} = \frac{16}{s^2 + 6.4s + 16}$$

(i) Peak overshoot

$$M_p = e^{\frac{-\pi \times \xi}{\sqrt{1-\xi^2}}}$$

$$= e^{-\frac{\pi \times 0.8}{\sqrt{1-(0.8)^2}}}$$

$$= 0.015 \text{ or } \mathbf{15\%}$$

(ii) Peak time

$$t_p = \frac{\pi}{\omega_d}$$

$$= \frac{\pi}{2.4}$$

$$= \mathbf{1.31 \text{ sec.}}$$

(iii) Damped natural frequency

$$\omega_d = \omega_n \sqrt{1-\xi^2}$$
$$= 4\sqrt{1-(0.8)^2}$$
$$= \mathbf{2.4 \text{ rad/sec.}}$$

(iv) Settling time t_s

$$t_s = \frac{4}{\xi \omega_n}$$

$$= \frac{4}{0.8 \times 4}$$

$$= \mathbf{1.25 \text{ sec.}}$$

Ans.

> $M_p = 15\%$
> $\omega_n = 4 \text{ rad/sec.}$
> $\omega_d = 2.4 \text{ rad/sec.}$
> $t_p = 1.31 \text{ sec.}$
> $t_s = 1.25 \text{ sec.}$

Example 2.6: For the given second order system, calculate the damping factor and natural frequency of damping.

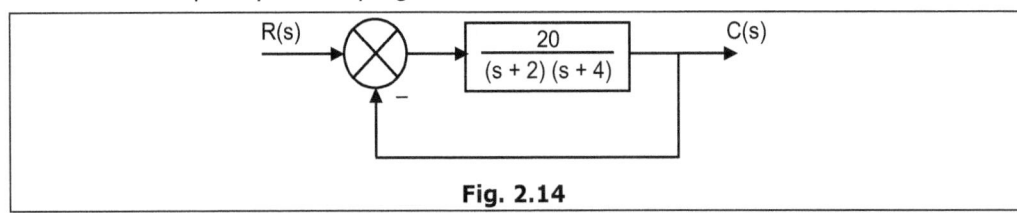

Fig. 2.14

Solution: To calculate $\omega_n = ?$

$\xi = ?$

Given: $G(s) = \dfrac{20}{(s+2)(s+4)}$

$H(s) = 1$

For any given system, close loop T.F. is,

$$\dfrac{C(s)}{R(s)} = \dfrac{G(s)}{1 + G(s)H(s)}$$

$$= \dfrac{\dfrac{20}{(s+2)(s+4)}}{1 + \dfrac{20}{(s+2)(s+4)}}$$

$$= \dfrac{20}{(s+2)(s+4) + 20}$$

$$\boxed{\text{T.F.} = \dfrac{C(s)}{R(s)} = \dfrac{20}{s^2 + 6s + 28}}$$

Compare this T.F. with the standard second order system T.F.

$$\dfrac{C(s)}{R(s)} = \dfrac{\omega_n^2}{s^2 + 2\xi\omega_n s + \omega_n^2}$$

We get,

$\omega_n^2 = 28$

$\therefore \quad \omega_n = \sqrt{28} = 5.29$ rad/sec.

and $\quad 2\xi\omega_n = 6$

$2\xi \times 5.29 = 6$

$\therefore \quad \xi = 0.5671$ or $\xi = 0.57$

Damping factor (ξ) = 0.56

Natural frequency of oscillations = 5.29 rad/sec.

Example 2.7: For the system shown in Fig. 2.15, find the closed loop T.F., damping ratio, natural frequency.

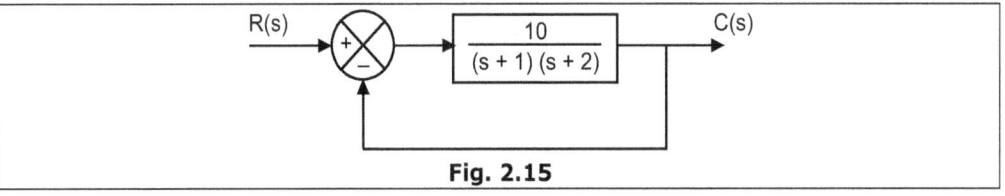

Fig. 2.15

Solution: Given: $G(s) = \dfrac{10}{(s+1)(s+2)}$

$H(s) = 1$

∴ Close loop T.F.

$$\text{T.F.} = \dfrac{C(s)}{R(s)} = \dfrac{G(s)}{1 + G(s)H(s)}$$

$$= \dfrac{\dfrac{10}{(s+1)(s+2)}}{1 + \dfrac{10}{(s+1)(s+2)}}$$

$$\boxed{\text{T.F.} = \dfrac{10}{s^2 + 3s + 12}}$$

Compare denominator $s^2 + 3s + 12$ with standard equation $s^2 + 2\xi\omega_n s + \omega_n^2$.

∴ $\omega_n^2 = 12$

$\omega_n = \sqrt{12} = $ **3.46 rad/sec.**

and $2\xi\omega_n = 3$

∴ $2\xi \times 3.46 = 3$

∴ $\xi = \dfrac{3}{2 \times 3.46} = $ **0.43**

| Damping ratio (ξ) = 0.43 |
| Natural frequency (ω_n) = 3.46 rad/sec. |

Example 2.8: Measurement conducted on a servo mechanism show the system response to be

$$C(t) = 1 + 0.2\, e^{-60t} - 1.2\, e^{-10t}$$

when subjected to a unit step input.

(a) Obtain the expression for the closed loop transfer function.
(b) Determine the natural frequency and damping ratio of the system.

Solution: Response of the given system is as follows:

$$C(t) = 1 + 0.2\, e^{-60t} - 1.2\, e^{-10t}$$

Taking Laplace transform,
We get,

$$C(s) = \dfrac{1}{s} + 0.2\dfrac{1}{(s+60)} - 1.2\dfrac{1}{(s+10)}$$

$$C(s) = \dfrac{(s+60)(s+10) + 0.2(s+10)s - 1.2s(s+60)}{s(s+10)(s+60)}$$

$$= \dfrac{s^2 + 70s + 600 + 0.2s^2 - 1.2s^2 - 72s + 2s}{s(s+10)(s+60)}$$

$$C(s) = \dfrac{600}{s(s^2 + 70s + 600)} \qquad \ldots (1)$$

Input is given as unit step
$$R(s) = \frac{1}{s}$$
Divide both sides of equation (1) by R(s),
$$\frac{C(s)}{R(s)} = \frac{s \times 600}{s(s^2 + 70s + 600)}$$

∴ $\quad$ T.F. $= \dfrac{C(s)}{R(s)} = \dfrac{600}{s^2 + 70s + 600} \quad$ (Closed loop T.F.)

Compare this T.F. with standard T.F.

$$\text{T.F.} = \frac{\omega_n^2}{s^2 + 2\xi\omega_n + \omega_n^2}$$

We get,
$$\omega_n^2 = 600$$
∴ $\quad \omega_n = 24.49$ rad/sec. $\quad$ (Natural frequency)
and $\quad 2\xi\omega_n = 70$
$\quad 2 \times \xi \times 24.49 = 70$
∴ $\quad \xi = 1.42 \quad$ (Damping ratio)

2.8 STEADY STATE ERRORS AND ERROR CONSTANTS

QUESTIONS
1. What is steady state error ? How is steady state error determined in feed back control ? **(4M)**
2. Define steady state errors. What is the effect of input on steady state error ? **(4M)**

- Steady state errors constitute an important aspect of system performance.
- The steady state error is a measure of system accuracy.
- These errors occur from the nature of inputs, type of the system and from non-linearities of system components like static friction, blacklash etc.
- The steady state performance of a stable control system is generally judged by its steady-state error to standard inputs.

Error Constants:
There are three types of error constants depending on input R(s).
1. Position error constant (K_p).
2. Velocity error constant (K_p).
3. Acceleration error constant (K_a).

2.8.1 Derivation of Steady-State Error

QUESTIONS
1. Derive relationship of steady state error in terms of open loop T.F. G(s) H(s). Find ess for step input. **(4M)**

Consider a unity feedback system as shown in Fig. 2.16.
Let,
$$\text{input} \rightarrow R(s) \qquad \ldots (2.15)$$
$$\text{output} \rightarrow C(s)$$
$$\text{Feedback signal} \rightarrow B(s)$$
and the difference between input and output is error signal → E(s).

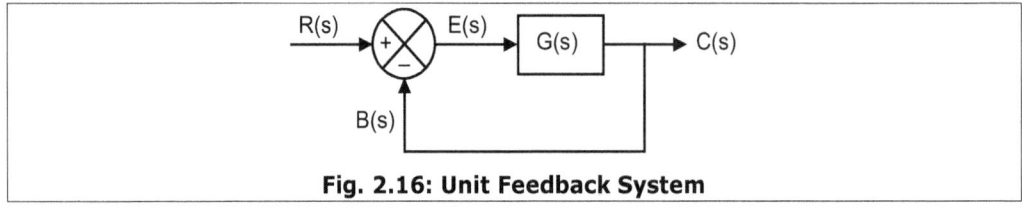

Fig. 2.16: Unit Feedback System

From Fig. 2.16, the transfer function of negative feedback is,

$$\frac{C(s)}{R(s)} = \frac{G(s)}{1 + G(s)} \qquad [\because H(s) = 1] \quad \ldots (2.16)$$

and $\quad C(s) = E(s) G(s) \qquad$ [Output = gain × input]

Equation (2.16) becomes,

$$\frac{E(s) G(s)}{R(s)} = \frac{G(s)}{1 + G(s)}$$

$$\therefore \quad E(s) = \frac{1}{1 + G(s)} R(s) \qquad \ldots (2.17)$$

The steady state error e_{ss}, may be found by the final value theorem as,

$$\therefore \quad e_{ss} = \lim_{t \to \infty} e(t)$$

$$= \lim_{s \to 0} s \cdot E(s)$$

$$= \lim_{s \to 0} s \cdot \frac{R(s)}{1 + G(s)} \qquad \left[\because E_s = \frac{R(s)}{1 + G(s)}\right]$$

For unity feedback, i.e. $H(s) = 1$

$$\therefore \quad e_{ss} = \lim_{s \to 0} \frac{s \cdot R(s)}{1 + G(s)} \qquad \ldots (2.18)$$

or when the feedback element is present,

$$e_{ss} = \lim_{s \to 0} \frac{s \cdot R(s)}{1 + G(s) H(s)} \qquad \ldots (2.19)$$

Steady-state errors for various standard test signals i.e. effect of standard input on steady-state error.

Equation (2.18) shows that the steady state error depends upon the input R(s) and the forward transfer function G(s). Thus, expression for steady-state errors for various types of standard test signals are derived below.

2.8.2 Unit Step Input

QUESTION

1. For type 0 system and for step input,
calculate, (i) Position error constant (k_p), (ii) Steady state error **(4M)**

Input, $r(t) = u(t)$

and $\quad R(s) = \dfrac{1}{s}$

From equation (2.18),

$$e_{ss} = \lim_{s \to 0} s \cdot \frac{R(s)}{1 + G(s)}$$

$$= \lim_{s \to 0} s \cdot \frac{1/s}{1 + G(s)}$$

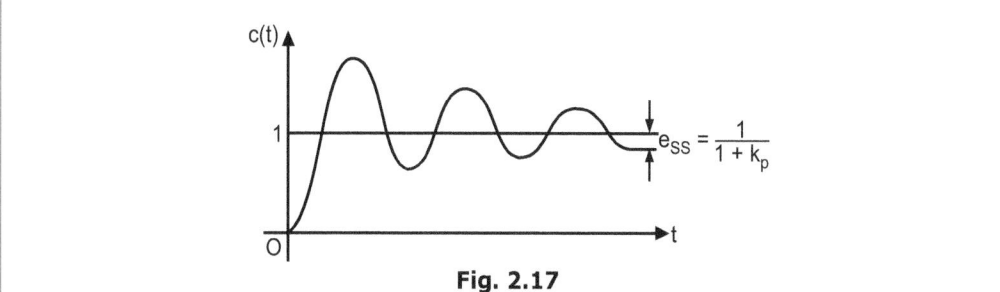

Fig. 2.17

$$= \lim_{s \to 0} \frac{1}{1 + G(s)}$$

$$= \frac{1}{1 + G(0)} = \frac{1}{1 + k_p} \qquad \ldots (2.20)$$

where, $\boxed{k_p = G(0)}$ *is defined as the position error constant.*

2.8.3 Unit Ramp Input

Input $r(t) = t$

and $R(s) = \dfrac{1}{s^2}$

Equation (2.18) becomes,

$$e_{ss} = \lim_{s \to 0} s \cdot \frac{R(s)}{1 + G(s)}$$

$$= \lim_{s \to 0} s \cdot \frac{\frac{1}{s^2}}{1 + G(s)}$$

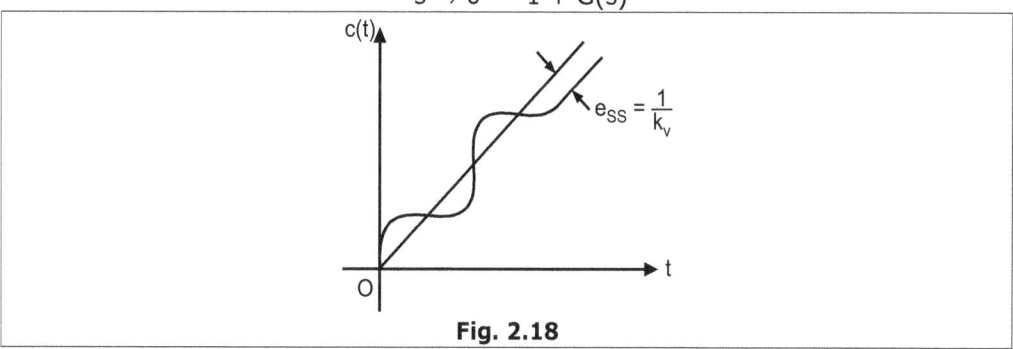

Fig. 2.18

$$= \lim_{s \to 0} \frac{1}{s + s\,G(s)} = \frac{1}{0 + s\,G(s)} = \frac{1}{k_v} \qquad \ldots (2.21)$$

where, $\boxed{k_v = \lim_{s \to 0} s \cdot G(s)}$ *is defined as the velocity error constant.*

2.8.4 Unit Parabolic (Acceleration) Input

$$\text{Input, } r(t) = \frac{t^2}{2}$$

and $$R(s) = \frac{1}{s^3}$$

Equation (2.4) becomes,

$$e_{ss} = \lim_{s \to 0} s \cdot \frac{R(s)}{1 + G(s)}$$

$$= \lim_{s \to 0} \frac{s \cdot \frac{1}{s^3}}{1 + G(s)}$$

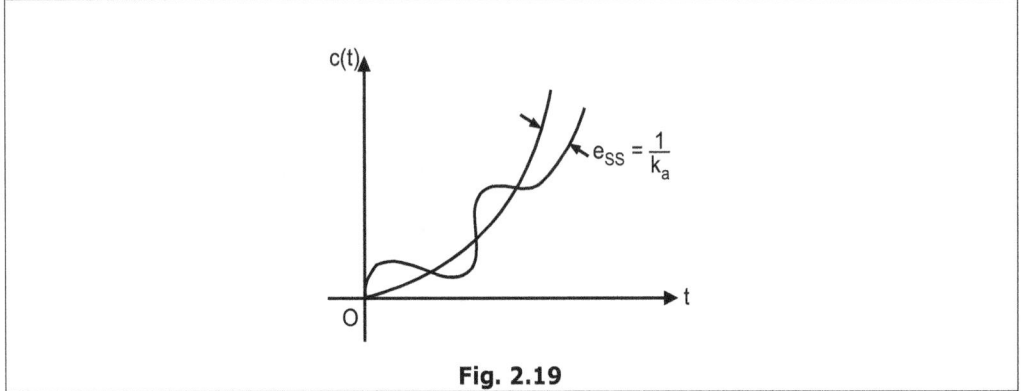

Fig. 2.19

$$= \lim_{s \to 0} \frac{1}{s^2 + s^2 G(s)} = \lim_{s \to 0} \frac{1}{s^2 G(s)} = \frac{1}{k_a} \quad \ldots (2.22)$$

where, $\boxed{k_a = \lim_{s \to 0} s^2 G(s)}$ *is defined as the acceleration error constant.*

2.9 TYPES OF FEEDBACK CONTROL SYSTEM

The open-loop transfer function of a unity feedback system can be written in two standard forms –
 (i) *the time-constant form,* and
 (ii) *the pole-zero form.*
In these two forms, G(s) is given as,

$$G(s)\,H(s) = G(s)\, \frac{k\,(T_{z1}\,s + 1)\,(T_{z2}\,s + 1)\,\ldots}{s^n\,(T_{p1}\,s + 1)\,(T_{p2}\,s + 1)\,\ldots} \text{ (time-constant form)}\ldots (2.23)$$

$$G(s)\,H(s) = G(s)\, \frac{k'\,(s + b_1)\,(s + b_2)\,\ldots}{s^n\,(s + a_1)\,(s + a_2)\,\ldots} \quad \text{(pole-zero form)} \quad \ldots (2.24)$$

$$[\because H(s) = 1]$$

The two equations given above have s^n **terms in the denominator. The value of n determines the type of feedback.**

Thus, the types of feedback control systems,
1. Type '0' system (n = 0)
2. Type '1' system (n = 1)
3. Type '2' system (n = 2)

2.9.1 Analysis of Type 0, 1, 2 Systems for Standard Inputs

QUESTIONS	
1. Determine the steady state error for a ramp input for a type 0, type 1 and type 2 systems.	(4M)
2. Describe how the type of system can be determined.	(4M)
3. Derive error coefficients, k_p, k_v and k_a relation for type '0' system.	(4M)

1. Type '0' System:

If n = 0, the steady-state errors to various standard inputs, obtained from equation (2.20), (2.21), (2.22) and (2.23) are,

$$e_{ss} \text{ (position)} = \frac{1}{1 + G(0)} = \frac{1}{1 + k_p} \quad \ldots (2.25)$$

$$e_{ss} \text{ (velocity)} = \lim_{s \to 0} \frac{1}{s\,G(s)} = \infty$$

$$e_{ss} \text{ (acceleration)} = \lim_{s \to 0} \frac{1}{s^2\,G(s)} = \infty$$

Thus, a system with n = 0 in G(s) has a constant position error and infinite velocity and acceleration errors.

where the position error constant is given by the open-loop gain of the transfer function in time-constant form.

2. Type-1 System:

If n = 1, the steady-state error for standard input is,

$$e_{ss} \text{ (position)} = \frac{1}{1 + G(0)} = \frac{1}{1 + \infty} = 0$$

$$e_{ss} \text{ (velocity)} = \lim_{s \to 0} \frac{1}{s\,G(s)} = \frac{1}{k_v} \quad \ldots (2.26)$$

$$e_{ss} \text{ (acceleration)} = \lim_{s \to 0} \frac{1}{s^2\,G(s)} = \infty$$

Thus, a system with n = 1 has zero position error, a constant velocity error and an infinite acceleration error at steady state.

3. Type-2 System:

If n = 2, the steady state errors to various standard inputs are –

$$e_{ss} \text{ (position)} = \frac{1}{1 + G(0)} = 0$$

$$e_{ss} \text{ (velocity)} = \lim_{s \to 0} \frac{1}{s\,G(s)} = 0$$

$$e_{ss} \text{ (acceleration)} = \lim_{s \to 0} \frac{1}{s^2\,G(s)} = \frac{1}{k_a} \quad \ldots (2.27)$$

Thus, a system with n = 2 has a zero position error, zero velocity and constant acceleration error at steady state.

Table 2.1: Steady State Errors for Various Standard Inputs

Type of input	Steady-state error		
	Type 0 system	Type 1 system	Type 2 system
Unit step	$\dfrac{1}{1+k_p}$	0	0
Unit ramp	∞	$\dfrac{1}{k_v}$	0
Unit parabolic	∞	∞	$\dfrac{1}{k_a}$
—	$k_p = \lim\limits_{s \to 0} G(s)$	$k_v = \lim\limits_{s \to 0} s\, G(s)$	$k_a = \lim\limits_{s \to 0} s^2\, G(s)$

SOLVED EXAMPLES

Example 2.9: The open loop transfer function of a feedback control system is given by,

$$G(s)\,H(s) = \dfrac{k(s+1)}{s(1+Ts)(1+2s)}$$

Determine the error coefficients and errors due to unit step input, unit ramp input and parabolic input if $k = 10$ and $T = 4$.

Solution: Put the values of k and T in the given T.F.

$$G(s)\,H(s) = \dfrac{10(s+1)}{s(1+4s)(1+2s)}$$

(i) $k_p = \lim\limits_{s \to 0} G(s)\,H(s) = \infty$

(ii) $k_v = \lim\limits_{s \to 0} s \cdot G(s)\,H(s) = \dfrac{10(0+1)}{(1+0)(1+0)} = 10$

(iii) $k_a = \lim\limits_{s \to 0} s^2 \cdot G(s)\,H(s) = 0$.

Errors due to,

(i) Unit step input $= \dfrac{1}{1+k_p} = 0$

(ii) Unit ramp input $= \dfrac{1}{k} = \dfrac{1}{10} = 0.1$

(iii) Unit parabolic input $= \dfrac{1}{k_a} = \infty$.

Example 2.10: A unity feedback system has the loop T.F.

$$G(s) = \dfrac{10(s+1)}{s(s+2)(s+5)}$$

Determine,
(i) System gain,
(ii) Step, ramp and parabolic error coefficients,
(iii) Steady state error when $r(t) = 3 + 10t$.

Solution: Given:

$$H(s) = 1$$

and

$$G(s) = \frac{10(s+1)}{s(s+2)(s+5)}$$

Open loop T.F.

$$G(s)H(s) = \frac{10(1+s)}{s \times 2(1+0.5s)\,5(1+0.2s)}$$

$$G(s) = \frac{(1+s)}{s(1+0.5s)(1+0.2s)}$$

Compare this open T.F. with standard open loop T.F.

$$G(s) = \frac{k(1+Tz_1 s)(1+Tz_2 s)}{s^n (1+Tp_1 s)(1+Tp_2 s)} \quad \ldots \text{(Refer equation 2.9)}$$

We get,

(i) System gain **k = 1**.

(ii) Step error coefficient.

$$k_p = \lim_{s \to 0} G(s)$$

$$= \lim_{s \to 0} \frac{(1+s)}{s(1+0.5s)(1+0.2s)}$$

$$= \frac{1}{0}$$

$$\boxed{k_p = \infty}$$

Ramp error coefficient

$$k_v = \lim_{s \to 0} s\, G(s)$$

$$= \lim_{s \to 0} \frac{s(1+s)}{s(1+0.5s)(1+0.2s)}$$

$$= \lim_{s \to 0} \frac{(1+s)}{(1+0.5s)(1+0.2s)}$$

$$\boxed{k_v = 1}$$

Parabolic error coefficient

$$k_a = \lim_{s \to 0} s^2\, G(s)$$

$$= \lim_{s \to 0} \frac{s^2 (1+s)}{s(1+0.5s)(1+0.2s)}$$

$$\boxed{k_a = 0}$$

(iii) $r(t) = 3 + 10t$

$\therefore \quad R(s) = \dfrac{3}{s} + \dfrac{10}{s^2}$

Steady state error

$e_{ss} = \displaystyle\lim_{s \to 0} \dfrac{s\,R(s)}{1 + G(s)}$

$\therefore \quad e_{ss} = \displaystyle\lim_{s \to 0} \dfrac{s\left(\dfrac{3}{s} + \dfrac{10}{s^2}\right)}{1 + \dfrac{(1+s)}{s(1+0.5s)(1+0.2s)}}$

$= \displaystyle\lim_{s \to 0} \dfrac{3}{1 + \dfrac{(1+s)}{s(1+0.5s)(1+0.2s)}} + \displaystyle\lim_{s \to 0} \dfrac{10}{s + \dfrac{(1+s)}{s(1+0.5s)(1+0.2s)}}$

$= \dfrac{3}{1 + \infty} + \dfrac{10}{0 + 1}$

$\therefore \quad \boxed{e_{ss} = 10}$

Example 2.11: A unity feedback system has the forward path transfer function.

$$G(s) = \dfrac{20(1+s)}{s^2(2+s)(4+s)}$$

Calculate its steady state error when the applied input is $r(t) = 40 + 20t + 5t^2$.

Solution: Given: $H(s) = 1$

$G(s) = \dfrac{20(1+s)}{s^2(2+s)(4+s)}$

$= \dfrac{20(1+s)}{s^2 \times 2(1+0.5s)\,4(1+0.25s)}$

$= \dfrac{20(1+s)}{8s^2(1+0.5s)(1+0.25s)}$

$G(s) = \dfrac{2.5(1+s)}{s^2(1+0.5s)(1+0.25s)}$

Applied input is $\quad r(t) = 40 + 20t + 5t^2$

Taking Laplace Transform

$\therefore \quad R(s) = \dfrac{40}{s} + \dfrac{20}{s^2} + \dfrac{5 \times 2}{s^3}$

$R(s) = \dfrac{40}{s} + \dfrac{20}{s^2} + \dfrac{10}{s^3}$

Steady state error,

$e_{ss} = \displaystyle\lim_{s \to 0} \dfrac{s \cdot R(s)}{1 + G(s)}$

$= \displaystyle\lim_{s \to 0} \dfrac{s\left[\dfrac{40}{s} + \dfrac{20}{s^2} + \dfrac{10}{s^3}\right]}{1 + \dfrac{2 \cdot s(1+s)}{s^2(1+0.5s)(1+0.25s)}}$

$$= \lim_{s \to 0} \frac{40 + \frac{20}{s} + \frac{10}{s^2}}{1 + \frac{2 \cdot s(1+s)}{s^2(1+0.5s)(1+0.25s)}}$$

$$= \lim_{s \to 0} \frac{40}{1 + \frac{2 \cdot s(1+s)}{s^2(1+0.5s)(1+0.25s)}}$$

$$+ \lim_{s \to 0} \frac{20}{s + \frac{2 \cdot s \cdot s(1+s)}{s^2(1+0.5s)(1+0.25s)}} + \lim_{s \to 0} \frac{10}{s^2 + \frac{2 \cdot s^2 \cdot s(1+s)}{s^2(1+0.5s)(1+0.25s)}}$$

$$= \frac{40}{1 + \infty} + \frac{20}{0 + \infty} + \frac{10}{0 + 2.5}$$

$$= 0 + 0 + 4$$

$$\boxed{e_{ss} = 4}$$

Example 2.12: The open loop T.F. of a servo system with unity feedback is

$$G(s) = \frac{10}{s(1+0.1s)}$$

Evaluate the static error constants (k_p, k_v, k_a) for the system. Obtain the steady error of the system when subjected to an input given by the polynomial.

$$r(t) = a_0 + a_1 t + \frac{a_2}{2} t^2$$

Solution: Given: $H(s) = 1$

For unity feedback system,

$$G(s) = \frac{10}{s(1+0.1s)}$$

Position Error Constant:

$$k_p = \lim_{s \to 0} G(s)$$

$$= \lim_{s \to 0} \frac{10}{s(1+0.1s)}$$

$$= \infty$$

$$\boxed{k_p = \infty}$$

Velocity Error Constant:

$$k_v = \lim_{s \to 0} s \cdot G(s)$$

$$= \lim_{s \to 0} \frac{s \times 10}{s(1+0.1s)}$$

$$= \frac{10}{1}$$

∴ $\boxed{k_v = 10}$

Acceleration Error Constant:

$$k_a = \lim_{s \to 0} s^2 G(s)$$

$$= \lim_{s \to 0} \frac{s^2 \times 10}{s(1 + 0.1s)}$$

$$= 0$$

$$\therefore \quad \boxed{k_a = 0}$$

To calculate steady state error, when

$$r(t) = a_0 + a_1 t + \frac{a_2}{2} t^2$$

Taking Laplace transform

$$R(s) = \frac{a_0}{s} + \frac{a_1}{s^2} + \frac{a_2}{s^3}$$

$$e_{ss} = \lim_{s \to 0} \frac{s \cdot R(s)}{1 + G(s)}$$

$$= \lim_{s \to 0} \frac{s \cdot \left[\frac{a_0}{s} + \frac{a_1}{s^2} + \frac{a_2}{s^3}\right]}{1 + \frac{10}{s(1 + 0.1s)}}$$

$$= \lim_{s \to 0} \frac{a_0}{1 + \frac{10}{s(1 + 0.1s)}} + \lim_{s \to 0} \frac{a_1}{s + \frac{10s}{s(1 + 0.1s)}} +$$

$$\lim_{s \to 0} \frac{a_2}{s^2 + \frac{10s^2}{s(1 + 0.1s)}}$$

$$= \frac{a_0}{1 + \infty} + \frac{a_1}{0 + 10} + \frac{a_2}{0 + 0}$$

$$= 0 + \frac{a_1}{10} + \infty$$

$$= \infty$$

$$\therefore \quad \boxed{e_{ss} = \infty}$$

Example 2.13: A unity feedback control system has

$$G(s) = \frac{k}{s(s + 2)(s^2 + 2s + 5)}$$

(i) For a unit ramp input it is designated that $e_{ss} \leq 0$. Determine the minimum value of k.

(ii) Determine e_{ss} if input $r(t) = 2 + 4t + \frac{t^2}{2}$. Assume $k = 10$.

Solution: Given: $H(s) = 1$

and
$$G(s) = \frac{k}{s(s + 2)(s^2 + 2s + 5)}$$

∴
$$G(s) = \frac{k}{s \times 2(1 + 0.5s) \times 5 \times (1 + 0.4s + 0.2s^2)}$$

$$= \frac{0.1k}{s(1 + 0.5s)(1 + 0.4s + 0.2s^2)}$$

(i) For unit ramp input

$$R(t) = t$$

Taking Laplace transform

∴
$$R(s) = \frac{1}{s^2}$$

Steady state error

$$e_{ss} = \lim_{s \to 0} \frac{s R(s)}{1 + G(s)}$$

$$= \lim_{s \to 0} \frac{s \times \frac{1}{s^2}}{1 + \frac{0.1k}{s(1 + 0.5s)(1 + 0.4s + 0.2s^2)}}$$

$$= \lim_{s \to 0} \frac{1}{s + \frac{0.1ks}{(1 + 0.5s)(1 + 0.4s + 0.2s^2)}}$$

∴
$$e_{ss} = \frac{1}{0 + 0.1k}$$

$$\boxed{e_{ss} = \frac{1}{0.1k}}$$

But it is given that $e_{ss} \leq 0.2$.

∴
$$0.2 = \frac{1}{0.1k}$$

∴
$$\boxed{k = 50}$$

∴ **Minimum value required for k is 50**.

(ii) Given:
$$k = 10$$

∴
$$G(s) = \frac{1}{s(1 + 0.5s)(1 + 0.4s + 0.2s^2)}$$

Input
$$r(t) = 2 + 4t + \frac{t^2}{2}$$

Taking Laplace transform

$$R(s) = \frac{2}{s} + \frac{4}{s^2} + \frac{1}{s^3}$$

Steady state error

$$e_{ss} = \lim_{s \to 0} \frac{s \cdot R(s)}{1 + G(s)}$$

$$= \lim_{s \to 0} \frac{s\left[\frac{2}{s} + \frac{4}{s^2} + \frac{1}{s^3}\right]}{1 + \frac{1}{s(1 + 0.5s)(1 + 0.4s + 0.2s^2)}}$$

$$= \lim_{s \to 0} \frac{2 + \frac{4}{s} + \frac{1}{s^2}}{1 + \frac{1}{s(1 + 0.5s)(1 + 0.4s + 0.2s^2)}}$$

$$= \lim_{s \to 0} \frac{2}{1 + \frac{1}{s(1 + 0.5s)(1 + 0.4s + 0.2s^2)}} +$$

$$\lim_{s \to 0} \frac{4}{s + \frac{s}{s(1 + 0.5s)(1 + 0.4s + 0.2s^2)}}$$

$$+ \lim_{s \to 0} \frac{1}{s^2 + \frac{s^2}{s(1 + 0.5s)(1 + 0.4s + 0.2s^2)}}$$

$$\therefore \quad e_{ss} = \frac{2}{1 + \infty} + \frac{4}{0 + 1} + \frac{1}{0 + 0} = 0 + 4 + \infty$$

$$= \infty$$

$$\therefore \quad \boxed{e_{ss} = \infty}$$

Example 2.14: A unity feedback control system has

$$G(s) = \frac{20(s + 4)}{s(s + 2)(s^2 + 2s + 2)}$$

If input $r(t) = 6t + 3t^2$ is given to the system, determine steady state error of the system.

Solution: Given: $H(s) = 1$

$$G(s) = \frac{20(s + 4)}{s(s + 2)(s^2 + 2s + 2)}$$

Input $\quad r(t) = 6t + 3t^2$

Taking Laplace transform

$$R(s) = \frac{6}{s^2} + \frac{3}{s^3}$$

The steady state error of the system is,

$$e_{ss} = \lim_{s \to 0} \frac{s R(s)}{1 + G(s)}$$

$$= \lim_{s \to 0} \frac{s\left[\frac{6}{s^2} + \frac{3}{s^3}\right]}{1 + \frac{20(s + 4)}{s(s + 2)(s^2 + 2s + 2)}}$$

Separate the numerator terms,

$$e_{ss} = \lim_{s \to 0} \frac{6}{s + \frac{20s(s+4)}{s(s+2)(s^2+2s+2)}} + \lim_{s \to 0} \frac{3}{s^2 + \frac{20s^2(s+4)}{s(s+2)(s^2+2s+2)}}$$

$$\therefore \quad e_{ss} = \frac{6}{0 + \frac{20 \times 4}{2 \times 2}} + \frac{3}{0 + 0}$$

$$= \frac{6}{20} + \frac{3}{\infty}$$

$$= \infty$$

∴ Steady state error

$$\boxed{e_{ss} = \infty}$$

Example 2.15: Find error coefficient for the given system.

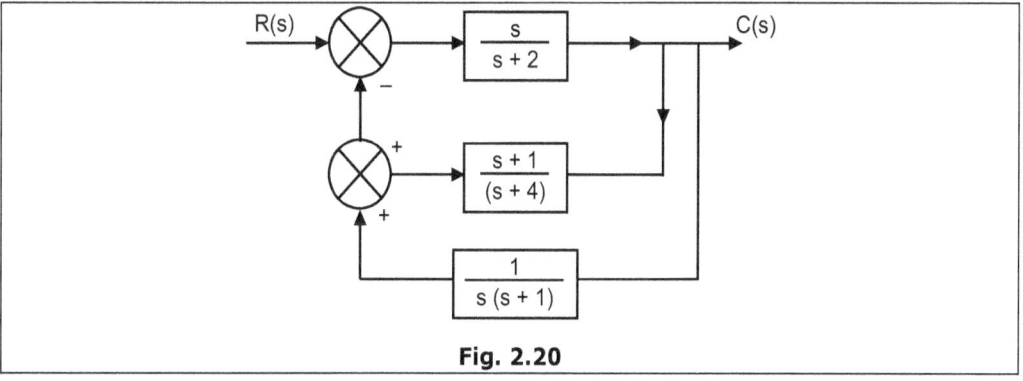

Fig. 2.20

Solution: To find open loop T.F, first we have to find H(s).

As shown in Fig. 2.20 $\frac{s+1}{s+4}$ and $\frac{1}{s(s+1)}$ blocks are connected in parallel, so add these two blocks.

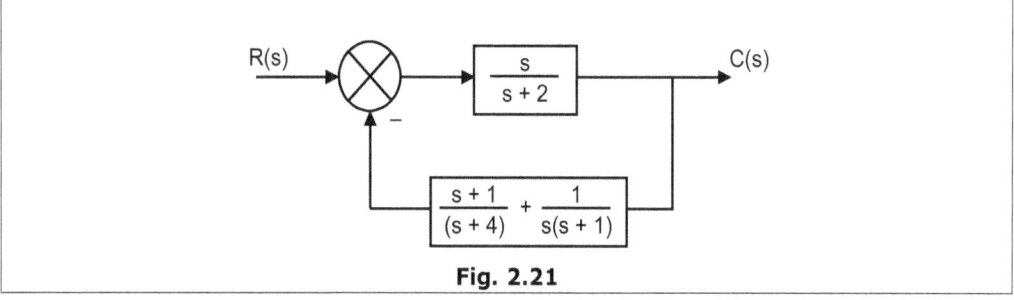

Fig. 2.21

As shown in above Fig. 2.21,

$$H(s) = \frac{s+1}{s+4} + \frac{1}{s(s+1)}$$

$$= \frac{s(s+1)^2 + (s+4)}{s(s+1)(s+4)}$$

$$= \frac{s^3 + 2s^2 + 2s + 4}{s(s+1)(s+4)}$$

Here, $\quad G(s) = \dfrac{s}{s+2}$

∴ Open loop T.F. is,

$$G(s)\,H(s) = \frac{s}{s+2} \cdot \frac{s^3 + 2s^2 + 2s + 4}{s(s+1)(s+4)}$$

∴ $$G(s)\,H(s) = \frac{s^3 + 2s^2 + 2s + 4}{(s+1)(s+2)(s+4)}$$

Position Error Constant:

$$k_p = \lim_{s \to 0} G(s)\,H(s)$$

$$= \lim_{s \to 0} \frac{s^3 + 2s^2 + 2s + 4}{(s+1)(s+2)(s+4)}$$

$$= \frac{4}{8}$$

$$= 0.5$$

∴ $\boxed{k_p = 0.5}$

Velocity Error Constant:

$$k_v = \lim_{s \to 0} s \cdot G(s)\,H(s)$$

$$= \lim_{s \to 0} \frac{s(s^3 + 2s^2 + 2s + 4)}{(s+1)(s+2)(s+4)}$$

$$= 0$$

∴ $\boxed{k_v = 0}$

Acceleration Error Constant:

$$k_a = \lim_{s \to 0} s^2\,G(s)\,H(s)$$

$$= \lim_{s \to 0} \frac{s^2(s^3 + 2s^2 + 2s + 4)}{(s+1)(s+2)(s+4)}$$

$$= 0$$

∴ $\boxed{k_a = 0}$

Example 2.16: A feedback system is shown in Fig. 2.22.

(a) Determine the steady state error for a unit ramp when k = 0.4 and $G_p(s) = 1$.

(b) Select an appropriate value for $G_p(s)$ so that the steady state error is equal to 0.01 for the unit ramp input.

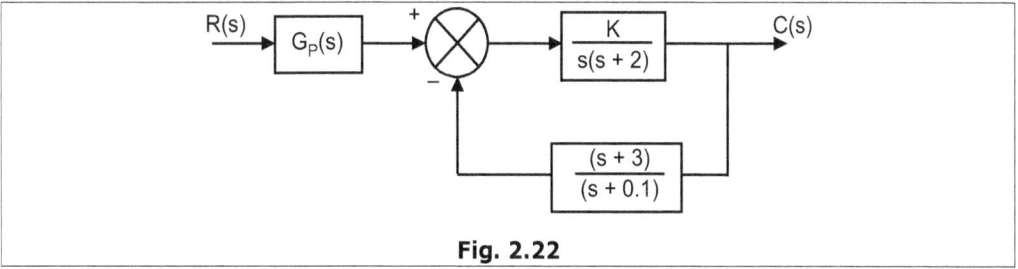

Fig. 2.22

Solution: From Fig. 2.9, open loop T.F.

$$G(s)\,H(s) = \frac{G_p(s)\,k}{s(s+2)} \times \frac{s+3}{s+0.1} \qquad \left(\because H(s) = \frac{s+3}{s+0.1}\right)$$

(a) Given:

$$G_p(s) = 1$$

and

$$k = 0.4$$

∴

$$G(s)\,H(s) = \frac{0.4\,(s+3)}{s(s+0.1)(s+2)}$$

Input is unit ramp

∴

$$r(t) = t$$

Taking L.T.

$$R(s) = \frac{1}{s^2}$$

The steady state error

$$e_{ss} = \lim_{s \to 0} \frac{s \cdot R(s)}{1 + G(s)\,H(s)}$$

∴

$$= \lim_{s \to 0} \frac{s \times \frac{1}{s^2}}{1 + \frac{0.4\,(s+3)}{s(s+0.1)(s+2)}}$$

$$= \lim_{s \to 0} \frac{1}{s + \frac{s \times 0.4 \times (s+3)}{s \times (s+0.1)(s+2)}}$$

$$= \frac{1}{0 + \frac{0.4 \times 3}{0.1 \times 0.2}}$$

$$= \frac{1}{6}$$

$$= 0.167$$

∴ $\boxed{e_{ss} = 0.167}$

(b) Find $G_p(s)$ if $e_{ss} = 0.01$

$$\therefore \quad e_{ss} = \lim_{s \to 0} \frac{s \times \frac{1}{s^2}}{1 + \frac{0.4\, G_p(s)\,(s+3)}{s(s+0.1)(s+2)}}$$

$$= \lim_{s \to 0} \frac{1}{s + 0.4 \frac{G_p(s)(s+3)}{(s+0.1)(s+2)}}$$

$$= \frac{1}{0 + \frac{G_p(s) \times 3 \times 0.4}{0.2}}$$

$$= \frac{1}{6\, G_p(s)}$$

$$0.01 = \frac{1}{6\, G_p(s)}$$

$\therefore \quad G_p(s) = 16.67$

$\therefore \quad \boxed{G_p(s) = 16.67}$

Example 2.17: Determine the ramp and parabolic error constants of a unity feedback control system whose open loop T.F. is, **(W-04)**

$$G(s) = \frac{k(1 + 2s)(1 + 4s)}{s^2(s^2 + s + 1)}$$

Solution: For ramp error constant

$$k_v = \lim_{s \to 0} s\, G(s)$$

$$= \lim_{s \to 0} \frac{k(1 + 2s)(1 + 4s)}{s^2(s^2 + s + 1)}$$

$$= \frac{k(1 + 0)(1 + 0)}{0(0 + 0 + 1)}$$

$$= \infty$$

$k_v = \infty$

For Parabolic error constant

$$k_a = \lim_{s \to 0} s^2\, G(s)$$

$$= \lim_{s \to 0} s^2 \cdot \frac{k(1 + 2s)(1 + 4s)}{s^2(s^2 + s + 1)}$$

$$= \frac{k(1 + 0)(1 + 0)}{(0 + 0 + 1)}$$

$$= k$$

$k_a = k$

Example 2.18: Determine the steady state error for unit ramp and unit parabolic input for a unity feedback system with

$$G(s) = \frac{k(s+2)(s+4)}{s^2(s+8)}$$ (W-04)

Solution: Steady state error for unit ramp input.

$$R(s) = \frac{1}{s^2}$$

$$e_{ss} = \lim_{s \to 0} s \cdot \frac{R(s)}{1+G(s)}$$

$$= \lim_{s \to 0} s \cdot \frac{1/s^2}{1 + \frac{k(s+2)(s+4)}{s^2(s+8)}}$$

$$= \lim_{s \to 0} s \cdot \frac{s^2(s+8)}{s^2(s+8) + k(s+2)(s+4)}$$

$$= 0 \times \frac{1}{1 + \frac{k(0+2)(0+4)}{0(0+8)}}$$

$$= 0 \times \frac{(0+8)}{0(0+8) + k(0+2)(0+4)}$$

$$= 0$$

Steady state error for unit parabolic input.

$$R(s) = \frac{1}{s^3}$$

$$e_{ss} = \lim_{s \to 0} s \cdot \frac{R(s)}{1+G(s)}$$

$$= \lim_{s \to 0} s \cdot \frac{1/s^3}{1 + \frac{k(s+2)(s+4)}{s^2(s+8)}}$$

$$= \lim_{s \to 0} s \cdot \frac{s^2(s+8)}{s^3[s^2(s+8) + k(s+2)(s+4)]}$$

$$= \frac{(0+8)}{(0+8) + k(0+2)(0+4)}$$

$$= \frac{8}{8+8k}$$

$$= \frac{1}{1+k}$$

Example 2.19: A unity feedback system has $G(s) = \dfrac{40(s+4)}{s(s^2+10s+16)}$ (S-05)

Determine,
(i) Type of system
(ii) All error coefficients.

Solution: Given: $G(s) = \dfrac{40(s+4)}{s(s^2+10s+16)}$

(i) Compare this equation with standard time-constant form
$$G(s) = \frac{k(T_{z_1}s + 1)(T_{z_2}s + 1)}{s^n (T_{p_1}s + 1)(T_{p_2}s + 1)}$$

For given T.F.
$$n = 0$$
∴ The given system is a Type '1' system.

(ii) Position error constant.
$$k_p = G(0)$$
$$= 0$$

Velocity error constant
$$k_v = \lim_{s \to 0} s \cdot G(s)$$
$$= \lim_{s \to 0} s \cdot \frac{40(s+4)}{s(s^2 + 10s + 16)}$$
$$= \frac{40(0+4)}{(0+0+16)}$$
$$= \frac{160}{6}$$
$$= 10$$

Acceleration error constant
$$k_a = \lim_{s \to 0} s^2 \cdot G(s)$$
$$= \lim_{s \to 0} s^2 \cdot \frac{40(s+4)}{s(s^2 + 10s + 16)}$$
$$= 0 \times \frac{40(0+4)}{(0+0+16)}$$
$$= 0$$

∴ All error constants are:
$$k_p = 0$$
$$k_v = 10$$
$$k_a = 0$$

Example 2.20: For a unity feedback system having open loop transfer function
$$G(s) = \frac{k(s+2)}{s(s^3 + 7s^2 + 12s)}$$ (S-07)

Find:
(i) Type of system (ii) k_p
(iii) k_v (iv) k_a

Solution: (i) **Given:** $G(s) = \dfrac{k(s+2)}{s(s^3 + 7s^2 + 12s)}$

$$= \frac{k(s+2)}{s^2(s^2 + 7s + 12)}$$

If we compare this T.F. with standard T.F., then here n = 2.
∴ Type of given system is **Type 2**.

(ii)
$$k_p = G(0)$$
$$= \frac{k(0+2)}{0(0+0+0)}$$
$$= \infty$$

(iii)
$$k_v = \lim_{s \to 0} s \cdot G(s)$$
$$= \lim_{s \to 0} s \cdot \frac{k(s+2)}{s(s^3 + 7s^2 + 12s)}$$
$$= \infty$$

$$k_a = \lim_{s \to 0} s^2 \cdot G(s)$$
$$= \lim_{s \to 0} s^2 \cdot \frac{(k+2)}{s^2(s^2 + 7s + 12)}$$
$$= \frac{(k+2)}{(0+0+12)}$$
$$= \frac{k+2}{12}$$

$$k_p = \infty$$
$$k_v = \infty$$
$$k_a = \frac{k+2}{12}$$

Example 2.21: For a control system, the open loop is given by T.F. $G(s) = \frac{20}{(s+1)(s^2+10s+6)}$. When the T.F. of feedback path is $H(s) = \frac{5}{s+3}$ and the system input is r(t) = 5, find e_{ss}.

Solution:
$$G(s)H(s) = \frac{100}{(s+1)(s+3)(s^2+10s+6)}$$
$$r(t) = 5$$
$$R(s) = \frac{5}{s} = 1$$

For input step input
$$e_{ss} = \lim_{s \to 0} s \cdot \frac{R(s)}{1 + G(s)H(s)}$$
$$= \lim_{s \to 0} s \cdot \frac{s}{s\left(1 + \frac{100}{(s+1)(s+3)(s^2+10s+6)}\right)}$$
$$= \lim_{s \to 0} \frac{5(s+1)(s+3)(s^2+10s+6)}{(s+1)(s+3)(s^2+10s+6) + 100}$$
$$= \frac{5(0+1)(0+3)(0+0+6)}{(0+1)(0+3)(0+0+6) + 100}$$
$$= \frac{5 \times 1 \times 3 \times 6}{1 \times 3 \times 6 \times 100}$$
$$e_{ss} = \frac{1}{20}$$

Example 2.22: A unity feedback system has open loop transfer function:
$$G(s) = \frac{10(s+1)}{s(s+2)(s+5)}$$
Calculate the static error coefficients and steady state error where $r(t) = 3 + 10t$.

(4M)

Solution: Given transfer function:
$$G(s) = \frac{10(s+1)}{s(s+2)(s+5)}$$
and $\quad r(t) = 3 + 10t$

Taking Laplace transform
$$H(s) = R(s) = \frac{3}{s} + \frac{10}{s^2} = \frac{3s + 10}{s^2}$$

(i) Position error coefficient:
$$k_p = \lim_{s \to 0} G(s) = \lim_{s \to 0} \frac{10(s+1)}{s(s+2)(s+5)}$$
$$\boxed{k_p = \infty}$$

(ii) Velocity error coefficient:
$$k_v = \lim_{s \to 0} s \cdot G(s) = \lim_{s \to 0} s \cdot \frac{10(s+1)}{s(s+2)(s+5)}$$
$$= \lim_{s \to 0} \frac{10(s+1)}{(s+2)(s+5)}$$
$$\boxed{k_v = 1}$$

(iii) Acceleration error coefficient:
$$k_a = \lim_{s \to 0} s^2 \cdot G(s) = \lim_{s \to 0} s^2 \cdot \frac{10(s+1)}{s(s+2)(s+5)}$$
$$= \lim_{s \to 0} = \lim_{s \to 0} \frac{10(s+1)}{s(s+2)(s+5)}$$
$$\therefore \boxed{k_a = \infty}$$

(iv) Steady state error:
$$e_{ss} = \lim_{s \to 0} \frac{s \cdot R(s)}{1 + G(s)H(s)}$$

Here, $\dfrac{1}{1 + G(s)H(s)} = \dfrac{1}{1 + \dfrac{10(s+1)}{s(s+2)(s+5)}}$

$$= \frac{s(s+2)(s+5)}{s(s+2)(s+5) + 10(s+1)}$$

and $\quad R(s) = \dfrac{3s + 10}{s^2}$

$\therefore \quad e_{ss} = \lim_{s \to 0} s \times \dfrac{3s + 10}{s^2} \times \dfrac{s(s+2)(s+5)}{s(s+2)(s+5) + 10(s+1)}$

$= \infty$

$\therefore \quad \boxed{e_{ss} = \infty}$

$$\boxed{\begin{array}{l} k_p = \infty \\ k_v = 1 \\ k_a = \infty \\ e_{ss} = \infty \end{array}}$$

Example 2.23: For unity feedback system having open loop T.F.
$$G(s) = \frac{k(s+2)}{s(s^3 + 7s^2 + 12s)}$$

Find:
(i) Type of the system.
(ii) Error coefficients.
(iii) Steady state error when input to the system is $\frac{R}{2}t^2$.

Solution: Given: $H(s) = 1$

To determine the type of system write $G(s)$ in time constant form.

$$G(s) H(s) = G(s) = \frac{k(s+2)}{s(s^3 + 7s^2 + 12s)}$$

$$= \frac{2k(1 + 0.5s)}{s^2(s^2 + 7s + 12)}$$

$$= \frac{2k(1 + 0.5s)}{s^2(s + 4)(s + 3)}$$

$$= \frac{2k(1 + 0.5s)}{s^2 \times 4 \times 3 (1 + 0.25s)(1 + 0.33s)}$$

$$\boxed{G(s) = \frac{\frac{2k}{12}(1 + 0.5s)}{s^2(1 + 0.25s)(1 + 0.33s)}}$$

comparing this with,

$$G(s) H(s) = G(s) = \frac{k(1 + Tz_1 s)(1 + Tz_2 s)}{s^n (1 + Tp_1 s)(1 + Tp_2 s)}$$

where,
$n = $ Type of the system

Here, $n = 2$

∴ **System is Type 2 system.**

(ii) Error Coefficients:

$$k_p = \lim_{s \to 0} G(s)$$

$$= \lim_{s \to 0} \frac{\frac{k}{6}(1 + 0.5s)}{s^2 (1 + 0.25s)(1 + 0.33s)}$$

$$= \infty$$

∴ $$k_v = \lim_{s \to 0} s \cdot G(s)$$

$$= \lim_{s \to 0} \frac{s \cdot \frac{k}{6}(1 + 0.5s)}{s^2 (1 + 0.25s)(1 + 0.33s)}$$

$$= \infty$$

$$k_a = \lim_{s \to 0} s^2 \cdot G(s)$$

$$= \lim_{s \to 0} \frac{s^2 \cdot \frac{k}{6}(1 + 0.5s)}{s^2(1 + 0.25s)(1 + 0.33s)}$$

$$= \frac{k}{6}$$

∴ Error coefficients are,

$$\boxed{\begin{array}{c} k_p = \infty \\ k_v = \infty \\ k_a = \dfrac{k}{6} \end{array}}$$

(iii) Steady state error when input

$$r(t) = \frac{R}{2} t^2$$

Taking L.T.

$$R(s) = \frac{R}{s^3}$$

$$e_{ss} = \lim_{s \to 0} \frac{s \cdot R(s)}{1 + G(s)}$$

$$= \lim_{s \to 0} \frac{s \cdot \frac{R}{s^3}}{1 + \frac{\frac{k}{6}(1 + 0.5s)}{s^2(1 + 0.25s)(1 + 0.33s)}}$$

$$= \lim_{s \to 0} \frac{R}{s^2 \left[1 + \dfrac{\frac{k}{6}(1 + 0.5s)}{s^2(1 + 0.25s)(1 + 0.33s)}\right]}$$

$$= \lim_{s \to 0} \frac{R}{s^2 + \dfrac{\frac{k}{6}(1 + 0.5s)}{(1 + 0.25s)(1 + 0.33s)}}$$

$$= \frac{R}{0 + \dfrac{\frac{k}{6}(1 + 0)}{(1 + 0)(1 + 0)}}$$

$$= \frac{6R}{k}$$

∴ $$\boxed{e_{ss} = \frac{6R}{k}}$$

Steady state error can also be determined as $e_{ss} = \dfrac{R}{K_a}$ as system is type 2 system, where, R is magnitude of the input.

$$\therefore \quad e_{ss} = \dfrac{R}{\dfrac{k}{6}} = \dfrac{6R}{k}$$

Example 2.24: For unity feedback system having

$$G(s) = \dfrac{10(s+1)}{s^2(s+2)(s+10)}$$

Determine:
(i) Type of the system.
(ii) Error coefficients.
(iii) Steady state error for input $r(t) = 1 + 4t + \dfrac{t^2}{2}$.

Solution: Given: Unit feedback system,

$$\therefore \quad H(s) = 1$$

To determine type of the system arrange G(s) H(s) in time-constant form.

$$G(s)\,H(s) = G(s) = \dfrac{10(s+1)}{s^2(s+2)(s+10)}$$

$$= \dfrac{10(s+1)}{s^2 \times 2(1+0.5s) \times 10(1+0.1s)}$$

$$= \dfrac{0.5(s+1)}{s^2(1+0.5s)(1+0.1s)}$$

Comparing this with standard time-constant form

$$G(s)\,H(s) = G(s) = \dfrac{k(1+Tz_1 s)(1+Tz_2 s)}{s^n(1+Tp_1 s)(1+Tp_2 s)}$$

where, n = Type of the system
Here, $n = 2$

∴ **Type of system is Type 2.**

(ii) Error Coefficients:

$$k_p = \lim_{s \to 0} G(s)$$

$$= \lim_{s \to 0} \dfrac{0.5(s+1)}{s^2(1+0.5s)(1+0.1s)}$$

$$= \infty$$

$$k_v = \lim_{s \to 0} s \cdot G(s)$$

$$= \lim_{s \to 0} s \times \dfrac{0.5(1+s)}{s^2(1+0.5s)(1+0.1s)}$$

$$= \infty$$

$$k_a = \lim_{s \to 0} s^2 G(s)$$

$$= \lim_{s \to 0} \frac{s^2 \times 0.5 (1 + s)}{s^2 (1 + 0.5s)(1 + 0.1s)}$$

$$= 0.5$$

∴ Error coefficients are

$$\boxed{\begin{array}{c} k_p = \infty \\ k_v = \infty \\ k_a = 0.5 \end{array}}$$

(iii) Steady state error for input

$$r(t) = 1 + 4t + \frac{t^2}{2}$$

Taking L.T.

$$R(s) = \frac{1}{s} + \frac{4}{s^2} + \frac{1}{s^3}$$

$$\therefore \quad e_{ss} = \lim_{s \to 0} \frac{s \cdot R(s)}{1 + G(s)}$$

$$= \lim_{s \to 0} \frac{s \left[\frac{1}{s} + \frac{4}{s^2} + \frac{1}{s^3}\right]}{1 + \frac{0.5(1 + s)}{s^2 (1 + 0.5s)(1 + 0.1s)}}$$

$$= \lim_{s \to 0} \frac{1 + \frac{4}{s} + \frac{1}{s^2}}{1 + \frac{0.5(1 + s)}{s^2 (1 + 0.5s)(1 + 0.1s)}}$$

Separate the numerator terms

$$= \lim_{s \to 0} \frac{1}{1 + \frac{0.5(1 + s)}{s^2 (1 + 0.5s)(1 + 0.1s)}} +$$

$$\lim_{s \to 0} \frac{4}{s + \frac{0.5(1 + s)}{s(1 + 0.5s)(1 + 0.1s)}} + \lim_{s \to 0} \frac{1}{s^2 + \frac{0.5(1 + s)}{(1 + 0.5s)(1 + 0.1s)}}$$

$$= \frac{1}{1 + \infty} + \frac{4}{0 + \infty} + \frac{1}{0 + 0.5}$$

$$= 0 + 0 + \frac{1}{0.5}$$

$$= 2$$

∴ $\boxed{e_{ss} = 2}$

Example 2.25: A unity feedback system has,
$$G(s) = \frac{40(s+2)}{s(s+1)(s+4)}$$

Determine:

(i) The type of system

(ii) All error coefficients and

(iii) Error for ramp input with magnitude 4.

Solution: Given: $H(s) = 1$

To determine type of system, arrange $G(s)\,H(s)$ in time constant form.

$$G(s)\,H(s) = G(s) = \frac{40(s+2)}{s(s+1)(s+2)}$$

$$= \frac{40 \times 2(1+0.5s)}{s(1+s) \times 4(1+0.25s)}$$

$$= \frac{20(1+0.5s)}{s(1+s)(1+0.25s)}$$

Comparing this with standard time-constant form,

$$G(s) = \frac{k(1+Tz_1s)(1+Tz_2s)}{s^n(1+Tp_1s)(1+Tp_2s)}$$

where, n = Type of the system

Here, n = 1.

So, the given system is **type 1 system.**

(ii) Error Coefficients

$$k_p = \lim_{s \to 0} G(s)$$

$$= \lim_{s \to 0} \frac{20(1+0.5s)}{s(1+s)(1+0.25s)}$$

$$= \frac{20(1+0)}{0(1+0)(1+0)}$$

$$= \frac{20}{0}$$

$$= \infty$$

$$k_v = \lim_{s \to 0} s\,G(s)$$

$$= \lim_{s \to 0} \frac{s \cdot 20(1+0.5s)}{s(1+s)(1+0.25s)}$$

$$= \lim_{s \to 0} \frac{20(1 + 0.5s)}{(1 + s)(1 + 0.25s)}$$

$$= \frac{20}{1}$$

$$= 20$$

$$k_a = \lim_{s \to 0} s^2 G(s)$$

$$= \lim_{s \to 0} \frac{s^2 \cdot 20(1 + 0.5s)}{s(1 + s)(1 + 0.25s)}$$

$$= \frac{0 \times 20(1 + 0)}{(1 + 0)(1 + 0)} = 0$$

$$\boxed{\begin{array}{l} k_p = \infty \\ k_v = 20 \\ k_a = 0 \end{array}}$$

(iii) Steady state error for ramp input is,

$$e_{ss} = \frac{A}{k_v}$$

$\because \quad A = $ Magnitude of ramp input

Here, $A = 4$ and $k_v = 20$.

$$\therefore \quad e_{ss} = \frac{4}{20}$$

$$= 0.2$$

$$\therefore \quad \boxed{e_{ss} = 0.2}$$

Example 2.26: For a system, $G(s) H(s) = \dfrac{k}{s^2(s + 2)(s + 3)}$.

Find the value of k to limit steady state error to 10 when input to the system is $1 + 10t + \dfrac{40}{2} t^2$.

Solution: Given: $G(s) H(s) = \dfrac{k}{s^2(s + 2)(s + 3)}$

Input is a combination of three inputs. So, first calculate their magnitudes.

$$r(t) = 1 + 10t + \frac{40}{2} t^2$$

$$\begin{aligned} A_1 &= \text{Step} = 1 \\ A_2 &= \text{Ramp} = 10 \\ A_3 &= \text{Parabolic} = 40 \end{aligned}$$

Now, find error coefficients

$$k_p = \lim_{s \to 0} G(s) H(s) = \lim_{s \to 0} \frac{k}{s^2(s + 2)(s + 3)} = \infty$$

$$k_v = \lim_{s \to 0} s G(s) H(s) = \lim_{s \to 0} \frac{s \cdot k}{s^2(s + 2)(s + 3)} = \infty$$

$$k_a = \lim_{s \to 0} s^2 G(s) H(s) = \lim_{s \to 0} \frac{s^2 \cdot k}{s^2(s + 2)(s + 3)} = \frac{k}{6}$$

∴ Steady state error is,

$$e_{ss} = e_{ss1} + e_{ss2} + e_{ss3}$$

$$= \frac{A_1}{1 + k_p} + \frac{A_2}{k_v} + \frac{A_3}{k_a}$$

$$10 = \frac{1}{1 + \infty} + \frac{10}{\infty} + \frac{40}{\left(\frac{k}{6}\right)} \quad [\because \text{Given : } e_{ss} = 10]$$

$$10 = \frac{240}{k}$$

∴ $k = 24$

∴ **Value of k is 24 to limit the steady state error to 10.**

Example 2.27: For a system shown in Fig. 2.23, determine type of the system, error coefficients and the error for the following inputs.
(i) $r(t) = 10$
(ii) $r(t) = 5t$
(iii) $r(t) = 10 + 5t + \frac{6}{2}t^2$ and

$$G_1 = \frac{20}{(s + 4)(s + 10)}, \quad H_1 = 10s$$

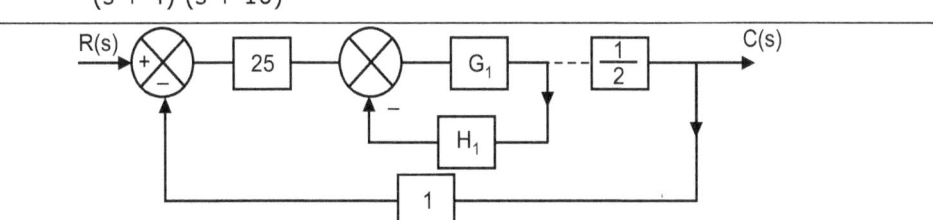

Fig. 2.23

Solution: First simplify the system.
1. Remove the inner closed loop.

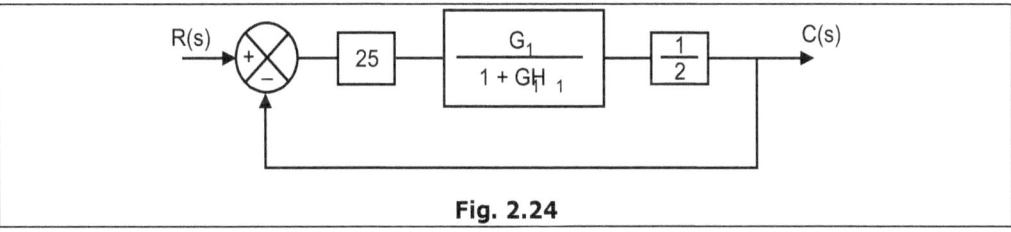

Fig. 2.24

$$\because \quad \frac{G_1}{1 + G_1 H_1} = \frac{\frac{20}{(s + 4)(s + 10)}}{1 + \frac{20}{(s + 4)(s + 10)} 10s}$$

$$= \frac{20}{(s + 4)(s + 10) + 200s}$$

$$= \frac{20}{s^2 + 214s + 40}$$

2. Now combining all blocks in series.

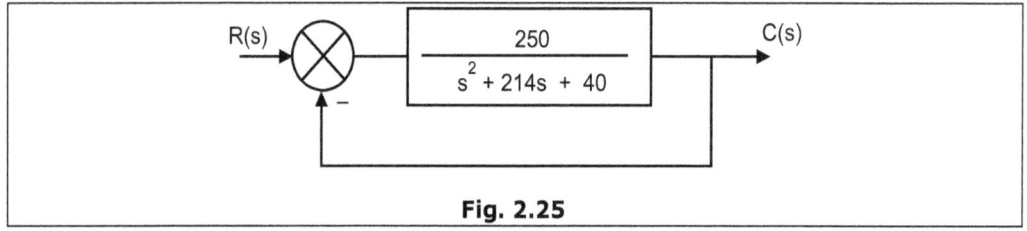

Fig. 2.25

$$\therefore \quad 25 \times \frac{20}{s^2 + 214s + 40} \times \frac{1}{2} = \frac{250}{s^2 + 214s + 40}$$

$$\therefore \quad G(s) = \frac{250}{s^2 + 214s + 40}, \quad H(s) = 1 \text{ System is unity feedback system.}$$

Now, comparing G(s) H(s) with standard time constant form

$$G(s) H(s) = G(s) = \frac{K (1 + Tz_1 s) (1 + Tz_2 s)}{s^n (1 + Tp_1 s) (1 + Tp_2 s)}$$

where, $\quad n = $ Type of system

$$n = 0$$

∴ **Type of system is type zero.**

Error coefficient:

$$k_p = \lim_{s \to 0} G(s)$$

$$= \lim_{s \to 0} \frac{250}{s^2 + 214s + 40}$$

$$= \frac{250}{40}$$

$$= \frac{25}{4}$$

$$k_v = \lim_{s \to 0} s\, G(s)$$

$$= \lim_{s \to 0} s \cdot \frac{250}{s^2 + 214s + 40}$$

$$= 0$$

$$k_u = \lim_{s \to 0} s^2\, G(s)$$

$$= \lim_{s \to 0} s^2 \cdot \frac{250}{s^2 + 214s + 40}$$

$$= 0$$

$$\therefore \quad \boxed{k_p = \frac{25}{4},\ k_v = 0,\ k_a = 0}$$

(i) r(t) = 10

Taking L.T.

$$R(s) = \frac{10}{s}, \quad A = 10$$

$$\therefore \quad e_{ss} = \frac{A}{1 + k_p}$$

$$= \frac{10}{1 + \frac{25}{4}}$$

$$\boxed{e_{ss} = 1.379}$$

(ii) r(t) = 5t

$$\therefore \quad R(s) = \frac{5}{s^2} \qquad \qquad \because A = 5$$

$$\therefore \quad e_{ss} = \frac{A}{k_v}$$

$$= \frac{5}{0} = \infty$$

$$\therefore \quad \boxed{e_{ss} = \infty}$$

(iii) $r(t) = 10 + 5t + \frac{6}{2}t^2$

$$A_1 = 10 \rightarrow \text{Step}$$
$$A_2 = 5 \rightarrow \text{Ramp}$$
$$A_3 = 6 \rightarrow \text{Parabolic}$$

$$\therefore \quad e_{ss} = \frac{A_1}{1 + k_p} + \frac{A_2}{k_v} + \frac{A_3}{k_a}$$

$$= \frac{10}{1 + \frac{2s}{4}} + \frac{5}{0} + \frac{6}{0}$$

$$= \infty$$

$$\boxed{e_{ss} = \infty}$$

As the system is type 0 system, the error is finite only for step input.

Example 2.28: Assuming r(t) = 0.1t and it is desired that $e_{ss} \leq 0.005$, find the range of values of k for error to be within the specified limit for the system shown in Fig. 2.26.

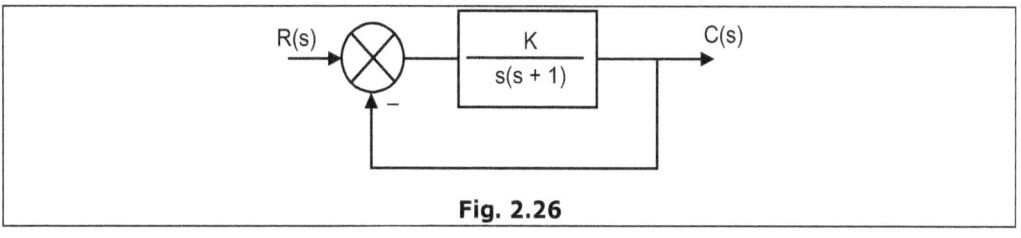

Fig. 2.26

From Fig. 2.26, the system is a unity feedback system.

$$G(s) = \frac{k}{s(s+1)} \text{ and } H(s) = 1$$

The input $r(t) = 0.1t$ i.e. ramp input with magnitude is 0.1.
We know that, for ramp input k_v controls the error.

$$\therefore \quad k_v = \lim_{s \to 0} s \cdot G(s)$$

$$= \lim_{s \to 0} \frac{s \cdot k}{s(s+1)}$$

$$= \frac{k}{0+1}$$

$$= k$$

Maximum e_{ss} allowed is 0.005.

$$\therefore \quad e_{ss} = \frac{A}{k_v}$$

$$0.005 = \frac{0.1}{k}$$

$$\therefore \quad k = \frac{0.1}{0.005}$$

$$k = 20$$

For any value of k greater than 20, e_{ss} will be less than 0.005.
∴ Range of k for $e_{ss} \leq 0.005$ is,

$$20 \leq k \leq \infty$$

Example 2.29: Determine the steady state error for following system for input 4t.

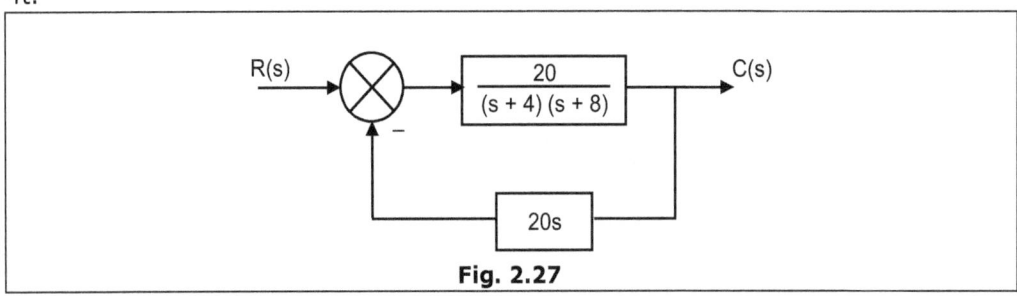

Fig. 2.27

Solution: For Fig. 2.27,

$$G(s) = \frac{20}{(s+4)(s+8)}$$

and $\quad H(s) = 20s$
∴ Open loop T.F.

$$G(s) H(s) = \frac{20}{(s+4)(s+8)} \times 20s$$

$$= \frac{400s}{(s+4)(s+8)}$$

Given input $r(t) = 4(t)$

$$\therefore \quad R(s) = \frac{4}{s^2}$$

Steady state error

$$e_{ss} = \lim_{s \to 0} \frac{s \cdot R(s)}{1 + G(s) H(s)}$$

$$= \lim_{s \to 0} \frac{s \times \frac{4}{s^2}}{1 + \frac{400s}{(s+4)(s+8)}}$$

$$= \lim_{s \to 0} \frac{4}{s + \frac{400s^2}{(s+4)(s+8)}}$$

$$= \frac{4}{0}$$

$$= \infty$$

$$\therefore \boxed{e_{ss} = \infty}$$

Example 2.30: For a system, $G(s) H(s) = \dfrac{k}{s(s+2)(s+5)}$ find the value of k limit steady state error to 5 when input to the system is $1 + 10t$.

Solution: Given:
$$G(s) H(s) = \frac{k}{s(s+2)(s+5)}$$

$$= \frac{k}{s \times 2(1 + 0.5s) \times 5(1 + 0.2s)}$$

$$= \frac{0.1 k}{s(1 + 0.5s)(1 + 0.2s)}$$

Input $r(t) = 1 + 10t$

$\therefore$ $R(s) = \dfrac{1}{s} + \dfrac{10}{s^2}$

$$= \frac{s + 10}{s^2}$$

Steady state error

$$e_{ss} = \lim_{s \to 0} \frac{s \cdot R(s)}{1 + G(s) H(s)}$$

$$= \lim_{s \to 0} \frac{s \times \frac{s+10}{s^2}}{1 + \frac{0.1k}{s(1 + 0.5s)(1 + 0.2s)}}$$

$$= \lim_{s \to 0} \frac{\frac{s+10}{s}}{1 + \frac{0.1k}{s(1 + 0.5s)(1 + 0.2s)}}$$

$$= \lim_{s \to 0} \frac{10(1 + 0.1s)}{s + \frac{0.1k}{(1 + 0.5s)(1 + 0.2s)}}$$

$$= \frac{10(1+0)}{0+\frac{0.1k}{(1+0)(1+0)}}$$

$$= \frac{10}{0.1k}$$

$$\therefore \quad 5 = \frac{10}{0.1k} \qquad [\because \text{ Given: } e_{ss} = 5]$$

$$\therefore \quad \boxed{k = 20}$$

To limit steady state value to 5, k should be 20.

Example 2.31: Input applied to the system is $r(t) = 0.2t$ and steady state error is ≤ 0.007, find the range value of k for a given system $H(s) = 1$.

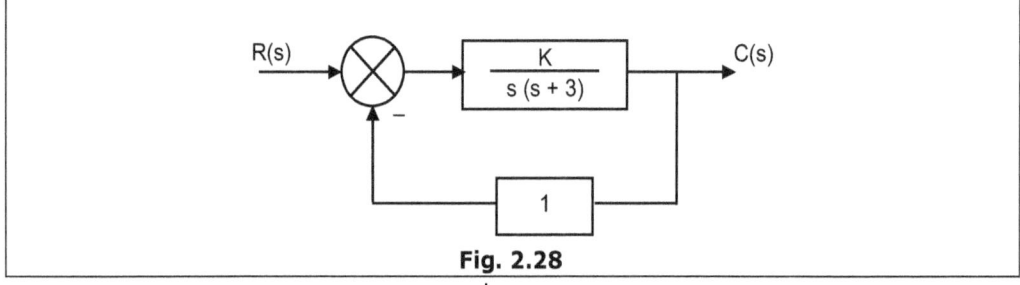

Fig. 2.28

Solution: Given: $\quad G(s) = \frac{k}{s(s+3)}, H(s) = 1$

$$\therefore \quad G(s)H(s) = G(s) = \frac{k}{s(s+3)}$$

$$r(t) = 0.2t$$

$$\therefore \quad R(s) = \frac{0.2}{s^2}$$

Steady state error

$$e_{ss} = \lim_{s \to 0} \frac{s \cdot R(s)}{1 + G(s)H(s)}$$

$$= \lim_{s \to 0} \frac{s \times \frac{0.2}{s^2}}{1 + \frac{k}{s(s+3)}}$$

$$= \lim_{s \to 0} \frac{0.2}{s\left(1 + \frac{k}{s(s+3)}\right)}$$

$$= \lim_{s \to 0} \frac{0.2}{s + \frac{k}{3(1+0.33s)}}$$

$$= \frac{0.2}{0 + \frac{k}{3(1+0)}}$$

$$= \frac{0.6}{k}$$

But $0 < e_{ss} \leq 0.007$.

So that the minimum value of e_{ss} is 0.

For $e_{ss} = 0$

$$0 = \frac{0.6}{k}$$

$$\therefore \boxed{k = \infty}$$

For $e_{ss} = 0.007$

$$0.007 = \frac{0.6}{k}$$

$$\therefore \boxed{k = 85.71}$$

$\therefore$ For $0 < e_{ss} \leq 0.007$
Range of k is **$85.71 \leq k \leq \infty$**.

Example 2.32: For a unity feedback system, $G(s) = \frac{500}{(s+10)}$ and $r(t) = 5$. Determine the steady state error. If it is required to reduce this existing error by 5% what will be the value of system gain?

Solution: Given:
$$G(s) = \frac{500}{(s+10)}$$
$$H(s) = 1$$
$$\therefore G(s)H(s) = G(s) = \frac{500}{(s+10)}$$
$$r(t) = 5$$
$$\therefore R(s) = \frac{5}{s}$$

Steady state error

$$e_{ss} = \lim_{s \to 0} \frac{s \cdot R(s)}{1 + G(s)}$$

$$= \lim_{s \to 0} \frac{s \cdot \frac{5}{s}}{1 + \frac{500}{1.0(1 + 0.1s)}}$$

$$= \lim_{s \to 0} \frac{5}{1 + \frac{50}{1 + 0.1s}}$$

$$= \frac{5}{1 + \frac{50}{1+0}}$$

$$= \frac{5}{51} = 0.098$$

$\therefore \boxed{e_{ss} = 0.098}$

Reduce this error by 5%.

Reduced new error by $0.098 \times \dfrac{5}{100} = 0.049$

∴ New error is $= 0.098 - 0.049$
$= \mathbf{0.093}$

$$G(s) = \dfrac{500}{10(1 + 0.1s)}$$

$$= \dfrac{50}{1 + 0.1s} = \dfrac{k}{1 + 0.1s}$$

$$e_{ss} = \lim_{s \to 0} \dfrac{s \cdot R(s)}{1 + G(s)}$$

$$= \lim_{s \to 0} \dfrac{s \times \dfrac{5}{s}}{1 + \dfrac{k}{1 + 0.1s}}$$

$$0.093 = \dfrac{5}{1 + k}$$

∴ $0.093 k + 0.093 = 5$

∴ $k = \dfrac{5 - 0.093}{0.093}$

$$\boxed{k = 52.70}$$

To reduce steady state error by 5%, gain should be 52.70.

Example 2.33: The unit step-response of a system is given by,
$$C(t) = \dfrac{5}{2} + 5t - \dfrac{5}{2}e^{-2t}$$

Find the transfer function of the system.

Solution: Given,
$$C(t) = \dfrac{5}{2} + 5t - \dfrac{5}{2}e^{-2t}$$

Where,

C(t)	C(s)
1	$\dfrac{1}{s}$
t	$\dfrac{1}{s^2}$
e^{-2t}	$\dfrac{1}{s+2}$

Take Laplace Transform,
$$C(s) = \dfrac{5}{2s} + \dfrac{5}{s^2} - \dfrac{5/2}{(s+2)}$$

∴ $$C(s) = \dfrac{5}{2}\left[\dfrac{1}{s} + \dfrac{2}{s^2} - \dfrac{1}{s+2}\right]$$

$$C(s) = \dfrac{10(s+1)}{s^2(s+2)}$$

Given response is a unit step.
Thus,
$$R(s) = \dfrac{1}{s}$$

∴ Transfer function $= \dfrac{C(s)}{R(s)}$

$$= \frac{\frac{10(s+1)}{s^2(s+2)}}{\frac{1}{s}}$$

$$= \frac{10(s+1)}{s(s+2)}$$

$$\boxed{T.F. = \frac{C(s)}{R(s)} = \frac{10(s+1)}{s(s+2)}}$$

Example 2.34: A control system is described by the differential equation

$$2\ddot{Y}(t) + 10\dot{Y}(t) + 12Y(t) = 12X(t)$$

Find its output response for unit step input y(t) as output and X(t) is input.

Solution: Given equation:

$$2\ddot{y}(t) + 10\dot{y}(t) + 12y(t) = 12X(t)$$

Take L.T.

$$2s^2 Y(s) + 10s Y(s) + 12 Y(s) = 12 X(s)$$

$$(2s^2 + 10s + 12) Y(s) = 12 X(s)$$

$$T.F. = \frac{Y(s)}{X(s)} = \frac{12}{2s^2 + 10s + 12}$$

∴ $\frac{C(s)}{R(s)} = X(t) = u(t)$

$$R(s) = X(s) = \frac{1}{s}$$

$$Y(s) = \frac{12}{s(2s^2 + 10s + 12)}$$

$$= \frac{12/2}{s(s^2 + 5s + 6)}$$

$$= \frac{6}{s(s+2)(s+3)}$$

Using partial fraction expansion,

$$Y(s) = 6\left[\frac{A}{s} + \frac{B}{s+2} + \frac{C}{s+3}\right]$$

$$A = \frac{1}{6}, B = -\frac{1}{6}, C = -\frac{1}{6}$$

∴ $Y(s) = \frac{1}{s} - \frac{1}{s+2} - \frac{1}{s+3}$

Taking inverse L.T. we get output response as

$$Y(t) = 1 - e^{-2t} - e^{-3t}$$

Example 2.35: A control system has T.F. = $\frac{C(s)}{R(s)} = \frac{3}{s+20}$. Determine its step response, ramp response and impulse response. Assume zero initial conditions. Sketch the response.

Solution: Given: T.F. = $\frac{C(s)}{R(s)} = \frac{3}{s+20}$

(i) Unit step response:

$$R(t) = u(t)$$

$$\therefore R(s) = \frac{1}{s}$$

$$\therefore C(s) = \frac{3}{s(s+20)}$$

Using partial fraction expansion,

$$C(s) = \frac{A}{s} + \frac{B}{s+20}$$

$$A = \frac{3}{20}, B = -\frac{3}{20}$$

$$\therefore C(s) = \frac{3}{20s} - \frac{3}{20(s+20)}$$

Taking inverse L.T.

$$C(t) = \frac{3}{20}[1 - e^{-20/t}]$$

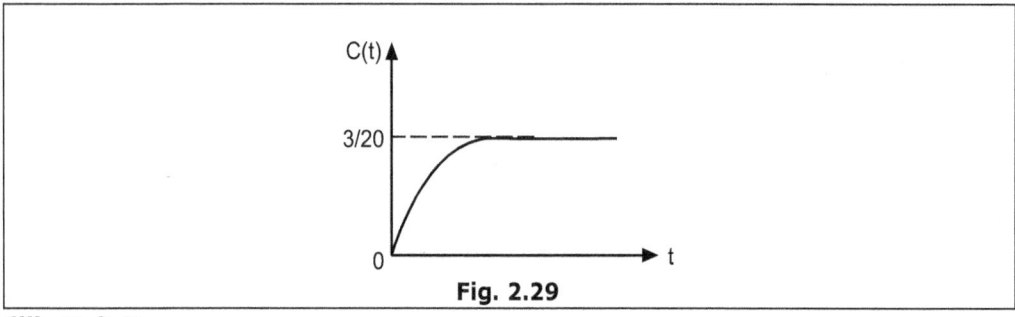

Fig. 2.29

(ii) Unit Ramp

$$R(t) = t$$
$$\therefore R(s) = 1/s^2$$

$$\therefore C(s) = \frac{3}{s^2(s+20)}$$

Using partial fraction expansion

$$C(s) = \frac{A}{s^2} + \frac{B}{s} + \frac{C}{s+20}$$

$$A = \frac{3}{20}, B = -\frac{3}{400}, C = \frac{3}{400}$$

$$\therefore C(s) = \frac{3}{20s^2} - \frac{3}{400s} + \frac{3}{400(s+20)}$$

$$= \frac{3}{20}\left[\frac{1}{s^2} - \frac{1}{20s} + \frac{1}{20(s+20)}\right]$$

Taking Inverse L.T.

$$C(t) = \frac{3}{20}\left[t - \frac{1}{20} + \frac{1}{20}e^{-20t}\right]$$

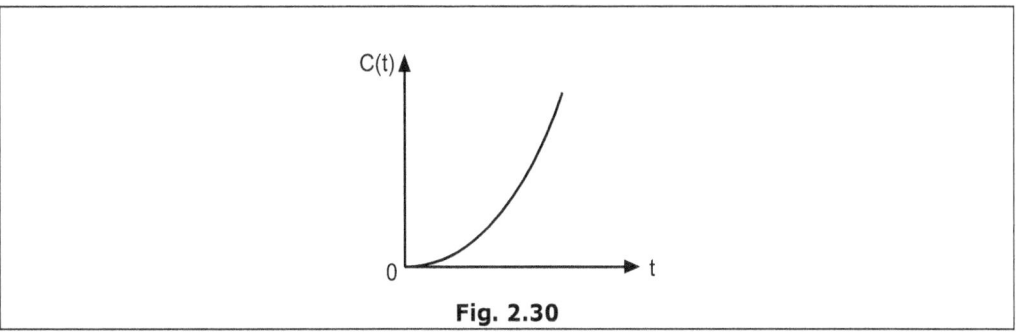

Fig. 2.30

(iii) Unit Impulse

$$R(t) = \delta(t)$$
$$\therefore \quad R(s) = 1$$

Taking Inverse L.T.

$$C(t) = 3e^{-20t}$$

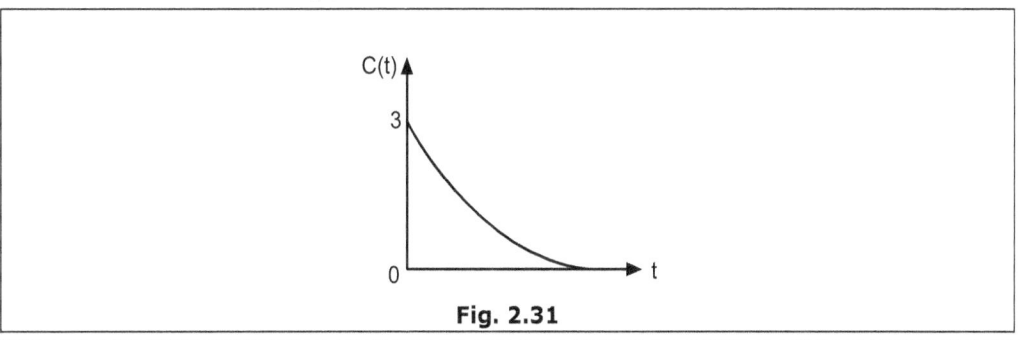

Fig. 2.31

Example 2.36: A feedback control system is given as,

$$G(s) = \frac{40}{s(s+2)(s+5)}, \quad H(s) = \frac{1}{s}$$

For a unit step input, determine the steady state error constants and errors.

Solution: $\quad G(s)\,H(s) = \dfrac{40}{s^2(s+2)(s+5)}$

(i) Position error constant

$$k_p = \lim_{s \to 0} G(s)\,H(s) = \lim_{s \to 0} \frac{40}{s^2(s+2)(s+5)}$$

$$= \infty$$

(ii) Velocity error constant

$$k_v = \lim_{s \to 0} s \cdot G(s)\,H(s) = \lim_{s \to 0} \frac{40}{s(s+2)(s+5)}$$

$$= \infty$$

(iii) Acceleration error constant

$$k_a = \lim_{s \to 0} s^2 \cdot G(s) H(s) = \lim_{s \to 0} \frac{40}{(s+2)(s+5)}$$

$$= \frac{40}{(0+2)(0+5)}$$

$$= 5.7$$

(iv) Steady state error $= \lim_{s \to 0} \frac{s R(s)}{1 + G(s) H(s)}$

$$\therefore \quad \frac{1}{1 + G(s) H(s)} = \frac{s^2 (s+2)(s+5)}{s^4 + 7s^3 + 10s^2 + 40}$$

For unit step input, $R(s) = \frac{1}{s}$

$$\therefore \quad \text{Steady state error} = \lim_{s \to 0} \frac{s^2 (s+2)(s+5)}{s^4 + 7s^3 + 10s^2 + 40}$$

$$= 0$$

Ans.
$$\boxed{\begin{array}{l} k_p = \infty \\ k_v = \infty \\ k_a = 5.7 \\ e_{ss} = 0 \end{array}}$$

Thus, **the system is a type-2 system.**

Example 2.37: For a unity feedback system whose open-loop transfer function is,

$$G(s) = \frac{50}{(1 + 0.1s)(1 + 2s)}$$

Find the position, velocity and acceleration error coefficients.

Solution: Given,

$$G(s) = \frac{50}{(1 + 0.1s)(1 + 2s)}$$

(i) Position error constant.

$$k_p = \lim_{s \to 0} G(s) = \lim_{s \to 0} \frac{50}{(1 + 0.1s)(1 + 2s)}$$

$$= \frac{50}{(1+0)(1+0)}$$

$$= 50$$

(ii) Velocity error constant

$$k_v = \lim_{s \to 0} s G(s) = \lim_{s \to 0} s \cdot \frac{50}{(1 + 0.1s)(1 + 2s)}$$

$$= 0 \times \frac{50}{(1+0)(1+0)}$$

$$= 0$$

(iii) Acceleration error constant

$$k_a = \lim_{s \to 0} s^2 G(s) = \lim_{s \to 0} s^2 \cdot \frac{50}{(1 + 0.1s)(1 + 2s)} = 0$$

Ans.
$$\boxed{\begin{array}{l} k_p = 50 \\ k_v = 0 \\ k_p = 0 \end{array}}$$

Thus, the system is a type-0 system.

Important Points

- **Time response** is the analysis of the control system or the analysis of output of the control system w.r.t. time.
- The response of a system to an applied excitation is called **time response** and it is a function of time, c(t).
- **Transient response** is defined as the part of the time response that goes to zero as time becomes very large.
- The part of the response that remains after the transient dies out is called **steady state response** $c_{ss}(t)$.
- If the steady state response of the output does not agree with the steady state exactly, the system is said to have a **steady-state error**.
- **Standard test signals** are:
  (i) Step input   (ii) Ramp input
  (iii) Parabolic input   (iv) Impulse input
- The **step** is a signal whose value changes from one level (usually zero) to another level A, in zero time.
- The **ramp** is a signal which starts at a value of zero and increases linearly with time.
- **Parabolic** signal is the integral of ramp input.
- A **unit impulse** is defined as a signal which has zero value everywhere except at t = 0 where its magnitude is infinite.
- **Types of Feedback control system:**
  (i) Time-constant form:
  $$G(s) = \frac{k(T_{z1} s + 1)(T_{z2} s + 1) \ldots}{s^n (T_{p1} s + 1)(T_{p2} s + 1) \ldots}$$

  (ii) Pole-zero form:
  $$G(s) = \frac{k'(s + b_1)(s + b_2) \ldots}{s^n (s + a_1)(s + a_2) \ldots}$$

- Types of feedback control systems.
    - (i) Type '0' system
    - (ii) Type '1' system
    - (iii) Type '2' system
- **Time constant** gives an indication of how fast the system tends to reach the final value.
- The **speed of the response** can be defined as the time for the output to reach to a particular percentage of its final value.
- **Delay time**, t_d is the time required for the response to reach to 50% of its final value.
- **Rise time**, t_r is the time required for the response to reach from 10% to 90% of the final value for over damped systems and 0 to 100% of the final value for undamped systems.
- **Peak time**, t_p is the time required for the response to reach the peak of the time response.
- **Settling time**, t_s is the time required for the response to reach and stay within a specified tolerance band of its final value.
- **Steady-state error**, e_{ss} gives the error between the actual output and desired output as 't' tends to infinity.
- **Error constant:**
    1. Position error constant (K_p).
    2. Velocity error constant (K_v).
    3. Acceleration error constant (K_p).

Practice Questions

1. Define and explain the following terms related to transfer function of a system.

    (i) Poles, (ii) Zeroes, (iii) Characteristic equation in order.

2. Define the poles and zeros of a transfer function.
3. Define steady state response and transient response.
4. What is meant by standard test signals ? State its necessity.
5. Sketch the step-signal and ramp signal.
6. State the concept of impulse input.

7. State the steady state errors and errors constants for (i) Unit step input, (ii) Ramp input, (iii) Unit parabolic unit.

8. Determine the position, velocity and acceleration constants of unity feedback control system whose open loop transfer function is,
$$G(s) = \frac{20}{s(s+1)(s+5)}$$

9. Define: (i) Rise time, (ii) Peak time, (iii) Peak overshoot, (iv) Settling time.

10. List the time response specifications of second order system.

11. Sketch
$$\text{Zeros} = -3, 3+j2, 1-j2$$
$$\text{Poles} = -4, -j3-3, -1-j \quad \text{on s-plane.}$$

12. For a given function, sketch the poles and zeros on s-plane.
$$F(s) = \frac{(s+1)(s+2)}{s^2+3s+6}$$

Previous Year MSBTE Questions and Answers (As Per 'E' Scheme)

1. What are the standard test signals used in time domain analysis ? State the need of these signals in control system. **(S-11)(4M)**

Ans. Refer Section 2.3.

2. Define damping. Show the effect of damping in the response of second-order control system. **(S-11)(4M)**

Ans. Refer Section 2.6 and 2.6.2.

3. Derive relationship of steady state error in terms of open loop T.F. G(S) H(S). Find ess for step input. **(S-12)(4M)**

Ans. Refer Section 2.8.1.

4. Derive error coefficient's Kp, Kv and Ka relation for Type 'O' system. **(S-12)(4M)**

Ans. Refer Section 2.8.1.

5. For given transfer function.
$$\text{T.F.} = \frac{10(S+8)}{S(S+4)(S^2+6S+25)}$$

Find:
(i) Poles, (ii) Zeros, (iii) Characteristic equation, (iv) Order of system. **(S-12)(8M)**

Ans. T.F. $= \dfrac{10(S+8)}{S(S+4)(S^2+6S+25)}$

(i) **Poles:**
  (i) $S = 0$
  (ii) $S + 4 = 0, \therefore S = -4$,
  (iii) $S^2 + 6S + 25 = 0$ which is quadratic equation.

For the quadratic equation

$$ax^2 + bx + c = 0$$

$$\text{The poles are} = \frac{-b \pm \sqrt{b^2 - 4ac}}{2a}$$

$$= \frac{-6 \pm \sqrt{6^2 - 4 \times 1 \times 25}}{2 \times 1}$$

$$= \frac{-6 \pm \sqrt{36 - 100}}{2}$$

$$= \frac{-6 \pm \sqrt{64}}{2}$$

$$= -3 \pm j4$$

∴ Poles are $-3 + j4$ and $3 - j4$.

The poles are 0, -4, $-3 + j4$ and $3 - j4$.

(ii) Zeros:

$$10(S + 8) = 0$$
$$S + 8 = 0$$
$$S = -8$$
$$\text{Zeros} = -8$$

(iii) Characteristic equation is

$$S(S + 4)(S^2 + 6S + 25) = 0$$
$$S(S^3 + 6S^2 + 25S + 4S^2 + 24S + 100) = 0$$
$$S^4 + 6S^3 + 25S^2 + 4S^2 + 24S^2 + 100 = 0$$
$$S^4 + 9S^3 + 49S^2 + 100S = 0$$

(iv) Order of system

The maximum power of S in characteristic equation is 4.

6. A unity feedback system has G(S)

$$G(S) = \frac{10(S + 1)}{S^2(S + 2)(S + 10)}$$

Find:

(i) Type of error, (ii) Error coefficient K_p, K_v and K_a, (iii) Steady state error for input.

(S-12) (8M)

$$r(t) = 1 + 4t = t^2/2$$

Ans.
$$G(S) = \frac{10(S + 1)}{S^2(S + 2)(S + 10)}, H(S) = 1$$

(i) Type of system = 2.

$$K_p = \lim_{S \to 0} G(S) H(S)$$

$$= \lim_{S \to 0} \frac{10(S + 1)}{S^2(S + 2)(S + 10)}$$

$$= \infty$$

$$K_v = \lim_{S \to 0} S \cdot G(S) H(S)$$

$$= \lim_{S \to 0} \frac{10(S + 1)}{S^2(S + 2)(S + 10)}$$

$$= \infty$$

$$K_a = \lim_{S \to 0} S^2 G(S) H(S)$$

$$= \lim_{S \to 0} \frac{10(S + 1)}{S^2(S + 2)(S + 10)}$$

$$= \frac{10}{2 \times 10}$$

$$= 0.5$$

(ii) Steady state error for input $r(t) = 1 + 4t + \frac{t^2}{2}$

$$R(S) = \frac{1}{S} + \frac{4}{S^2} + \frac{1}{S^3}$$

$$= \frac{S^2 + 4S + 1}{S^3}$$

Steady state error $e_{ss} = \lim_{S \to 0} S \times E(S)$

$$= \lim_{S \to 0} \frac{S \, R(S)}{1 + G(S) H(S)}$$

$$= \lim_{S \to 0} \frac{\frac{S(S^2 + 4S + 1)}{S^3}}{\{1 + 10(S + 1)/S^2(S + 2)(S + 10)\}}$$

$$= 0.1$$

7. Find out the poles and zeros of the following: **(W-12) (4M)**

$$T.F. = \frac{S^4 - 4}{s(s^2 + 5s + 6)}$$

Ans. $\frac{(s + 2)(s - 2)}{s(s + 3)(s + 2)}$

Zeros: −2, +2

Poles: 0, −3, −2

8. Draw the standard test signals used in time domain analysis. State the mathematical expression in Laplace transform of each. **(W-12) (4M)**

Ans. Refer Sections 2.3.1, 2.3.2 and 2.3.3.

9. Why standard test signals are required? State Laplace representation of all standard trust signals. **(W-12) (4M)**

Ans. Refer Sections 2.3, 2.3.1, 2.3.2 and 2.3.3.

10. Explain the effect of damping on response of control system with neat sketch. **(W-12) (4M)**

Ans. Refer Section 2.6.2.

11. A system has open loop transfer function $G(s) = \dfrac{4}{s(s+2)(1+0.5s)}$ and unity feedback. Find the steady state error for r(t) = 3t. **(W-12) (4M)**

Ans. Similar to Problem 2.19.

12. Find out the type of the system and error coefficients for the system with $G(s)\,H(s) = \dfrac{(s+3)}{s(1+0.6s)(1+0.35s)}$. **(W-12) (4M)**

Ans. Similar to Problem 2.19.

13. Derive the expression of output response of a 1st order system for unit step input.

(W-12) (4M)

Ans. Refer Section 2.5.

★★★

STABILITY

About This Chapter ...

- Introduction to Stability
- Analysis of Stability
- Root Locations on s-plane
- Routh's Stability Criterion
- Numerical Problems

3.1 INTRODUCTION TO STABILITY

- After transient behaviour, if system reaches the steady state value, then system is called **stable system**.
- Stability of a closed-loop feedback system is very important to control system design.
- Unstable closed loop system has generally no practical value. So, it is very important to check whether the designed system is stable or not.
- If it is stable, then for what range of system parameter is it stable? How can it be made stable by varying the system parameters, if it is unstable? All these things are important while designing the system.
- The stability of a feedback system is related to the location of roots of the characteristic equation of the system transfer function.
- The Routh-Hurwitz Method is used for assessing system stability. In this technique, without actually computing roots of the characteristic equation; it gives the number of roots on right half of the s-plane. This method gives the range of system parameter for a stable system.
- Other methods to determine stability are:
    1. Root locus
    2. Nyquist criterion
    3. Bode plot
    4. Polar plot

3.2 THE CONCEPT OF STABILITY

QUESTION

1. Describe the concept of stability with respect to absolute, relative and marginal stability. **(4M)**

- Stability in a system implies that small changes in the system input, in initial conditions or in system parameters, do not result in large changes, in the system output.
- Stability is a very important characteristic of the transient performance of a system.
- The concept of stability can be understood by considering a right circular cone placed on a plane horizontal surface.
- If the cone is resting on its base and is tipped slightly it returns to its original position. **This position is called stable.**

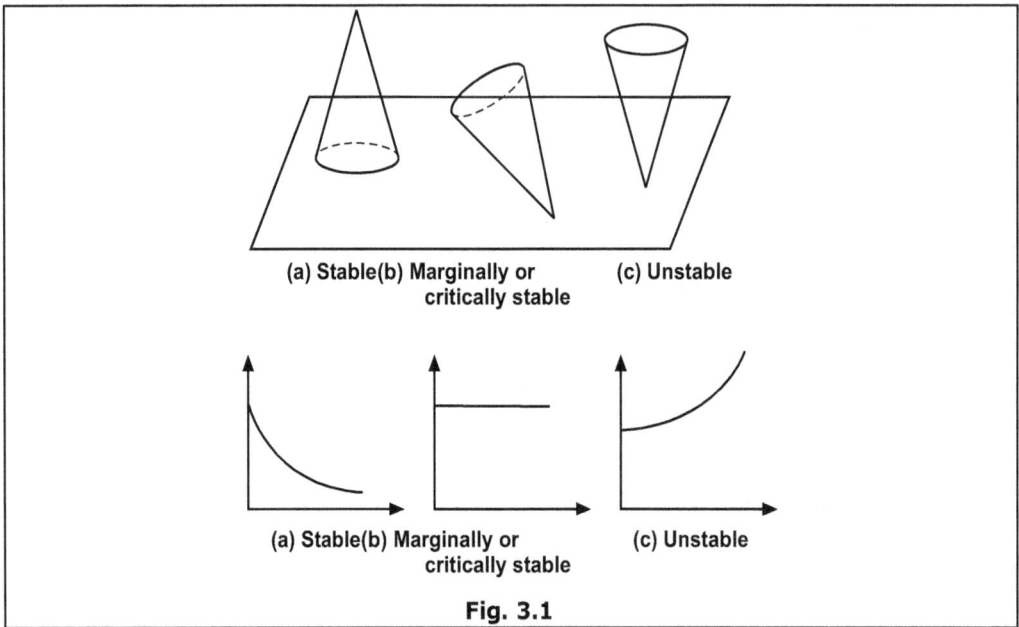

(a) Stable (b) Marginally or critically stable (c) Unstable

(a) Stable (b) Marginally or critically stable (c) Unstable

Fig. 3.1

- If the cone rest on its side and is displaced slightly it rolls and leaves the position. This is called **critically** or **marginally stable.**
- If the cone is placed on its tip and released, it falls onto its side and is called **unstable.**
- The stability of a dynamic system is defined in a similar manner.

3.3 ANALYSIS OF STABILITY

QUESTIONS

1. Explain in brief conditionally stable and relative stable system. **(4M)**
2. Define the terms: (i) Stable system, (ii) Unstable system, (iii) Critical system, (iv) Conditional stable system. **(4M)**
3. Explain the concept of marginal stability. Draw neat sketch to represent it on s-plane. **(4M)**

3.3.1 Stable System

To improve the system performance, every working system is designed to be stable within the boundaries of parameter variations permitted by the stability considerations.

A linear time-invariant system is stable if it satisfies the following conditions:

(i) When the system is excited by a bounded input, the output is also bounded.

(ii) In the absence of the input, the output tends to zero irrespective of the initial conditions.

Generally, stability concerns a free system relative to its transient behaviour.

Definition:

The system is stable if it produces a bounded output for a bounded input.

3.3.2 Unstable system

A linear time invarient system is unstable if the system is excited by a bounded input and produces an unbounded output response.

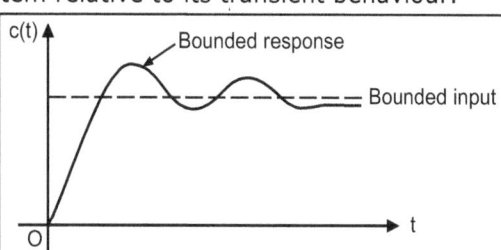

Fig. 3.2: Bounded Input Bounded Output for Stable System

i.e. once any bounded input is given, and system output goes on increasing and the designer does not have any control on it.

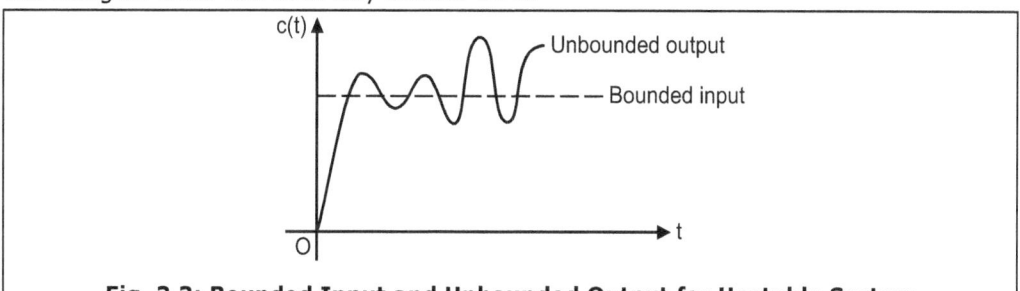

Fig. 3.3: Bounded Input and Unbounded Output for Unstable System

Definition:

If the system input is bounded, but the system output does not remain within the plus or minus 2% bound of the desired output, the system is said to be unstable.

For analysis and design purposes, we can classify the stability of control system as,

(i) *absolutely stable system,* and

(ii) *relatively* or *conditionally stable system.*

3.3.3 Absolutely Stable System

- *If a system is stable for all variations then it is called absolutely stable system.*
- If a linear time invariant system is excited by a bounded input, then the response of system is bounded and controllable.

However, 'absolute stability' refers only to the condition of whether the system is stable or not in 'yes' or 'no'.

3.3.4 Relatively Stable System

- Once the system is found to be stable it is of interest to determine how stable it is, and this degree of stability is a measure of relative stability.

Definition:

Relative stability is a quantitative measure of how fast the transients die out in the system.

- When the input is given to a linear time invariant system for a conditionally stable system its output is bounded.
- i.e. *the stability of system depends on the condition or parameter or inputs of the system, so also called **conditionally stable system.***

If it is required to find relative stability of system about a line $s = -\sigma_1$ i.e. all roots must lie to the left of the line $s = -\sigma_1$.

To determine this relative stability, substitute,

$$s = z - \sigma_1$$

If the new characteristic equation satisfies the Routh criterion, then it indicates that all the roots of the original characteristic equation are more negative than $-\sigma_1$.

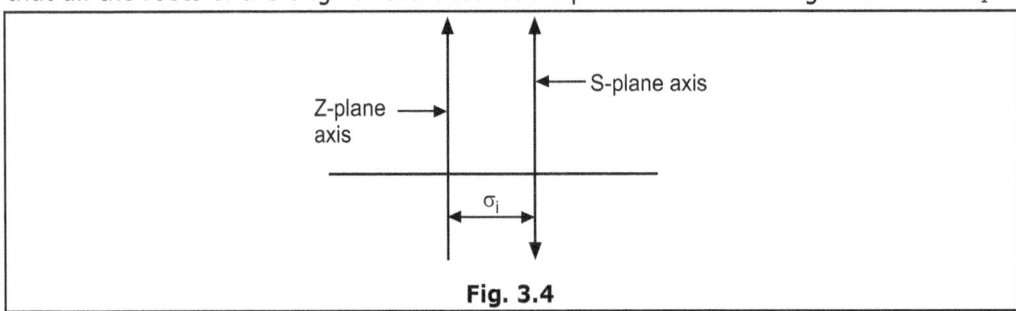

Fig. 3.4

3.3.5 Marginally or Limitedly Stable System (Critically)

- Sometimes, the system output is within ± 2% bound of the desired output.
- **However, the output of the system does not settle down to a constant value and keeps fluctuating within the desired output bounds. Such a system is said to be limitedly or marginally stable system.**
- The output usually oscillates in a finite range or remains steady at some value. Such systems are not stable as their response does not decay to zero. Also, they are not defined as unstable because their output does not go on increasing infinitely.

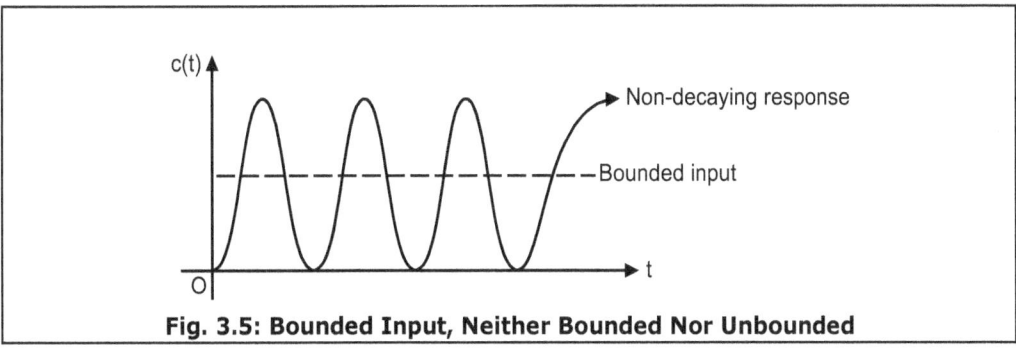

Fig. 3.5: Bounded Input, Neither Bounded Nor Unbounded

Definition:

If the output of the system oscillates within a finite range, such that it is neither a stable nor an unstable system, then it is called a *marginally or limitedly stable system*.

3.4 ROOT LOCATIONS IN S-PLANE FOR STABLE AND UNSTABLE SYSTEM

- There are various methods of determining the stability of any control system.
- The stability of linear time-invariant system can be determined by checking the locations of the roots of the characteristic equation of the system.
- For absolute stability, only the information on the characteristic equation root with respect to jω-axis of the s-plane is necessary.
- But it is not necessary to solve for the exact roots.
- **s-plane** contains imaginary and real axis.
- The imaginary axis divides the complex plane (s-plane) into two halfs, the left half and right half plane as shown in Fig. 3.6.

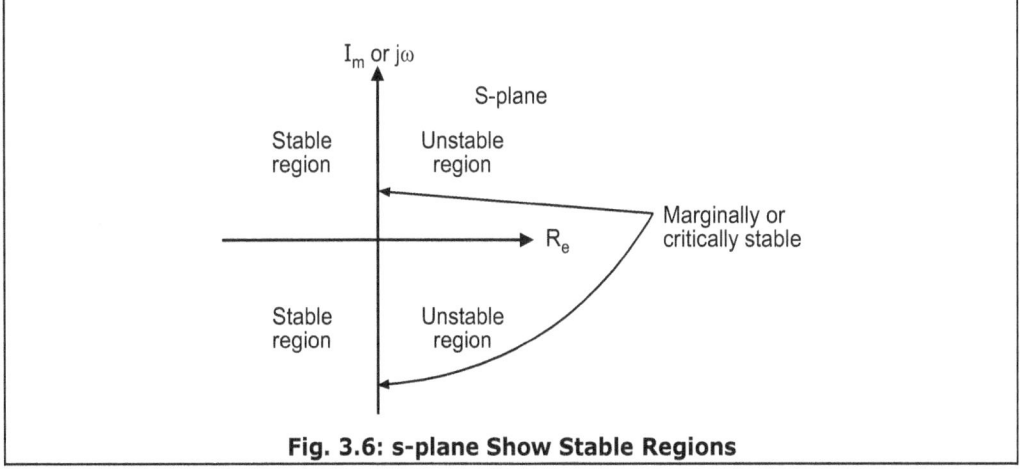

Fig. 3.6: s-plane Show Stable Regions

By referring Fig. 3.6.

Absolutely Stable System:

If all the roots of the characteristic equation lie on the left half of the s-plane i.e. if the real parts of all roots are negative, then the system is said to be absolutely stable.

Critically Stable System:

If the system has one or more pair of roots lying in the imaginary axis i.e. with real parts equal to zero and no roots lie on right half of the plane, the system is said to be critically or marginally or limitedly stable system.

Unstable System:

If one of the roots lies in the right half of the plane i.e. it has positive real parts, then the system is said to be unstable.

In case of complex systems, it is not always easy to determine the roots of the characteristic equation. In such a case, the Routh's and Hurwitz stability criterion is applied.

3.4.1 Special Cases

QUESTION

1. State advantages of Routh's stability criterion. **(4M)**

In applying the Routh's stability criterion, certain difficulties arise causing the breakdown of the Routh's test.

Case I: *'When the first term in any row of the Routh array is zero while the rest of the row has at least one non-zero term'.*

Because of the zero, terms in the next row becomes infinite value and Routh's test breaks down.

To overcome this difficulty, the following methods are used.

Method I:

Replace 0, by ϵ, a small positive number and proceed to evaluate the rest of the Routh array.

Take limit as $\epsilon \to 0$ from positive side for each first column term and check the sign changes.

3.5 ROUTH'S STABILITY CRITERION
(ROUTH'S HURWITZ CRITERION)

QUESTION

1. State and explain Routh Hurwitz stability criterion with suitable example. **(4M)**

This criterion is an algebraic method that provides information on the absolute stability of the linear time invarient system that has a characteristic equation with constant coefficients.

The criterion also tests the locations of the roots of the characteristic equations on the s-plane.

This criterion is based on arranging the coefficients of the characteristic equation into an array, called the Routh's array as –

Consider the characteristic equation –

$$q(s) = a_0 s^n + a_1 s^{n-1} + a_2 s^{n-2} + \ldots + a_{n-1} s + a_n = 0$$

Routh Array:

s^n	a_0	a_2	a_4	a_6	......
s^{n-1}	a_1	a_3	a_5	....	......
s^{n-2}	b_1	b_2	b_3	....	......
s^{n-3}	c_1	c_2	....	....	......
s^{n-4}	d_1	d_2			
$\vdots$	$\vdots$	$\vdots$			
$\vdots$	$\vdots$	$\vdots$			
s^2	e_1	a_n			
s^1	f_1				
s^0	a_n				

... (3.9)

The coefficients $b_1, b_2, \ldots$ are evaluated as,

$$b_1 = \frac{a_1 a_2 - a_0 a_3}{a_1}$$

$$b_2 = \frac{a_1 a_4 - a_0 a_5}{a_1}$$

This process is continued till we get a zero as the last coefficient in the third row. Similarly,

$$c_1 = \frac{b_1 a_3 - a_1 b_2}{b_1}$$

$$c_2 = \frac{b_1 a_5 - a_1 b_3}{b_1}$$

and

$$d_1 = \frac{c_1 b_2 - b_1 c_2}{c_1}$$

$$d_2 = \frac{c_1 b_3 - b_1 c_3}{c_1}$$

In the process of generating the Routh array, the missing terms are regarded as zero. Also all the elements of any row can be divided by positive constants.

Statement:

The Rouths stability criterion states that,

For a system to be stable, it is necessary and sufficient that each term of the first column of Routh array (equation 3.7) of its characteristic equation be positive if $a_0 > 0$. If this condition is not met, the system is unstable and number of sign changes of the terms of the first column of the Routh array corresponds to the number of roots of the characteristic equation in the right half of the s-plane.

The Rouths and Hurwitz criterion are equivalent as elements of the first column of the Routh array can be interpreted in terms of Hurwitz determinants as follows:

$$b_1 = \frac{a_1 a_2 - a_0 a_3}{a_1} = \frac{\begin{vmatrix} a_1 & a_0 \\ a_3 & a_2 \end{vmatrix}}{a_1} = \frac{\Delta_2}{\Delta_1}$$

Similarly,

$$c_1 = \frac{D_3}{D_2}$$

$$d_1 = \frac{D_4}{D_3}$$

Thus, the condition of positiveness of the Hurwitz determinants corresponds to the condition of positiveness of elements of the first column of the Routh array.

SOLVED EXAMPLES

Example 3.1: Consider the forth order system with the characteristic equation.

$$s^4 + 8s^3 + 18s^2 + 16s + 5 = 0$$

Solution: The Routh array for this system is,

s^4	1	18	5
s^3	8	16	0 (For the missing term)
s^2	$\frac{8 \times 18 - 1 \times 16}{8} = 16$	$\frac{8 \times 5 - 1 \times 0}{8} = 5$	
s^1	$\frac{16 \times 16 - 8 \times 5}{16} = 13.5$	0	
s^0	5		

The elements of first column are all positive and hence the system is **stable**.

Example 3.2: Consider the following characteristic equation

$$3s^4 + 10s^3 + 5s^2 + 5s + 2 = 0$$

Solution: The Routh array is given below.

s^4	3	5	2
s^3	10	5	0
s^2	$\frac{5 \times 10 - 3 \times 5}{10} = 3.5$	$\frac{10 \times 2 - 3 \times 0}{10} = 2$	0
s^1	$\frac{3.5 \times 5 - 10 \times 2}{3.5} = \frac{2.95}{3.5}$	0	
s^0	2		

All the elements in the first column are not positive. So, the system becomes **unstable**.

Example 3.3: Consider the given characteristic equation

$$s^5 + s^4 + 2s^3 + 2s^2 + 3s + 5 = 0$$

The Routh array is,

s^5	1	2	3
s^4	1	2	5
s^3	ε	-2	
s^2	$\dfrac{2\varepsilon + 2}{\varepsilon}$	5	
s^1	$\dfrac{-4\varepsilon - 4 - 5\varepsilon^2}{2\varepsilon + 2}$		
s^0	5		

(i) From the Routh array, the first element in 3rd row is 0. This is replaced by ε i.e. $\varepsilon \to 0$.

(ii) The first element in the 4th row is now $\dfrac{2\varepsilon + 2}{\varepsilon}$ which has a **positive sign** as $\varepsilon \to 0$.

(iii) The first element in the 5th row is now $\dfrac{-4\varepsilon - 4 - 5\varepsilon^2}{2\varepsilon + 2}$ which has a limiting value of -2 as $\varepsilon \to 0$.

From this we have found that there are two sign changes in the first column and hence the system is **unstable** having two poles at the right half of s-plane.

Method 2:

Another method to overcome this problem is to replace s by $\dfrac{1}{z}$ in the characteristic equation and rearranging, we get,

$$\left(\frac{1}{z}\right)^5 + \left(\frac{1}{z}\right)^4 + 2\left(\frac{1}{z}\right)^3 + 2\left(\frac{1}{z}\right)^2 + 3\left(\frac{1}{z}\right) + 5 = 0$$

Taking L.C.M.

$$5z^5 + 3z^4 + 2z^3 + 2z^2 + z + 1 = 0$$

The Routh array is,

z^5	5	2	1
z^4	3	2	1
z^3	$-\dfrac{4}{3}$	$-\dfrac{2}{3}$	
z^2	$\dfrac{1}{2}$	1	
z^1	2		
z^0	1		

Two sign changes in the first column indicate two roots in the right half of the s-plane. Hence, the system is **unstable**.

Case 2: When all the elements in any one row of Routh array is zero:

- The polynomials whose coefficients are the elements of the row just above the row of zero's the Routh array is called an **auxiliary equation.**
- This polynomial gives the number and location of root pairs of the characteristic equation which are symmetrically located in the s-plane. The *order of the auxiliary polynomial is always even.*
- Because of a zero in the array, the Routh's tests breaks down.
- This difficulty is overcome by replacing the row of zeros in the Routh's array by a row of coefficient of the polynomial generated by taking derivative of the auxiliary polynomial.
- **Advantages of Routh's Criterion:**
    1. Determines stability of closed loop system.
    2. Simple method.
    3. It progress systematically.
    4. Frequently used to determine absolute and relative stability of a system.
    5. Determines range of k for stable operation.
- **Disadvantages of Routh's Criterion:**
    1. Valid only for real coefficients of characteristic equation.
    2. Exact location of poles is not known.
    3. Only idea of stability known.
- **Applications of the Routh's Criterion:**
    1. Finding range of k for stable operation.
    2. Finding stability of system (stable or unstable).
    3. Position on s-plane.

SOLVED EXAMPLES

Example 3.4: Consider the sixth order system with the characteristic equation

$$s^6 + 2s^5 + 8s^4 + 12s^3 + 20s^2 + 16s + 16 = 0$$

Routh array is,

s^6	1	8	20	16
s^5	2	12	16	
s^4	2	12	16	
s^3	0	0	0	

The elements in s^3 row are zero, the Routh's test breaks down.

∴ Taking auxiliary equation for s^4 row.

$$A(s) = 2s^4 + 12s^2 + 16$$

The derivative of the polynomial w.r.t. s is,

$$\frac{d}{ds} A(s) = 8s^3 + 24s$$

Completing array,

s^6	1	8	20	16
s^5	2	12	16	0
s^4	2	12	16	0
s^3	8	24	0	
s^2	6	16	0	
s^1	2.67	0		
s^0	16			

No sign changes in the first column of new array.

∴ **The system is stable.**

By solving the roots of auxiliary equation,

$$2s^4 + 12s^2 + 16 = 0$$

Put $s^2 = x$

∴ $2x^2 + 12x + 16 = 0$

∴ $x = \dfrac{-12 \pm \sqrt{144 - 128}}{4} = -3 \pm 1$

∴ $x = -4, -2$ i.e. $s^2 = -2$

or $s = \pm j\sqrt{2}$ or $s^2 = -4$

∴ $s = \pm j2$

The root is located on imaginary axis.

∴ The system is **marginally stable.**

Example 3.5: Determine the range of k for which the system becomes stable. For given Fig. 3.7.

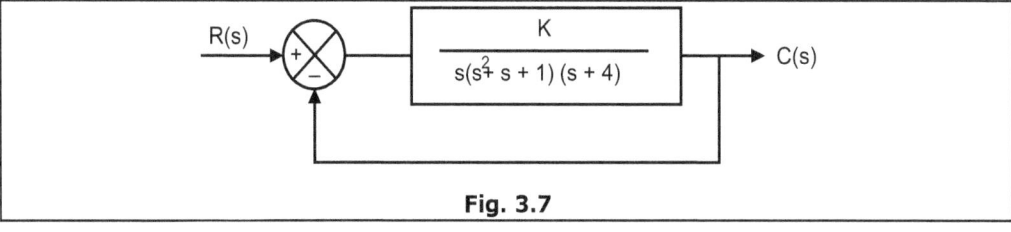

Fig. 3.7

Sol.: The closed-loop transfer function is,

$$\frac{C(s)}{R(s)} = \frac{k}{s(s^2 + s + 1)(s + 4) + k}$$

Thus, characteristic equation is,
$$s(s^2 + s + 1)(s + 4) + k = 0$$
or $\quad s^4 + 5s^3 + 5s^2 + 4s + k = 0$

The Routh array for this equation is,

s^4	1	5	k
s^3	5	4	
s^2	21/5	k	
s^1	$\dfrac{16.8 - 5k}{4.2}$	0	
s^0	k		

For a stable system, all signs of elements in the first column are positive.
Thus, condition of system stability requires
$$k > 0$$
and $\quad (16.8 - 5k) > 0$

Therefore, for stabiity, k should be in the range.
$$16.8 > k > 0$$

Example 3.6: By Routh's criterion, determine the stability of the system represented by the following characteristic equations. For systems found to be unstable, determine the number of roots of characteristic equation in the right half s-plane.

(a) $s^4 + 2s^3 + 8s^2 + 4s + 3 = 0$

Solution:

s^4	1	8	3
s^3	2	4	0
s^2	6	3	0
s^1	3	0	
s^0	3		

All the elements in the first column of Routh array are positive.

∴ System is **stable**.

(b) $s^5 + s^4 + 3s^3 + 9s^2 + 16s + 10 = 0$

Sol.: Routh array is,

s^5	1	3	16
s^4	1	9	10
s^3	−6	6	0
s^2	61/6	10	
s^1	$\dfrac{726}{61}$	0	
s^0	10		

Sign changes in the first column of array.

Thus, system is **unstable**.

Example 3.7: Determine the stability of the closed-loop system using Routh's criteria.

$$G(s) = \frac{2}{s(s+1)(s+2)}$$

Sol.: The transfer function of closed-loop T.F.

$$\frac{C(s)}{R(s)} = \frac{G(s)}{1 + G(s)H(s)} \qquad (H(s) = 1)$$

$$= \frac{\frac{2}{s(s+1)(s+2)}}{1 + \frac{2}{s(s+1)(s+2)} \cdot 1}$$

$$= \frac{2}{s(s+1)(s+2) + 2}$$

∴ The characteristic equation is,

$$1 + GH = s(s+1)(s+2) + 2 = 0$$
$$= s^3 + 3s^2 + 2s + 2 = 0$$

Routh array is,

s^3	1	2
s^2	3	2
s^1	4/3	0
s^0	2	

All the signs in first column of the array is positive. Thus, the system is **stable**.

Example 3.8: The loop transfer function of a unity feedback system is $\frac{k}{s(1+0.4s)(1+0.2s)}$. Find the restriction on k so that the closed-loop system is absolutely stable.

Solution: $$G(s) = \frac{k}{s(1+0.4s)(1+0.2s)}$$

The characteristic equation of a closed-loop system is,

$$1 + GH = 0$$
$$= s(1+0.4s)(1+0.2s) + k$$
$$= s(1 + 0.65s + 0.1s^2) + k$$
$$= s^3 + 6.5s^2 + 10s + 10k = 0$$

Routh array becomes,

s^3	1	10
s^2	6.5	10 k
s^1	$\frac{65 - 10k}{6.5}$	0
s^0	10k	

If the system is stable, there should be no pole lying on the right half of the s-plane.

i.e. No sign changes in the first column of array.

Hence,

$k > 0$ and $65 - 10k > 0$.

∴ The restriction on k is,

$$\boxed{0 < k < 6.5}$$

Example 3.9: Determine the stability by Hurwitz criterion.

$$s^3 + s^2 + s + 4 = 0$$

Solution: Highest term is s^3.

∴ Solve upto D_3 i.e. 3×3 determinants.

$$H = \begin{vmatrix} 1 & 4 & 0 \\ 1 & 1 & 0 \\ 0 & 1 & 4 \end{vmatrix}$$

$$D_1 = |1| > 0, \quad D_2 = \begin{vmatrix} 1 & 4 \\ 1 & 1 \end{vmatrix} = -3 < 0$$

$$D_3 = \begin{vmatrix} 1 & 4 & 0 \\ 1 & 1 & 0 \\ 0 & 1 & 4 \end{vmatrix} = 1(4-0) - 4(4-0) + 0 = 4 - 16 = -12$$

as D_2 is less than zero, system is unstable.

Example 3.10: Determine the values of k and b_1, so that the system whose open loop transfer function is

$$G(s) = \frac{k(s+1)}{s^3 + bs^2 + 3s + 1}$$

oscillates at a frequency of oscillations of 2 rad/sec. Assume unity feedback.

Solution: The characteristic equation is,

$$s^3 + bs^2 + 3s + 1 + k(s+1) = 0$$

or $s^3 + bs^2 + (k+3)s + k(k+1) = 0$

The Routh array is,

s^3	1	k + 3
s^2	b	k + 1
s^1	$(k+3) - \frac{(k+1)}{b}$	0
s^0	k + 1	

The system will have a sustained oscillations if row No. 3 is zero i.e.

$$\frac{b(k + 3) - (k + 1)}{b} = 0$$

i.e.
$$b = \frac{k + 1}{k + 3}$$

The subsidiary equation of row number 2 is,

$$bs^2 + (k + 1) = 0$$

$$s^2 = -\frac{(k + 1)}{b} = (j\omega)^2 = (j_2)^2 = -4$$

(∵ ω = 2 rad/sec)

Putting $b = \frac{k + 1}{4}$ in equation (1), we get,

$$\frac{k + 1}{4} = \frac{k + 1}{k + 3}$$

$$k + 3 = 4$$

∴ $k = 1$

$$b = \frac{k + 1}{4} = \frac{1 + 1}{4} = \frac{1}{2}$$

$$= 0.5$$

Example 3.11: Find out the conditions for stability for the systems whose characteristic equations are given below. The case where stability is suggested for real values of k. Determine the values of k which will cause sustained oscillations.

$$s^4 + 20s^3 + 224s^2 + 1240s + 2400 + k = 0$$

Solution: The Routh's array is,

s^4	1	224	2400 + k
s^3	20	1240	0
s^2	162	2400 + k	0
s^1	$1240 - \frac{(2400 + k)20}{162}$	0	
s^0	2400 + k		

For stability

2400 + k > 0 or k > −2400

Also $1240 - \frac{(2400 + k)}{162} > 0$ or k < 7644

The range of k for stability is,

−2400 < k < 7644

If k = 7644, then the first column is (1, 20, 162, 10044).

Example 3.12: The characteristic equation of a feedback control system is $s^3 + 3ks^2 + (k + 2) s + 4 = 0$. Determine the range of k for which the system is stable.

Solution: The Routh's array is,

s^3	1	k + 2
s^2	3k	4
s^1	$\dfrac{3k^2 + 6k - 1}{3k}$	
s^0	4	

For stability,

$$3k > 0 \text{ i.e. } k > 0$$

and $\quad 3k^2 + 6k - 4 > 0$ i.e. $k > -1 \pm 1.53$

i.e. $k > 0.53$

The range of k is thus,

$$\boxed{\infty > k > 0.53}$$

Example 3.13: The characteristic equation of a feedback control system is,

$$s^4 + 20ks^3 + 5s^2 + 10s + 15 = 0$$

Find the range of k for which the system is stable.

Solution: The Routh's array is,

s^4	1	5	15
s^3	20k	10	
s^2	$5 - \dfrac{1}{2k}$	15	
s^1	$10 - \dfrac{600 k^2}{10k - 1}$	0	
s^0	15		

The system will be stable, if,

$$20k > 0 \text{ i.e. } k > 0$$

$$5 - \frac{1}{2k} > 0 \text{ or } 5 > \frac{1}{2k} \text{ or } k > \frac{1}{10}$$

Also,

$$10 - \frac{600 k^2}{10k - 1} > 0$$

i.e. $-600 k^2 + 100k - 10 > 0$

gives a complex root. Hence, the system is unstable.

Examples on Relative Stability

Example 3.14: Consider the characteristic equation
$$s^3 + 7s^2 + 25s + 39 = 0$$
Check the relative stability for line $s = -1$.

Solution: Shift the origin at $s = -1$.

So substitute $s = z - 1$ where $\sigma = -1$.

$(z-1)^3 + 7(z-1)^2 + 25(z-1) + 39 = 0$

$z^3 - 3z^2 + 3z - 1 + 7z^2 - 14z + 7 + 25z - 25 + 39 = 0$

$z^3 + 4z^2 + 14z + 20 = 0$

The Rouths array for above equation is,

z^3	1	14
z^2	4	20
z^1	9	
z^0	20	

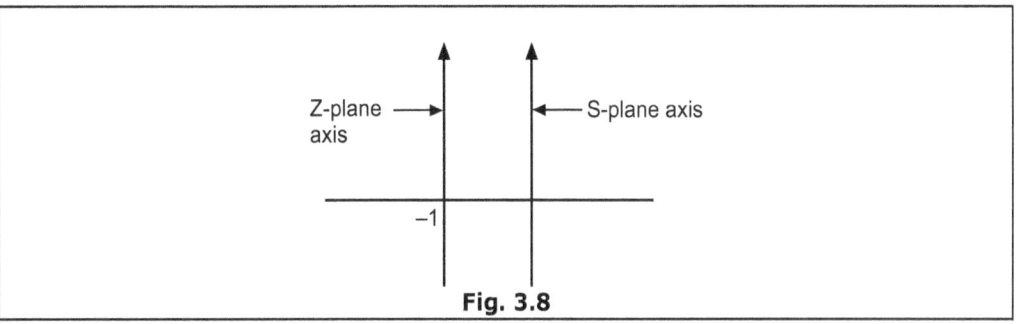

Fig. 3.8

All elements of the first column of Rouths array are positive; hence all roots of z polynomial lie on the left of $s = -1$ in the s-plane.

Example 3.15: A system has $G(s) = \dfrac{2}{s(s+1)(s+2)}$, $H(s) = 1$, with Routh's criterion, determine its relative stability about the line $s = -1$.

Solution: Determining stability about the line $s = -1$ means finding whether there is any root to the right of $s = -1$.

If there is any root on the right of $s = -1$ line, the system is unstable about the line $s = -1$.

The characteristic equation
$$1 + G(s)H(s) = 0$$

$\therefore \quad 1 + \dfrac{2}{s(s+1)(s+2)} = 0$

$s(s^2 + 3s + 2) + 2 = 0$

$s^3 + 3s^2 + 2s + 2 = 0$

To find stability about $s = -1$ replace s by $z - 1$
i.e. $s = z - 1$

$\therefore$ $(z - 1)^3 + 3(z - 1)^2 + 2(z - 1) + 2 = 0$

$z^3 - 3z^2 + 3z - 1 + 3z^2 - 6z + 3 + 2z - 2 + 2 = 0$

$z^3 - z + 2 = 0$

The Routh array is,

z^3	1	−1
z^2	0	2
z_1	∞	
z^0	2	

Since first element of z^2 row is 0, replace it by a small positive number ε.
The new routh array is,

z^3	1	−1	
z^2	ε	2	sign change
z^1	$\dfrac{-\varepsilon - 2}{\varepsilon}$	0	sign change
z^0	2		

where, $\displaystyle\lim_{\varepsilon \to 0} \dfrac{-\varepsilon - 2}{\varepsilon} = -\infty$.

There are two sign changes so two roots are on the right of $s = -1$ line. Hence, system is not stable about $s = -1$ line.

Example 3.16: Determine the range of values of k such that the characteristic equation has roots more negative than $s = -1$.

$s^3 + 3(k + 1)s^2 + (7k + 5)s + (4k + 7) = 0$

Solution: To find stability about $s = -1$.

Put $s = z - 1$.

$\therefore$ $(z - 1)^3 + 3(k + 1)(z - 1)^2 + (7k + 5)(z - 1) + (4k + 7) = 0$

$z^3 - 3z^2 + 3z - 1 + (3k + 3)(z^2 - 2z + 1) + (7k + 5)(z - 1) + (4k + 7) = 0$

$z^3 - 3z^2 + 3z - 1 + 3kz^2 - 6kz + 3k + 3z^2 - 6z + 3 + 7kz - 7k +$
$\hspace{8cm} 5z - 5 + 4k + 7 = 0$

$z^3 + 3kz^2 + (2 + k)z + 4 = 0$

The Routh array is,

z^3	1	$2 + k$
z^2	$3k$	4
z^1	$\dfrac{3k(k + 2) - 4}{3k}$	0
z^0	4	

System will be stable about −1 only if the following conditions are satisfied.

1. $3k > 0$

   i.e. $k > 0$

2. $\dfrac{3k(k+2) - 4}{3k} > 0$

$\therefore 3k(k+2) - 4 > 0$

$\therefore k^2 + 2k - 1.33 > 0$

$(k + 2.52)(k - 0.526) > 0$

$k > -2.52$ and $k > 0.526$

To make a system stable about $s = -1$, range of k should be

$\boxed{0.526 < k < \infty}$

Example 3.17: Check the stability of the following characteristic equation about the $s = -2$ line

$$q(s) = s^2 + 5s + 2$$

Solution: For checking stability about $s = -2$ line

Put $s = z - 2$

$\therefore \quad (z-2)^2 + 5(z-2) + 2 = 0$

$z^2 - 2z + 4 + 5z - 10 + 2 = 0$

$z^2 + 3z - 4 = 0$

The Routh array is,

z^2	1	− 4
z^1	3	0
z^0	− 4	← sign change

There is one sign change and hence system is unstable about line $s = -2$.

There is one root on the right half side of the line $s = -2$.

Example 3.18: The open-loop T.F. of a unity feedback control system is given as,

$$G(s) = \dfrac{k}{s(1 + Ts)}$$

Determine the values of k and T required, so that there are no roots to the right of the line $s = -a$.

Solution: Given: $G(s) = \dfrac{k}{s(1 + Ts)}$, $H(s) = 1$.

The characteristics equation is,
$$1 + G(s)H(s) = 0$$
$$1 + \frac{k}{s(1+Ts)} = 0$$
$$s + Ts^2 + k = 0$$
Put $\quad s = z - a$
$$\therefore T(z-a)^2 + (z-a) + k = 0$$
$$T(z^2 + 2az + a^2) + z - a + k = 0$$
$$Tz^2 + (1-2Ta)z + (Ta^2 - a + k) = 0$$

The Routh array is,

z^2	T	$Ta^2 - a + k$
z^1	$1 - 2Ta$	0
z^0	$Ta^2 - a + k$	

For a stable system,

1. $1 - 2Ta > 0$
    $Ta < 0.5$
    $$T < \frac{0.5}{a}$$

2. $Ta^2 - a + k > 0$
    $k > -(Ta^2 - a)$

EXAMPLES ON STABLE, UNSTABLE, MARGINALLY STABLE SYSTEMS

Example 3.19: Find the roots of the characteristic equation for systems whose open-loop transfer functions are given below. Locate the roots in the s-plane and indicate stability of each system.

(a) $G(s)H(s) = \dfrac{1}{(s+2)(s+4)}$

(b) $G(s)H(s) = \dfrac{5(s+3)}{s(s+3)(s+8)}$

(c) $G(s)H(s) = \dfrac{5}{s(s+2)}$

Solution:

(a) $\quad G(s)H(s) = \dfrac{1}{(s+2)(s+4)}$

Characteristic equation is $1 + G(s)H(s) = 0$.
$$1 + \frac{1}{(s+2)(s+4)} = 0$$
$$(s+2)(s+4) + 1 = 0$$
$$s^2 + 6s + 9 = 0$$
$$(s+3)(s+3) = 0$$
$$s_1 = -3 \text{ and } s_2 = -3$$

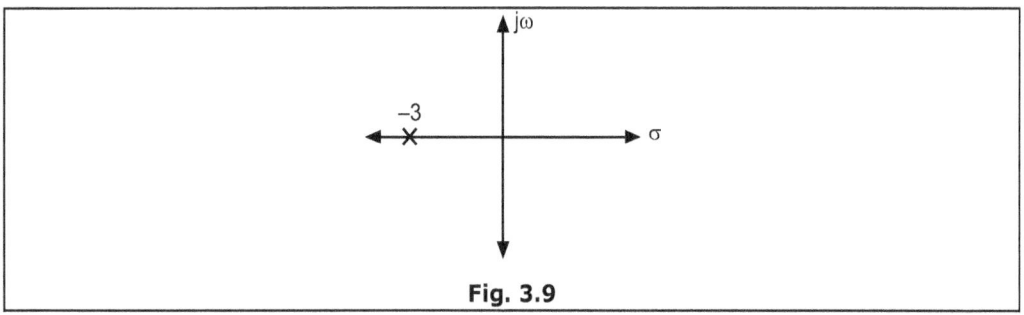

Fig. 3.9

Both roots lie on the left half of the s-plane as shown in Fig. 3.9. Hence, the system is stable.

(b) $\quad G(s) \cdot H(s) = \dfrac{5(s+3)}{s(s+3)(s+8)}$

Characteristic equation is,

$$1 + G(s)H(s) = 0$$

$\therefore \quad 1 + \dfrac{5(s+3)}{s(s+3)(s+8)} = 0$

$s(s^2 + 11s + 24) + 5s + 15 = 0$

$s^3 + 11s^2 + 29s + 15s = 0$

Roots of equation are,

$s_1 = -0.683$, $s_2 = -7.317$ and $s_3 = -3$.

All roots lie on the left half of the s-plane.

Hence the system is stable.

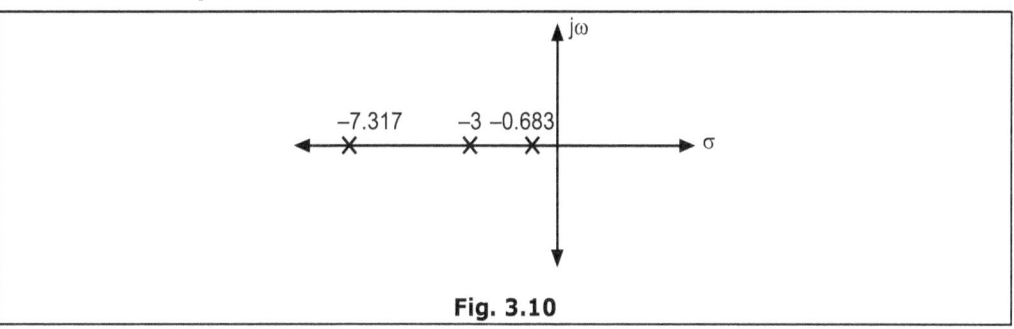

Fig. 3.10

(c) $\quad G(s)H(s) = \dfrac{5}{s(s+2)}$

The characteristic equation is,

$1 + G(s)H(s) = 0$

$1 + \dfrac{5}{s(s+2)} = 0$

$\therefore \quad 1 + \dfrac{5}{s(s+2)} = 0$

$$s^2 + 2s + 5 = 0$$
$$s_1 = -2 + j2$$
and $$s_2 = -2 - j2$$

The roots are complex conjugates and lie on the left half of the s-plane so that the system is stable.

Location of roots is shown in Fig. 3.11.

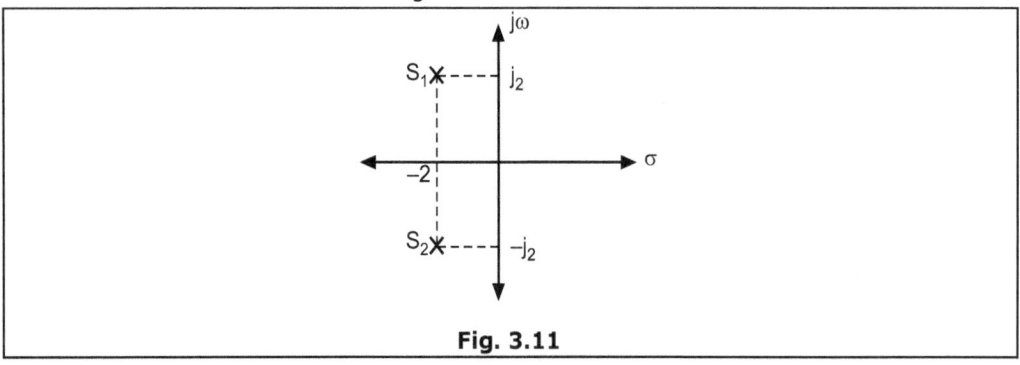

Fig. 3.11

Example 3.20: By means of the Routh criterion, determine stability of systems represented by the following characteristic equations. For a system to be unstable, determine the number of roots of the characteristic equation in the right half of the s-plane.

(i) $s^4 + 2s^3 + 8s^2 + 4s + 3 = 0$.

Solution: The Routh array is,

s^4	1	8	3
s^3	2	4	0
s^2	6	3	0
s^1	3	0	0
s^0	3		

All elements of the first column of Rouths array are positive. Hence, the system is stable.

(ii) $s^4 + 2s^3 + s^2 + 4s + 2 = 0$

Solution: The Routh array is,

	s^4	1	1	2
	s^3	2	4	0
sign change	s^2	-1	2	0
sign change	s^1	8	0	0
	s^0	2	0	0

One element of the first column of Routh array is negative and hence, the system is unstable.

Sign changes twice and hence there are two roots on the right of 's' plane.

(iii) $s^5 + s^4 + 3s^3 + 9s^2 + 16s + 10 = 0$.

Solution: The Routh array is,

s^5	1	3	16
s^4	1	9	10
s^3	−6	6	0
s^2	10	10	0
s^1	12	0	0
s^0	10	0	0

One element in the first column of Routh array is negative. **Hence, the system is unstable.**

There are two sign changes in the first column **hence there are two roots on the right half of the s-plane.**

(iv) $s^6 + 3s^5 + 5s^4 + 9s^3 + 8s^2 + 6s + 4 = 0$.

Solution: The Routh array is,

s^6	1	5	8	4
s^5	3	9	6	0
s^4	2	6	4	
s^3	0	0	0	
s^2				
s^1				
s^0				

All elements of the fourth row are zero. Hence write auxiliary equation i.e. polynomial of row.

$$A(s) = 2s^4 + 6s^2 + 4$$

Differentiating above equation with respect to s, we get,

$$\frac{dA(s)}{ds} = 8s^3 + 12s$$

The new Routh array is,

s^6	1	5	8	4
s^5	3	9	6	0
s^4	2	6	4	0
s^3	8	12	0	0
s^2	3	4	0	0
s^1	1.33	0	0	0
s^0	4	0	0	0

All elements of first column are positive. **Hence, the system is not unstable.**

To calculate the roots of the auxiliary equation,

$$2s^4 + 6s^2 + 4 = 0$$
$$s^4 + 3s^2 + 2 = 0$$

Put $s^2 = x$

$$x^2 + 3x + 2 = 0$$
$$(x + 2)(x + 1) = 0$$

∴ $x = -2$ and $x = -1$

i.e. $s^2 = -2$ and $s^2 = -1$

∴ $s = \pm j\sqrt{2}$ and $s = \pm j1$

There are two pairs of roots on the imaginary axis. **Hence, the system is limitedly stable.**

(v) $s^3 - 3s + 2 = 0$.

Solution: Since coefficient of s is negative and s^2 term is missing in the characteristic equation, the **system is unstable**. To determine roots in right half, Routh array is,

s^3	1	-3
s^2	0	2
s^1	∞	

Since the first element of second row is zero, Routh test breaks so substitute a small positive number ε in place of zero.

s^3	1	-3	
s^2	ε	2	
s^1	$\dfrac{-3\varepsilon - 2}{\varepsilon}$	0	← sign change
s^0	2		← sign change

The first element of s^1 row is $\dfrac{-3\varepsilon - 2}{\varepsilon}$.

∴ $\lim\limits_{\varepsilon \to 0} \dfrac{-3\varepsilon - 2}{\varepsilon} = \lim\limits_{\varepsilon \to 0} -3 - \dfrac{2}{\varepsilon}$

$= -\infty$

Since there are two sign changes in Rouths array, two roots lie on right of the 's' plane.

(vi) $s^5 + 2s^4 + 2s^3 + 4s^2 + 11s + 10 = 0$.

Solution: Routh array is,

s^5	1	2	11
s^4	2	4	10
s^3	0	6	0
s^2	∞		
s^1			
s^0			

Since the first element of 3rd row is zero, we have to substitute ε in place of zero.

∴ The new Routh array is,

s^5	1	2	11
s^4	2	4	10
s^3	ε	6	0
s^2	$\dfrac{4\varepsilon - 12}{\varepsilon}$	$\dfrac{10\varepsilon}{\varepsilon}$	0 ← sign change
s^1	$\dfrac{6(4\varepsilon - 12) - 10\varepsilon^2}{4\varepsilon - 12}$	0	0 ← sign change
s^0	10		

∴ $\displaystyle\lim_{\varepsilon \to 0} \dfrac{4\varepsilon - 12}{\varepsilon} = -\dfrac{12}{\varepsilon} \to$ Negative number

and $\displaystyle\lim_{\varepsilon \to 0} 6\dfrac{(4\varepsilon - 12)}{(4\varepsilon - 12)} = \lim_{\varepsilon \to 0}\dfrac{10\varepsilon^2}{4\varepsilon - 12} = 6 \to$ Positive number.

Since there are two sign changes in the first column of Routh array, the **system is unstable** and **two roots lie on the right half of the s-plane.**

(vii) $s^5 + s^4 + 2s^3 + 2s^2 + s + 1 = 0.$

Solution: The Routh Array is,

s^5	1	2	1
s^4	1	2	1
s^3	0	0	0
s^2			
s^1			
s^0			

Since all elements of third row are zero, write auxiliary equation i.e. polynomial of s^4 row.

∴ $\qquad A(s) = s^4 + 2s^2 + 1$

Differentiate A(s) w.r.t. s,

$$\dfrac{dA(s)}{ds} = 4s^3 + 4s$$

Replace zeros of s^3 row by coefficients of above equation. The new Routh array is,

s^5	1	2	1
s^4	1	2	1
s^3	4	4	0
s^2	1	1	0
s^1	0	0	0
s^0			

Again all elements of row s^1 are zero. Hence, write auxiliary equation of row s^2.
$$A(s) = s^2 + 1$$
Differentiate w.r.t. s,
$$\frac{dA(s)}{ds} = 2s$$

The new Routh array is,

s^5	1	2	1
s^4	1	2	1
s^3	4	4	0
s^2	1	1	0
s^1	2	0	0
s^0	1	0	0

Since all elements of first column are positive, **system is stable.**

Let us find the roots of first auxiliary equation. These are the roots of characteristic equation also.
$$A(s) = s^4 + 2s^2 + 1 = 0$$
Put $s^2 = x$
∴ $$A(s) = x^2 + 2x + 1 = 0$$
$$(x + 1)^2 = 0$$
∴ $$(x + 1)(x + 1) = 0$$
$$x + 1 = 0 \quad \text{or} \quad x + 1 = 0$$
$$x = -1 \quad \text{or} \quad x = -1$$
i.e. $$s^2 = -1 \quad \text{or} \quad s^2 = -1$$
$$s^2 = \pm j\sqrt{1} \quad \text{and} \quad s = \pm\sqrt{1}$$

These are repeated on the jω axis and hence system is **marginally** or **limitedly stable.**

Roots are shown in Fig. 3.12.

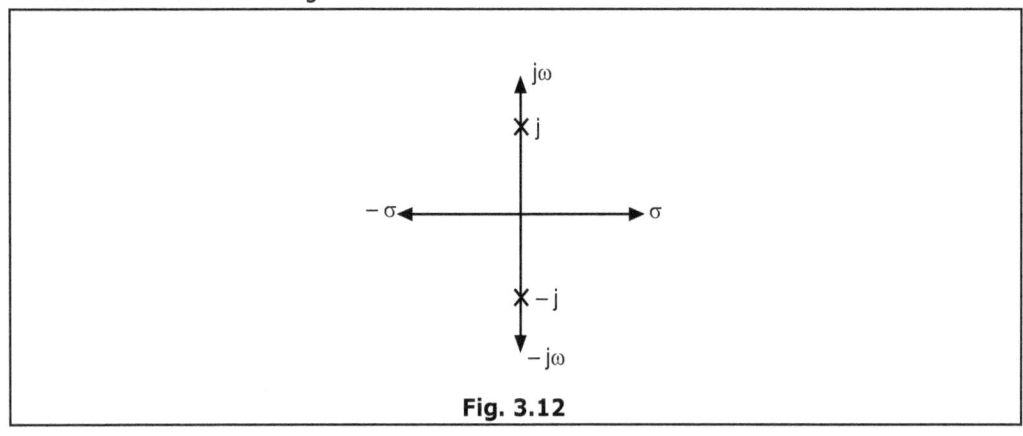

Fig. 3.12

(viii) $s^5 + s^4 + 4s^3 + 24s^2 + 3s + 63 = 0$.

Solution: The Routh array is,

s^5	1	4	3
s^4	1	24	63
s^3	−20	−60	0
s^2	21	63	0
s^1	0	0	0
s^0			

Since all elements of s^1 row are zero, we have to write auxiliary equation for s^2 row.

$$\therefore \quad A(s) = 21s^2 + 63$$

Differentiate w.r.t. s,

$$\therefore \quad \frac{dA(s)}{ds} = 42s$$

Replacing s^1 row by the coefficient of the above equation, the new Routh array is,

s^5	1	4	3	
s^4	1	24	63	
s^3	−20	−60	0	← sign change
s^2	21	63	0	← sign change
s^1	42	0	0	
s^0	63	0	0	

Two sign changes in the first column and hence the system is unstable.

Let us find out roots from the auxiliary equations.

$$21s^2 + 63 = 0$$
$$21s^2 = -63$$
$$s^2 = -3$$
$$s = \pm j\sqrt{3}$$

(ix) $s^6 + 4s^5 + 3s^4 − 16s^2 − 64s − 48 = 0$.

Solution: The Routh array is,

s^6	1	3	−16	−48
s^5	4	0	−64	0
s^4	3	0	−48	0
s^3	0	0	0	0

Since all elements of s^3 row are zero, we have to write auxiliary equation i.e. equation of s^4 row.

$$A(s) = 3s^4 - 48$$

Differentiate w.r.t. s

$$\frac{dA(s)}{ds} = 12s^3$$

The new Routh array is,

s^6	1	3	−16	−48
s^5	4	0	−64	0
s^4	3	0	−48	0
s^3	12	0	0	0
s^2	0	−48	0	0

Since the first element of s^2 row is zero, put ε in place of 0 and calculate the other elements. The new Routh array is,

s^6	1	3	−16	−48
s^5	4	0	−64	0
s^4	3	0	−48	0
s^3	12	0	0	0
s^2	ε	−48	0	0
s^1	$\frac{576}{\varepsilon}$	0		
s^0	−48			

As $\lim_{\varepsilon \to 0} \frac{576}{\varepsilon} = +\infty$

Therefore, sign changes in the first column, **hence the equation is unstable.**

Calculate roots from auxiliary equation.

$$A(s) = 3s^4 - 48 = 0$$

Put $s^2 = x$

$$= 3x^2 - 48 = 0$$
$$3x^2 = 48$$
$$x^2 = 16$$
∴ $\quad x = \pm 4$

$s^2 = 4$ and $s^2 = -4$

$s^2 = \pm 2$ and $s = \pm j_2$

Location of roots on s-plane shown in Fig. 3.13.

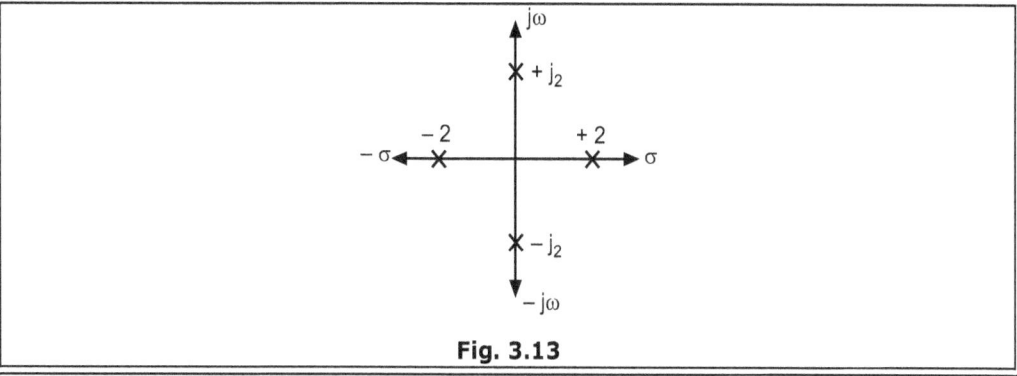

Fig. 3.13

Example 3.21: Find the range of values of k for the system to be stable.
$$q(s) = s^4 + 20\,ks^3 + 5s^2 + 10s + 15 = 0$$

Solution: The Routh array is,

s^4	1	5	15
s^3	20 k	10	0
s^2	$\dfrac{100\,k - 10}{20\,k}$	15	0
s^1	$\dfrac{\dfrac{10\,(100\,k - 1)}{20k} - 15 \times 20\,k}{\dfrac{100\,k - 10}{20\,k}}$	0	0
s^0	15	0	0

For a system to be stable all elements of first column must be positive.

∴ $\dfrac{100\,k - 10}{20\,k} > 0$

i.e. $10\,k - 1 > 0$

$k > 0.1$

and $\dfrac{1000\,k - 100 - 6000\,k^2}{100\,k - 10} > 0$

Value of k is complex and hence the system is always unstable.

Example 3.22: The characteristic equation for a certain feedback control system is given below. Determine the range of values of k for which the system is stable.
$$q(s) = s^4 + 4s^3 + 13s^2 + 36s + k = 0$$

Solution: The Routh array for the given characteristic equation is,

s^4	1	13	k
s^3	4	36	0
s^2	4	k	0
s^1	$\dfrac{144 - 4k}{4}$	0	0
s^0	k		

For a stable system, all elements of the first row must be zero.

Hence, $\dfrac{144 - 4k}{4} > 0$ and $k > 0$

i.e. $36 - k > 0$

∴ $k < 36$ and $k > 0$

∴ The range of k is,

$$\boxed{0 < k < 36}$$

Example 3.23: For the characteristic equation given below find the value of k for which the system is marginally or limitedly stable. Also find the frequency of oscillations for this value of k.

$$q(s) = s^4 + 22s^3 + 10s^2 + s + k = 0$$

Solution: System can be marginally stable if all elements of any row of Routh array are zero.

The Routh array for the given characteristic equation is,

s^4	1	10	k
s^3	22	1	0
s^2	9.95	k	0
s^1	$\dfrac{9.95 - 22k}{9.95}$	0	0
s^0	k	0	0

If we put $k = 0$ in s^0 row then $k = 0$ makes original equation as,

$$q(s) = s^4 + 22s^3 + 10s^2 + s = 0$$

i.e. s^0 term is missing and system will unstable so we cannot make $k = 0$.

∴ We have to substitute,

$$\dfrac{9.95 - 22k}{9.95} = 0$$ which makes all elements of s^1 row as zero.

∴ $9.95 - 22k = 0$

and $k_{mar} = \mathbf{0.4524}$

so that if $k = 0.4524$, system will be marginally or limitedly stable.

Frequency of oscillations is calculated from the roots of auxiliary equations. Here, the equation is equation of s^2 row.

∴ $A(s) = 9.95 s^2 + k_{mar} = 0$

∴ $9.95 s^2 + 0.4524 = 0$

$s^2 = -0.04526$

$$s^2 = \pm j0.2136$$

$= \pm j\omega$

where, ω is frequency of oscillations.

$$\boxed{\omega = 0.2132 \text{ rad/sec.}}$$

Example 3.24: Find the range of values of k for system to be stable.
$$q(s) = s^3 + 1040s^2 + 48{,}500s + 400000k = 0$$

Solution: The Routh array is,

s^3	1	48,500
s^2	1040	4,00,000 k
s^1	$\dfrac{50440000 - 400000\,k}{1040}$	0
s^0	4,00,000 k	0

For the system to be stable, all the coefficients in the first column of the Routh array must have the same sign so that,

$$\frac{50440000 - 400000\,k}{1040} > 0$$

or $\quad\quad\quad\quad k < 126.1$
and $\quad\quad\quad 4{,}00{,}000\,k > 0$
$\therefore\quad\quad\quad\quad\quad k > 0$
$\therefore$ Condition for stability of the overall system is,
$$\boxed{0 < k < 126.1}$$

Example 3.25: The closed loop transfer function of a unity feedback control system is given by,
$$G(s) = \frac{k}{(s+2)(s+4)(s^2 + 6s + 2s)}$$

By applying the Routh criterion, discuss the stability of the closed-loop system as a function of k. Determine the value of k which will cause sustained oscillations in the closed loop system. What are the corresponding oscillation frequencies?

Solution: Given: $G(s) = \dfrac{k}{(s+2)(s+4)(s^2 + 6s + 2s)}$, $H(s) = 1$

First find the characteristic equation $1 + G(s)\,H(s) = 0$

i.e. $1 + \dfrac{k}{(s+2)(s+4)(s^2 + 6s + 25)} = 0$

$\therefore\ (s+2)(s+4)(s^2 + 6s + 25) + k = 0$
$\quad (s^2 + 6s + 8)(s^2 + 6s + 25) + k = 0$
$\quad s^4 + 12s^3 + 69s^2 + 198s + (200 + k) = 0$

The Routh array is,

s^4	1	69	200 + k	
s^3	12	198	0	
s^2	52.5	200 + k	0	
s^1	$\dfrac{10395 - 12\,(200 + k)}{52.5}$	0	0	
s^0	(200 + k)	0	0	

For the system to be stable, it must satisfy the following conditions.

$$200 + k > 0$$
$$k > -200$$

But k cannot be negative, hence k > 0.

and $10395 - 12 \times 200 - 12k > 0$

$$12k < 7995$$
$$k < 666.25$$

i.e. the range of k for a stable system is,

$$\boxed{0 < k < 666.25}$$

Marginally Stable:

For sustained oscillations, system should be marginally stable so make all elements of s^1 row zero.

$$\therefore 10395 - 12(200 + k) = 0$$

$$k_{mar} = 666.25$$

To find frequency of oscillations, we have to write auxiliary equation for s^2 row.

i.e.
$$A(s) = 52.5s^2 + (200 + k) = 0$$
$$= 52.5s^2 + (200 + 666.25) = 0 \quad [\because \text{Put, } k_{max} = 666.25]$$
$$= 52.5s^2 + 866.25 = 0$$
$$= 52.5s^2 + 866.25 = 0$$

$\therefore$
$$s^2 = -16.5$$
$$s = \pm j4.06$$

Compare with $s = j\omega$. (Here, $\omega = -4.06$)

But ω cannot be negative.

Hence, frequency of oscillations is 4.06 rad/sec.

Example 3.26: The open loop transfer function of a feedback system is,

$$G(s)H(s) = \frac{k(s+5)}{s(1+Ts)(1+2s)}$$

Parameters k and T are represented on a plane with k on X-axis and T on Y-axis. Determine the region on which a closed loop system is stable.

Solution: $G(s)H(s) = \dfrac{k(s+5)}{s(1+Ts)(1+2s)}$

The characteristic equation is,

$$1 + G(s)H(s) = 0$$
$$1 + \frac{k(s+5)}{s(1+Ts)(1+2s)} = 0$$

$s(1 + Ts)(1 + 2s) + k(s + 5) = 0$

$s(1 + 2s + Ts + 2Ts^2) + ks + 5k = 0$

$2Ts^3 + (2 + T)s^2 + (k + 1)s + 5k = 0$

The Routh array is,

s^3	$2T$	$k + 1$
s^2	$T + 2$	$5k$
s^1	$\dfrac{(T + 2)(k + 1) - 10kT}{T + 2}$	0
s^0	$5k$	0

For a stable system, all elements of the first column must be positive, hence,

$$5k > 0$$

i.e. $\quad k > 0$

and $\quad \dfrac{(T + 2)(k + 1) - 10kT}{T + 2} > 0$

$(T + 2)(k + 1) - 10kT > 0$

$kT + T + 2k + 2 - 10kT > 0$

$2k + T + 2 - 9kT > 0$

$$k < \dfrac{T + 2}{9T - 2}$$

For positive values of T and k, we get the graph shown in Fig. 3.14.

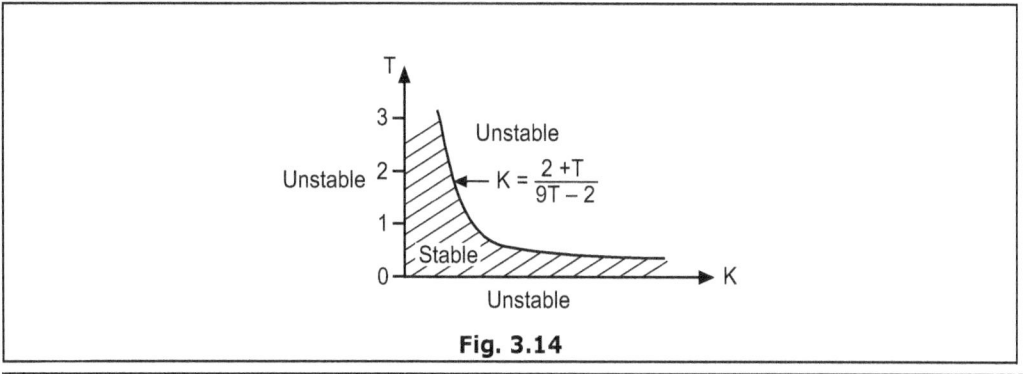

Fig. 3.14

Example 3.27: A negative feedback system has a loop transfer function.

$$G(s)H(s) = \dfrac{k(s + 2)}{s(s - 1)}$$

(i) Find the value of gain when ξ of the closed loop root is equal to 0.707.

(ii) Find the value of the gain when the closed loop system has two roots on the imaginary axis.

Solution: Characteristic equation is,

$$1 + G(s)H(s) = 0$$

$$1 + \frac{k(s+2)}{s(s-1)} = 0$$

$$s^2 - s + ks + 2k = 0$$

$$\therefore s^2 + (k-1)s + 2k = 0$$

(i) $\xi = 0.707$, $k = ?$

Compare characteristic equation with standard equation $s^2 + 2\xi\omega_n s + \omega_n^2 = 0$

We get, $\omega_n^2 = 2k$

$\therefore \omega_n = \sqrt{2k}$

and $2\xi\omega_n = (k-1)$

$$\xi = \frac{k-1}{2\sqrt{2k}} \qquad (\because \omega_n = \sqrt{2k})$$

$$\xi \times 2\sqrt{2k} = k - 1$$

$$0.707 - 2\sqrt{2k} = k - 1$$

$$1.414 \times \sqrt{2k} = k - 1 \text{ (Square both sides)}$$

$$1.99(2k) = k^2 - 2k + 1$$

$$k^2 - 6k + 1 = 0$$

$\therefore$ $\boxed{k = 0.17}$ and $\boxed{k = 5.82}$

If we take $k = 0.17$, ξ is negative; hence we have to consider **k = 5.82**.

The Routh array for equation $s^2 + (k-1)s + 2k = 0$ is,

s^2	1	2k
s^1	k - 1	0
s^0	2k	

When system has roots on the imaginary axis, then the system becomes marginally stable and hence one of the row of Routh array must have all elements zero.

$\therefore$ $k - 1 = 0$

$$k = 1$$

The auxiliary equation is,

$$s^2 + 2k = 0$$

$\therefore$ $k = 1$

$\therefore$ $s^2 + 2 = 0$

$$s^2 = -2$$

$$s = \pm j\sqrt{2}$$

so that the closed loop system has $\pm j\sqrt{2}$ roots on the imaginary axis, then the value of k is 1.

Example 3.28: A system oscillates with frequency ω, if it has poles at s = ± jω and no poles in the right half of s-plane. Determine the values of k and a, so that the system shown in Fig. 3.15 oscillates at a frequency 2 rad/sec.

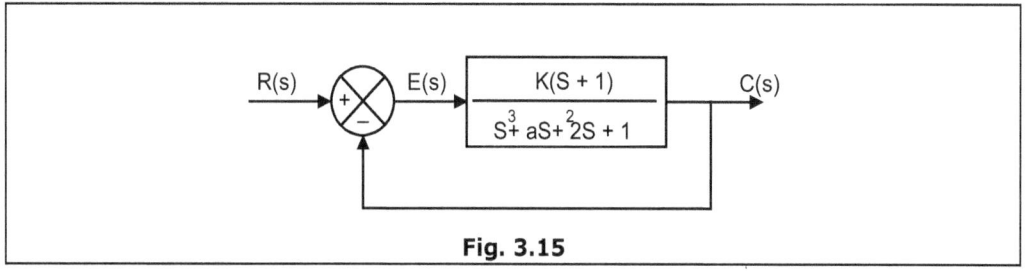

Fig. 3.15

Solution: From Fig. 3.15,

$$G(s) = \frac{k(s+1)}{s^3 + as^2 + 2s + 1}, \quad H(s) = 1$$

The characteristic equation is,

$$1 + G(s)H(s) = 0$$

$$1 + \frac{k(s+1)}{s^3 + as^2 + 2s + 1} = 0$$

$$s^3 + as^2 + 2s + 1 + ks + k = 0$$

$$s^3 + as^2 + (2+k)s + (1+k) = 0$$

The Routh array is,

s^3	1	2 + k	0
s^2	a	1 + k	0
s^1	$\frac{a(2+k) - (1+k)}{a}$	0	0
s^0	1 + k	0	0

It is given that the system has poles on jω axis only, hence the system is marginally stable.

To calculate roots, make the elements of s^1 row zero.

$$\therefore \quad \frac{a(2+k) - (1+k)}{a} = 0$$

$$a(2+k) = 1+k$$

$$a = \frac{1+k}{2+k}$$

The auxiliary equation i.e. equation of s^2 row is,

$$A(s) = as^2 + (1+k) = 0$$

$$as^2 = -(1+k)$$

$$s^2 = -\frac{k+1}{a} \qquad \left(\text{Put } a = \frac{1+k}{2+k}\right)$$

$$= -\frac{k+1}{\frac{1+k}{2+k}}$$

∴ $s^2 = -(2+k)$

∴ $s = \pm j\sqrt{k+2} = \pm j\omega$

∴ $j\omega = j\sqrt{k+2}$

∴ $\omega = \sqrt{k+2}$

But $\omega = 2$ rad/sec. given.

∴ $2 = \sqrt{k+2}$

$4 = k+2$ (Squaring above term)

∴ $\boxed{k = 2}$

and $a = \frac{k+1}{k+2}$

$a = \frac{3}{4} = 0.75$

so that to oscillate a system at 2 rad/sec. **k = 2 and a = 0.75**.

Example 3.29: Determine the stability of the system, whose open loop transfer function has poles at s = 0, s = −1 and s = − 4 and zero at s = − 2, gain k of forward path is 10.

Solution: Given: Poles at G(s) H(s) are at s = 0, s = − 1 and s = − 4 and zero at s = − 2, k = 10.

∴ $G(s)H(s) = \dfrac{10(s+2)}{s(s+1)(s+4)}$

The characteristic equation,

$1 + G(s)H(s) = 0$

∴ $1 + \dfrac{10(s+2)}{s(s+1)(s+4)} = 0$

$s(s+1)(s+4) + 10(s+2) = 0$

$s(s^2 + 5s + 4) + 10s + 20 = 0$

$s^3 + 5s^2 + 14s + 20 = 0$

The Routh array is,

s^3	1	14
s^2	5	20
s^1	10	0
s^0	20	

All elements in the first column of Routh array are positive.
Hence, the system is stable.

Example 3.30: A feedback control system has a characteristic equation

$$s^3 + (1 + k)s^2 + 10s + (5 + 15k) = 0$$

The parameter k must be positive. What is the maximum value k can assume before the system becomes unstable ? When k is equal to the maximum value, the system oscillates. Determine the frequency of oscillation.

Solution: The given characteristic equation is,

$$s^3 + (1 + k)s^2 + 10s + (5 + 15k) = 0$$

Routh array is,

s^3	1	10	0
s^2	$(1 + k)$	$5 + 15k$	0
s^1	$\dfrac{10(1 + k) - (5 + 15k)}{(1 + k)}$	0	0
s^0	$5 + 15k$	0	0

For the system to be stable, conditions are,

$$5 + 15k > 0$$
$$k > -1.33 \qquad \text{(But k cannot be negative)}$$

and $10(1 + k) - (5 + 15k) > 0$

$$10 + 10k - 5 - 15k > 0$$
$$5 - 15k > 0$$
$$k < 1$$

So the range of k for the system to be stable,

$$\boxed{0 < k < 1}$$

Maximum value of k is 1.

When k = 1, system oscillates.

So that auxiliary equation is equation of row s^2 with k = 1.

i.e. $\qquad A(s) = 2s^2 + 20$

∴ $\qquad s^2 = -10$

$$s = \pm j\sqrt{10}$$
$$= j\omega$$

∴ $\qquad \omega = \sqrt{10}$ rad/sec. frequency of oscillations.

Example 3.31: Examine the stability of (S-07)
$$s^4 + 6s^3 + 26s^2 + 56s + 80 = 0 \text{ by Routh's criterion}$$
Solution: Characteristics equation is,

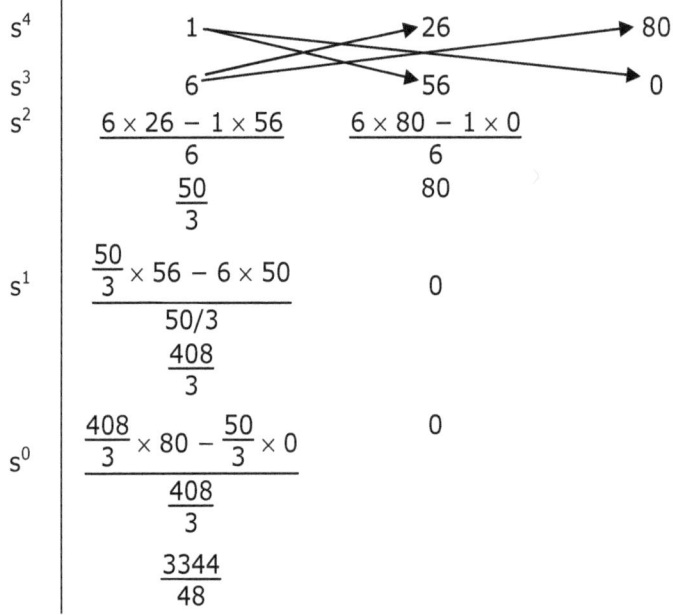

All elements in the first column are positive. Thus, the system is stable.

Example 3.32: Find the restrictions on k, so that the system whose transfer function is given below is absolutely stable. (S-08)

$$G(s) = \frac{k}{s(1 + 0.55)(1 + 0.1s)}$$

$$H(s) = 1$$

Solution: The characteristic equation of the closed-loop system is,

$$1 + GH = 0$$

$$= 1 + \frac{k}{s(1 + 0.5s)(1 + 0.1s)} 1$$

$$= s(1 + 0.5s)(1 + 0.1s) + k$$

$$= (s + 0.5s^2)(1 + 0.1s) + k$$

$$= 0.05s^3 + 0.6s^2 + s + k$$

Routh array becomes,

s^3	0.05	1
s^2	0.6	k
s^1	$\dfrac{0.6 - 0.05k}{0.6}$	0
s^0	k	

If the system is stable, there should not be any pole lying on the right half of the s-plane.

    i.e. no sign changes in the first column of array.
Hence,   k > 0 and 0.6 − 0.005 > 0
∴   The restriction on k is,

$$\boxed{0 < k < 0.6}$$

Example 3.33: A unity feedback system is characterized by the open loop transfer function $G(s) = \dfrac{k(s + 13)}{s(s + 3)(s + 7)}$.

Using Routh criteria, calculate the range of values of k for the system to be stable.   **(S-09, S-12) (8M)**

Solution: Given: $G(s) = \dfrac{k(s + 13)}{s(s + 3)(s + 7)}$

$$H(s) = 1$$

The characteristic equation of the closed loop system is,
$$1 + G(s)H(S) = 0$$
$$1 + \dfrac{k(s + 13)}{s(s + 3)(s + 7)} = 0$$
$$s(s + 3)(s + 7) + k(s + 13) = 0$$
$$s^3 + 10s^2 + (21 + k)s + 3k = 0$$

Routh array becomes,

s^3	1	21 + k	0
s^2	10	13k	0
s^1	$\dfrac{10(21 + k) - 13k}{10}$		
s^0	3k		

For a stable system, no sign changes in first column.
Hence, k > 0 and 210 + 7k > 0

$$\boxed{0 < k < -30} \quad \begin{bmatrix} \therefore\ 210 > -7k \\ \therefore\ k > -30 \end{bmatrix}$$

Example 3.34: By means of Rouths criteria, determine the stability of the system represented by the characteristics equation
$$s^4 + 2s^3 + 8s^2 + 4s + 3 = 0 \quad\quad \text{(4M)}$$

Solution: The given characteristic equation,
$$s^4 + 2s^3 + 8s^2 + 4s + 3 = 0$$

The Routh array for this equation is,

s^4	1	8	3
s^3	2	4	0
s^2	6	3	
s^1	3	0	
s^0	3		

All terms in the first columns are positive. **Hence, the given system is stable.**

Important Points

- The **system is stable** if it produces a bounded output for a bounded input.
- A linear time-invariant system is **unstable** if the system is excited by bounded input and produces an unbounded output response.
- If the system input is bounded, but the system output does not remain within the plus or minus 2% bond of the desired output, the system is said to be **unstable**.
- If a system is stable for all variations then it is called **absolutely stable system.**
- **Relative stability** is a quantitative measure of how fast the transient die out in the system.
- The output of the system does not settle down to a constant value and keep fluctuating within the desired output bounds. Such a system is said to be **limitedly** or **marginally stable system.**
- **s-plane** contains imaginary and real axis.
- If all the roots of the characteristic equation i.e. on the left half of the s-plane, then the system is said to be **absolutely stable.**
- If the system has one or more pair of roots lying in the imaginary axis and no roots on the right half of the plane, the system is said to be **critically** or **marginally** or **limitedly stable.**
- If one of the roots in the right half of the plane i.e. it has positive real parts, then the system is said to be **unstable.**
- The criterion based on ordering the coefficients of the characteristics equation into array is called the **Routh's array.**
- **Routh's stability criterion** states that, for a system to be stable, it is necessary and sufficient that each term of first column of Routh array of its characteristics equation be positive if $a_0 > 0$. If this condition is not met, the system is unstable and number of the Routh array corresponds to the number of roots of the characteristic equation of the right half of the s-plane.
- The polynomials whose coefficients are the elements of the row just above the zero of the zero's Routh array is called an **auxiliary equation.**

Practice Questions

1. State the concept of stability.
2. Define:
   (i) Stable,

(ii) Unstable,

(iii) Absolutely stable,

(iv) Relatively stable system.

3. State the Routh's criterion.

4. Test whether the following unity feedback system whose open loop T.F. is, $G(s) = \dfrac{2}{s(s+1)(s+2)}$ is stable or not by Routh's stability criterion.

5. Determine the stability of the system by Routh's criterion, whose characteristic equation is,

    $s^4 + 2s^3 + 8s^2 + 4s + 3 = 0$

6. Determine the range of k for the stability of unity feedback system whose open loop transfer function is,

    $$G(s) = \dfrac{k}{s(s+1)(s+2)}$$

7. Define: (i) Absolutely Stable system, (ii) Relatively Stable System, (iii) Marginally Stable System.

Previous Year MSBTE Questions and Answers (As Per 'E' Scheme)

1. Explain the concept of marginal stability. **(S-11) (4M)**

Ans. Refer Section 3.3.5.

2. Define the terms:

    (i) Stable system, (ii) Unstable system, (iii) Critical stable system, (iv) Conditionally stable system. **(S-12) (4M)**

Ans. Refer Section 3.3.1, 3.3.2 and 3.3.5.

3. Consider fifth order system with characteristic equation given by

    $S^5 + S^4 + 2S^3 + 2S^2 + 3S + 5 = 0$ **(S-12) (8M)**

Ans. Similar to Example 3.20 (vii).

4. A system has

    $G(S) H(S) = \dfrac{K(S+13)}{S(S+3)(S+7)}$

    where, K is positive.

    Determine the range of K values for system stability. **(S-12) (8M)**

Ans. Refer Example 3.33.

5. Explain the concept of marginal stability. Draw sketch to represent it on s-plane.

(W-12) (4M)

Ans. Refer Section 3.3.5.

6. For the system with characteristic equation.

   $s^4 + 6s^3 + 21s^2 + 36s + 20 = 0$, find the stability of the system with Routh's stability criterion.

(W-12) (4M)

Ans. Similar to Problem 3.20.

7. State any four advantages of frequency response analysis. **(W-12) (4M)**

Ans. Refer Section 3.5.

8. Find the range of K for stability of a unity feedback system with:

   $G(s) = \dfrac{K}{s(s+4)(s^2+3s+2)}$ **(W-12) (8M)**

Ans. Refer Section 3.32.

✱✱✱

FREQUENCY RESPONSE

About This Chapter ...

After reading this chapter students can understand –
- Introduction
- Frequency Response Specifications
- Frequency Response of a Closed Loop System
- Methods Used in Frequency Response
- Advantages and Disadvantages of Frequency Response
- Numerical Problems

4.1 INTRODUCTION

- Consider a linear system with a sinusoidal input.
$$r(t) = A \sin \omega t$$
- Under steady-state, the steady state output may be written as,
$$C(t) = B \sin (\omega t + \phi)$$
- **The magnitude and phase relationship between the sinusoidal input and steady state output of a system is known as frequency response.** Whereas in linear time invariant systems, the frequency response is independent of the amplitude and phase of the input signal.

Definition:

Frequency response of a system is defined as the steady state response of the system to a sinusoidal input signal.

The frequency response test on a system or a component is performed by keeping the amplitude A fixed and determining B and ϕ for a suitable range of frequency.

The frequency response is easily evaluated from the sinusoidal transfer function which can be obtained by replacing s with $j\omega$ in the system transfer function T(s).

The transfer function $T(j\omega)$ obtained, is a complex function of frequency and has both magnitude and phase angle. These characteristics are then represented by graphical plots. There are various graphical techniques to represent the sinusoidal transfer function $T(j\omega)$.

The frequency response test is not recommended for systems with a very large time constant.

The system transfer function can be converted to a frequency response function, by substituting $s = j\omega$.

Thus, the overall transfer function is,

$$T(s) = \frac{C(s)}{R(s)} = \frac{G(s)}{1 + G(s) H(s)} \quad \ldots (4.1)$$

$$T(j\omega) = \frac{C(j\omega)}{R(j\omega)} = \frac{G(j\omega)}{1 + G(j\omega) H(j\omega)} \quad \ldots (4.2)$$

The transfer function thus, obtained is a complex function of frequency and has both a magnitude and a phase angle. These characteristics are represented by graphical plots.

4.2 FREQUENCY RESPONSE SPECIFICATIONS

QUESTIONS

1. Define the following frequency response specifications :
   (i) Cut-off frequency, (ii) Resonant frequency, (iii) Gain-cross-over frequency, (iv) Phase-cross-over frequency **(4M)**
2. Define the following terms related with frequency response :
   (i) Resonant frequency, (ii) Cut-off frequency, (iii) Gain margin, (iv) Phase margin. **(8M)**

In the design of linear control systems, using the frequency domain methods, it is necessary to define a set of specifications. The frequency response is shown in Fig. 4.1.

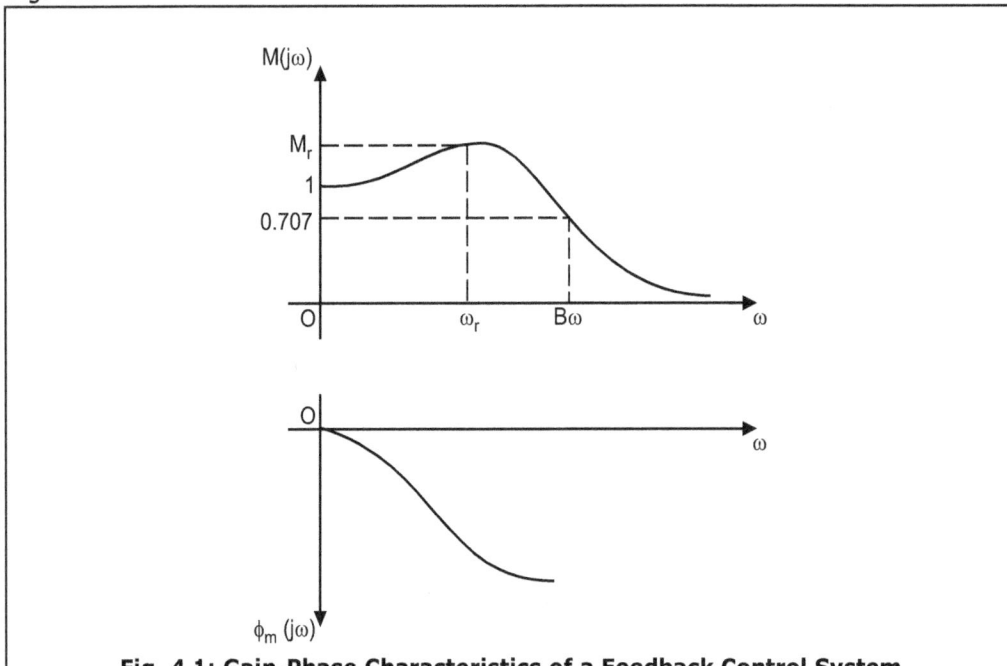

Fig. 4.1: Gain-Phase Characteristics of a Feedback Control System

The frequency domain specifications are –

1. **Peak Response M_r:**

   It is defined as the maximum value of $|M(j\omega)|$ shown in Fig. 4.1.

   The magnitude of M_r gives an indication of the relative stability of a stable feedback control system.

   A large M_r corresponds to a large maximum overshoot of step response in the transient response.

   M_r ranges between 1.1 and 1.5.

2. **Resonant Frequency ω_r:**

   This is the frequency at which the resonance peak M_r occurs. This indicates the speed of the transient response.

3. **Bandwidth:**

   It is defined as the range of frequency at which the magnitude of $|M(j\omega)|$ drops to 70.7% of its zero frequency value or 3 dB from the zero frequency value.

   Large bandwidth corresponds to a faster rise time and when bandwidth is small, signals of relatively low frequencies are passed and the time response will be slow.

4. **Cut-off Rate:**

   It is the slope of the log-magnitude curve near the cut-off frequency.

   The cut-off rate indicates the stability of the system to distinguish the signal from noise.

5. **Phase Margin (ϕ_{pm}) : (Phase cross-over frequency)**

   - It is a measure of relative stability.
   - Let ϕ be the phase angle of the system at unity gain. The phase margin is $180 + \phi$. The frequency at which gain is unity, ω_1 is called the **gain cross over frequency**.

     For an open-loop transfer function,

     $$|G(j\omega)\,H(j\omega)|_{\omega=\omega_1} = 1$$

     $\therefore \quad |G(j\omega)\,H(j\omega)|_{\omega=\omega_1} = |1| < \phi$

     $\therefore \quad$ Phase Margin is $180 + \phi$

   - **The phase margin indicates how much the system angle can be increased to cause the system to become unstable from a stable condition.**

6. **Gain Margin: (Gain cross-over frequency)**
- *It is the amount of gain in 'dB' that can be allowed to increase before the system becomes unstable.*
- The frequency ω_2 where phase angle of the transfer function is $-180°$ is called the **phase cross over frequency**.

$$\text{Gain Margin} = \frac{1}{|G(j\omega_2) H(j\omega_2)|}$$

The gain margin indicates how much gain can be increased to cause system instability.

The gain margin and phase margin are evaluated for all frequency domain methods. The graphical methods are –

(i) Bode plot

(ii) Polar plot

4.3 FREQUENCY RESPONSE OF CLOSED LOOP SYSTEM

For the single loop control system, the closed loop transfer function is,

$$M(s) = \frac{C(s)}{R(s)} = \frac{G(s)}{1 + G(s) H(s)} \quad \ldots (4.3)$$

Under the steady-state $s = j\omega$.

$$M(j\omega) = \frac{C(j\omega)}{R(j\omega)} = \frac{G(j\omega)}{1 + G(j\omega) H(j\omega)} \quad \ldots (4.4)$$

The sinusoidal steady-state T.F. $M(j\omega)$ may be in terms of magnitude and phase i.e.,

$$M(j\omega) = |M(j\omega)| \angle M(j\omega) \quad \ldots (4.5)$$

or $M(j\omega)$ can be expressed in terms of real and imaginary parts.

$$M(j\omega) = \text{Re}[M(j\omega)] + j\, \text{Im}[M(j\omega)] \quad \ldots (4.6)$$

The magnitude of $M(j\omega)$ is,

$$|M(j\omega)| = \left|\frac{G(j\omega)}{1 + G(j\omega) H(j\omega)}\right| = \frac{|G(j\omega)|}{1 + |G(j\omega) H(j\omega)|} \quad \ldots (4.7)$$

and phase of $M(j\omega)$ is,

$$\angle M(j\omega) = \phi M(j\omega) = \angle G(j\omega) - \angle[1 + G(j\omega) H(j\omega)] \quad \ldots (4.8)$$

The magnitude and phase of the frequency response carry great significance on the system performance.

4.4 METHODS USED IN FREQUENCY RESPONSE

The frequency response characteristics have two plots:
(1) Magnitude function, and
(2) Phase function.
There are various methods of frequency response analysis.

1. **Polar plot:**
   It is a plot of magnitude versus phase angle as ω is varied from zero to infinity in polar co-ordinates.
2. **Bode plot:**
   This plot illustrates the relative stability of a system. There are two plots: (i) Magnitude, (ii) Phase versus frequency ω in logarithmic scale.
3. **Magnitude Vs. Phase plot:**
   It is a plot of magnitude versus phase on rectangular co-ordinates as ω is varied.

4.5 ADVANTAGES AND DISADVANTAGES OF FREQUENCY RESPONSE ANALYSIS

QUESTION
1. State any four advantages of frequency response analysis. **(4M)**

Advantages:
1. Easy to get frequency response test with good accuracy.
2. Design of open loop transfer function for specified closed loop performance is easier in frequency domain than time domain.
3. Effects of noise disturbance and parameter variations are easy to visualize.

Disadvantages:
1. The methods can be applied only to linear systems when these methods applied to non-linear systems, the results of analysis and design are not exact.
2. Even for linear systems, there is no exact relations between frequency response and step response for higher order system.
3. This method is suitable only for the time constants upto few minutes.
4. Obtaining frequency response practically is time consuming.

4.6 BODE PLOT

Bode plot illustrates the relative stability of the system. So, one of the most useful representation of transfer function is a logarithmic plot which consists of two graphs or plots.

- **Graph I:** Magnitude versus frequency (Magnitude plot).
- **Graph II:** Phase angle versus frequency (Phase angle plot).

In Graph I the logarithm of magnitude of G (jω) is plotted in decibel on y-axis and log frequency is plotted on x-axis.

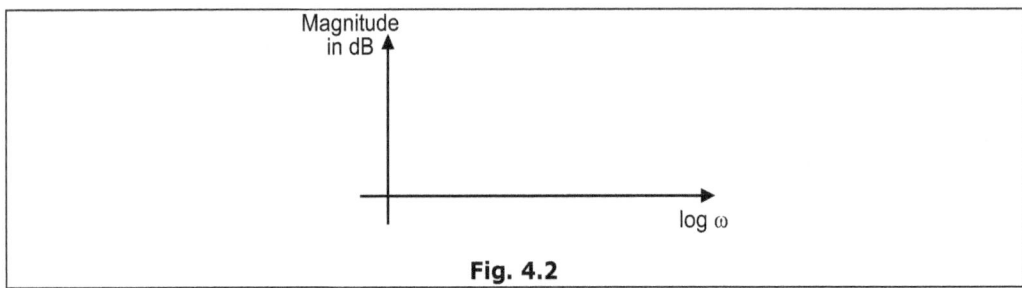

Fig. 4.2

In Graph II, the phase angle of G (jω) is plotted on y-axis while log frequency is plotted on x-axis.

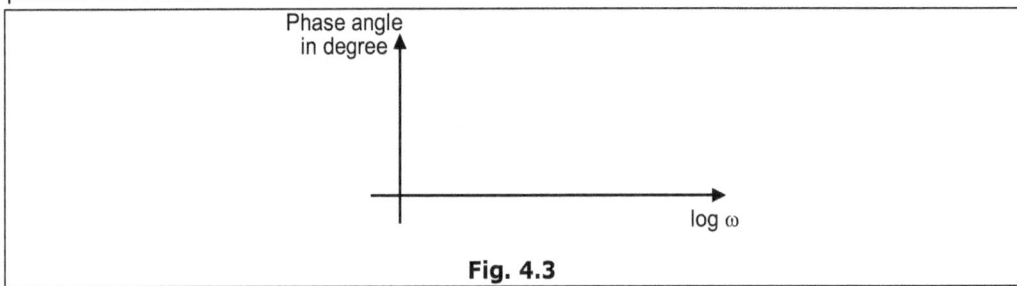

Fig. 4.3

Need:
1. Bode plot uses logarithmic scale so it covers large range of frequency.
2. Stability of the system can be easily found out.
3. From plot easy to measure gain cross-over and phase cross-over frequencies.

Logarithmic Scales:
Why to use?
Logarithmic scales are used because they considerably simplify their construction, manipulation and interpretation.

A logarithmic scale is used because the magnitude and phase angle may be graphed or plotted over a greater range of frequencies than with linear frequency axis.

For example, Let G (jω) have values 2, 5, 10 at frequencies 10, 100, 500 rad/s.

If a linear scale is used for x-axis then if we assume scale as 1 cm = 10 Hz, then between 10 and 100 we need 10 cms and 100 and 500 we need 400 cms of graph paper. This scale is very long. To get the clarity of graph paper we have to compress the scale.

As normal scale fails to give correct representation and full range of frequency both logarithmic scales are used.

How to use log scales?
Log-scale uses the principle that, when the ratio between two points is same, the two points will be separated equally. For example, 10, 100, 1000, 10,000, etc.

Then,

$$\frac{100}{10} = \frac{1000}{100} = \frac{10000}{1000} = \frac{0.01}{0.001}$$ etc. will be in log scales.

Commercially available semi-log paper shown in Fig. 4.4.

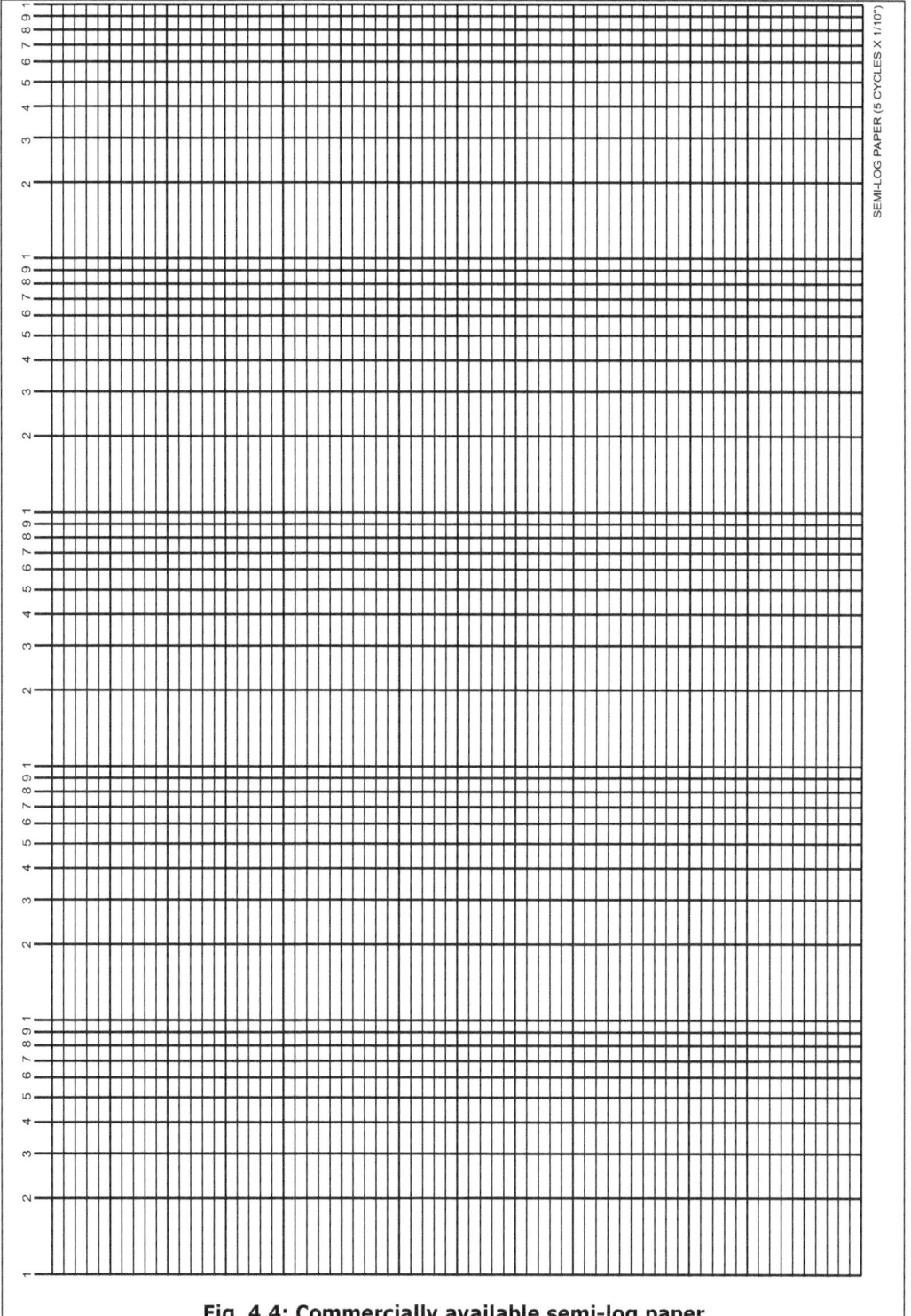

Fig. 4.4: Commercially available semi-log paper

How to read the scale on log paper?

From Fig. 4.4,

1. Left hand side numbers are written as 1, 2, 3, 4, 5, 6, 7, 8, 9 and again same cycle of 1 – 9 repeats (5 cycles are available). This is X-axis.

2. Y-axis is normal scale i.e. equidistant. Each bold line is one inch and subdivided into 0.1 inch each with 0.5 inch slightly darker.

- **Scale Marking:**

1. **X-axis:**

   - Suppose we choose left-most 1 as $0.1 \frac{rad}{s}$ (in first cycle) then, Next 1 is $(0.1 \times 10) = 1 \frac{rad}{s}$ (in second cycle).

     Next 1 is $(1 \times 10) = 10 \frac{rad}{s}$ (in third cycle).

     Next 1 is $(10 \times 10) = 100 \frac{rad}{s}$ (in forth cycle), etc.

   - Similarly,

     Left most 2, is $0.2 \frac{rad}{s}$ (first cycle).

     Next 2 as $(0.2 \times 10) = 2 \frac{rad}{3}$ (in second cycle).

     Next 2 as $(2 \times 10) = 20 \frac{rad}{s}$ (in third cycle).

     i.e. (2 × value of 2 in previous cycle).

The whole scale appears as in Fig. 4.5.

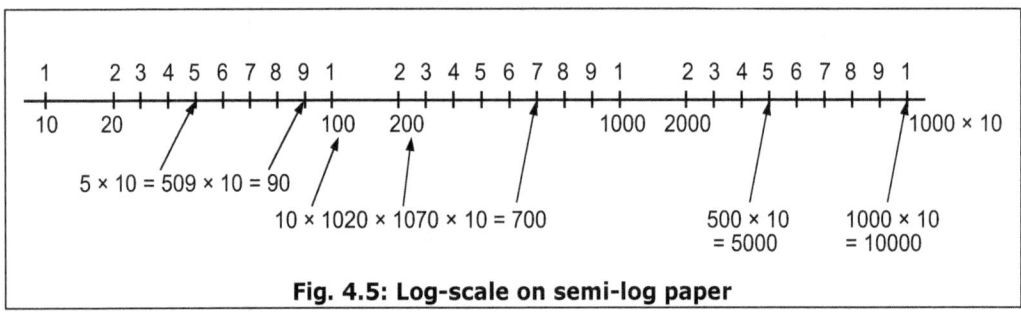

Fig. 4.5: Log-scale on semi-log paper

Hence, for above examples, scales are –

1. 0.1, 0.2, 0.3, 0.4, 0.5, 0.6, 0.7, 0.8, 0.9, (first cycle).
2. 1, 2, 3, 4, 5, 6, 7, 8, 9, (second cycle).
3. 10, 20, 30, 40, 50, 60, 70, 80, 90, (third cycle).
4. 100, 200, 300, 400, 500, 600, 700, 800, 900, (forth cycle).
5. 1000, 2k, 3k, 4k, 5k, 6k, 7k, 8k, 9k, (fifth cycle).

Hence, by choosing left most 1 properly. All other frequencies automatically fixed.

- **Y-axis:** This ordinary scale which are used in simple graph paper on which magnitude (dB), and phase angle (degrees) on y-axis using some suitable scale are plotted.

4.6.1 Standard Form of G (jω)

Consider,

$$G(s) = \frac{p(s)}{q(s)} = \frac{a_0 s^m + a_1 s^{m-1} + a_2 s^{m-2} + \ldots}{b_0 s^n + b_1 s^{n-1} + b_2 s^{n-2} + \ldots}$$

This equation is factorised in general type.

$$= \frac{k_1 s^g (s+a)(s+b) \ldots}{s^k (s+c)(s+d)}$$

[In equation only one term i.e. either s^g or s^k is present].

$$= \frac{k_1 s^g \left(1 + \frac{s}{a}\right)\left(1 + \frac{s}{b}\right) \ldots}{s^k \left(1 + \frac{s}{c}\right)\left(1 + \frac{s}{d}\right) \ldots}$$

where,

$$k_1 = \frac{k \, ab \ldots}{cd \ldots}$$

Put $s = j\omega$

$$\therefore \quad G(j\omega) = \frac{k_1 (j\omega)^g \left(1 + j\frac{\omega}{a}\right)\left(1 + j\frac{\omega}{b}\right) \ldots}{(j\omega)^k \left(1 + j\frac{\omega}{c}\right) + \left(1 + j\frac{\omega}{d}\right) \ldots} \quad \ldots (4.9)$$

This is the standard form of equation while plotting Bode plot.
The possible factors of G (jω) in equation (4.10) are,
1. Constant factor k,
2. Poles at origin $\frac{1}{(j\omega)^k}$ of order k.
3. Zeros at origin $(j\omega)^g$ of order g.
4. Finite poles at $\frac{1}{\left(1 + \frac{j\omega}{b}\right)}$.
5. Finite zeros at $\left(1 + \frac{j\omega}{b}\right)$.
6. Second order poles $\frac{1}{1 + j2\xi\omega - \omega^2}$.
7. Second order zeros $(1 + 2j\xi\omega - \omega^2)$.

If any transfer function containing few of the above factors, then we have to reduce the G (jω) to the form of equation (4.9) as a first step.

4.6.2 To Plot the Slop Lines and Angles on Bode Plot

Let poles and zeros at origin $(j\omega)^{\pm p}$.

Magnitude of $j\omega$ i.e.

$|(j\omega)^{\pm p}|$ in dB is,

$$2 \log_{10} |(j\omega)^{\pm p}| = \pm 20\, p \log_{10} \omega \text{ dB} \qquad \ldots (4.10)$$

- For $\omega \geq 0$

The equation for given p represents as **straightline** in either semilog or rectangular co-ordinates. The slopes of these are determined by taking derivative of equation (4.10) with respect to $\log_{10} \omega$.

$$\therefore \frac{d}{d \log_{10} \omega} (\pm 20\, p \log_{10} \omega) = \pm 20\, p \text{ dB/decade} \qquad \ldots (4.11)$$

These straight lines pass through 0-dB axis at $\omega = 1$. Thus, a unit change in $\log_{10} \omega$ corresponds to a change of $\pm 20\, p$ dB in magnitude.

Furthermore, a unit change in $\log_{10} \omega$ is equivalent to **decade of variation in ω**, i.e. from 1 to 10, 10 to 100 and so on, in semi-log co-ordinates.

Therefore, the slope of the straight lines in equation (4.10) are said to be $\pm 20p$ dB/decade of frequency.

In place of the decades, sometimes **octaves** are used to represent the separation of two frequencies.

The frequencies ω_1 and ω_2 are separated by octave if $\frac{\omega_2}{\omega_1} = 2$.

Thus, the number of decades between any two frequencies ω_1 and ω_2 is given by,

$$\text{Number of decades} = \log_{10}\left(\frac{\omega_2}{\omega_1}\right) \qquad \ldots (4.12)$$

$$\text{Number of octaves} = \frac{\log_{10}(\omega_2/\omega_1)}{\log_{10} 2} = \frac{1}{0.301} \text{ decades} = \textbf{3.32 decades}$$

$$\ldots (4.13)$$

e.g. $\pm 20\, p$ dB/decade $= \pm 20 \infty\, 0.301 \cong 6\, p$ dB/octave

$$\boxed{\angle (j\omega)^{\pm p} = \pm p \times 90^0}$$

4.6.3 Steps for Constructing Bode Plot

1. Bring the given $G(j\omega)$ in standard form.
2. Put $s = j\omega$.
3. List the factors present.
4. Choose suitable y and x-scales for magnitude curve and draw the magnitude curve for each.

5. Draw the resultant plot.
6. Write phase equation for each phase term present.
7. See the largest frequency term present, and choose the starting point on log scale.
8. Prepare phase table.
9. Draw the phase plot to suitable scale.

Gain Margin Calculation:

10. Observe the resultant **phase curve** and find ω where **phase curve crosses −180°**. This is called **phase cross-over frequency** i.e. $\omega = \omega_{pc}$.
11. For this value of ω_{pc} go to resultant magnitude curve. For this find out how many db below 0 db is the resultant curve. This is **gain margin.**

Phase Margin Calculations:

12. From the resultant magnitude curve find where the resultant crosses 0 dB axis. Thus the **gain cross-over frequency, ω_{gc}.**
13. For gain cross-over frequency ω_{gc}, go to phase curve and find out phase angle ϕ.

$$\therefore \quad \text{Phae Margin} = 180° + \phi$$

Thus, **system is stable for positive values of gain and phase margin.**

4.6.4 Bode Plot for Gain K

i.e. for $G(s) = K$

$K = $ Constant

- **Magnitude Plot:**

Put $s = j\omega$

$\therefore \quad G(j\omega) = k$

The log magnitude is

$$= 20 \log_{10} |G(j\omega)|$$
$$= 20 \log_{10} k$$
$$= 20 \text{ dB (for } k = 10)$$

So, magnitude plot is straight line passing through 20 dB.

- **Phase Vs. log ω plot:**

Phase angle $\phi = \angle G(j\omega)$

$= \angle k = 0$, For k > 0

$= -180°$, For k < 0

So, for a positive values of k the Bode plot is a straight line with equation for phase angle equal to 0° for all ω and phase angle is − 180° for all ω for negative values of k.

Bode Plot:

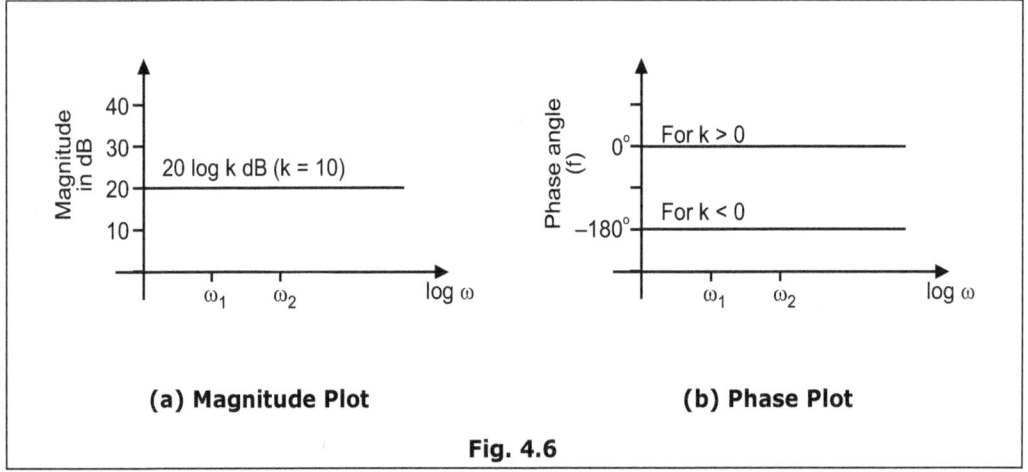

(a) Magnitude Plot   (b) Phase Plot

Fig. 4.6

4.6.5 Bode Plot for Poles and Zeros at Origin

- **Poles at origin** $\left(\dfrac{1}{s}\right)$

  i.e. $$G(s) = \dfrac{1}{(s)^p}$$

  Put $$G(j\omega) = \dfrac{1}{(j\omega)^p}$$

- **Magnitude Vs. log ω plot:**

  Given,
  $$G(j\omega) = (j\omega)^{-p}$$

  Log magnitude is,
  $$20 \log_{10} G(j\omega) = 20 \log (j\omega)^{-p}$$
  $$= -20 \, p \log_{10} (j\omega) \text{ dB}$$

  The magnitude is depends on p.

  For p = 1, the straight line passes through (0 dB, ω = 1) at slope = − 20 dB/dec.

  For p = 2, the straight line passes through 0 dB at ω = 1, at slope = − 4 dB/dec. and so on.

- **Phase Vs. log ω plot:**

  $$G(j\omega) = \dfrac{1}{(j\omega)^p} = (j\omega)^{-p} \quad \phi = \pm 20 \, p$$

  For p = 1, $\angle G(j\omega) = \angle G(j\omega)^{-1} = -90 \times 1 = -90°$

  For p = 2 $\angle G(j\omega) = \angle G(j\omega)^{-2} = -90 \times 2 = -180°$

  For p = 3 $\angle G(j\omega) = \angle G(j\omega)^{-3} = -90 \times 3 = -270°$ and so on.

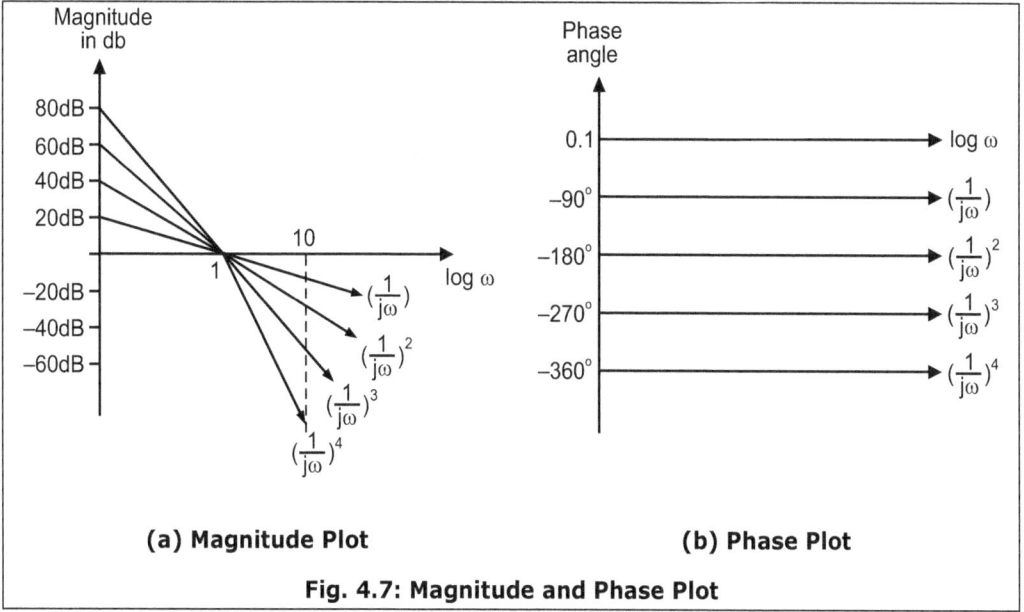

(a) Magnitude Plot (b) Phase Plot

Fig. 4.7: Magnitude and Phase Plot

- **Zeros at origin $(j\omega)^{+p}$:**

    Let $\quad G(j\omega) = (j\omega)^{+p}$

- **Magnitude Vs. log ω plot:**

    $$G(j\omega) = (j\omega)^{+p}$$

    Log magnitude is,

    $$M = 20 \log G(j\omega)$$
    $$= 20 \log (j\omega)^p$$
    $$= 20 p \log (j\omega)$$

    For p = 1, the straight line passes through 0 db, ω = 1, at slope = 20 dB/dec. [From equation (4.11)].

    For p = 2, the straight line passes through 0 db, ω = 1 at slope = 20 × 2 = 40 dB/dec. [Slope = 20 p db/dec. equation 4.11)].

    For p = 3, the straight line passes through 0 db, ω = 1 at slope = 20 × 3 = 60 db/dec. and so on.

- **Phase Vs. log ω plot:**

    Let, $\quad G(j\omega) = (j\omega)^p \quad\quad$ Use $\phi = 90 \times p$

    ∴ For p = 1 $\quad \phi = \angle (j\omega)^1 = 90 \times 1 = 90°$

    For p = 2 $\quad \phi = \angle (j\omega)^2 = 90 \times 2 = 180°$

    For p = 3 $\quad \phi = \angle (j\omega)^3 = 90 \times 3 = 270°$

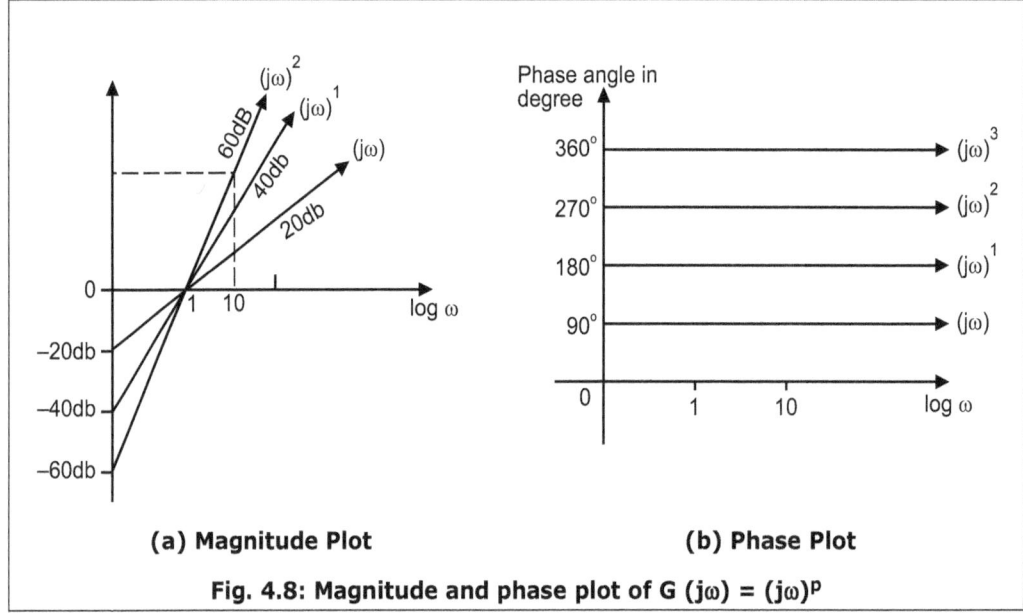

(a) Magnitude Plot (b) Phase Plot

Fig. 4.8: Magnitude and phase plot of G (jω) = (jω)^p

4. **Bode plot for $G(s) = \dfrac{1}{1 + sT}$:**

   Put s = jω

   ∴ $\qquad G(j\omega) = \dfrac{1}{1 + j\omega T}$

   $|G(j\omega)| = \dfrac{1}{\sqrt{1 + \omega^2 T^2}}, \quad \phi = \angle G(j\omega) = \angle \dfrac{1}{1 + j\omega T}$

   $\qquad\qquad\qquad\qquad\qquad\qquad\qquad\qquad = -\tan^{-1} \omega T$

- **Magnitude Vs. log ω plot:**

   Log magnitude is,

   $$M = 20 \log_{10} \dfrac{1}{\sqrt{1 + \omega^2 T^2}}$$

   Equate real and imaginary part.

   ∴ $\qquad\qquad 1 = \omega T$

   ∴ $\qquad\qquad \omega = \dfrac{1}{T}$ is the corner frequency

   ∴ At $\qquad\qquad \omega = \dfrac{1}{T}$

   $$M = 20 \log_{10} \dfrac{1}{\sqrt{2}} = -3 \text{ db}$$

   Case I: $\qquad \omega << \dfrac{1}{T}$

   i.e. $\qquad\qquad \omega T << 1$

   ∴ ωT is neglected.

Then,
$$M = 20 \log_{10} \frac{1}{\sqrt{1 + \omega^2 + T^2}}$$
$$= 20 \log_{10}(1)$$
$$= 0 \text{ dB}$$

Case II: $\omega >> \frac{1}{T}$

i.e. $\omega T >> 1$

∴ $$M = 20 \log_{10} \frac{1}{\sqrt{1 + \omega^2 T^2}}$$
$$= 20 \log_{10}\left(\frac{1}{\omega T}\right)$$

Let $\omega = \frac{1}{2T}$

$M = 20 \log_{10}(2) = -1 \text{ db}$

$\omega T = 2$

$M = 20 \log_{10}\left(\frac{1}{2}\right) = -7 \text{ dB}$

Hence, magnitude plot has two part $\omega << \frac{1}{T}$ and $\omega >> \frac{1}{T}$.

M varies with slop – 20 db/dec.

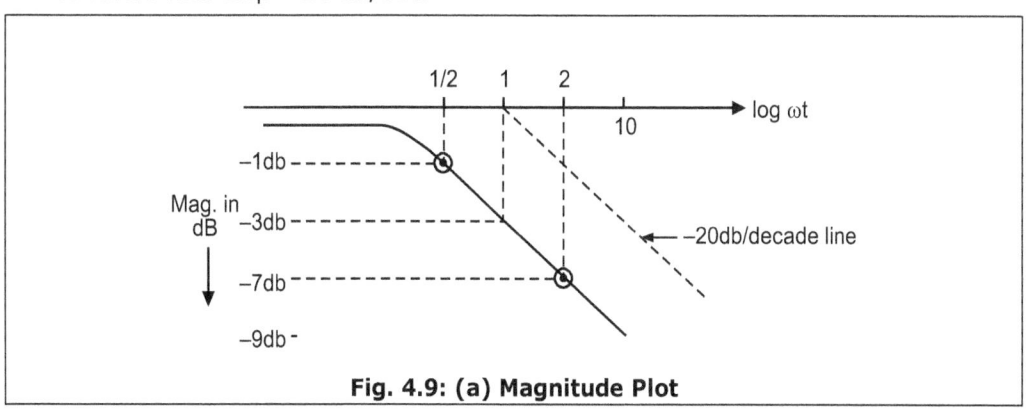

Fig. 4.9: (a) Magnitude Plot

- **Phase Vs. log ω plot:**

At $\omega T = 0$ $\phi = -\tan^{-1} \omega T$
$= 0$

$\omega T = 0.01$ $\phi = -0.57°$

$\omega T = 1$ $\phi = -5.7°$

$\phi = -45°$

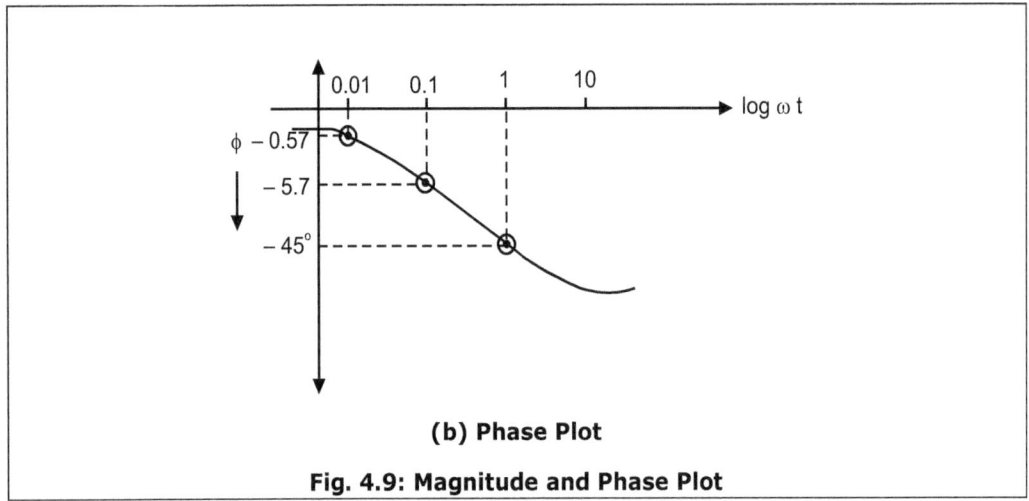

(b) Phase Plot

Fig. 4.9: Magnitude and Phase Plot

5. **Bode plot for**

$$G(s) = 1 + sT$$

Put

$$s = j\omega$$

$$G(j\omega) = (1 + j\omega T)^1$$

Log magnitude is,

$$|G(j\omega)| = \sqrt{1 + \omega^2 T^2}$$

∴

$$M = 20 \log_{10} \sqrt{1 + \omega^2 T^2}$$

- **Magnitude Vs. log ω plot:**

Equal real and imaginary part.

∴ $\omega T = 1$

∴ $\omega = \dfrac{1}{T}$ is the corner frequency (centre frequency)

So, we can plot magnitude plot at three values of ω i.e.

$\omega < \dfrac{1}{T}$, $\omega > \dfrac{1}{T}$ and $\omega = \dfrac{1}{T}$

or $\omega T < 1$, $\omega T > 1$ and $\omega T = 1$

At $\omega T << 1$ $M = 20 \log_{10} 1 = 0$

$\omega T >> 1$ $M = 20 \log \omega T$

which is a straight line having a slope of + 20 dB/dec.

[∵ $(1 + j\omega T)^{+1}$ ∴ slope = + 20 p = + 20 × 1 = 20 db/dec.]

This is a straight line approximation, hence correction has to be applied at corner frequency one octave to left and one to the right.

At $\omega T = 1$

$$M = 20 \log_{10} \sqrt{1 + 1}$$
$$= 3 \text{ dB}$$

At $\omega T < 1$ i.e. $\omega T = \dfrac{1}{2}$

$$\therefore \quad M = 20 \log_{10} \sqrt{1 + \left(\dfrac{1}{2}\right)^2}$$
$$= 1 \text{ dB}$$

At $\omega T > 1$ i.e. $\omega T = 2$

$$\therefore \quad M = 20 \log_{10} \sqrt{1 + 2^2}$$
$$= 7 \text{ dB}$$

Phase Vs. log ω plot :

$$\phi = \angle G(j\omega)$$
$$= \tan^{-1} \omega T$$

At

$\omega T = 0$ $\phi = 0$

$\omega T = 1$ $\phi = 45°$

$\omega T = 0.01$ $\phi = +0.57°$

$\omega T = 0.1$ $\phi = +5.7°$

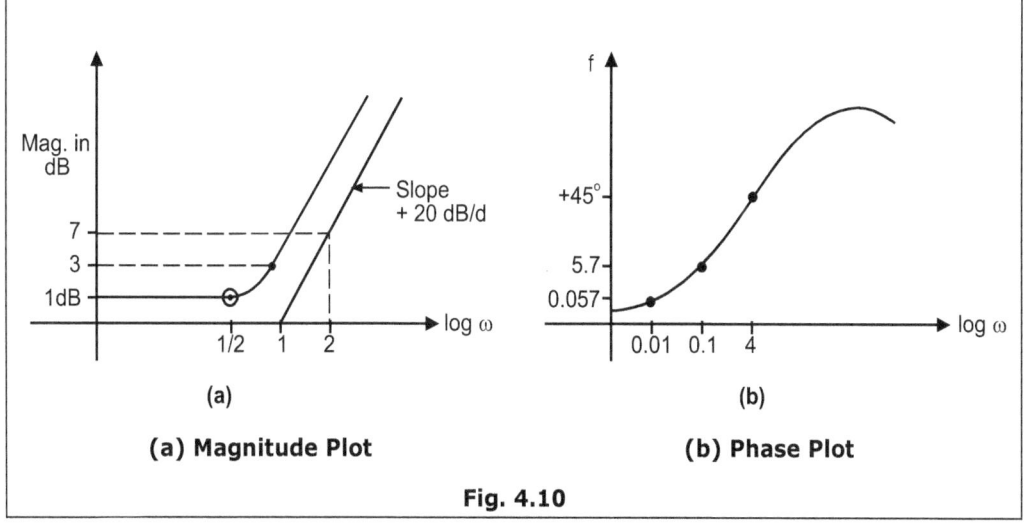

(a) Magnitude Plot   (b) Phase Plot

Fig. 4.10

Example 4.1: Draw a + 20 dB/dec. line passing through $\omega = 1$, 10 dB.

Sol. : As we know decade means two frequencies 10 times apart i.e. $\omega = 0.1$ and 1, $\omega = 10$ and $\omega = 10$, 100 are one decade apart.

1. Mark point ω = 1, 10 db as shown in Fig. 4.11.
2. Now from ω = 1 move to the next decade i.e. ω = 10.
3. At ω = 10, the line will up by 20 db more than value at ω = 1, i.e. 20 db more than 10 db i.e. 30 db.
4. Join the points ω = (10, 30 db) and ω = (1, 10 db).

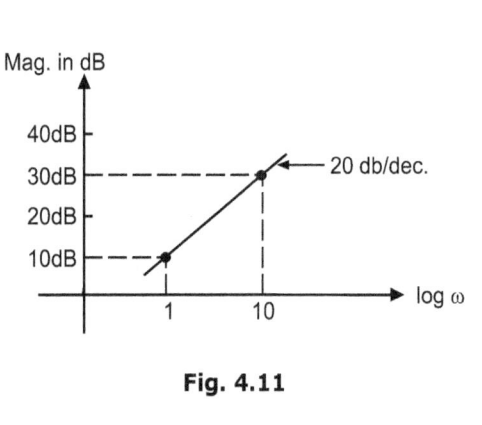

Fig. 4.11

Example 4.2: Draw a 40 db/dec. line passing through ω = 1, 10 db till ω = 5.

Sol. : 1. Mark point ω = 1, 10 db point shown in Fig. 4.11.

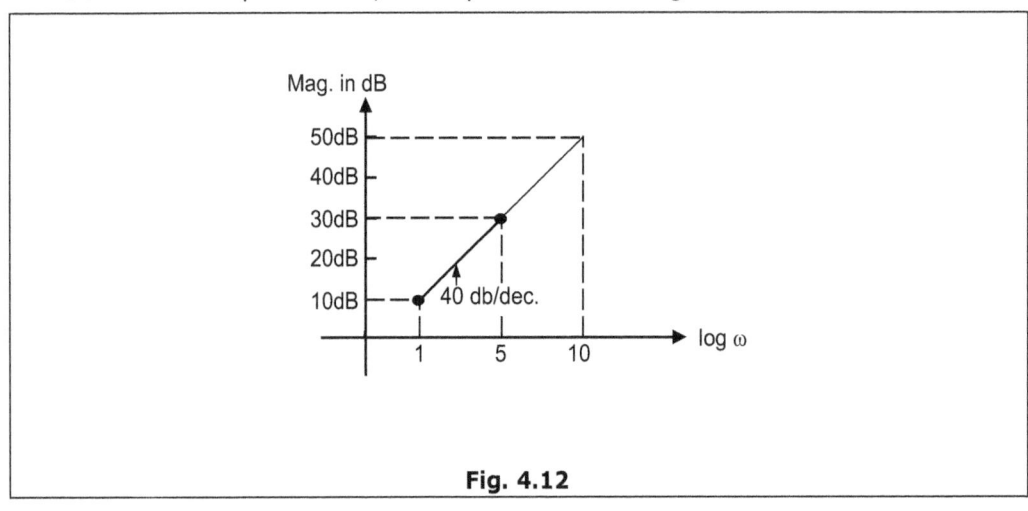

Fig. 4.12

2. Now, mark the next decade at ω = 10.
3. Slope is + 40 db in one decade i.e. line move up by + 40 db from its value ω = 1.
   i.e. 10 db + 40 db = 50 db at ω = 10.
4. Joint points ω = 1, 10 db and ω = 10, 50 db.
5. Darken the line between ω = 1 and ω = 5.

Example 4.3: Draw a slope line between ω = 2 and ω = 5 at − 40 db/dec. value at ω = 2 is 10 db.

Sol. :

1. Mark ω = 2, 10 db as shown in Fig. 4.13.
2. Move to the next decade i.e. ω = 20.
3. Lines lopes – 40 db in one decade so go down by 40 db with respect to the value at ω = 2, i.e. 10 db – 40 db = – 30 db.
4. Join (ω = 2, 40 db) and (ω = 20, – 30 db). Draw line only between ω = 2 to ω = 5.

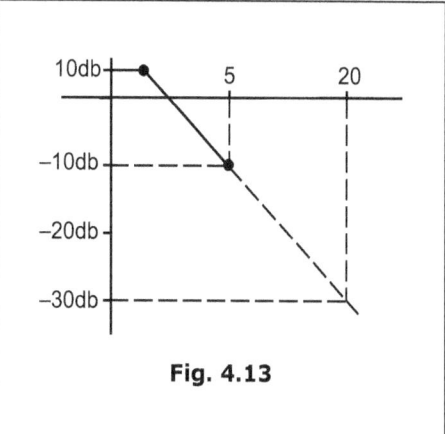

Fig. 4.13

Fig. 4.14 shows the various slope lines.

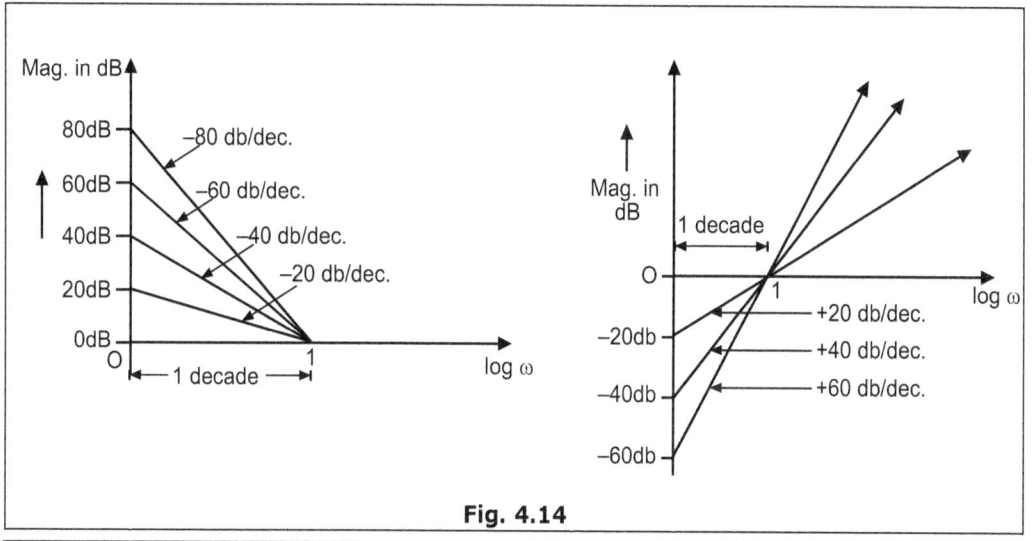

Fig. 4.14

Example 4.4: Sketch the bode plots and determine the gain cross-over and phase cross-over frequencies.

$$G(s) = \frac{10}{s(1 + 0.5s)(1 + 0.1s)}$$

Sol.: Step 1:

Given G(s) is in standard form.

Put s = jω.

$$\therefore \quad G(j\omega) = \frac{10}{j\omega(1 + j\,0.5\,\omega)(1 + j\,0.1\,\omega)}$$

This is the standard form.

Step 2: The following factors are present.

1. Pole at origin: $\dfrac{1}{j\omega}$.

2. First order pole: $\dfrac{1}{1 + j\,0.5\,\omega}$.

3. First order pole: $\dfrac{1}{1 + 0.1\,\omega}$

Prepare table for **magnitude plot.**

Sr. No.	Factor	Corner Frequency	Asymptotic log magnitude characteristic
1	$\dfrac{1}{j\omega}$	None	Straight line of constant slope − 20 db/dec. passing through $\omega = 1$.
2	$\dfrac{1}{(1 + j\,0.5\,\omega)}$	$\omega_1 = 2$	Straight line of constant slope − 20 db/dec. originating from $\omega_1 = 2$.
3	$\dfrac{1}{(1 + j\,0.1\,\omega)}$	$\omega_2 = 10$	Straight line of constant slope of − 20 db/dec. originating from $\omega_2 = 10$.
4	10	None	Straight line of constant slope of 0 db/sec. starting from $20 \log_{10} 10 = 20$ db point.

where, corner frequency is found by equating real and imaginary part.

For example,

1. $j\omega = 0$ so, no corner frequency
2. $1 + j\,0.5\,\omega$,

$$0.5\,\omega = 1$$

∴ $\omega = 2$ is the corner frequency

3. $1 + j\,0.1\,\omega$

$$0.1\,\omega = 1$$

∴ $\omega = 10$ is the corner frequency

Powers of all these terms are − 1.

∴ Slopes are − 20 db/dec. for each term.

Step 3: Magnitude plot for individual factors are shown by dotted line and resultant line is shown dark. (Fig. 4.15).

Step 4: Choose y-axis scale 1 cm = 20 db.

Here largest first order is $(1 + j\,0.1\,\omega)^{-1}$

∴ Choose x-axis starting point as 0.1 rad/sec.

Thus, x-axis printed 1 will have 0.1, 1, 10, 100, 1000 frequency.

Step 5: Write the phase equation.

1. For $\dfrac{1}{j\omega}$ $\phi = \angle (j\omega)^{-1} = -90 \times 1 = -90°$

2. For $\dfrac{1}{1 + j\,0.5\,\omega}$ $\phi = -\tan^{-1}(0.5\,\omega)$

3. For $\dfrac{1}{1 + j\,0.1\,\omega}$ $\phi = -\tan^{-1}(0.1\,\omega)$

∴ $\phi(j\omega) = -90° - \tan^{-1}(0.5\,\omega) - \tan^{-1}(0.1\,\omega)$

Step 6: The frequency range is from $\omega = 0.1$ to $\omega = 1000$.

Step 7: Prepare table for phase plot.

$\phi = -90° - \tan^{-1}(0.5\,\omega) - \tan^{-1}(0.1\,\omega)$

Sr. No.	ω	ϕ
1	0	$-90°$
2	0.1	$-93.43°$
3	1	$-122.3°$
4	2	$-146.31°$
5	5	$-184.76°$
6	10	$-213.7°$

Step 8: Draw the phase plot where smallest $\phi = -90°$ and largest $\phi = -213.7°$. So scale choosen as $30° = 1$ unit and starting scale is $-90°$ (Fig. 9.37).

Step 9: From phase resultant curve find 'ω' where phase curve crosses $-180°$. This is phase cross-over frequency $\omega_{pc} = 5$ rad/sec.

Step 10: For this value of ω_{pc}, go to the magnitude resultant curve which is dB below line. Hence, GM is positive. Thus, GM is dB.

∴   GM = 20 dB

Step 11: Phase margin calculation – From the magnitude resultant find where the resultant crosses 0 db line. This is gain cross-over frequency $\omega_{gc} = 4.2$ rad/sec.

Step 12: For this value of ω_{gc}, go to the phase curve and find out how much is the phase angle ϕ, $\phi = -130°$, ∴ pm $= 180 + \phi = 180 - 130 = 50°$.

Stability,
1. Gm = 21 dB.
2. pm = 50°.
3. Gain cross-over frequency $\omega_{gc} = 4.2$ rad/sec.
4. Phase cross-over frequency $\omega_{pc} = 0.5$ rad/sec. system is stable.

Magnitude and phase plots are shown in Fig. 4.15.

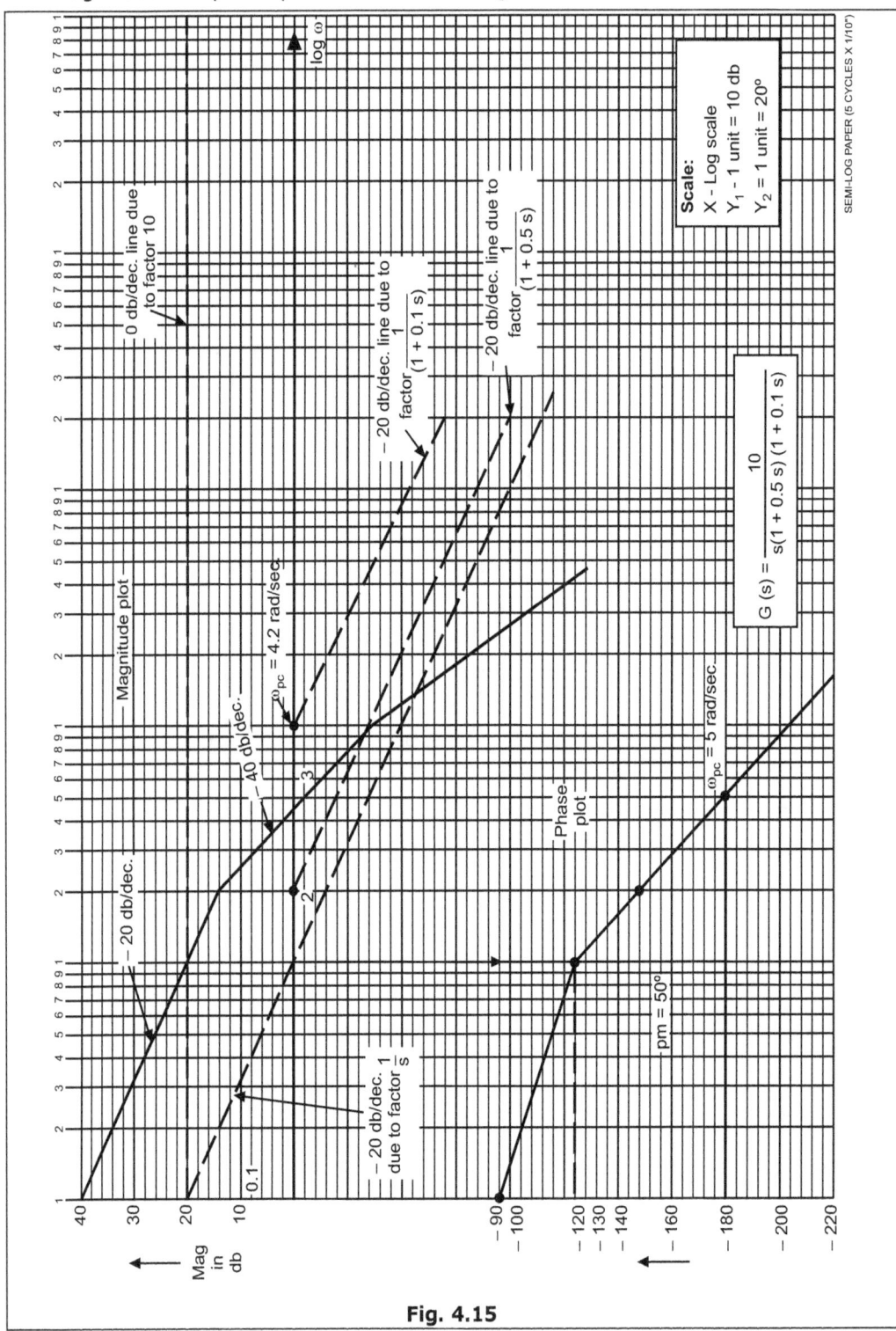

Fig. 4.15

SOLVED EXAMPLES

Example 4.5: Draw the Bode plot for a system

$$G(s)H(s) = \frac{100}{s(s+1)(s+2)}$$

Find
(a) Gain margin, (b) Phase margin
(c) Gain cross-over frequency, (d) Phase cross-over frequency

Sol.: Step 1: Bring given $G(s)H(s)$ in standard form.

$$G(s)H(s) = \frac{50}{s(1+s)(1+0.5s)}$$

$$= \frac{100}{s(1+s)\,2(1+0.5s)}$$

$$= \frac{50}{s(1+s)(1+0.5s)}$$

Put $s = j\omega$

$$\therefore \quad G(j\omega)H(j\omega) = \frac{50}{j\omega(1+j\omega)(1+j0.5\omega)}$$

Step 2: The following factors are present.

1. Pole at origin: $\frac{1}{j\omega}$.

2. First order pole: $\frac{1}{1+j\omega}$ i.e. $(1+j\omega)^{-1}$

3. First order pole: $\frac{1}{1+j0.5\omega}$ i.e. $(1+j0.5\omega)^{-1}$

Prepare table:

Sr. No.	Factor	Corner Frequency	Asymptotic log magnitude characteristic
1	50	None	Straight line of slope 0 db/dec. starting from point $20\log_{10}50 = 34$ db.
2	$\frac{1}{j\omega}$	None	Straight line of slope − 20 db/sec. passing through $\omega = 1$.
3	$\frac{1}{1+j\omega}$	1	Straight line of slope − 20 db/dec. originating from $\omega = 1$.
4	$\frac{1}{1+0.5\omega}$	2	Straight line of slope − 20 db/dec. originating from $\omega = 2$.

Step 3: Choose y-axis scale 1 cm = 20 dB.
Here largest first order is $(1+j0.5\omega)^{-1}$
Thus, choose x-axis starting point at 0.1 rad/sec. 0.1, 1, 10, 100, 1000 frequencies.

Step 4: Draw the resultant magnitude curve. (Fig. 4.16).
Draw the individual lines as per magnitude plot table.

$$\text{Resultant slope} = \text{Sum of all individual slopes}$$
$$= -20\,\text{db/dec} - 20\,\text{db/dec} - 20\,\text{db/dec}.$$
$$= -60\,\text{dB/dec}.$$

Step 5: Write the phase equation.

1. For $\dfrac{1}{j\omega}$ $\phi = -90°$

2. For $\dfrac{1}{1+j\omega}$ $\phi = -\tan^{-1}\omega$

3. For $\dfrac{1}{1+j\,0.5\,\omega}$ $\phi = -\tan^{-1}(0.5\,\omega)$

∴ Phase equation is,

$$\phi = -90° - \tan^{-1}\omega - \tan^{-1}(0.5\,\omega)$$

Step 6: Prepare table for phase plot.

Sr. No.	ω rad/sec.	φ
1	0	– 90°
2	0.1	– 98.6°
3	0.2	– 107°
4	0.5	– 130.6°
5	1	– 161.6°
6	1.4	– 179.5°
7	2	– 198.4°

Step 7: Draw the phase plot (Fig. 4.16).
where,   smallest $\phi = -90°$
              largest $\phi = -198.4°$

∴ Scale choosen as 30° = 1 unit starting from – 90°.

Step 8: Gain margin calculations – From phase resultant curve find ω where phase curve crosses – 180°. This is phase cross-over frequency.

$$\omega_{pc} = 1.4 \text{ rad/sec.}$$

Step 9: For this value of ω_{pc}, go to the magnitude resultant curve which is 27 db below 0 db. Hence, gain margin is positive.

∴   GM = 27 db

Step 10: Phase margin calculations – From the magnitude resultant curve find where the resultant crosses 0 dB line. This is gain cross-over frequency ω_{gc}. In graph ω_{gc} = 4.45 rad/s.

Step 11: For this value of ω_{gc}, go to the phase curve and find out how much is the phase angle φ.

$$\phi = -127°$$

∴   Phase margin = + 180 + φ
                         = 180 – 127
                         = **53°**

Stability :
           GM = 27 db
           PM = 53°
           ω_{gc} = 4.45 rad/sec.
           ω_{pc} = 1.4 rad/sec.

Thus, **system is stable.**
Magnitude and phase plots are shown in Fig. 4.16 as shown on next page.

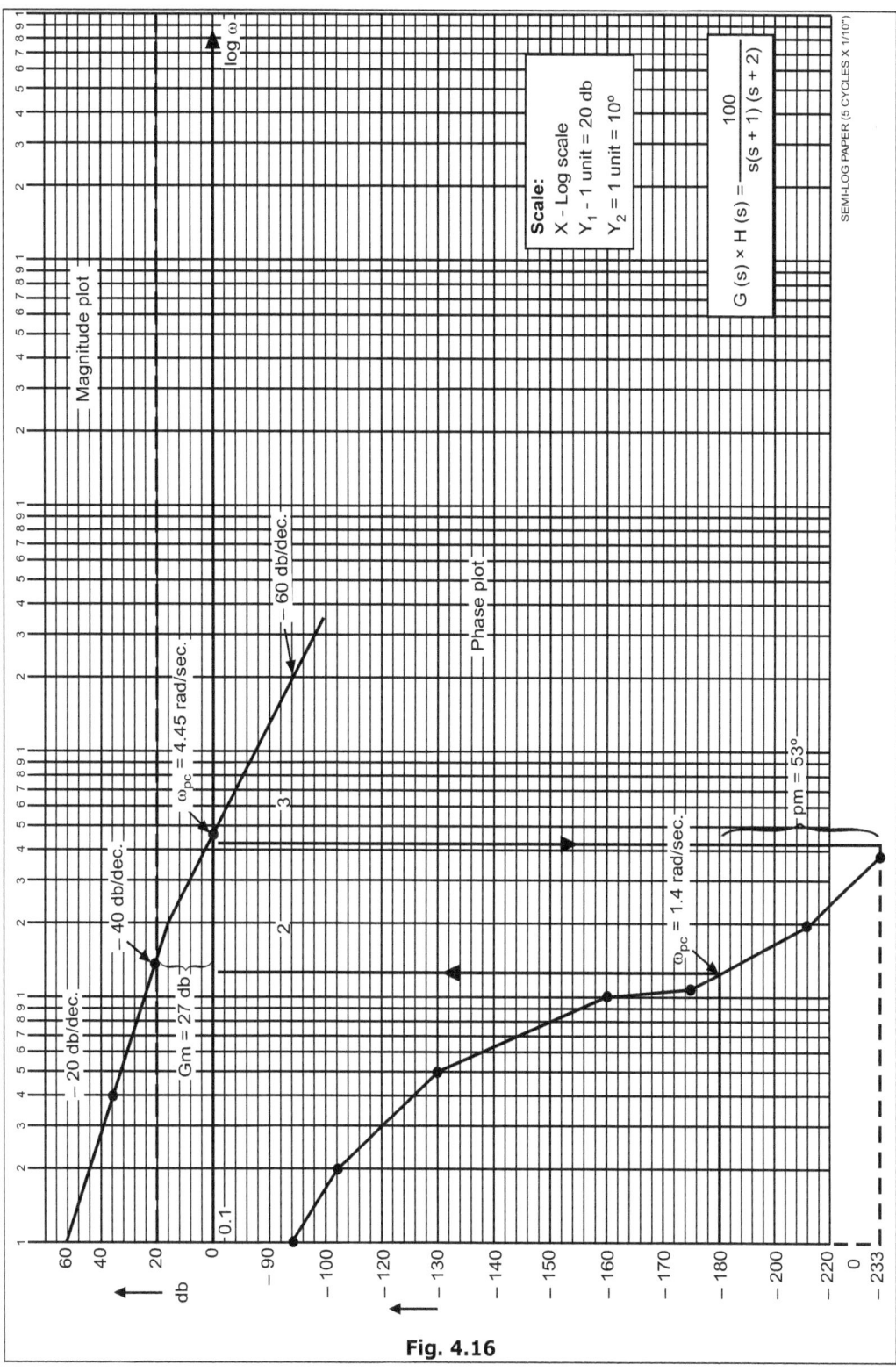

Fig. 4.16

Example 4.6: Draw the bode plot for the system having,
$$G(s) = \frac{10}{s(1 + 0.01s)(1 + 0.1s)}, \quad H(s) = 1$$

Determine: (i) The gain cross-over frequency and corresponding phase margin. (ii) The phase cross-over frequency and corresponding phase margin.

Sol.: **Step 1:** Bring given function into standard form.
$$G(s) = \frac{10}{s(1 + 0.01s)(1 + 0.1s)}$$

It is in standard form only.

Put $s = j\omega$

$$\therefore \quad G(j\omega) = \frac{10}{j\omega(1 + j\,0.01\omega)(1 + j\,0.1\omega)}$$

Step 2: Factors present are –

1. Constant = 10.
2. Poles at origin = $\frac{1}{j\omega}$.
3. First order pole = $\frac{1}{1 + j\,0.1\,\omega}$.
4. First order pole = $\frac{1}{1 + j\,0.01\,\omega}$.

Step 3: Prepare table for magnitude plot.

Sr. No.	Factor	Corner frequency rad/sec.	Asymptotic log magnitude curve
1.	10	None	Straight line of 0 db/dec. Straight from point 20 log 10 = 20 db.
2.	$\frac{1}{j\omega}$	None	Straight line of – 20 db/dec. passing through $\omega = 1$.
3.	$\frac{1}{1 + j\,0.1\,\omega}$	10 $\left(\begin{array}{c} 1 = 0.1\,\omega \\ \therefore \omega = 10 \end{array}\right)$	Straight line of – 20 db/dec. originating from $\omega = 10$.
4.	$\frac{1}{1 + j\,0.01\,\omega}$	100 $\left(\begin{array}{c} \therefore 1 = 0.01\,\omega \\ \therefore \omega = 100 \end{array}\right)$	Straight line of – 20 db/dec. originating from $\omega = 100$.

Step 4: Choose y-axis 1 cm = 20 db. Here largest first order factor is $(1 + j\,0.01\,\omega)$. Thus, choose x-axis starting as 0.1 rad/sec. as ω. i.e. X-axis having scales. 0.1, 1, 10, 100, 1000 as frequencies for each printed 1.

Step 5 : Draw resultant. The magnitude for each factor.
(i) Constant : 20 db. (ii) $j\omega^{-1}$: – 20 db/dec.
(iii) $(1 + j\,0.01\,\omega)^{-1}$: – 20 db/dec. (iv) $(1 + j\,0.1\,\omega)^{-1}$: – 20 db/dec.

The total algebraic sum is + 20 – 20 – 20 – 20 = – 40 db/dec.

Therefore, draw at line slopping – 40 db/dec. from starting point $\omega = 0.01$ till the first change point $\omega = 10$.

Step 6: Phase plot. $\angle G(j\omega) = \angle \frac{1}{j\omega} + \angle \frac{1}{(1 + j\,0.1\,\omega)} + \angle \frac{1}{(1 + j\,0.01\,\omega)}$

$$\therefore \quad \phi = -90 - \tan^{-1} 0.1\,\omega - \tan^{-1} 0.01\,\omega$$

Phase plot table.

Sr. No.	ω rad/sec.	ϕ
1	0	– 90°
2	0.1	– 90.6°
3	0.5	– 93.15°
4	1	– 96.3°
5	5	– 119°
6	10	– 141°

Bode plot is shown on graph on next page.

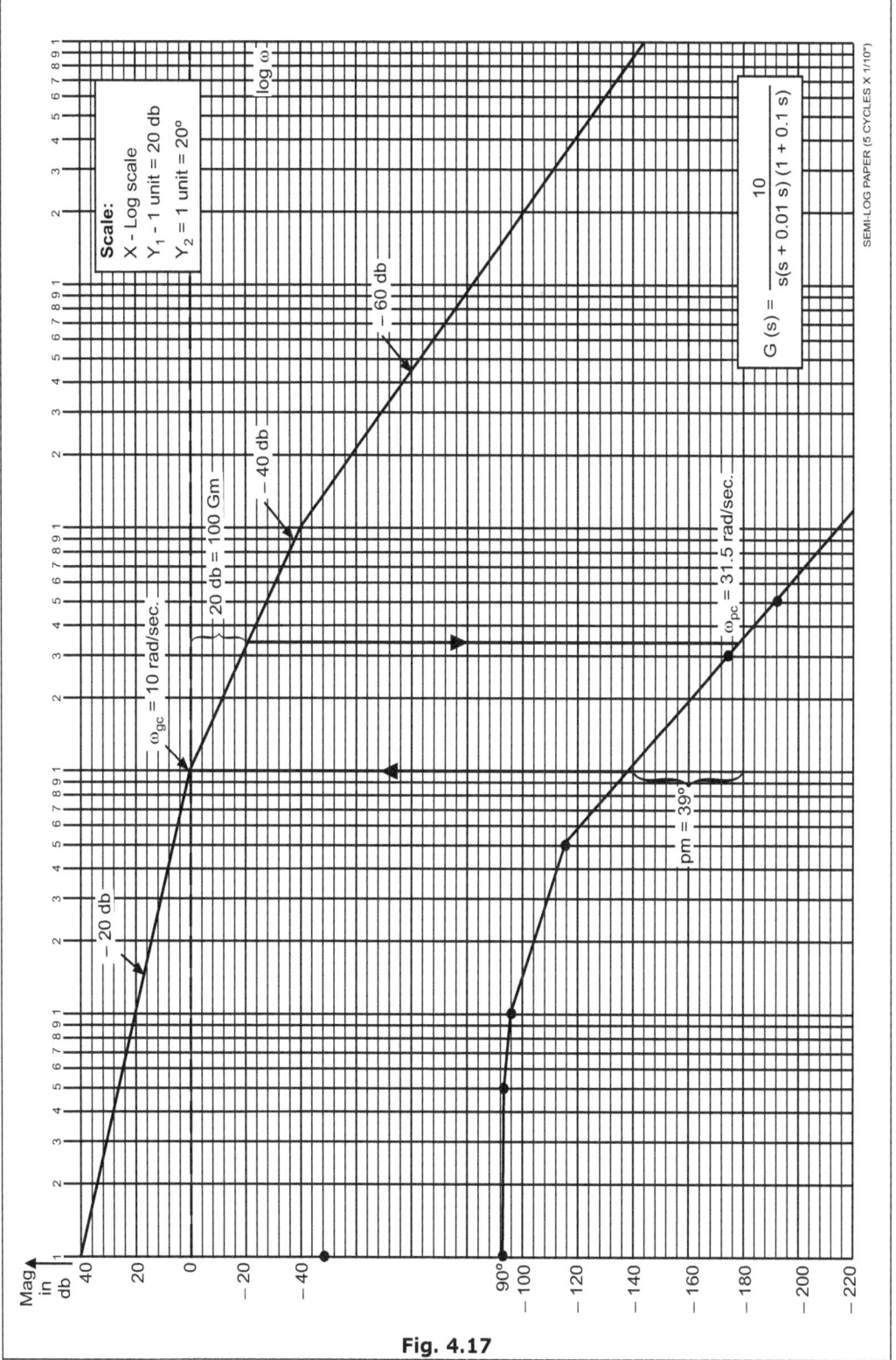

Fig. 4.17

Ans. (i) Gain cross-over frequency = 10 rad/sec.
(ii) Phase cross-over frequency = 31.5 rad/sec.
(iii) Gain margin = 20 db.
(iv) Phase margin = 39°.

Example 4.7: Sketch the Bode plot for the transfer function,

$$G(s) = \frac{ks^2}{(1 + 0.2s)(1 + 0.02s)}$$

Determine the system gain k for the gain cross-over frequency to be 5 rad/sec.

Sol.: Step 1 : Bring G(s) in standard form.

Let k = 1.

Put s = jω.

$$\therefore \quad G(j\omega) = \frac{(j\omega)^2}{(1 + j\,0.2\,\omega)(1 + j\,0.02\,\omega)}$$

This is the standard form.

Step 2: The following are present.
1. Zero at origin $(j\omega)^2$.
2. First order pole: $\frac{1}{(1 + j\,0.2\,\omega)}$.
3. First order pole: $\frac{1}{(1 + j\,0.02\,\omega)}$.

Prepare table for magnitude plot.

To find the corner frequencies equate real and imaginary parts of poles.

(i) $1 = 0.2\,\omega$.
∴ ω = **5 rad/sec.**
(ii) $1 = 0.02\,\omega$.
∴ ω = **50 rad/sec.**
∴ **Corner frequencies** are 5 and 50 rad/sec.

Sr. No.	Factor	Corner frequency	Asymptotic log magnitude characteristic
1.	$(j\omega)^2$	None	Straight line of constant slope 40 db/dec. passing through ω = 1.
2.	$\frac{1}{1 + j\,0.2\,\omega}$	$\omega_1 = 5$	Straight line of constant slope – 20 db/dec. originating from ω = 5.
3.	$\frac{1}{1 + j\,0.02\,\omega}$	$\omega_2 = 50$	Straight line of constant slope – 20 db/dec. originating from ω = 50.

Step 3: If the gain cross-over frequency is required to be **5 rad/sec**. For this the plot has to be brought down by 28 db. Hence,

$$20\,\log_{10} k = -28$$

∴ k = 0.04.

Step 4: The magnitude plot is shown in the figure where the individual factors are shown by dotted lines and resultant is shown by dark line.

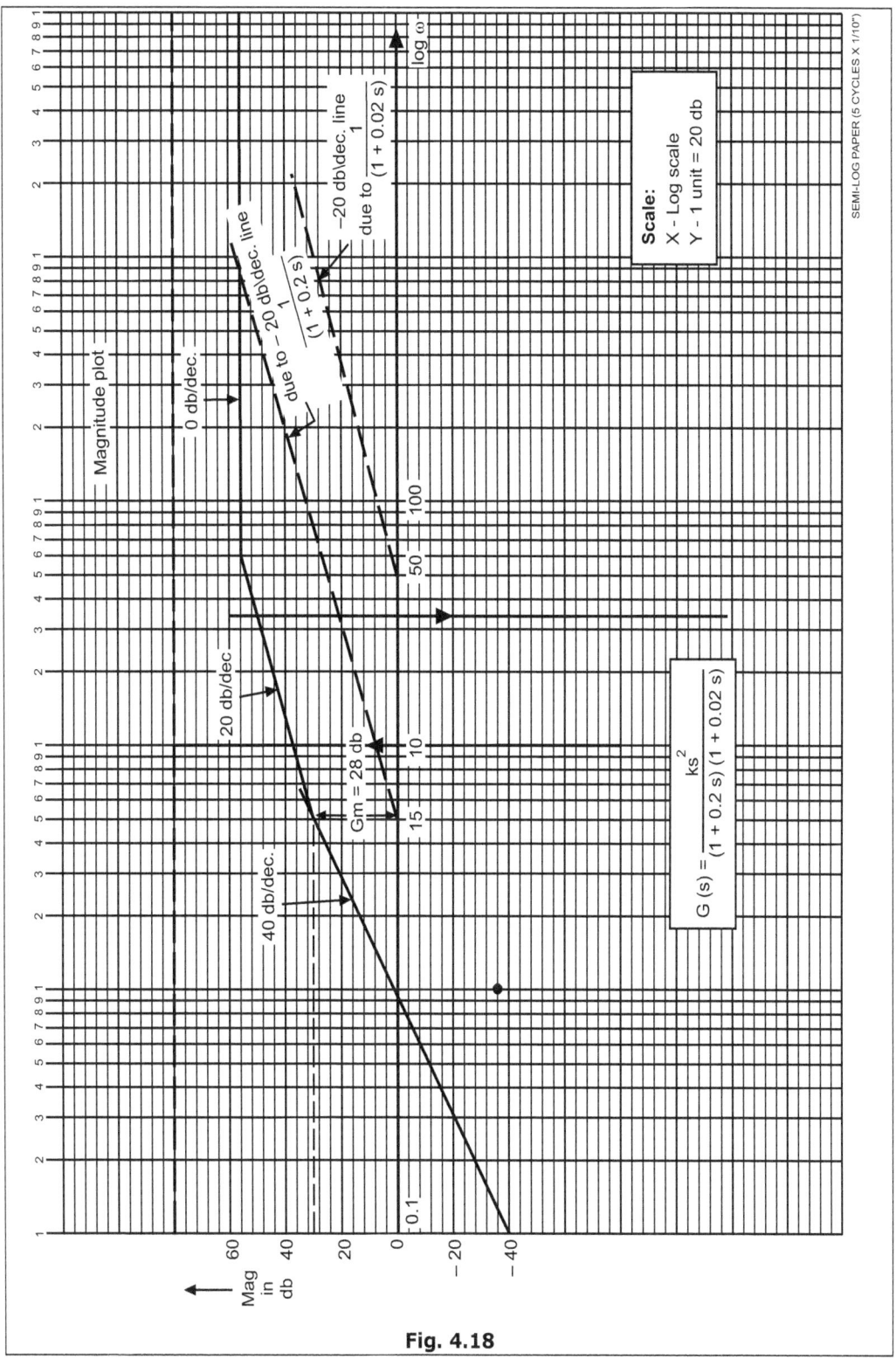

Fig. 4.18

Example 4.8: Draw the Bode plot for a system having,

$$G(s) = \frac{3}{s(1 + 0.05s)(1 + 0.2s)}, \quad H(s) = 1$$

Determine,
(i) Gain cross-over frequency and phase margin.
(ii) Phase cross-over frequency and gain margin.
(iii) Stability.

Sol.: Step 1: Bring G(s) in standard form
Put $s = j\omega$.

$$\therefore \quad G(j\omega) = \frac{3}{j\omega(1 + j\,0.05\,\omega)(1 + j\,0.02\,\omega)}$$

Step 2: The following points are present.

(i) Pole at origin: $\frac{1}{j\omega}$.

(ii) First order pole: $\frac{1}{1 + j\,0.05\,\omega}$.

(iii) First order pole: $\frac{1}{1 + j\,0.2\,\omega}$.

Step 3: Corner frequency by equating real and imaginary parts.

(i) $0.05\,\omega = 1$.
$\therefore$ $\omega = 20$ **rad/sec.**

(ii) $0.2\,\omega = 1$
$\therefore$ $\omega = 5$ **rad/sec.**

Step 4: Prepare table for magnitude plot.

Sr. No.	Factor	Corner frequency rad/sec.	Asymptotic log magnitude characteristic c
1.	3	None	Straight line of 0 db/dec. starting from $20\log_{10} 3 = 9.5$ db.
2.	$\frac{1}{j\omega}$	None	Straight line of -20 db/dec. passing through $\omega = 1$.
3.	$\frac{1}{1 + j\,0.05\,\omega}$	20	Straight line of -20 db/dec. originating from $\omega = 20$.
4.	$\frac{1}{1 + j\,0.2\,\omega}$	5	Straight line of -20 db/dec. originating from $\omega = 5$.

Step 5: Choose y-axis scale 1 cm = 20 db. Here largest first order is $(1 + j\,0.05\,\omega)$.

Thus, choose x-axis starting point 0.1 rad/sec. Thus, x-axis print 1 will have 0.1, 1, 10, 100, 1000 frequency.

Step 6: Write the phase equation.

(i) For $\dfrac{1}{j\omega} = (j\omega)^{-1}$

$\phi = \angle (j\omega)^{-1}$
$= -90 \times 1 = \mathbf{90°}$

(ii) For $\dfrac{1}{1 + j\,0.05\,\omega} = (1 + j\,0.05\,\omega)$

$\phi = \angle (1 + j\,0.05\,\omega)^{-1}$
$= -\tan^{-1} 0.05\,\omega$

(iii) For $\dfrac{1}{1 + j\,0.2\,\omega} = (1 + j\,0.2\,\omega)^{-1}$

$\therefore \phi = \angle (1 + j\,0.2\,\omega)^{-1}$
$= -\tan^{-1} 0.2\,\omega$

$\therefore \quad \phi(j\omega) = -90° - \tan^{-1} 0.05\,\omega - \tan^{-1} 0.2\,\omega$

Step 7: Prepare table for the phase plot

$\therefore \quad \phi = -90° - \tan^{-1} 0.05\,\omega - \tan^{-1} 0.2\,\omega$

Sr. No.	ω rad/sec.	ϕ
1	0	$-90°$
2	0.1	$-91.4°$
3	0.5	$-97°$
4	1	$-104.2°$
5	3	$-149°$
6	5	$-180°$
7	10	$-211°$

Step 8: Draw the phase plot.
Where smallest $\phi = -90°$ and largest $\phi = -211°$. So scale chosen as $20° = 1$ unit and starting scale is $-90°$.

Step 9: Gain margin calculation.
From phase resultant curve find 'ω' where phase curves crosses $-180°$.
This is phase cross-over frequency $\omega_{pc} = 10$ rad/sec.

Step 10:
For this value of ω_{pc}, goto the magnitude resultant curve which is **17 db** below **0 db** line.

Hence, Gain margin is positive **system is stable.**

Step 11: Phase margin calculations.
From the magnitude resultant curve, find where the resultant crosses 0 db line. This is gain cross-over frequency $\omega_{gc} = 3$ rad/sec.

Step 12:
For this value of ω_{gc}, go to the phase curve and find out how much is the phase angle ϕ.

$\therefore \quad$ PM $= 180 + \phi$
$= 180 - 132$
$= \mathbf{48°}$

Ans.

(i)	Gain cross-over frequency	= 5 rad/sec.
(ii)	Phase cross-over frequency	= 10 rad/sec.
(iii)	Gain margin	= 17 db
(iv)	Phase margin	= 48°

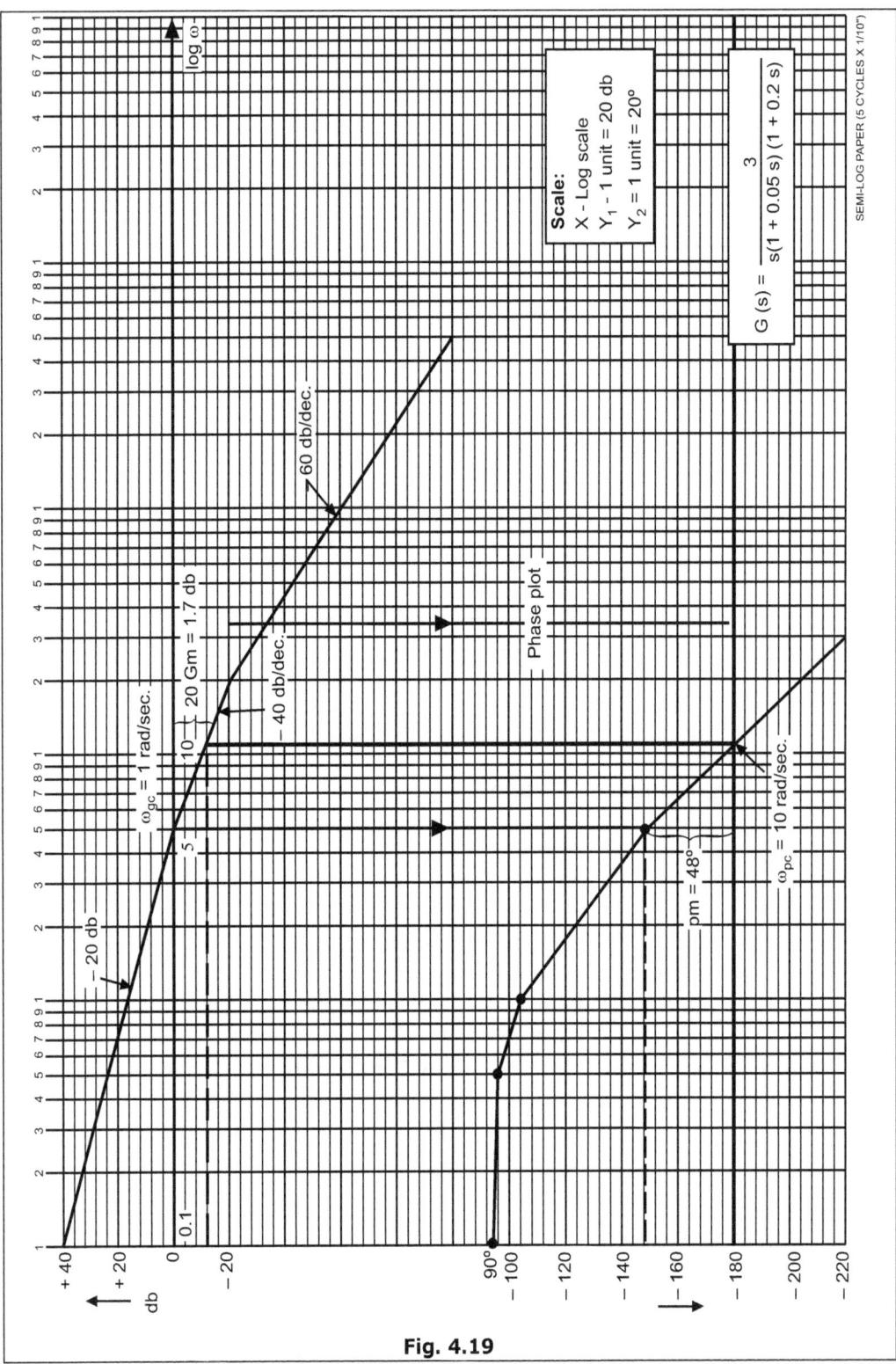

Fig. 4.19

Example 4.9: A certain unity feedback control system is given by,

$$G(s) = \frac{k}{s(1+s)(1+0.1s)}$$

Draw the Bode plot for the system. Determine from plot, the value of k so as to have,

(i) Gain margin = 10 db. (ii) Phase margin = 50°.

Sol.: Step 1: Put $s = j\omega$ in given T.F.

$$G(j\omega) = \frac{k}{j\omega(1+j\omega)(1+j0.1\omega)}$$

Step 2: Let $k = 1$.
Magnitude plot.

Sr. No.	Factor	Corner frequency	Asymptotic log magnitude characteristic
1.	$\frac{1}{j\omega}$	None	Straight line of – 20 db/dec. passing through $\omega = 1$.
2.	$\frac{1}{1+j\omega}$	1	Straight line of – 20 db/dec. originating from $\omega = 1$.
3.	$\frac{1}{1+j0.01\omega}$	10	Straight line of – 20 db/dec. originating from $\omega = 10$.

Step 3 : Phase plot.

$$\phi = -90° - \tan^{-1}\omega - \tan^{-1}0.1\omega$$

Sr. No.	ω rad/sec.	ϕ
1	0	– 90°
2	0.1	– 96.3°
3	0.5	– 119.4°
4	1	– 140.7°
5	3	– 178.3°
6	5	– 195°
7	10	– 219°

Step 4:
(i) For Gm to be 10 db the magnitude plot has to be shifted-up by,

$$19.5 - 10 = 9.5 \text{ db}$$
$$20 \log_{10} k = 9.5 \quad (\because 19.5 \text{ db is the Gm from plot})$$

∴ $\boxed{k = 2.98}$

(ii) For pm to be 50° the value of ω at $-180° + 50 = -130°$ is 0.73 rad/sec. and Gm is – 5 db.

Thus, to have pm, 50° the magnitude plot to be shifted down by 5 db so that $\omega_{gc} = 0.73$ rad/sec.

$$20 \log_{10} k = -5$$

∴ $\boxed{k = 0.56}$

Note: From examination point of view there is no need to write the details steps. Once you understand how to plot the Bode plot.
The following should be directly in solution.
(i) Standard form of T.F. (ii) Corner frequency. (iii) Table for magnitude plot.
(iv) Equation of phase angle and table for phase plot.
(v) Gain margin, phase margin, ω_{pc} and ω_{gc} directly on plot.

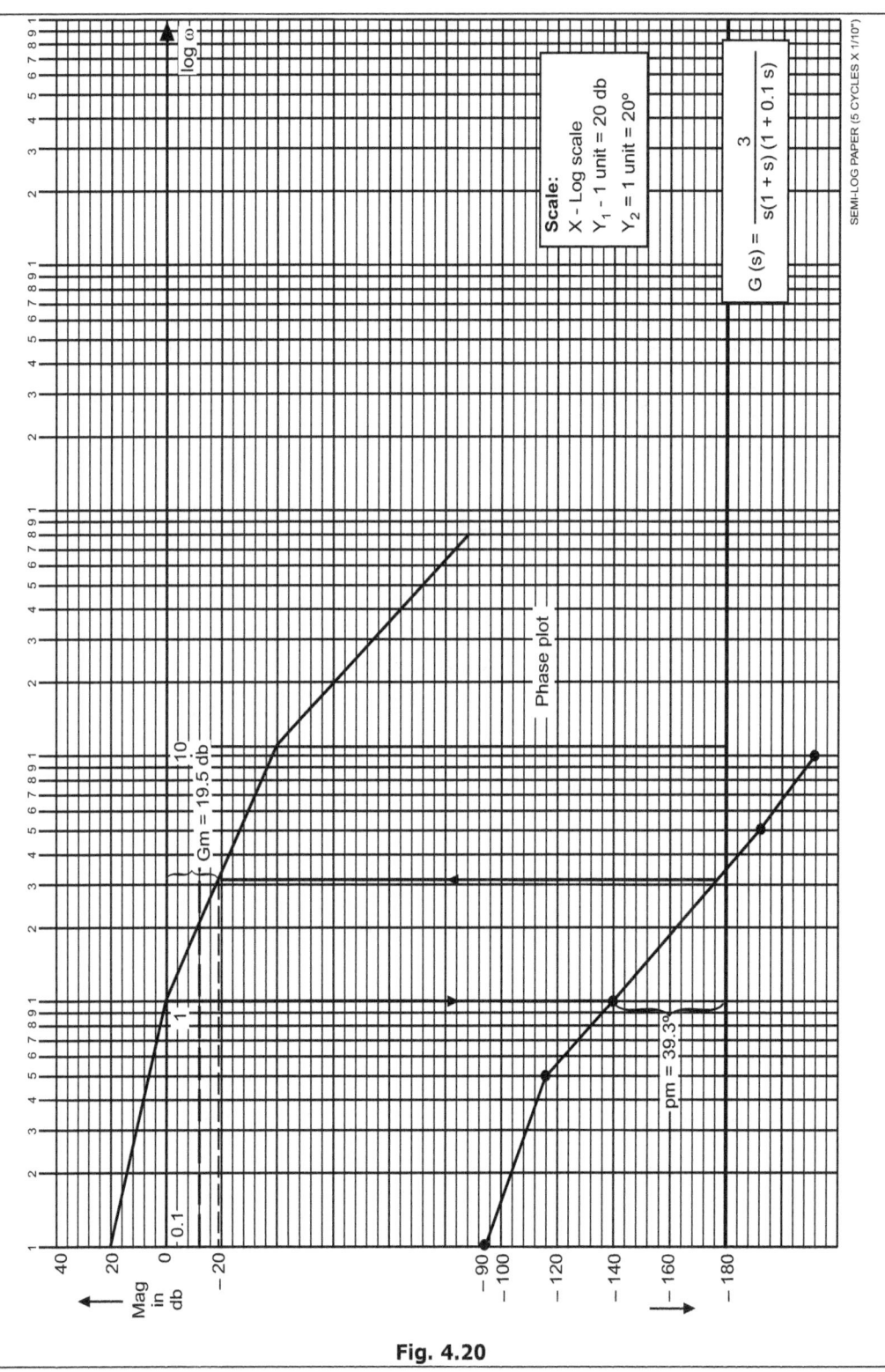

Fig. 4.20

Important Points

- **Frequency response** of a system is defined as the steady state response of the system to a sinusoidal signal.
- **Peak response** is defined as the maximum value of $|M(j\omega)|$.
- **Resonant frequency** ω_r is the frequency at which the response peak M_r occurs.
- **Bandwidth** is defined as the range of frequency at which the magnitude of $|M(j\omega)|$ drops to 70.7% of its zero frequency value.
- **Cut-off rate** is the slope of the log magnitude curve near the cut-off frequency.
- The **phase margin** indicates how much the system angle can be increased to cause the system to become unstable from a stable condition.
- **Gain Margin** is the amount of gain in 'dB' that can be allowed to increase before the system reaches instability.
- The frequency at which gain is unity is called **gain cross-over frequency.**
- The frequency where phase angle of transfer function is $-180°$ is called **phase cross-over frequency.**

Practice Questions

1. Define frequency response.
2. Draw the frequency response and list its specifications.
3. Define :
   - (i) Peak response,
   - (ii) Phase margin,
   - (iii) Gain margin,
   - (iv) Cut-off rate.
4. Define :
   - (i) Gain cross-over frequency,
   - (ii) Phase cross-over frequency.
5. State the advantages of frequency response.

Previous Year MSBTE Questions and Answers (As Per 'E' Scheme)

1. Define the following frequency response specifications:

    (i) Response peak,

    (ii) Bandwidth,

    (iii) Cut-off frequency,

    (iv) Resonant frequency. **(W-12) (4M)**

Ans. Refer Section 4.2.

2. State any four advantages of frequency response analysis. **(W-12) (4M)**

Ans. Refer Section 4.5.

✻✻✻

PROCESS CONTROL AND CONTROL ACTIONS

About This Chapter ...

After reading this chapter students can understand –
- Process Control System
- Process Characteristics
- Role of Controllers in Process Industry
- Introduction to Controllers
- Control Actions
- Composite Controllers (Control Actions)
- Controllers
- Composite Controller Modes

5.1 INTRODUCTION

- A process is defined as a set of operations that perform physical or chemical transformation or a series of transformation in which the fluid or solid materials are converted into suitable or useful state.
- Such process might be a production process, plant, transportation of matter and energy.
- A process forms part of a set of production or processing functions executed in and by means of process hardware such as pipes, tanks, motors shafts etc.
- The performance of process variables such as temperature, pressure, flow, level etc.
- The control of process variables is achieved by the control equipment.
- The process control is therefore, an engineering science of measuring one or more of these process variables and automatically controlling them to the desired level called set points or reference points.

5.2 PROCESS CONTROL SYSTEM (W-12)

QUESTION

1. Draw the block diagram of process control system and describe each element.

(W-12)(4M)

- In process control, the basic objective is to regulate the value of certain variables within a specified limit.

- To regulate these process variables, we use a controller and a final control element which regulate the process variable in accordance with the reference value or set point.

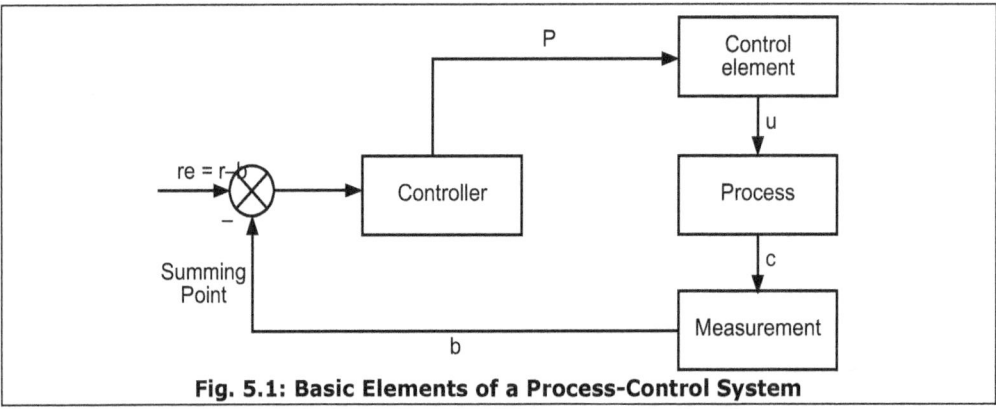

Fig. 5.1: Basic Elements of a Process-Control System

- **Process:**

  Process consists of several regulated operations. Many variables may be involved in such a process and it may be desirable to control these variables at the same time. In a single variable process, only one variable is to be controlled. In multivariable processes, in which many variables, perhaps inter-related, are involved may require regulation.

- **Measuring Element:**

  It measures or senses the actual value of the control variable and converts it into proportional feedback variable.

- **Error Detector:**

  It compares the feedback variable with the set point signal so as to generate deviation on error signal.

- **Controller:**

  It generates the correct signal depending upon the magnitude of deviation which is then applied to the final control element. The controller may be pneumatic, hydraulic, electronic or analog or digital computer which solves certain equations to produce a proper output.

- **Final Control Element:**

  Depending upon the signal from controller, the final control elements adjust the manipulated variable so as to drive the control variable towards the set point. Hence, the final control element directly influences the process.

5.3 MODES OF CONTROL ACTION

- A controller is used to eliminate or reduce the error (differentiate between set point and the measured value) by generating a correction signal to the final control element.

- Modern industrial controllers are usually made to produce one or a combination of six basic control actions called modes of control, common to the industrial automatic controllers.

- *An automatic controller produces the control signal is called as control action.*

  Control actions are classified as –

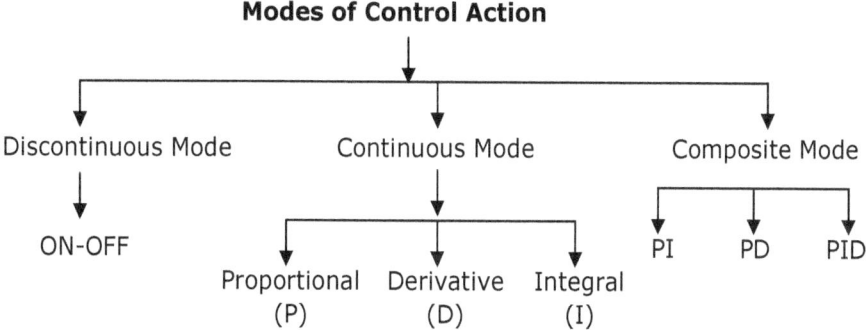

1. Discontinuous mode.
2. Two Position or ON-OFF Controllers.
3. Continuous Modes.
    (i) Proportional (P) Controller.
    (ii) Derivative (D) Controller.
    (iii) Integral (I) Controller.
4. Composite Controllers.
    (i)   Proportional + Integral (PI) Controller.
    (ii) Proportional + Derivative (PD) Controller.
    (iii) Proportional + Integral + Derivative (PID) Controller.

5.4 DISCONTINUOUS MODE

- In this type of controller output varies only in two levels ON and OFF, so it is called Discontinuous Mode Control Action.

5.4.1 ON-OFF Controllers

QUESTIONS

1. State the principle of ON-OFF control. Write its standard equation and define neutral zone. **(4M)**
2. State the advantages and disadvantages of ON-OFF control action (two each). **(4M)**
3. Explain ON-OFF control action with simple example. What is natural zone concept? **(4M)**

- In ON-OFF control action, the output has only two states, fully ON and fully OFF or 1 or 0.
- An ON-OFF controller operates on the manipulated variable only when the measured output crosses the set point.
- Fig. 5.2 shows the block diagram of ON-OFF controller in which output signal m(t) from the controller remains at maximum M_1 or minimum M_2 value, depending on whether the error signal 'e' is positive or negative.

  ∴ Output equation is,

  $$m(t) = M_1 \text{ for } e > 0 \quad \ldots (5.1)$$
  $$m(t) = M_2 \text{ for } e < 0 \quad \ldots (5.2)$$

  Therefore, M_1 and M_2 are constants. Minimum value of M_2 is either zero or $-M_1$.

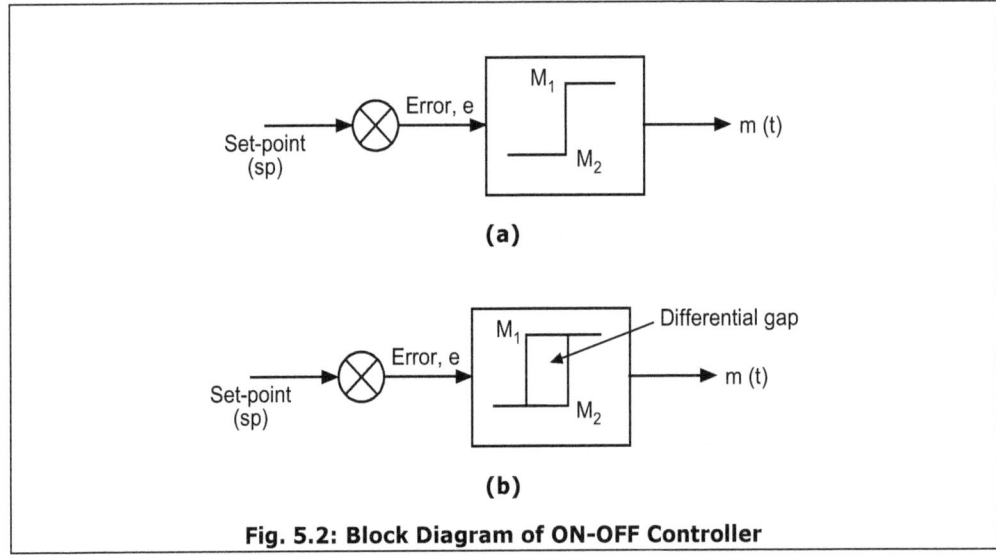

Fig. 5.2: Block Diagram of ON-OFF Controller

- In conditioning system, when the temperature falls below a certain reference level, the error is positive the output is maximum (M_1) i.e. 100% controller output will stop the air supply to the air conditioner.

- When the temperature rises above a certain reference level, error will be negative i.e. output is zero i.e. M_2. Now, controller output will start the electric supply to air conditioner.

- **Neutral Zone:**
  - If the error is positive, heater (as explained in example 1) is **ON** and if the error is negative, heater is **OFF**. To avoid the frequent operation of ON-OFF mechanism, a **neutral zone** or **differential gap** is kept as shown in Fig. 5.3.
  - Practically, there is an overlap when e_p increases through zero and when it decreases through zero. On this overlap the controller output does not change thus, range $2\Delta e$ is known as the neutral zone.

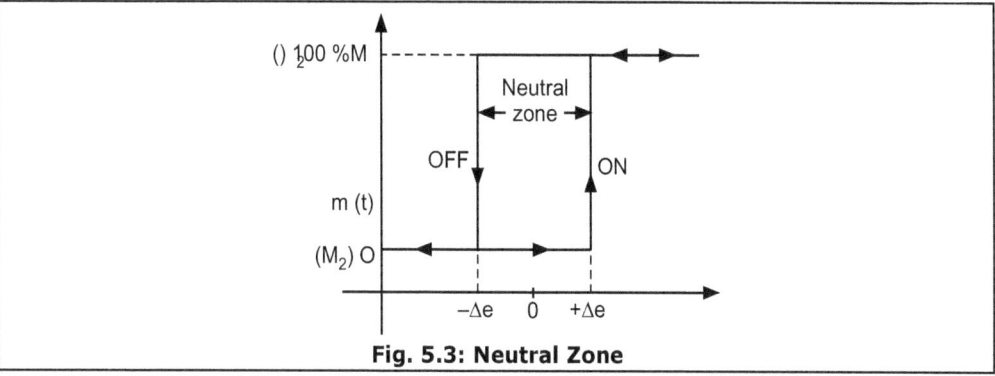

Fig. 5.3: Neutral Zone

- The range through which the actuating error signal must move before switching occurs is called the Neutral zone.
- To prevent excessive cycling, to reduce losses of components and arching at relay contacts, neutral zones are purposely kept.
- In Fig. 5.3 $2\Delta E$ is the neutral zone. It is decided by the accuracy required. But during the zone, the controller output does not change.

- **Features of Control Action:**

It is usually associated with overshoot and the undershoot. Because of the mechanical friction at electrical contacts, the controller goes on slightly below the set point and goes-off above the set point as shown in Fig. 5.4.

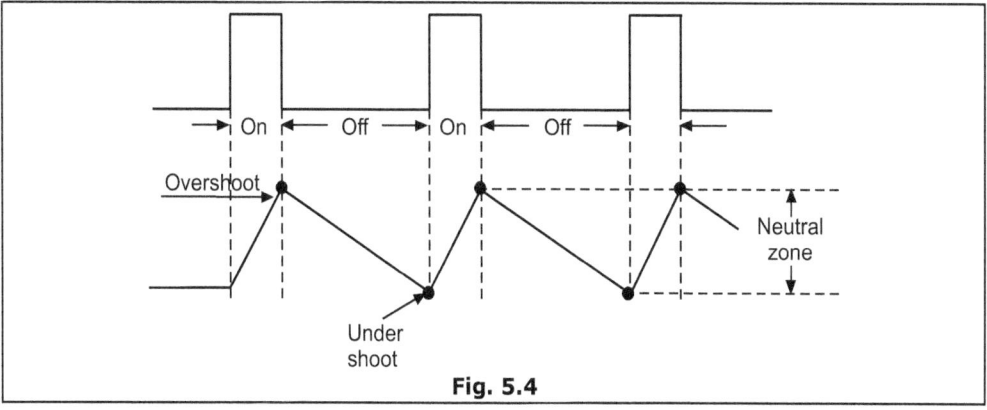

Fig. 5.4

From Fig. 5.4, it is seen that heat is **ON** for short period and **OFF** for more time period.

As the heater is ON, the temperature starts to rise and when heater becomes off, temperature drops and so we get a triangular waveform.

When heater is ON, temperature increases and **overshoot** occurs and when heater is off, temperature drops and **undershoot** occurs. i.e. finite warm-up time and cool-off time of heat produces overshoots and undershoots.

ON-OFF control action is suitable under conditions as –

1. When fast corrective action is required.
2. Process response is slow.
3. Change in load is small and slow.
4. Small or no dead zone.

- **Advantage:**
    1. Simple and economical.

- **Disadvantage:**
    1. Not suitable for complex systems.

- **Applications:**

    Used in,
    1. Room heaters.
    2. Refrigerators.
    3. Level control of water tanks.
    4. Widely used in industrial and domestic control systems.
    5. Air conditioners.

5.5 CONTINUOUS MODE

- In continuous mode, the controller continuously adjust the manipulated variable so that the input to the process is approximately in balanced with process demand.

5.5.1 Proportional Controller

QUESTIONS

1. State the expression for proportional controller and define (i) Proportional band and (ii) Offset. **(4M)**
2. Describe the action of proportional controller with offset. **(4M)**

- A proportional (P) controller continuously adjusts the manipulated variable so that the input to the process is approximately in balanced with the process demand.

- In proportional control, the output of the controller is proportional to the error.

- Proportional controller is essentially an amplifier with an adjustable gain.
- The relationship between output of the control m(t) and the error signal e, is shown in block diagram Fig. 5.5.

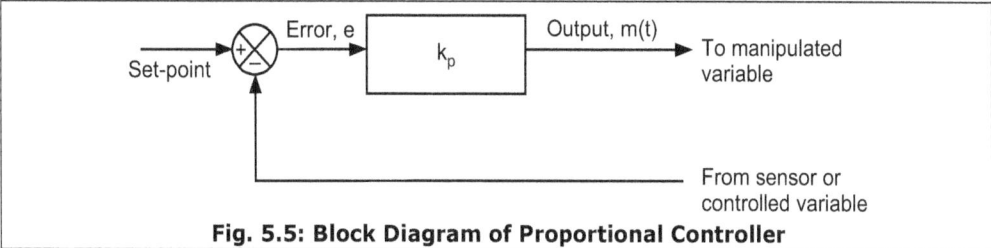

Fig. 5.5: Block Diagram of Proportional Controller

The output equation is,
$$m(t) = k_p \, e(t) \qquad \ldots (5.3)$$
where, $m(t)$ = Output
k_p = A constant called proportional gain
e = Error signal
$M(s) = k_p \, E(s)$

- The value of change in the controller output for a given change in actuating error signal depends on the proportional band of the instrument.

- **Proportional Band:**
    - **The range of error to cover the 0% to 100% controller output is called the proportional band,** because the one-to-one correspondence exists only for error in this range.

- The transfer function response curve of a wideband and narrow band proportional controller is shown in Fig. 5.6.

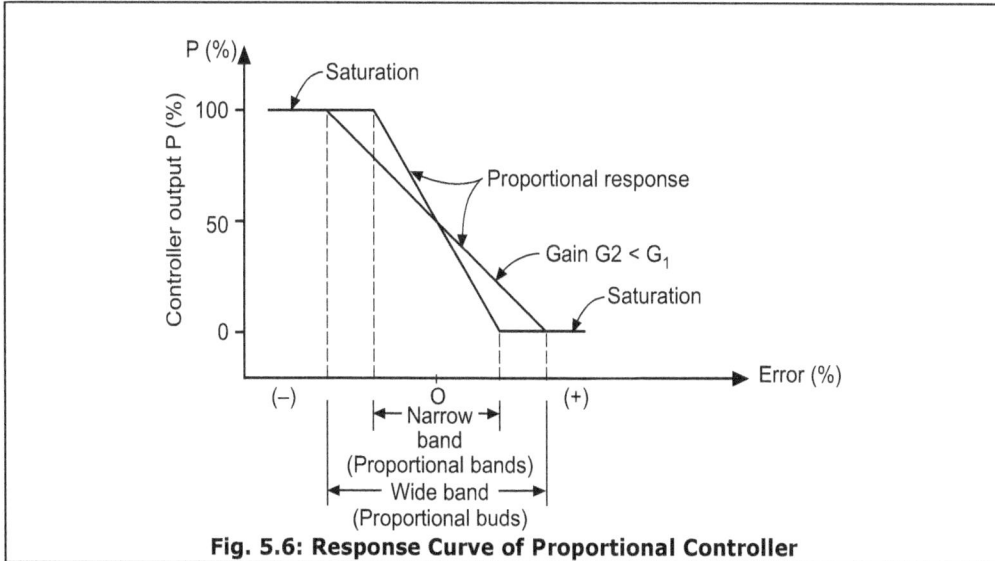

Fig. 5.6: Response Curve of Proportional Controller

- From response curve, it is evident that in case of wide band proportional controller the large change in the input is required to produce a small change in the process output whereas in case of narrow-band proportional controller a small change in the input produces a large change in the output.

- If the proportional band is reduced to zero then it becomes an ON-OFF controller. Thus, narrowing the proportional band increases the gain.
    - **Note that the proportional band is dependent on the gain.**
    - A high gain means large response to an error, but also a narrow band within which the output is not saturated.

    The proportional band is defined by the equation,

    $$PB = \frac{100}{k_p} \quad \ldots (5.4)$$

- **Characteristics of Proportional Mode:**
    1. If error is zero, the output is a constant equal to P_o
    2. If there is error, for every 1% of error a correction of $k_p\%$ is added to or subtracted from P_o, depending on the direction of the controller.
    3. There is a band of error about zero of magnitude PB within which the output is not saturated at 0% or 100%.

- **Offset:**
    - **An important characteristic of the proportional mode is that it produces a permanent residual error in the operating point of the controlled variable. When a change in load occurs, this error is referred to as offset.**
    - Offset can be minimised by a larger constant k_p, which also reduces the proportional band.
    - Consider a system under the nominal load with the controller at 50% and the error as zero, to see how offset occurs is shown in Fig. 5.7.

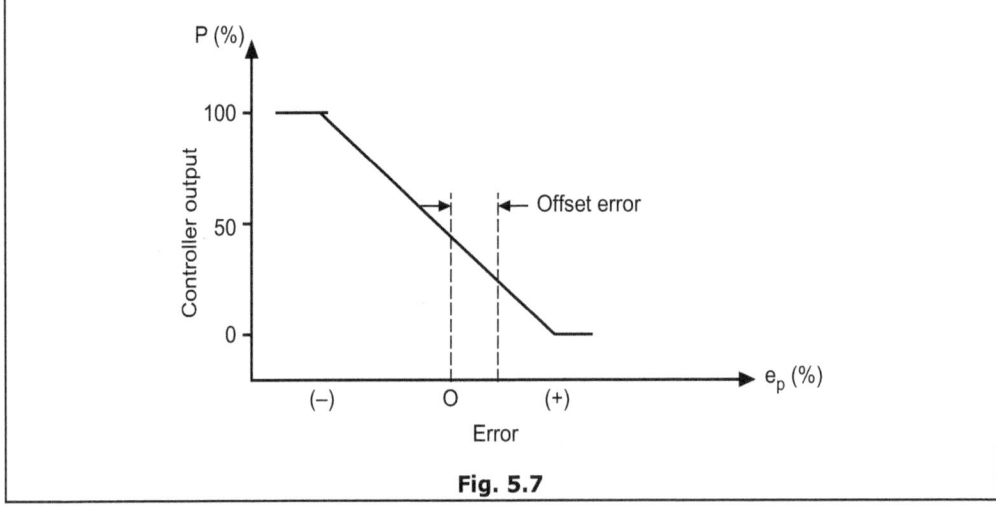

Fig. 5.7

- An offset error occurs if a proportional controller requires a new nominal output following a load change.

- If transient error occurs, the system responds by changing the controller output in correspondence with the transient to effect a return to zero error.

- However, suppose, a load change occurs that requires a permanent change in controller output to produce the zero error state.

- Because, a one-to-one correspondence exists between the controller output and error, it is clear that a new zero error controller output can never be achieved.

- Instead, the system produces a small permanent offset in reaching a compromise position of the controller output under new loads.

- **Effect of Offset**
    - The offset error limits the use of the proportional mode to only a few cases, particularly those where a manual reset of the operating point is possible to eliminate offset.
    - Proportional control is generally used in processes where large load changes are unlikely or with moderate to small process lag times.
    - Fig. 5.7 shows that if k_p is made very large, the PB becomes very small and proportional mode acts like ON/Off mode.
    - ON/Off mode exhibits oscillations about the setpoint. i.e. for high gain, the proportional mode causes oscillations of the error.

The worst result is obtained when there is dead time or transfer lag is present in the system.

Also, a problem occurs when the offset is larger than the time required for stability.

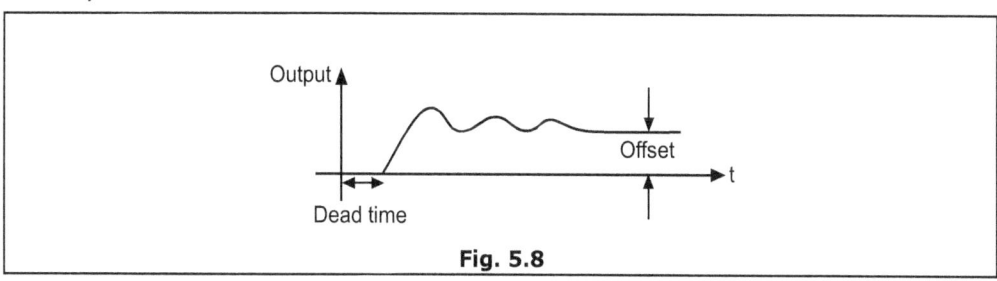

Fig. 5.8

The proportional control action is not suitable for following conditions:
1. If load changes are rapid, that exist for long period.
2. Process reaction rate is fast.
3. There is considerable dead time.

- **Disadvantage:**
It produces offset in the output when load changes occur.

- **Application:**

    It is used where,
    (i) Manual reset of operating point is possible,
    (ii) Load changes are small and
    (iii) No dead time exists.

SOLVED EXAMPLES

Example 5.1:

A liquid level control system linearly converts displacement of 2 to 3 metres in a control signal of 4 to 20 mA. A relay is a control element to open or close a control valve. The relay switches ON at 11 mA and opens at 9 mA.

Determine
(i) Relationship between liquid level and control signal.
(ii) The neutral zone.

Solution:

(i) Given:

Height	Current
2 m	4 mA
3 m	20 mA

$$P = k_p e_p + P_o$$

$$2\,m = k_p (4\,mA) + P_o \quad \ldots (1)$$

$$3\,m = k_p (20\,mA) + P_o \quad \ldots (2)$$

Subtract equation (1) from (2)

$$+1 = 16 \times 10^{-3} k_p + 0$$

$$k_p = 0.0625 \text{ m/mA (slope)}$$

$$P_o = 1.75 \text{ m (Intercept)}$$

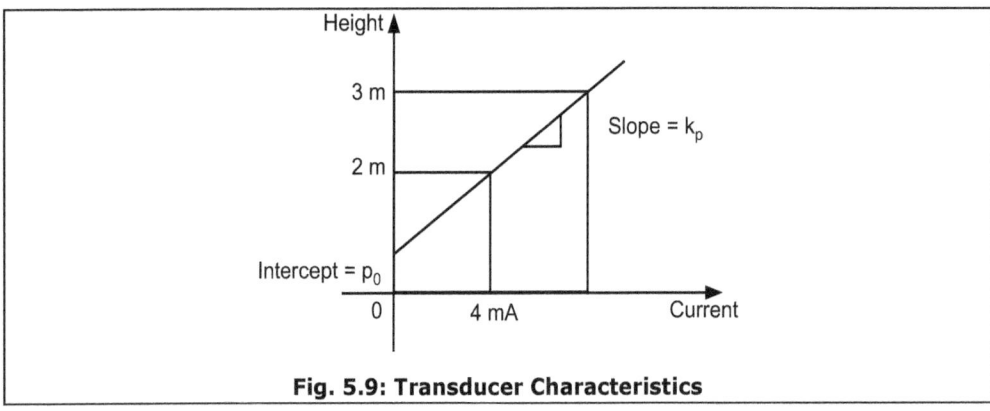

Fig. 5.9: Transducer Characteristics

∴ Relationship between displacement (h) and control signal (i.e. current) is

$$h = k_p i + P_o$$

(ii) The relay closes at 11 mA = h_{max}

$$h_{max} = k_p(i) + P_o$$
$$= 0.0625 (11) + 1.75$$
$$= \mathbf{2.4375 \text{ m}}$$

Relay opens at 9 mA

$$h_{min} = k_p(i) + P_o$$
$$= 0.0625 (9) + 1.75$$
$$= \mathbf{2.3125 \text{ m}}$$

∴ Neutral zone = $h_{max} - h_{min}$
$$= 2.4375 - 2.3125$$
$$= \mathbf{0.1250 \text{ m}}$$

5.5.2 Integral Controller

- Offset of plain proportional controller is removed (reset) in the integral controller.

- In integral (I) control mode, the value of controller output m(t) is changed at the rate proportional to the error signal e.

- The steady-state error or offset in the proportional control is eliminated by including integral control action in the controller.

- The output signal m(t) can have non-zero value when the error signal e is zero. This is impossible in proportional control because a non-zero control signal requires a non-zero error signal.

- **The output equation of integral controller** is,

$$\boxed{m(t) = \frac{1}{T_i} \int_0^t e \, dt} \qquad \ldots (5.5)$$

- Laplace transform is,

$$M(s) = \frac{1}{T_i s} E(s) \qquad \ldots (5.6)$$

where, T_i = Integral time setting (reset times) of the controller

- For zero error, the value of output remains stationary.
- If the value of error signal 'e' is doubled, then the value of output m(t) varies twice as fast.
- The integral control mode, continuously integrating the area under the error curve. It eliminates the offset by forcing the addition (or removal) of mass or energy which should have been added (or removed) in the past.
- A block diagram of integral control action is shown in Fig. 5.10.

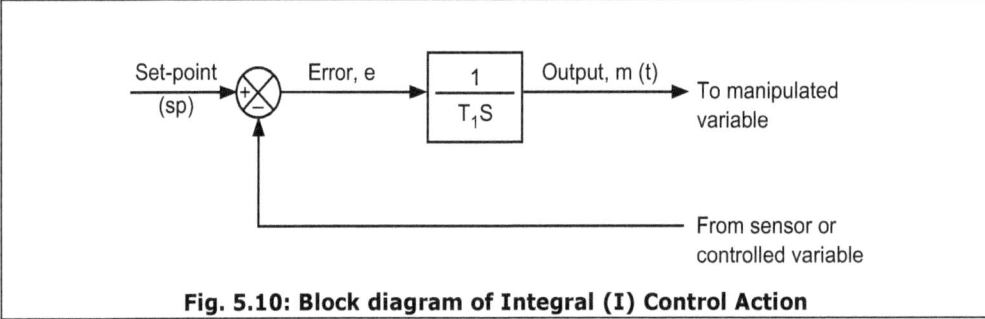

Fig. 5.10: Block diagram of Integral (I) Control Action

Response Curve of Integral Control Action (Characteristics):

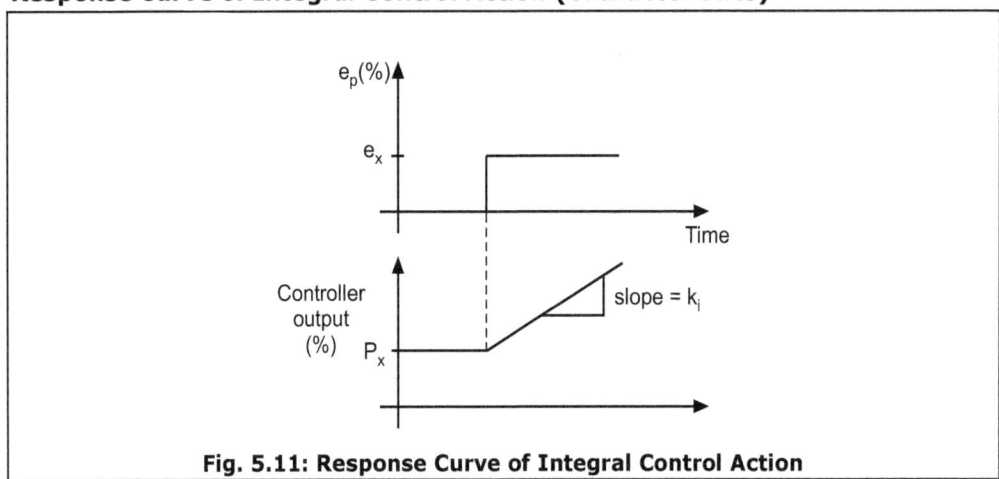

Fig. 5.11: Response Curve of Integral Control Action

1. The controller stays fixed when the error is zero. This controller output value remains what it was when the error reached zero.
2. Controller output changes at the rate of k_p percentage per second for every 1% of error (e_p).
3. There are delays in controller output change and time error reduction.

5.5.3 Derivative Controller

QUESTION

1. State the principle of derivative control with mathematical expression and its characteristics. **(4M)**

- In derivative control action, the output signal of the controller is a function of the rate at which the error is changing.
- Derivative control action provides the means of obtaining a controller with high sensitivity.
- Derivative control predicts actuating (process) errors before they have evolved and takes corrective action in advance of that occurrance and tends to increase the stability of the system.
- The output equation of derivative controller is

$$m(t) = T_d \frac{de(t)}{dt} \quad \ldots (5.7)$$

where, T_d = Derivative time of the controller

Laplace transform is,

$$M(s) = T_d \cdot S\, E(s) \quad \ldots (5.8)$$

- A block diagram of derivative control action is shown in Fig. 5.12.

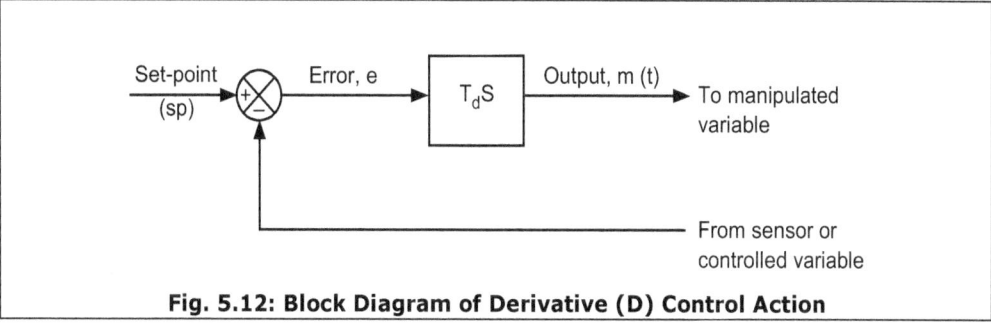

Fig. 5.12: Block Diagram of Derivative (D) Control Action

- The derivative control mode acts on the rate at which the error signal changes, it can also cause unnecessary upsets, such as reacting to a sudden set point change by the operator, amplifying noise, causing when the measurement signal changes in steps.
- **Since derivative control operates on the rate of change of error and not the error itself, it is always used in combination with proportional or P + I control action.**

Response of Derivative Control (Characteristics):

1. No output if error is zero or constant.
2. When error changes with time, the controller output changes T_d percent for every 1% per second change in error.

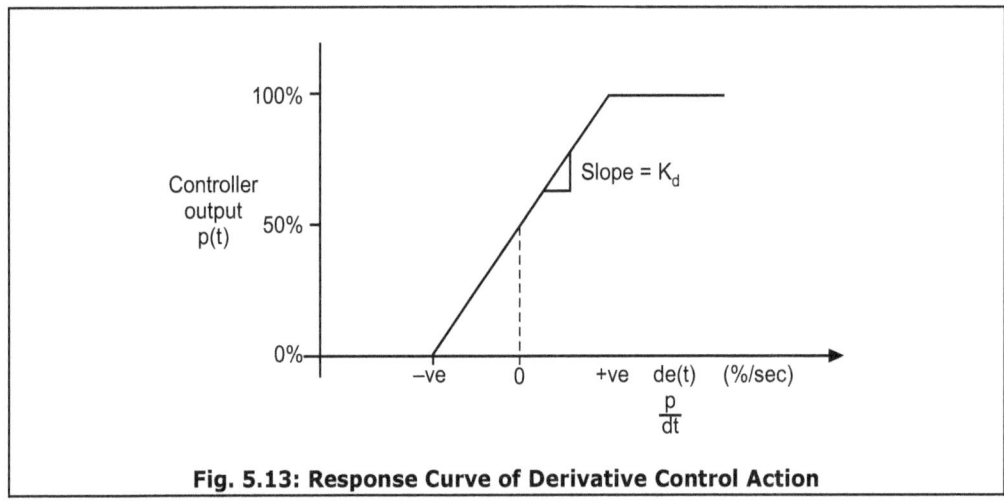

Fig. 5.13: Response Curve of Derivative Control Action

5.6 COMPOSITE CONTROLLERS (CONTROL ACTION)

Composite control action means the combination of two continuous control action.

Control requirements do not fit any one of the P, I or D control actions. We can combine these basic control actions to get advantages of each of them and eliminate limitations of the individual control actions.

i.e.

1. P + I control action (PI) 2. P + D control action (PD) 3. P I D control action.

5.6.1 PI Control Action

QUESTIONS	
1. Explain PI control action. State its equation. State the limitations of PI controller.	(8M)
2. Explain PI control action. State advantages of PI control (any two).	(6M)

- In proportional plus-integral (PI) control, the output is proportional to a linear combination of the input error and the time integral of the input error.
- **The output equation of PI controller** is,

$$m(t) = k_p \left(e(t) + \frac{1}{T_i} \int_0^t e(t) \right) \quad \ldots (5.9)$$

Its Laplace transform is,

$$M(s) = k_p \left[1 + \frac{1}{T_i s} \right] E(s) \quad \ldots (5.10)$$

- The integral time T_i varied by providing a knob. It adjusts the integral control action.

- The inverse of T_i is called the reset rate which is the number of times per minute that the proportional part of the control action is duplicated.
- Reset is measured in terms of repeats per minute.
- Fig. 5.14 show the block diagram of proportional plus integral (PI) control action.

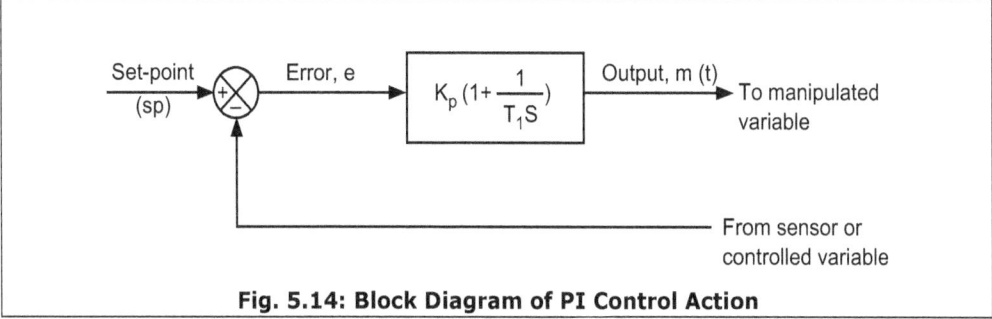

Fig. 5.14: Block Diagram of PI Control Action

Response Controller:

- The integral action eliminates the inherent offset of the proportional control and the proportional control gives one-to-one correspondence of error to output.

  This is explained in Fig. 5.15 (a).

  1. The controller output is fixed at the value when error reached zero, until the error is zero.

  2. The correction is done by the proportional term, when the error is not zero. The integral term increases or decreases the accumulated value of $P_{i(0)}$ depending on sign of the error and the required control action.

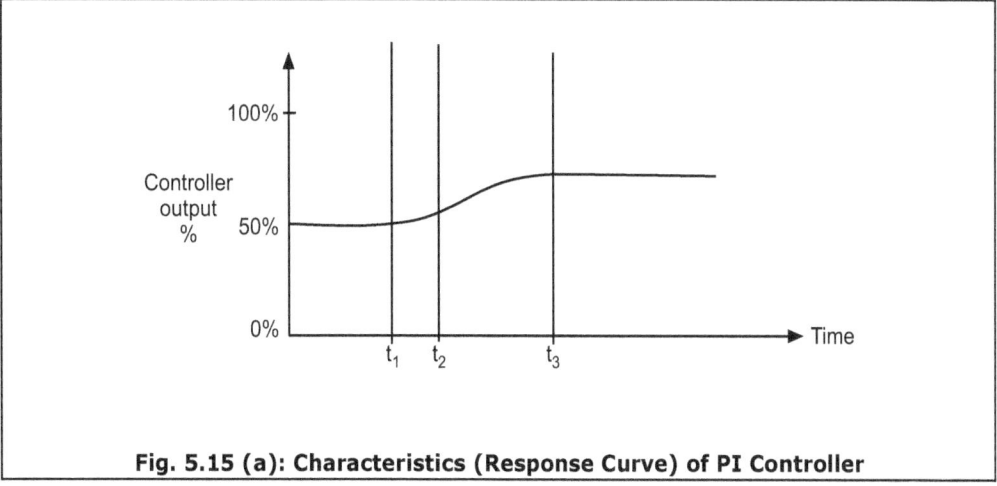

Fig. 5.15 (a): Characteristics (Response Curve) of PI Controller

5.6.2 Proportional and Derivative (PD) Controller

QUESTION

1. What is meant by PD controller? Explain. **(4M)**

- Another combination of control actions which involve the proportional and derivative control (PD) is also required in industrial processes.
- In proportional-plus-derivative (PD) control, the derivative (or rate) action causes the controller output to vary as the rate of change of the actuating error signal varies.
- The output equation of PD controller is,

$$m(t) = k_p \left(e(t) + T_d \frac{de(t)}{dt} \right) \quad \ldots (5.11)$$

where,
$$T_d = \text{Derivative time}$$

Its Lapace transform is,

$$M(s) = k_p (1 + T_d S) \, E(s) \quad \ldots (5.12)$$

- T_d is the derivative time - the time interval by which the rate action advances the offset of the proportional control action.
- A block diagram of proportional pulse derivative (PD) control action is shown in Fig. 5.15.

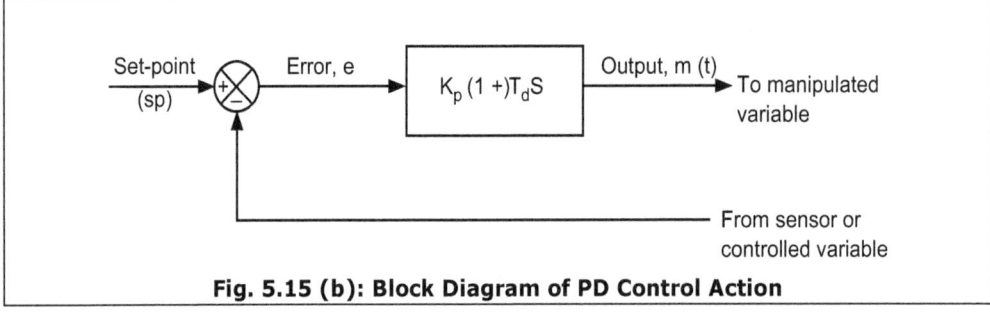

Fig. 5.15 (b): Block Diagram of PD Control Action

- This system cannot eliminate the offset error of proportional control. However, this system can handle fast changes in load which change the controlled variable fast i.e. b(t).

Response of PD Controller (Characteristics):

Consider a hypothetical example where the error $e_p(t)$ changes as shown in Fig. 5.16 (a).

Controller output with PD control action. Output = 50% when error (e_p) = 0% as shown in Fig. 5.16 (b).

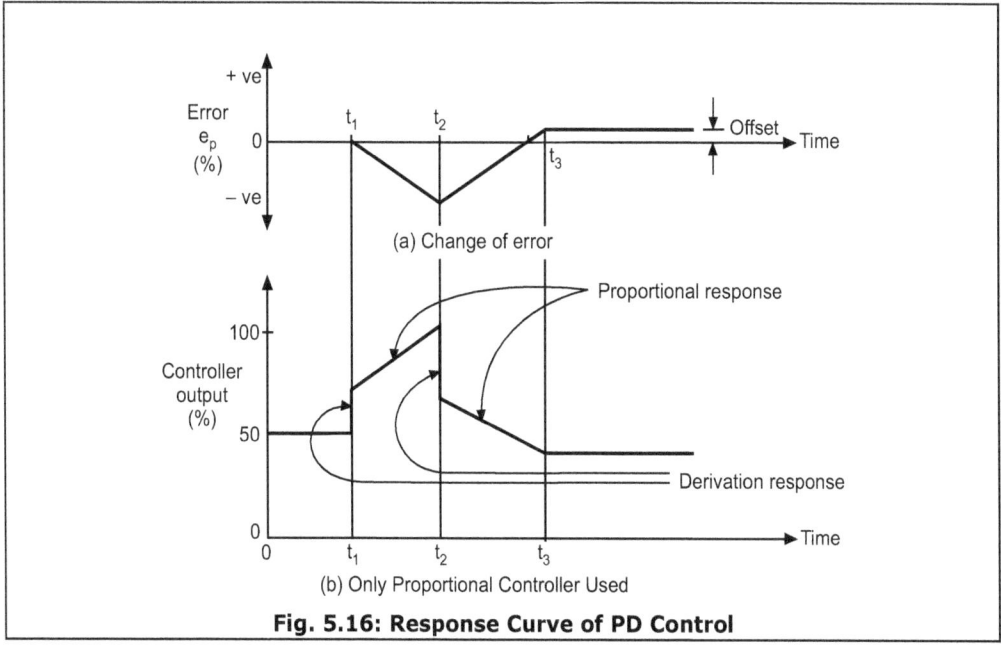

Fig. 5.16: Response Curve of PD Control

1. Offset of proportional control cannot be eliminated.
2. Controller output changes very fast in response to rate of change of error (e_p).

- Derivative time is the time interval by which the rate action advances effect of proportional control action.
- For a constant actuating signal, derivative control has no action on it. Hence, it is always used in combination with proportional or PI action.

- **Advantage:**

  It improves the damping ratio and reduces the maximum overshoot.

- **Limitations:**

  1. It is effective only during the transient state.
  2. If error is constant, it is not useful.

5.6.3 PID Control Action

QUESTION

1. Explain PID control action. **(8M)**

- It is a powerful but complex control action. This combination has an advantage of each of the three individual control actions.
- In proportional plus integral plus derivative (PID) control, also called three mode controller.

- The output equation of PID controller is,

$$m(t) = k_p \left[e(t) + \frac{1}{T_i} \int_0^t e\, dt + T_d \frac{de(t)}{dt} \right] \quad \ldots (5.13)$$

- Its Laplace transform is,

$$M(s) = k_p \left[1 + \frac{1}{T_i S} + T_d \cdot S \right] E(s) \quad \ldots (5.14)$$

- A block diagram of PID control action is shown in Fig. 5.17.

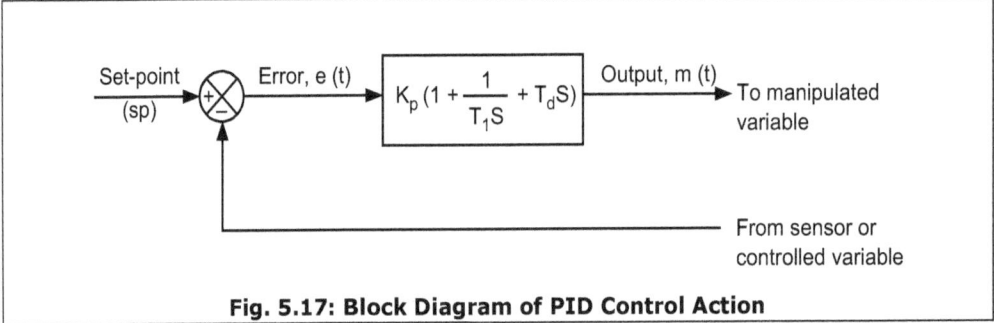

Fig. 5.17: Block Diagram of PID Control Action

Response of PID Controller (Characteristics):

- If the error signal is a ramp, then the output (Fig. 5.18).

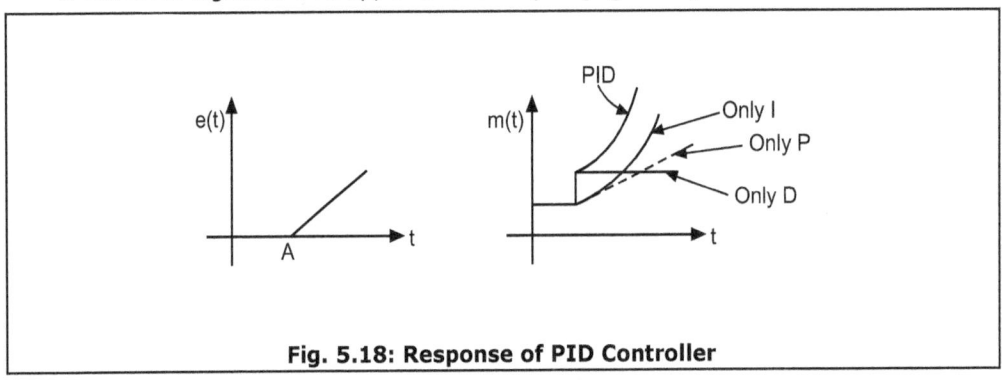

Fig. 5.18: Response of PID Controller

PID control action is a compromise between the advantages of PI and PD control.

Offset is eliminated by the integral action.

Derivative action lowers the maximum deviation and eliminates the oscillations that occur in PI control.

Derivative action in addition increases the speed of response to set point changes.

Response of control system to unit-step shown in Fig. 5.19.

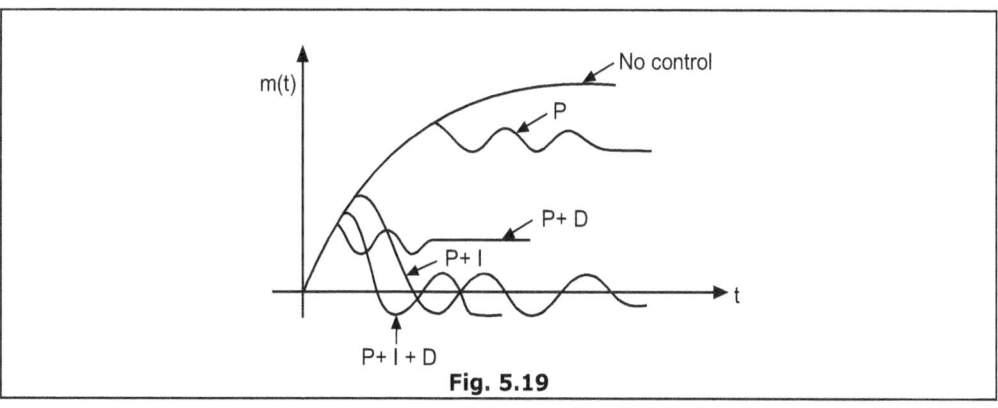
Fig. 5.19

5.7 COMPARISON OF P, PI, PD AND PID CONTROLLER

Sr. No.	Parameter	P-Type	PI-Type	PD-Type	PID-Type
1.	Deviation	High maximum	High maximum	Smallest maximum	–
2.	Period of oscillation	Moderate	Long	Smallest	–
3.	Offset	Maximum	No offset	Smaller than P-type	A compromise between PI and PD
4.	Time required for oscillations to stop	Considerable	Large	Shortest	–
5.	Output equation	$m(t) = k_p\, e(t)$	$m(t) = k_p \left(e + \dfrac{1}{T_i} \int_0^t e(t)\, dt \right)$	$m(t) = k_p \left(e + T_d \dfrac{de(t)}{dt} \right)$	$m(t) = \left[e + \dfrac{1}{T_i} \int_0^t e(t) \cdot dt + T_d \cdot \dfrac{de(t)}{(dt)} \right]$

Important Points

- **Process control** system consists of:
  (i) Process
  (ii) Measuring element
  (iii) Error detector
  (iv) Controller and
  (v) Final control element
- **Process characteristics:**
  (i) Process load
  (ii) Process lag
  (iii) Control lag
  (iv) Dead time
  (v) Error of deviation

- The **automatic controller** compares the actual value of the plant output with the desired output or value.
- The manner in which the automatic controller produces the control signal is called **control action**.
- An automatic controller produces the control signal called as **control action.**

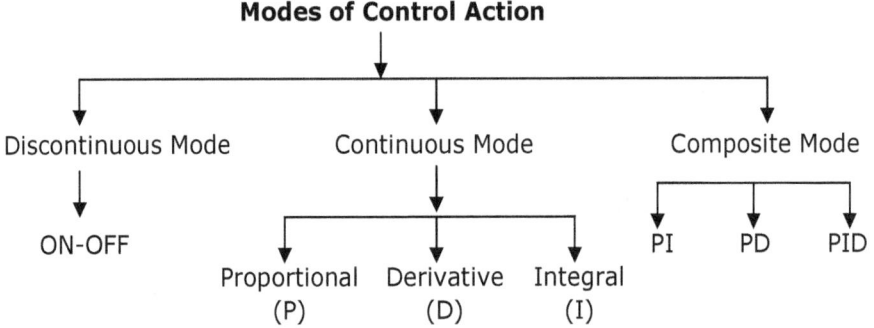

- The range through which the actuating error signal must move before switching occurs is called **neutral zone.**
- To prevent excessive cycling, to reduce losses of components and arching at relay contacts, neutral zones are purposely kept.
- **Proportional control action** is widely used to control action where the output of controller is a linear function of the error signal.
- Departure from set point is called **offset.**
- The offset is eliminated by adding integral action to the proportional control action.

Practice Questions

1. What is meant by control action?
2. Give the classification of control action.
3. State the concept of ON-OFF control action with example.
4. What is meant by Neutral zone?
5. State the advantage, disadvantage and application of ON-OFF control action.
6. List the continuous control action. State the proportional control action.
7. What are composite control actions? State any one.
8. Draw the electronic ON-OFF controller.

9. Draw the electronic integral and derivative controller.

10. Draw the electronic PID controller.

11. What is the limitation of proportional control actions and how is it overcome?

12. Explain proportional (P) Controller using electronic circuit. Draw its response.

Previous Year MSBTE Questions & Answers (As Per 'E' Scheme)

1. State the principle of derivative control action. Write its standard equation and draw its output response. **(S-11) (4M)**

Ans. Refer Section 5.5.3.

3. Compare P, I and D control action on the basis of (i) Nature of output, (ii) Response of error, (iii) Equation, (iv) Application. **(S-11) (4M)**

Ans. Refer Section 5.7.

4. Explain ON-OFF control action with simple example. What is neutral zone concept? **(S-12) (4M)**

Ans. Refer Section 5.4.1.

5. Draw neat diagram of process control system. State function of each element. **(S-12) (4M)**

Ans. Refer Section 5.2.

6. Compare P-control with PID control action. (any six points) **(S-12) (4M)**

Ans.

P control	PID control
1. Offset is present.	1. Offset is absent.
2. Amplifies noise.	2. Eliminates noise.
3. Moderate response speed.	3. Fast speed.
4. Moderate stability.	4. High stability.
5. Controller output is proportional to error.	5. Controller output is proportional to magnitude duration, rate of change error.
6. $P_{out} = K_p E_p + P_o$	6. $P_{out} = K_p E_p + K_p K_{io} \int E_p(t)\, dt + P_o$
7. Simple design.	7. Complex design.

7. Explain PI control section. State advantages of PI control (any two). **(S-12) (6M)**

Ans. Refer Section 5.6.1.

8. Define: (i) Neutral Zone, (ii) Proportional band and state the modes of control actions. **(W-12) (4M)**

Ans. Refer Sections 5.4.1 and 5.5.1.

9. Draw the block diagram of process control system and describe each element. **(W-12) (4M)**

Ans. Refer Section 5.2.

10. State the principle of derivative control with mathematical expression and its characteristics. **(W-12) (4M)**

Ans. Refer Section 5.5.3.

11. State any two advantages and two disadvantages of ON-OFF controller. **(W-12) (4M)**

Ans. Refer Section 5.4.1.

12. Name the continuous and composite modes of control actions. Compare P, I and D control actions w.r.t. **(W-12) (4M)**

    (i) Mathematical expression, (ii) Response to error, (iii) Offset, (iv) Stability

Ans. Refer Sections 5.3, 5.5, 5.5.2 and 5.5.3.

✱✱✱

SERVO SYSTEM

About This Chapter ...

After reading this chapter students can understand –
- Introduction
- A.C. and D.C. Servo Systems
- Servo Components
- Potentiometer as Error Detector
- Synchro as Error Detector
- Servomotors
- D.C. Servomotor
- Stepper Motor

6.1 INTRODUCTION

- **In automatic control system the word 'servo' or 'servomechanism' deals with the control of 'position'** (mechanical position or time derivatives of position such as velocity, acceleration).
- Actuators are the devices whose output is the mechanical motion (translatory/rotary). The actuators are characterised by power output and speed-torque relationship to match the load. These could be electrical, hydraulic or pneumatic.
- An actuator in a control system performs many tasks to manipulate the controlled process or plant.
- For example, it may open or close a valve in a hydraulic or steam or chemical process, turn a rod of link with respect to its neighbouring link, move a transformer tap, moves up or down the control rods of a nuclear reactor etc.
- Because of the flexibility inherent in a transmitting electrical power and desirable speed-torque relations which are linear, electrical actuators (i.e. motors) are widely used in control systems except in low speed but high torque applications where hydraulic actuators are still in use. Penumatic actuators are not in use because they suffer from leakages and inaccuracies.
- D.C. and A.C. motors are the two types of electric actuators. In low power rating, these are known as **servomotors**. D.C. motors are costlier than ac motors because of the commutation gear. But D.C. motors have linear characteristics and higher **stalled torque/inertia** ratio.
- So in this chapter, we have to study servocomponents which are mainly used for positioning the load.

6.2 SERVO SYSTEM

- In automatic control system the position of the final element or load is controlled, is known as servo system.
- For example, mechanical position or velocity, acceleration.

6.3 A.C. AND D.C. SERVO SYSTEMS

6.3.1 D.C. Position Control System (D.C. Servosystem)

QUESTIONS

1. Draw the block diagram and explain each block of servo system. Define servo system. **(4M)**
2. Draw neat diagram of D.C. position control system and describe. **(4M)**

- A generalized servosystem is used to position some final element, say a load shaft being driven by motor through gear system. Such a d.c. position control system is shown in Fig. 6.2 in which the driving motor is geared to the load to be moved.

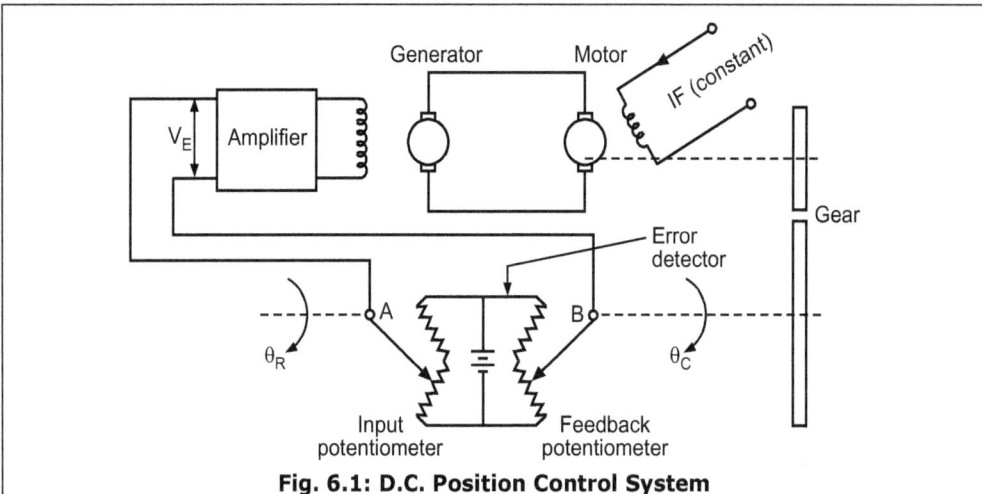

Fig. 6.1: D.C. Position Control System

- Here θ_C denotes the output position and θ_R denotes the desired or reference position.
- Both the quantities are measured and compared using an error detector (potentiometer pair), whose output voltage is V_E and that is proportional to the error in angular position $\theta_E = \theta_R - \theta_C$.
- The voltage $V_E = K_p \theta_E$ is amplified and used to control the field current of a D.C. generator which supplies the armature current to the driving motor.
- The gears are mechanically connected to a motor that positions the load.

Operation:

- Assume K_p = 100 volts/rad, and the output shaft position be 0.5 rad, and corresponding to this condition the slider arm B has a voltage of + 50 volts.

- Let the slider arm A be set at + 50 volts. Then, error signal will be zero (i.e. $V_E = 0$). Hence, the motor has zero output torque, so that the load stays stationary at 0.5 rad.
- Now, assume that, the new desired position of load is 0.6 rad. To achieve this, the arm A is placed at + 60 volts position, while arm B at the + 50 volt position.
- This makes an error signal of + 10 volts.
- Now, this error signal is amplified and fed to the servomotor which generates an output torque that repositions the load.
- The system comes to a steady position only when the error signal becomes zero that is the arm B reaches the position corresponding to 0.6 rad (i.e. + 60 volts).

- **Applications:**
  D.C. position systems are used as –
  (i) Machine tool control.
  (ii) Constant-tension control of sheet rolls in paper mills.
  (iii) Control of sheet metal thickness in hot rolling mills.
  (iv) Radar tracking systems.
  (v) Missile guidance systems etc.

6.3.2 (A.C. Position Control System) A.C. Servosystem

QUESTION

1. Describe the working of A.C. position control system with a neat diagram. **(4M)**

Consider the system shown in Fig. 6.2 in which the position of the mechanical load is controlled in accordance with the position of the reference shaft.

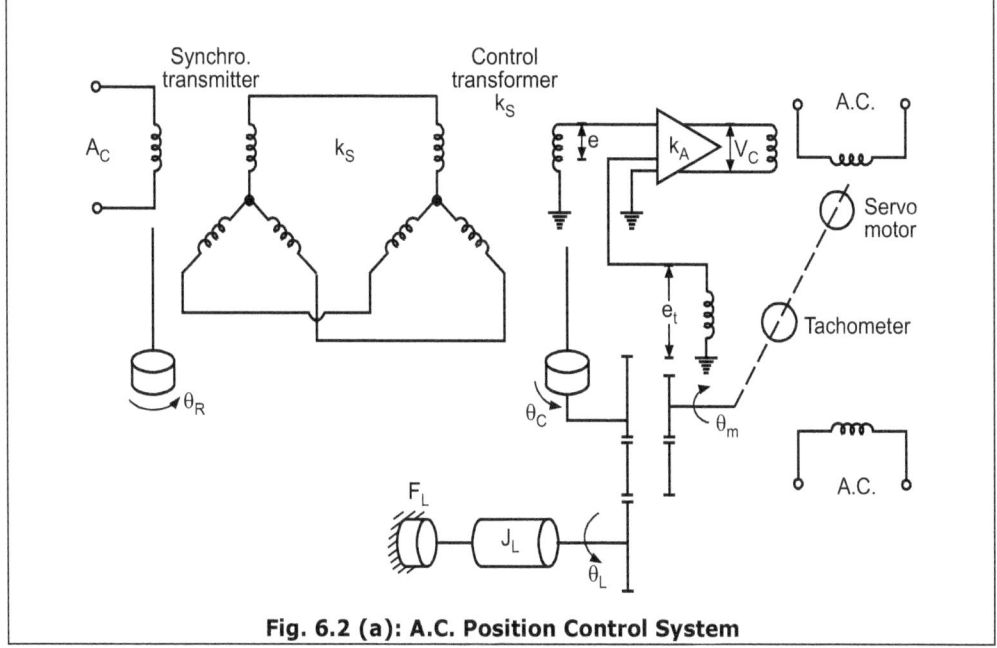

Fig. 6.2 (a): A.C. Position Control System

The components used in this system are –
(i) Synchro transmitter-control transformer pair as error detector.
(ii) A.C. amplifier for signal amplification.
(iii) A.C. servomotor to drive load shaft through gearing.
(iv) A.C. tachometer for providing feedback.

- The servomotors are provided with two carrier voltages 90° out of phase with each other.
- For this reference motor phase and synchro transmitter rotor coil is excited directly from carrier supply.
- Where control voltage is obtained by amplifying the error signal.

Transfer Function:

The operating point of A.C. servomotor is ($V_c = 0$, $\theta_m = 0$) as the motor is stationary under steady D.C. conditions.

From signal flow graph in Fig. 6.2 (b), the transfer function is,

$$\frac{\theta_C(s)}{\theta_R(s)} = \frac{k_m\, k_A\, k_s n}{\tau_m s^2 + (1 + k_m\, k_A\, k_t)\, s + k_m\, k_A\, k_s n}$$

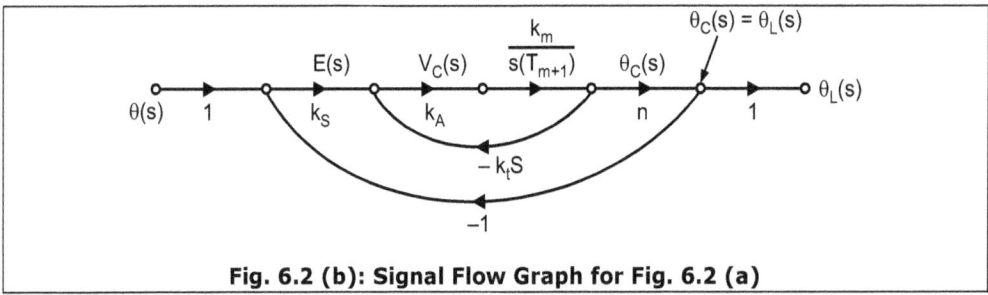

Fig. 6.2 (b): Signal Flow Graph for Fig. 6.2 (a)

Where,
k_m = Motor gain, rad/volts.
τ_m = Motor time constant; sec.
k_s = Synchro sensitivity; volts/rad.
k_t = Tachometer constant; volts/rad/sec.
k_A = Amplifier gain.
n = Gear ratio = $\dfrac{\theta_C}{\theta_m} = \dfrac{\theta_L}{\theta_m}$

6.4 SERVO-COMPONENTS

The components which are used for controlling the position of load. These are –
(i) Potentiometer.   (ii) Synchro transmitter and synchro receiver.
(iii) A.C. and D.C. servomotors.   (iv) A.C. and D.C. tachometer.
(v) Amplidyne.   (vi) Stepper motor.

6.4.1 Potentiometer as Error Detector

QUESTIONS

1. Sketch the potentiometer as an error detector. (4M)
2. Draw and explain potentiometer as an error detector. (4M)
3. Explain potentiometer as error detector. (4M)

In feedback control system, a pair of potentiometers is used as an error detector which are connected as shown in Fig. 6.3.

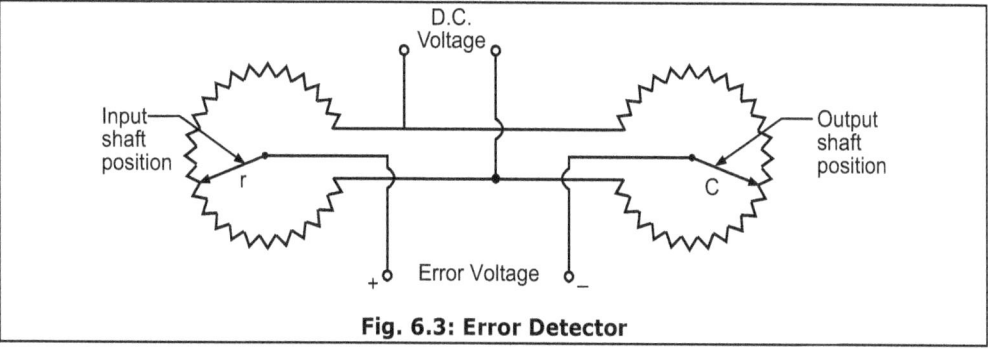

Fig. 6.3: Error Detector

- The D.C. voltage is applied between the fixed terminals as shown.
- Initially the positions of both the sliding contacts are at minimum i.e. zero position, so that the error signal (voltage) is zero.
- When the position of the sliding contact of input potentiometer changes error voltage is produced between the two variable terminals as shown.

  ∴ The voltage,
  $$V = k_s (\theta_r - \theta_c)$$

where,

  θ_r = Input angular displacement.
  θ_c = Output angular displacement.
  k_s = Sensitivity of the error detector; V/degree.

This can be represented by the block diagram as shown in Fig. 6.4.

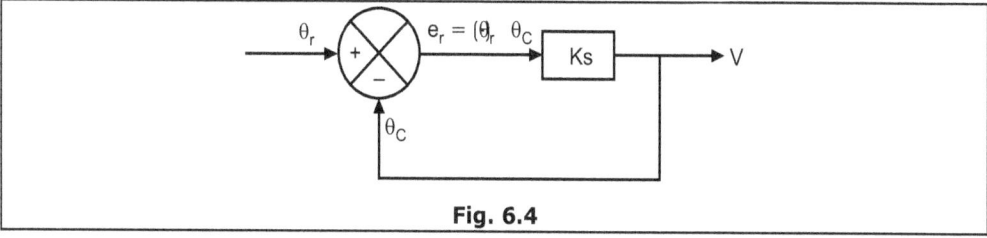

Fig. 6.4

- Now, the position of the output sliding contact also changes corresponding to the input sliding contact and the error voltage becomes zero.
- The output sliding contact is steady till the input does not change its position.

Error detector for linear positioning is shown in Fig. 6.5.

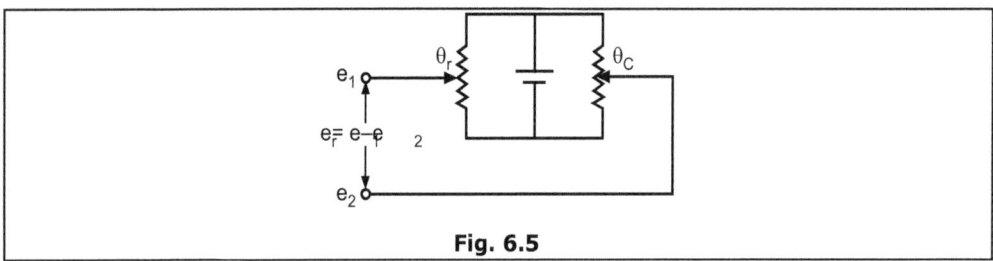

Fig. 6.5

- **Advantages:**
    1. It is possible to get an error voltage.
    2. Error voltage with necessary amplification drives the motor in both directions.
    3. Possible to change load positions.
    4. Behaviour is much linear.
    5. A.C. servomotor will also rotate in both directions.
- **Disadvantages:**
    1. Most error detectors give angular displacement upto 300° only.
    2. Large number of turns reduces resolution.
    3. Power dissipation is small, so cannot be used for high power operations.
    4. Also not useful for high frequency operations.
- **Applications:**
    1. For A.C. and D.C. position control system.
    2. Error voltage developed can be used to drive A.C. and D.C. servomotor and so position control system can be obtained.

6.5 SYNCHROS

- Synchros are small motor like components widely used for remote transmission of shaft position in A.C. servo-mechanisms.

Definition:

A synchro is an electromagnetic transducer commonly used to convert an angular position of a shaft into an electric signal.

- The basic synchro unit is called a synchro transmitter.
- A synchros basically consists of a wound rotor and a wound stator, that can be arranged to give adjustable mutual coupling between the winding on the two members.
- It is inherently balanced, has a good reliability and also has a useful operating angle of 360° which is capable of continuous rotation.

6.5.1 Synchro Error Detector

QUESTIONS

1. Draw neat diagram of synchro as an error detector. Explain its operation. **(6M)**

- The output of the synchro-transmitter is applied to the stator windings of a synchro-control-transformer (called synchro receiver).
- *The construction of the the synchro control transformer is similar in construction to that of the synchro transmitter except for the shape of the rotor.*
- The shape of the synchro-control-transformer is cylindrical in shape so that the air gap is practically uniform.
- The pair of transmitter and control transformer acts as an error detector.

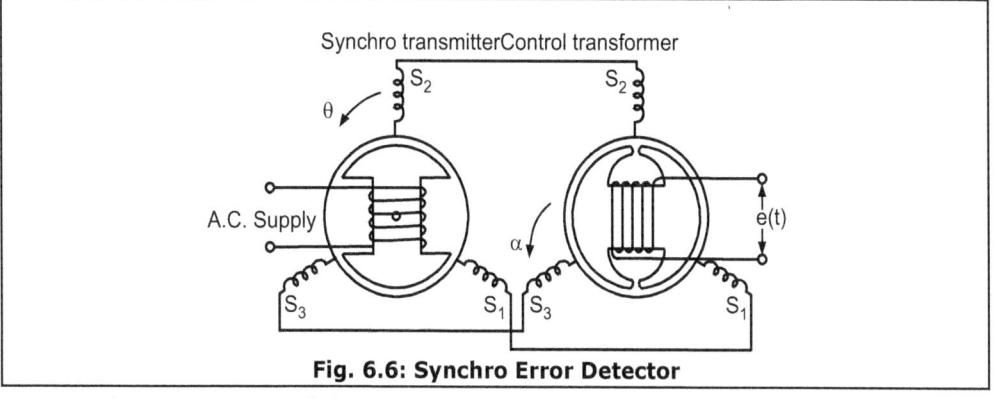

Fig. 6.6: Synchro Error Detector

- Circulating currents of the same phase but of different magnitudes flow through the two sets of stator coils.
- This establishes an identical flux pattern in the air gap of the control transformer (considering voltage drops in resistances and leakage reactances of two sets of stator coils are usually small).
- Thus, the control transformer flux axis is in the same position as that of the synchro-transmitter rotor.
- The voltage induced in the control transformer rotor is proportional to the cosine of the angle between the two rotors and is given by –

$$e(t) = k' V_r \sin \phi \sin \omega t \qquad \ldots (6.8)$$

where,

ϕ = Angular displacement between the two rotors.

- When $\phi = 90°$ i.e. the two rotors are at right angles, then the voltage induced in the control transformer rotor is zero. This position is known as electrical zero position (null position) of the synchro-control transformer.

In Fig. 6.10, the transmitter and control transformer rotors are shown in electrical zero position.

Operation:

Let us consider the rotor of the transmitter rotate through an angle θ in the direction indicated and let the control transformer also rotate in the same direction through an angle α which gives the result as net angular separator of $\phi = (90° - \theta + \alpha)$ between the two rotors.

- From equation (5.8), the voltage at the rotor terminals of the control transformer is,

$$e(t) = k' V_r \sin(\theta - \alpha) \sin \omega_c t \qquad \ldots (6.9)$$

- As the angular displacement between the two rotors is small, then,

$$e(t) = k' V_r (\theta - \alpha) \sin \omega_c t \qquad \ldots (6.10)$$

- From equation (5.10), we can say that the synchro-transmitter *control transformer pair acts as an error detector which gives voltage signal at the rotor of control transformer proportional to the angular difference between the transmitter and control transformer shaft position.*

  From equation (5.10), the signal representing the discrepancy between the two shaft positions is,

$$e_m(t) = k_s (\theta - \alpha) \qquad \ldots (6.11)$$

  where,

  k_s = Sensitivity of error detector, rms/rad

  $(\theta - \alpha)$ = Angular difference of the shafts of the synchro pair

- **Features of Synchro Error Detector:**
  - The rotor of the synchro control transformer is made cylindrical in shape so that the air gap is practically uniform. This is an essential feature for control transformer, since its rotor terminals are connected to an amplifier. Therefore, the change in the rotor output impedance with rotation of the shaft must be minimized.
  - The stator windings of the control transformer has a higher impedance per phase. This feature permits several control transformers to be fed from a single transmitter.

6.6 SERVOMOTORS

- A.C. and D.C. servomotors are commonly used as power devices in electrical control systems.
- A.C. servomotors are suitable for low power applications. They are rugged, light in weight and have no brush contacts such as in D.C. servomotors.
- The error signal derived from synchros is amplified by amplifiers to produce a control signal for the servomotor.

6.6.1 Difference from Normal 2 Phase Induction Motor

QUESTION

1. State how an AC servometer differs from a normal 2-phase induction motor. Draw its torque-speed characteristics. **(4M)**

An A.C. servomotor is basically a two-phase induction motor except for some special design features.

- A two-phase induction motor consists of two stator windings placed 90° apart in space and excited by a.c. voltages which differ in time phase by 90°.
- Fig. 6.7 shows the schematic diagram of a two phase induction motor.

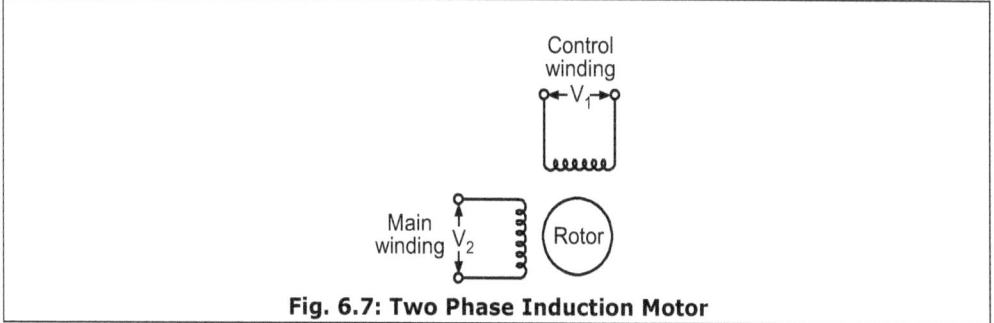

Fig. 6.7: Two Phase Induction Motor

- Here, two voltages of equal magnitude and 90° phase difference are applied to the two stator phases, that makes their respective fields 90° apart in both time and space resulting in a magnetic field of constant magnitude rotating at synchronous speed.
- The direction of rotation depends on the phase relationship between the voltages V_1 and V_2.
- If the field sweeps over the rotor, voltages are induced in it producing current in the short-circuited rotor.
- The interaction of the rotating magnetic field and rotor current produces a torque in the rotor.
- The general torque-speed characteristics of a two phase induction motor is shown in Fig. 6.8.

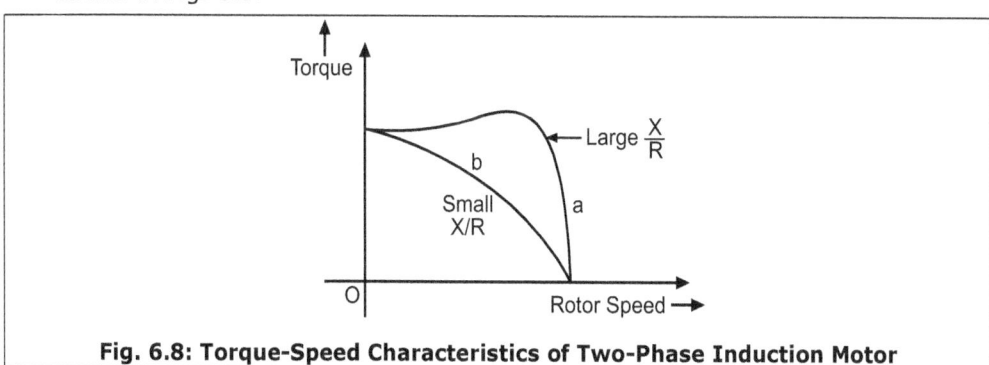

Fig. 6.8: Torque-Speed Characteristics of Two-Phase Induction Motor

- As shown in Fig., the shape of the characteristic depends on the ratio X/R (i.e. rotor reactance to rotor resistances).
- In general, the X/R ratio is kept high to obtain maximum torque close to the 5% slip.

- An A.C. servomotor differs in two ways from a normal induction motor.
    1. The rotor resistance of the servomotor is high, so its X/R ratio is small. This makes the torque-speed characteristic nearly linear as compared to highly non-linear characteristic with large X/R ratio in induction motor.
    2. The rotor construction is usually squirrel cage or drag cup type. The diameter of the rotor is kept small to reduce the insertia and thus we obtain good acceleration whereas drag-cup construction is used for very low inertia applications.

Also in servo applications, the voltages to the two stator windings are rarely balanced.

6.6.2 Two-phase A.C. Servo Motors

QUESTIONS
1. State the principle of AC servomotors. Also draw its schematic diagram. **(4M)**
2. Draw and explain the schematic of 2-phase a.c. servomotor. **(4M)**
3. Draw the schematic diagram of AC servo system and the elements. State any two advantages of it. **(4M)**

Fig. 6.9 shows the A.C. servomotor.

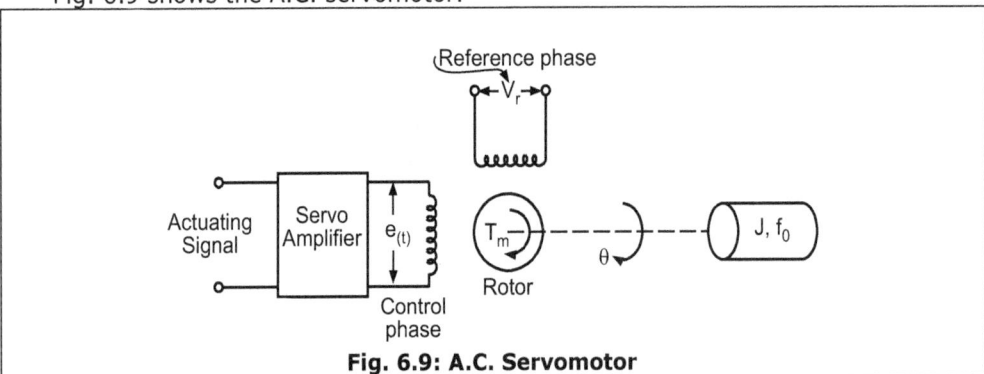

Fig. 6.9: A.C. Servomotor

- One of the phase known as reference phase is excited by a constant voltage.
- The other phase known as control phase is energized by a voltage which is 90° out of phase with respect to voltage of the reference phase.
- The control phase voltage is supplied from the servo-amplifier with variable magnitude and polarity.

    i.e. ± 90° phase angle with respect to the reference phase.

- As the control phase signal changes its sign, the direction of rotation of the motor also reverses.

6.6.3 Torque-speed Characteristics of A.C. Servomotor

Fig. 6.10 (a) and (b) shows the torque-speed characteristic of the A.C. servomotor.

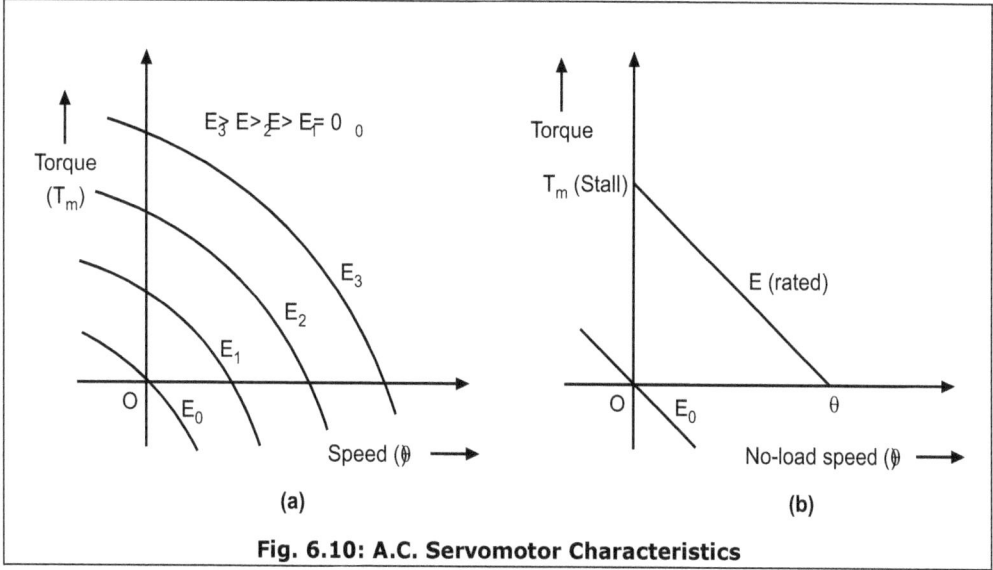

Fig. 6.10: A.C. Servomotor Characteristics

- Starting torque of the servomotor under unbalanced operation is proportional to E i.e. the rms value of the sinusoidal control voltage e(t).
- A family of torque-speed curves with variable rms control voltage is shown in Fig. 6.10 (a).
- All these curves having negative slopes and the curve for zero control voltage goes through the origin and the motor develops de-accelerating torque.
- As shown in Fig. 6.10 (a), the torque-speed curves are non-linear, but at low-speed (origin) the curves are nearly linear and equidistant.
- Thus, the torque varies linearly with speed and control voltage.
- The curves are approximated to linear characteristics. The approximation is valid for motors operating at high speed as shown in Fig. 6.10 (b).

6.7 D.C. SERVOMOTOR

QUESTION

1. State how a D.C. servomotor differs from a normal D.C. motor. State the advantages of D.C. servomotor.

- D.C. servomotor have many advantages in control systems. The speed of the D.C. servomotor can be controlled easily and accurately.
- The speed-torque relation is linear.
- They are expensive and the commutator also requires maintenance.
- But, advanced commutator design make it maintenance free.
- The speciality of the D.C. motor is high starting torque and easy speed control.

The D.C. servomotor has two important equations

1. Back emf e_b which is proportional to speed θ and flux ϕ.

$$\therefore \quad e_b \propto \frac{\phi z \theta}{60}\left(\frac{P}{A}\right)$$

or $\quad e_b = k_m \phi \omega_m$

2. Also torque is proportional to ϕ and armature current i_a.

$$\therefore \quad T \propto i_a$$

How D.C. servomotor differs from normal D.C. motor?

- A DC motor has a two wire connection.
- All drive power is supplied over these two wires think of a light bulb.
- When you turn ON DC motor, it just starts spinning round and round i.e. with constant speed.
- Most DC motors are pretty fast about 5000 RPM.
- With DC motor, its speed is controlled using a technique called PWM.
- The normal DC motor is like bulb it has no electronics of it own and it requires a large amount of drive to be supplied to it.
- The function of the servo is to receive a control signal that represents a desired output position of the servo shaft and apply power to its DC motor until its shaft turns to that position.
- It uses position sensing device to determine the rotational position of the shaft, so it knows which way the motor must run to move the shaft to the commanded position.
- The shaft typically does not rotate freely round and round like a DC motor but rather than can only turn 200 degrees or so back and forth.
- The servo has a 3 wire connection power, ground and control.
- The power source must be constantly applied, the servo has its own drive electronics that draw current from the power lead to drive the motor.
- The control signal is PWM, but here the duration of the positive going pulse determines the position of the servo shaft.
- The servo motor is one used to control something through the use of feedback.

The d.c. servomotor operates in two modes.

(1) Armature controlled.
(2) Field controlled.

6.7.1 Armature Controlled D.C. Servomotor

In armature control, the field is energized by a constant voltage and so the flux is constant.

Consider the armature-controlled D.C. servomotor shown in Fig. 6.11.

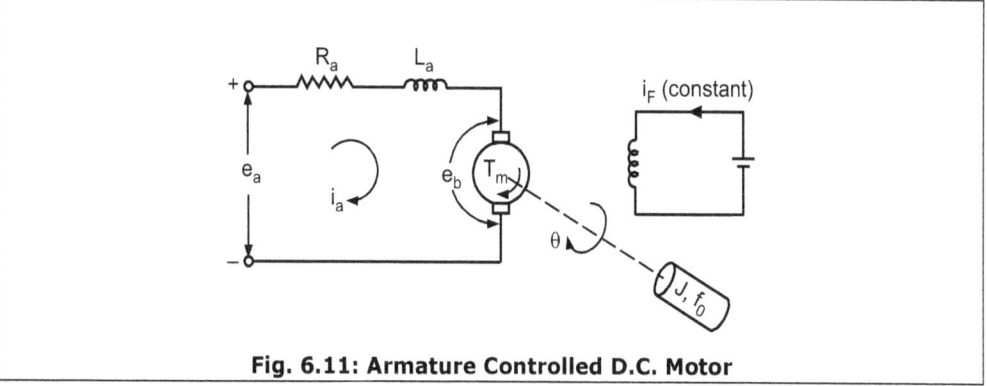

Fig. 6.11: Armature Controlled D.C. Motor

where, R_a = Armature resistance; Ω.

L_a = Armature inductance; H.

i_a = Armature current; A.

i_f = Field current; A.

e_a = Applied armature voltage; V.

e_b = Back e.m.f. (v).

T_m = Motor torque; Nm.

θ = Angular displacement of motor shaft; rad.

J = Equivalent movement of inertia of motor and load to motor shaft; kg-m².

f_o = Equivalent viscous friction coefficient of motor and load referred to motor shaft (Nm/rad/s).

For servo applications, D.C. motors are generally used in the linear range of the magnetization curve.

Thus, the air gap flux ϕ is directly proportional to the field current.

i.e. $$\phi = k_f i_f \qquad \ldots (6.17)$$

where,

$$k_f = \text{Constant}$$

In armature controlled d.c. motor, field current is always kept constant, so that,

$$T_m = k_T i_a \qquad \ldots (6.18)$$

where,

$$k_T = \text{Motor torque constant}$$

Also, the back e.m.f. of the motor is proportional to the speed is given as,

$$e_b = k_b \frac{d\theta}{dt} \qquad \ldots (6.19)$$

Apply KCL to the circuit shown in Fig. 6.15 gives,

$$L_a \frac{di_a}{dt} + R_a i_a + e_b = e_a \qquad \ldots (6.20)$$

The torque equation is,

$$J \frac{d^2\theta}{dt^2} + f_0 \frac{d\theta}{dt} = M = k_T i_a \qquad \ldots (6.21)$$

Now, take the Laplace transform of equation (6.18) and (6.19) by assuming zero initial conditions, we get,

$$E_b(s) = k_b s \theta(s) \qquad \ldots (6.22)$$
$$(L_a s + R_a) I_a(s) = E_a(s) - E_b(s) \qquad \ldots (6.23)$$
$$(Js^2 + f_0 s) \theta(s) = T_m(s) = k_T I_a(s) \qquad \ldots (6.24)$$

Therefore, the transfer function of armature controlled d.c. motor is,

$$\boxed{G(s) = \frac{\theta(s)}{E_a(s)} = \frac{k_T}{s[(R_a + sL_a)(Js + f_0) + k_T k_b]}} \qquad \ldots (6.25)$$

The inductance (L_a) of armature circuit is usually negligible.

Therefore, the transfer function is,

$$\boxed{\frac{\theta(s)}{E_a(s)} = \frac{k_T/R_a}{Js^2 + s(f_0 + k_T k_b/R_a)}} \qquad \ldots (6.26)$$

Let,

$$f = f_0 + k_T k_b/R_a$$

Then, the transfer function becomes,

$$\boxed{\frac{\theta(s)}{E_a(s)} = \frac{k_T/R_a}{s(Js + f)}} \qquad \ldots (6.27)$$

6.7.2 Field Controlled d.c. Servomotor (S-08)

QUESTION
1. Draw the field controller D.C. servomotor. Derive its transfer function. (S-08) (4M)

The field controlled d.c. motor is shown in Fig. 6.12 as given below:

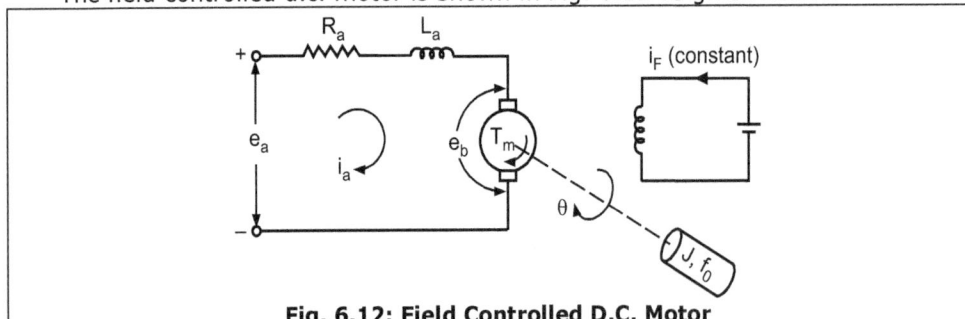

Fig. 6.12: Field Controlled D.C. Motor

where, R_f = Field winding resistance; Ω.

L_f = Field winding inductance; H.

e = Field control voltage; V.

i_f = Field current; A.

T_m = Motor torque; Nm.

J = Equivalent moment of inertia of motor and load referred to motor shaft; kg-m².

f = Equivalent viscous friction coefficient of motor and load referred to motor shaft; Nm/rad/s.

θ = Angular displacement of motor shaft (rad).

In the field controlled D.C. motor, armature current is kept constant.

Thus,
$$T_m = k_1 k_f i_f i_a = k_T' i_f$$

where,

$k_T' \Rightarrow$ Constant

The equation of the field circuit is,

$$L_f \frac{di_f}{dt} + R_f i_f = e_f \qquad \text{... (6.28)}$$

The torque equation is,

$$J \frac{d^2\theta}{dt^2} = f \frac{d\theta}{dt} = T_m = k_T' i_f \qquad \text{... (6.29)}$$

Taking Laplace transform of equation (6.28) and (6.29), assuming zero initial conditions, we get,

$$(L_f s + R_f) I_f(s) = E_f(s) \qquad \text{... (6.30)}$$

$$(Js^2 + fs) \theta(s) = T_m(s) = k_T' I_f(s) \qquad \text{... (6.31)}$$

From the above equations, the transfer function of the d.c. motor is obtained as –

$$\frac{\theta(s)}{E_f(s)} = \frac{k_T'}{s(L_f s + R_f)(Js + f)}$$

$$\boxed{\frac{\theta(s)}{E_f(s)} = \frac{k_m}{s(\tau_f s + 1)(\tau_{me} s + 1)}} \qquad \text{... (6.32)}$$

where,

$$k_m = \frac{k_T'}{R_f f}, \text{ Motor gain constant.}$$

$$\tau_f = \frac{L_f}{R_f}, \text{ Time constant of field circuit.}$$

and $\tau_{me} = \frac{J}{f}$, Mechanical time constant.

For small size D.C. motors, field control is advantageous because that requires a low power servo amplifier.

For large size motors, it is cheaper to use armature controlled D.C. motor.

6.7.3 Comparison between Armature Controlled and Field Controlled D.C. Servomotors

QUESTION

1. Give the comparison between armature controlled and field controlled D.C. servomotor. **(4M)**

	Field Controlled		Armature Controlled
1.	Simple design of amplifier because of low power requirement.	1.	Amplifier must be designed for large power rating.
2.	In field circuit, no back e.m.f. is produced.	2.	Back e.m.f. provides damping.
3.	Large time constant.	3.	Small time constant.
4.	This is an open loop system.	4.	This is a closed loop system.
5.	Armature current is kept constant.	5.	Field current is kept constant.
6.	Error voltage is applied to the field winding.	6.	Error voltage is applied to the armature winding.

6.7.4 Comparison between D.C. and A.C. Servomotor

QUESTIONS

1. Distinguish between A.C. servomotor and D.C. servomotor. **(4M)**
2. Compare AC and DC servomotors (6 points). **(4M)**

D.C. Servomotor	A.C. Servomotor
1. For small size, they deliver high output.	1. Designed for low power output. $\left(\frac{1}{2} \text{ to } 100 \text{ watts}\right)$
2. Amplifier used for D.C. motor has a drift.	2. A.C. amplifiers have no drifts.
3. More efficiency.	3. Less efficiency as rotor resistance is large (η = 5 to 20%).
4. Commutator is present in d.c. motors, so more maintenance is required.	4. Commutator is absent, so requires less maintenance.
5. No slip rings. Hence slip losses are zero.	5. Slip rings produce slip loses.
6. It is a noisy motor.	6. Relatively smooth operation.

6.8 STEPPER MOTOR

QUESTION

1. List the types of stepper motor. Describe the working of any one type.

- **Stepper motor is an electromechanical device which actuates a train of pulses of step angular or linear movements in response to a train of input pulses on one-to-one basis i.e. one step actuation for each pulse input.**

- A stepper motor is an actuator element of incremental motion control systems such as –

  Computer peripherals like printers, tape drives, capstan drives etc., for *machine tool and process control systems.*

  The most widely used stepper motor are of *two types*.

  1. *Variable reluctance motor.*
  2. *Permanent magnet motor.*

6.8.1 Variable Reluctance Stepper Motor

QUESTIONS

1. Explain the principle of working of a variable reluctance stepper motor with suitable diagram. (4M)
2. Draw the variable reluctance type stepper motor. Describe its operation. (4M)
3. State the principle and operation of stepper motor. List any four characteristics. (4M)
4. Draw and explain variable reluctance type stepper motor. (4M)

- A variable reluctance stepper motor consists of only one or several stacks of stator and rotors.
- Stator have a common frame whereas rotors have a common shaft as shown in the cross-sectional view of Fig. 6.13 for a 3-stack motor.

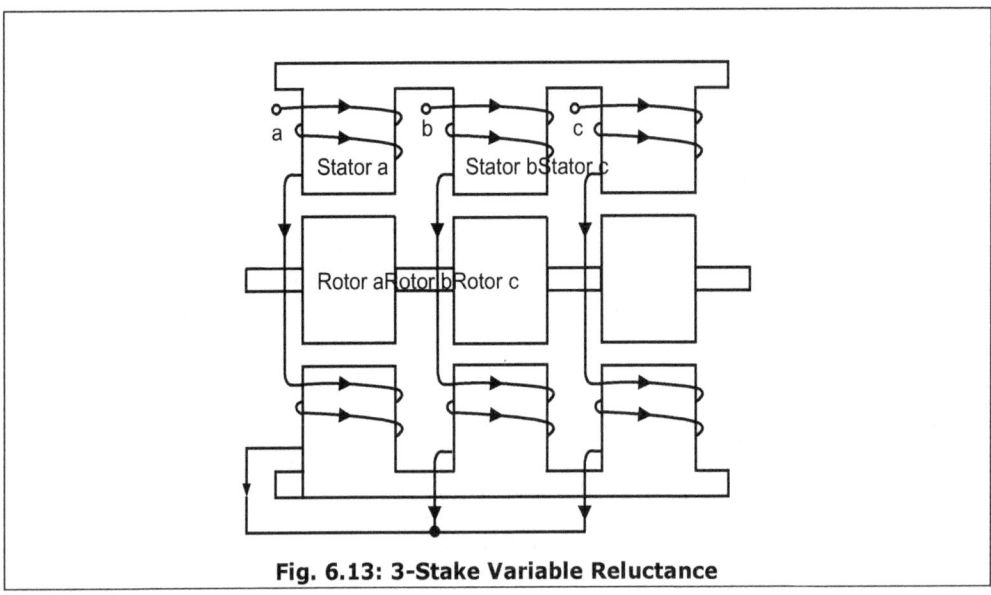

Fig. 6.13: 3-Stake Variable Reluctance

The toothed structure is shown in Fig. 6.14 (a).

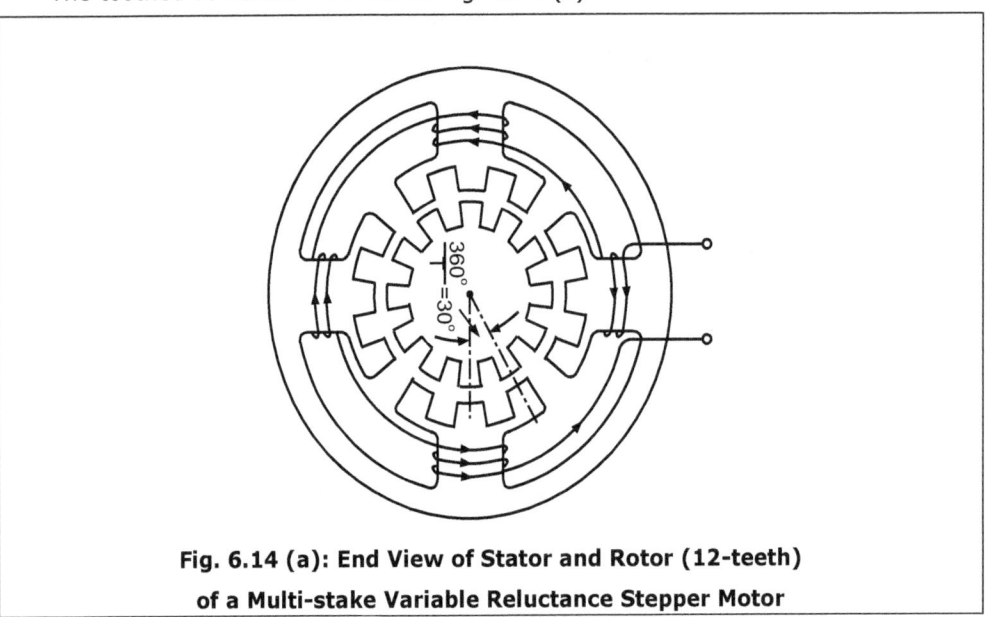

Fig. 6.14 (a): End View of Stator and Rotor (12-teeth) of a Multi-stake Variable Reluctance Stepper Motor

- Here, the stator and rotor teeths are of same size and are aligned as shown in Fig. 6.14 (b).
- The stators are pulse excited whereas the rotors are unexcited.

To understand the working of stepper motor, let us consider a particular stator and rotor set shown in Fig. 6.14 (b).

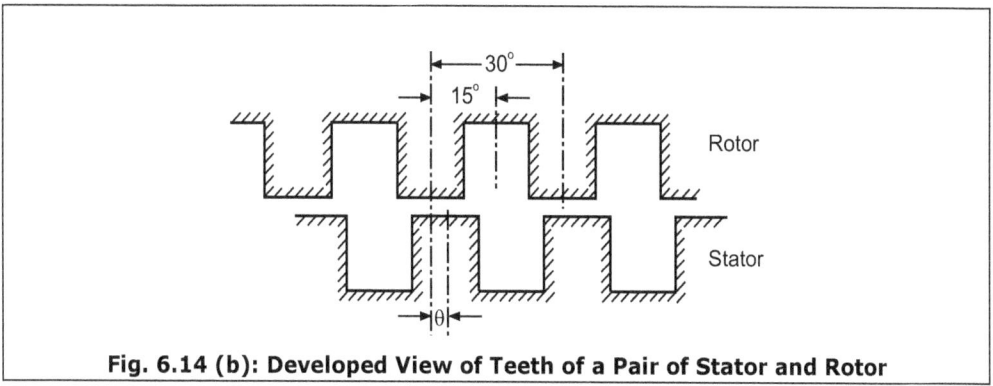

Fig. 6.14 (b): Developed View of Teeth of a Pair of Stator and Rotor

- If the stator is excited, the rotor is pulled into the nearest reluctance position, i.e. the position where the stator and rotor are aligned.
- The angular misalignment θ occurs because of the static torque acting on the rotor.
- There are two positions of zero torque.
  (i) For θ = 0, the rotor and stator teeth are aligned and
  (ii) For $\theta = \dfrac{360°}{2 \times T} = \dfrac{180°}{T}$, where, T – Number of rotor teeth.

  Rotor teeth are aligned with the stator slots.

Torque-Angle Characteristics:

The torque-angle characteristic for one stack of a stepper motor is shown in Fig. 6.14 (c).

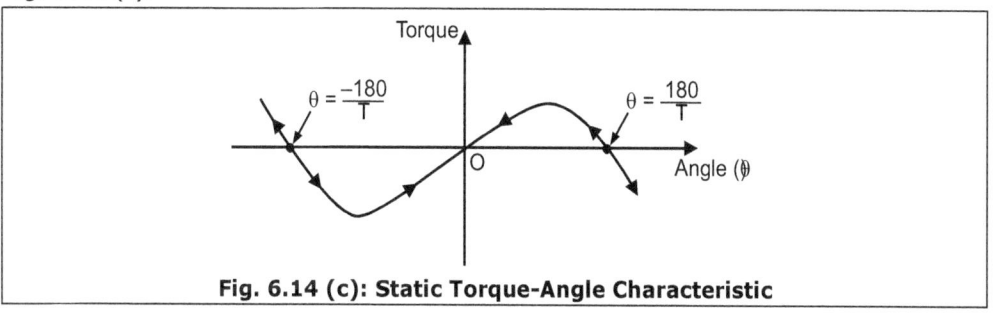

Fig. 6.14 (c): Static Torque-Angle Characteristic

(i) Teeth aligned position θ = 0, is a stable position i.e. slight disturbance from this position in either direction brings the rotor back to it.

(ii) Tooth slot aligned position $\theta = \dfrac{180}{T}$ is unstable i.e. slight disturbance from this position in either direction makes the rotor move away from it.

The teeth on all the rotors are perfectly aligned but the stator teeths differ by an angular displacement of,

$$\alpha = \dfrac{360}{nT}$$

where,

n = Number of stacks

Fig. 6.14 (d) shows the developed diagram of a 3-stack stepper motor in such a way that the stack 'c' rotor teeth are aligned with its stator.

Therefore,

$$\alpha = \frac{360}{nT}$$

$$= \frac{360}{3 \times 12}$$

$$= 10°$$

where,

n = Number of rotor teeth = 12

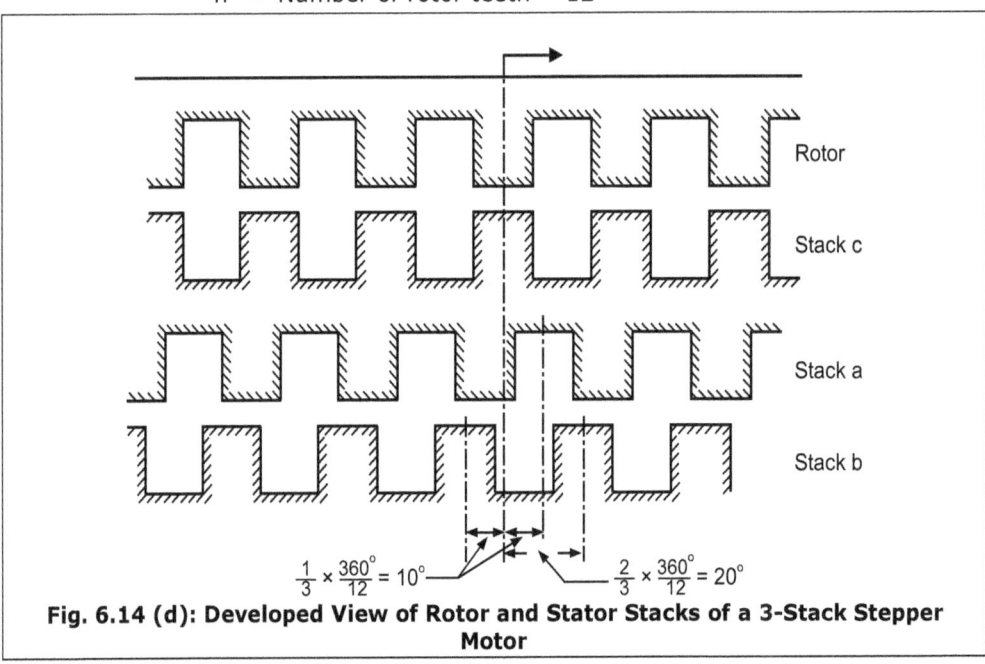

Fig. 6.14 (d): Developed View of Rotor and Stator Stacks of a 3-Stack Stepper Motor

- In a 3-stack or multiple stack rotor, the number of phases is equal to the number of stacks.
- If 'Phase a' stator is pulse excited, the rotor will move by 10° in the direction shown.
- Now if 'Phase b' stator is excited, the rotor will move in opposite direction by 10° (direction as shown).
- If the pulse train sequence is abcadb, then the rotor moves in incremental motion in the indicated direction.
- For the pulse train sequence bacba, the rotor moves in the opposite direction.

- Hence, directional control is possible with three or more phases.

Voltage Equation:

Let,
$e(t)$ = Voltage applied per stack
R = Winding resistance per stack
$L(\theta)$ = Winding inductance per stack
$i(t)$ = Current per stack
$\theta(t)$ = Angular position of rotor

Apply KVL for stator winding,

$$e(t) = R_i(t) + \frac{d\lambda}{dt}$$

where,

$$\lambda = \text{flux linkages of stator winding} = i\, L(\theta)$$

Therefore,

$$e(t) = R_i(t) + L(\theta)\frac{di}{dt} + i\frac{dL(\theta)}{dt}$$

$$e(t) = R_i(t) + L\theta\frac{di}{dt} + i\underbrace{\frac{dL(\theta)}{d\theta} \cdot \frac{d\theta}{dt}}_{} \quad \ldots (6.32)$$

Transformer e.m.f.   Speed e.m.f.

6.8.2 Permanent-Magnet Stepper Motor

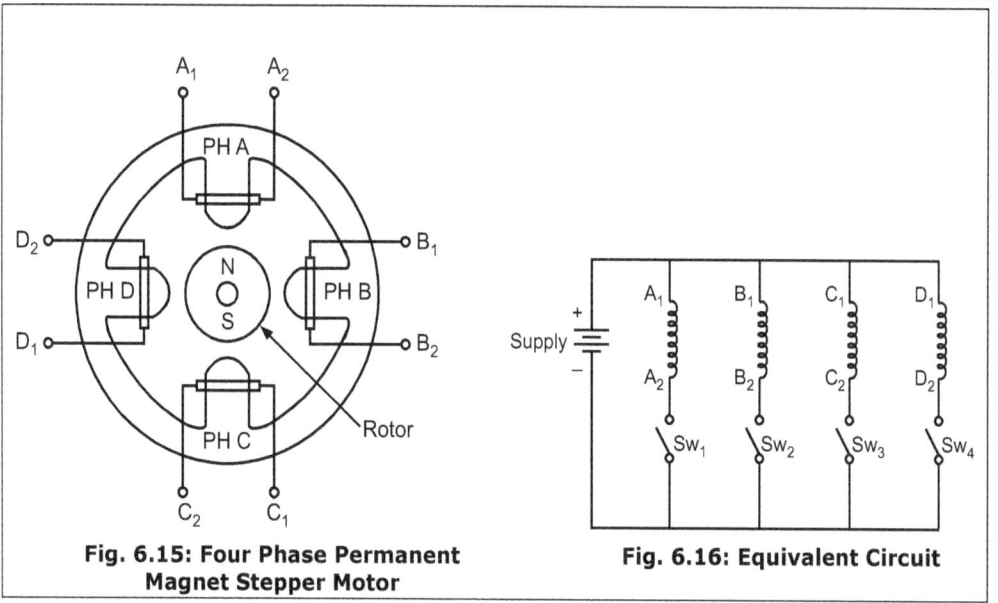

Fig. 6.15: Four Phase Permanent Magnet Stepper Motor

Fig. 6.16: Equivalent Circuit

Permanent magnet type motors work on the reaction between an electromagnetic field and a permanent magnet.

- The stator of this type may be multipole stator which has four poles.
- Exciting coils are wound around the poles.
- The rotor is a smooth cylindrical type. It is made by ferrite material which is permanently magnetised.
- As soon as the voltage pulses are applied to the various phases with the help of a driving circuit, the rotor makes a 90° revolution called as step for each input voltage pulse.

    (1) First Sw_1 is closed exciting phase A. We have N pole in phase A due to its excitation. Due to the electromechanical torque developed, rotor rotates to adjusts in magnetic axis with the magnetic axis of the stator.

    (2) Next phase B is excited with switch Sw_2, disconnecting phase A. Due to this rotor further rotates to adjust its magnetic axis with N pole of phase B. Hence it rotates through 90° called as step.

Similarly, when phase C and phase D are sequentially excited the rotor tends to rotate through 90° every time. When such a sequence is repeated, it results into step motion of a permanent magnet stepper motor. Further reduction in step angle can be achieved by increasing the number of rotor poles.

Step angle α_S is given by,

$$\alpha_S = \frac{360°}{2\,Pm}$$

where,   P = Number of poles.

m = Number of phases in the exciting winding.

6.8.3 Use of Stepper Motor in Control System

QUESTION

1. State four applications of stepper motor.

The stepper motor is used by two ways in control system.

(i) Open loop mode.   (ii) Closed loop mode.

(i) Open Loop Mode:

The stepper motor is a digital device that gives angular displacement as the output determined by the number of input pulses.

The system is open loop and so load is connected directly to the motor shaft without feedback as shown in Fig. 6.17.

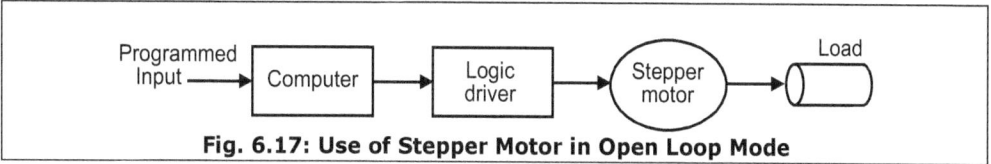

Fig. 6.17: Use of Stepper Motor in Open Loop Mode

(ii) Close Loop Mode:

In closed loop mode, the stepper motor is used like a conventional servomotor.

A signal from the output is feedback to the input and is used to operate a gate controlling the pulses from the pulse generator as shown in Fig. 6.18.

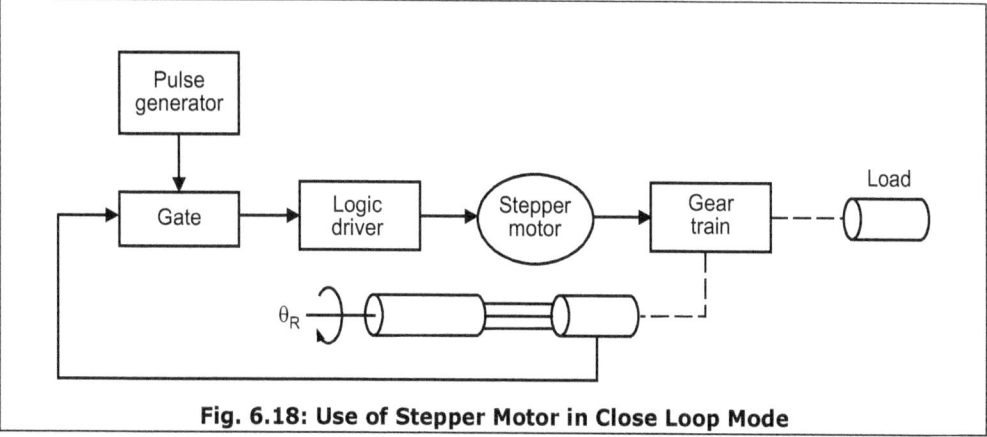

Fig. 6.18: Use of Stepper Motor in Close Loop Mode

6.8.4 Comparison between Stepper Motor and D.C. Servomotor

	Stepper Motor		D.C. Servomotor
1.	Stepper motor is an electromechanical device which actuates a train of pulses of step angular or linear movements.	1.	Servomotor is a device which gives angular movement.
2.	Used for motion control system such as printers, tape drives, capstan drives etc.	2.	Used in D.C. position control system.
3.	Types: (a) Variable reluctance motor. (b) Permanent motor magnet motor.	3.	Types: (a) Field controlled D.C. servomotor. (b) Armature controlled D.C. servomotor.
4.	It is immune to noise because it gives its output in terms of 1's and 0's.	4.	It is a noisy motor.

Important Points

- In an automatic control system, the word servo or **servomechanism** deals with the control of position.
- D.C. position control system is used to position some final element, say a load shaft being driven by the motor through a gear system.
- Potentiometers are single reliable devices for measuring mechanical displacement-linear or angular.
- In feedback control system, the pair of potentiometer is used as an **error detector**.
- A **synchro** is an electromagnetic transducer commonly used to convert the angular position of a shaft into an electric signal.
- When the rotor axis and stator coil s_2 align with each other, then the angular displacement is zero, more flux linkages with coil s_2, so maximum voltage is induced in coil s_2 and terminal voltage between s_3 and s_1 becomes zero. This is called the electrical zero position of the **synchrotransmitter.**
- **Rotary encoder** is generally used in control system in changing rotary displacement into coded signal.
- **Stepper motor** is an electromechanical device which actuates a train of pulses of step angular or linear movements in response to a train of input pulses on a one-to-one basis.

Practice Questions

1. Define the term 'servomechanism' or actuator.
2. Draw and explain the D.C. position control system.
3. Draw and explain the A.C. position control system.
4. How is potentiometer used as error detector ?
5. List the advantages, disadvantages and applications of potentiometer error detector.
6. Define synchro.
7. Draw the construction and explain the operation of synchro transmitter.
8. Draw and explain how synchro is used as an error detector.
9. What is an electrical zero position of a synchro transmitter ?
10. Define synchro transmitter.

11. Compare A.C. servomotor and two-phase induction motor.

12. Draw A.C. servomotor and explain its working.

13. Draw the torque-speech characteristic of A.C. servomotor.

14. Give two important equations of D.C. servomotor and state its two operating modes.

15. Draw field controlled D.C. servomotor and derive its transfer function.

16. What is the use of stepper motor ? List its types.

17. Draw the construction of reluctance type stepper motor and explain.

18. Give the applications of stepper motor.

19. Give the comparison between armature controlled and field controlled D.C. servomotor.

Previous Year MSBTE Questions & Answers (As Per 'E' Scheme)

1. What is synchro ? (S-11) (2M)

Ans. Refer Section 6.5.

2. Draw and explain potentiometer as an error detector. (S-11, W-12) (4M)

Ans. Refer Section 6.4.1.

3. Explain the working of variable reluctance stepper motor. (S-11) (4M)

Ans. Refer Section 6.8.1.

4. Differentiate between armature controlled and field controlled C servomotor (any four points). (S-11) (4M)

Ans. Refer Section 6.7.3.

5. State how a AC servomotor differs from a normal 2-phase induction motor. Draw its torque-speed characteristics. (S-11) (4M)

Ans. Refer Sections 6.6.1 and 6.6.3.

6. Compare DC servomotor with armature controlled and field controlled (any six points). (S-12) (4M)

Ans. Refer Section 6.7.3.

7. Draw neat diagram of synchro as an error detector. Explain its operation. (S-12) (6M)

Ans. Refer Section 6.5.1.

8. Draw neat diagram of D.C. position control system and describe. (S-12) (4M)

Ans. Refer Section 6.2.1.

9. Explain A.C. servomotor operation with neat diagram. Compare AC servomotor with normal induction motor. (any six points) (S-12) (8M)

Ans. Refer Sections 6.6.2 and 6.6.1.

10. Draw the block diagram and explain each block of servo system. Define servo system. (W-12) (4M)

Ans. Refer Section 6.2.1, 6.2.

11. Compare AC and DC servomotors. (6 points) (W-12) (4M)

Ans. Refer Section 6.7.4.

12. How is AC servomotor different from a normal 2-phase induction motor? Explain. Draw the torque-speed characteristic of AC servomotor. (W-12) (4M)

Ans. Refer Sections 6.6.1 and 6.6.3.

13. Draw and explain variable reluctance type stepper motor. (W-12) (4M)

Ans. Refer Section 6.8.1.

14. Draw the schematic diagram of AC servo system and the elements. state any 2 advantages of it. (W-12) (4M)

Ans. Refer Section 6.6.2.

✱✱✱